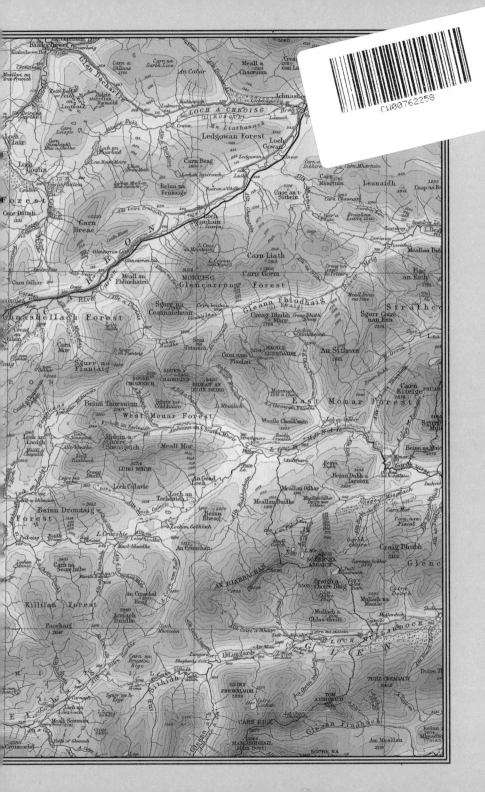

Rails to
Kyle of Lochalsh

The Story of the
Dingwall and Skye Railway
including the
Strathpeffer Branch

by
David McConnell

THE OAKWOOD PRESS

ISBN 0 85361 513 6

Typeset by Oakwood Graphics.
Repro by Ford Graphics, Ringwood, Hants.
Printed by Alpha Print (Oxford) Ltd, Witney, Oxon.

A Cumming 4-6-0 engine with the 'Lewisman' passes Badicaul on its way to Kyle in the 1930s. The island of Raasay is in the background.   *Drawing by Aurore McConnell*

Title Page: The view from above Achnashellach, looking south-west down Strath Carron, in the days of the Dingwall & Skye Railway, as a train heads for Glen Carron. Loch Dughaill is in the centre of the scene with Loch Carron is in the distance. This drawing, which is a version of the *Illustrated London News* drawing on page 52, was specially produced for the book to show the correct height and steepness of the hills that were exaggerated by the artist of the London journal.
Drawing by Aurore McConnell

Published by
The Oakwood Press
P.O. Box 122, Headington, Oxford, OX3 8LU.

Contents

Much is visible in this magnificent aerial view of Kyle of Lochalsh in 1961, looking north, with the active railway pier indicating the largest source of employment for the village. The frequently operated Skye ferry has just departed for Kyleakin, and beside its jetty is the Lochalsh Hotel that expanded over the decades from the original Station Hotel building at the railway's opening in 1897. The main street lies across the centre of the picture, and towards the lower right are the railway cottages and, on its own overlooking the sea, the station master's house. Just in front, and to the right, of the smaller road bridge, the signal box can be seen, while on the other side of the bridge is the engine shed, and further along, the turntable is discernible at the end of the siding. The route of the railway is visible for over a mile from the pier, as it passes by the Pladaig shore and continues to hug the coast towards the hamlet of Badicaul at the extreme top-centre of the picture. The higher ground on the left of the view is the Plock of Kyle. For some of the features, this photograph can be compared with the 25 inch Ordnance Survey map of 1902 (*see page 172*).   *Hunting Aerofilms Ltd*

Chapter One

Before the Skye Railway

The establishment of the Skye railway, initially in 1870 and subsequently in 1897 - winding its way from Dingwall south-westwards through the beautiful and remote country of Ross-shire in the direction of the mountainous 'misty isle' - verified a prophecy, made over two centuries previously by a famous soothsayer from the Isle of Lewis in the Outer Hebrides. He was Kenneth MacKenzie, who was also referred to as Coinneach Odhar*, and later as the Brahan Seer because he worked on the Brahan estate, near Strathpeffer; and his words were that 'the day will come when long strings of carriages, without horses, shall run between Dingwall and Inverness, and more wonderful still, between Dingwall and the Isle of Skye'. However, within the 100 years prior to these long strings of carriages, in the form of steam trains between the Highland capital of Inverness and Skye, various travellers - who were more akin to explorers - provided written illustrations of what it was then like to make their way across the West, while recording aspects of the scenery and the social conditions.

In 1773, Dr Samuel Johnson, the English philosopher, poet and lexicographer, and his much younger companion of law, James Boswell of Edinburgh, were among the earliest travellers to write about the West Highlands and islands. They were accompanied on horseback by Boswell's servant and on foot by two Highlanders who rented the horses to them and who were employed to guide them from Inverness to Glenelg. They headed westwards by the old military road through Glen Moriston, Glen Shiel and over the steep, 1,100 ft-high Mam Ratagan Pass towards Glenelg. Johnson was alarmed on the ascent of the pass, which he described as 'a high hill on which a road is cut, but so steep and narrow, that it is very difficult', explaining that:

> Upon one of the precipices, my horse, weary with the steepness of the rise, staggered a little, and I called in haste to the Highlander to hold him. This was the only moment of my journey in which I thought myself endangered.

'It is a terrible steep climb', wrote Boswell, 'notwithstanding the road is formed slanting along it; however, we made it out'. They were dissatisfied with their stay at the inn at Glenelg where, according to Boswell, their room was 'damp and dirty, with bare walls, and a variety of bad smells'. They were also little fed, and Johnson declared the fact thus:

> Of the provisions, the negative catalogue was very copious. Here was no meat, no milk, no bread, no eggs, no wine. Whisky we might have, and I believe at last they caught a fowl and killed it.

They did have some success. Johnson continued:

> We had some bread, and with that we prepared ourselves to be contented, when we had a very eminent proof of Highland hospitality.

For then, a gentleman's servant who had kept them company as they made their way through Glen Shiel, 'came to us again', as Johnson added, 'with a present from his master, of rum and sugar':

> The gentleman, well knowing the penury of the place, had this attention to two men, whose

---

* Pronounced 'Co-in-*yach* Oar' ('ch' as in 'loch'), meaning 'Brown Kenneth'.

1

names, perhaps, he had not heard, by whom his kindness was not likely to be ever repaid, and who could be recommended to him only by their necessities.

Johnson summed up the remoteness of the West with these words:

To the southern inhabitants of Scotland, the state of the mountains and the islands is equally unknown with that of Borneo or Sumatra. Of both, they have only heard a little, and guess the rest.

On the following day, Johnson, Boswell and the servant were ferried southwards from Glenelg across the Sound of Sleat to Armadale in Skye, to meet Lord MacDonald of Sleat*.

John Knox, a Scottish philanthropist who made his fortune as a bookseller in London, carried out a six-months' tour of the West Highlands and islands in 1786 on behalf of the newly-formed British Society for Extending the Fisheries,† with the aim of establishing suitable sites for fishing-stations. Having surveyed Skye, he crossed by the Kyle Rhea# ferry to the mainland at Glenelg, and he briefly explained how horses and cattle were made to swim the narrows:

My course being northward, I had an agreeable passage through that part of the channel called Kyle Rhea which, though no more than a quarter of a mile wide, has a depth of water sufficient for the largest ships. Here, the flood-tide runs at seven miles an hour; but at the lowest ebb, this strait is the usual passage where horses and black cattle are swam across between Skye and the mainland; for though this is the principal passage to that great island, it is not accommodated with a horse-ferry. When horses are to be taken over, they are pushed off the rock into the water. A small boat with five men attends, four of them holding the halters of a pair on each side of the boat. When black cattle are to cross the kyle, one is tied by the horn to a boat; a second is tied to the first; and a third to the second; and so on, to eight, ten or twelve.

From Kintail, Knox travelled towards Loch Carron:

The ridge which we were now crossing presented much improvable land almost to the summit. The views, on the descent northwards, were equal to those we had left; they were composed of verdant glens, pouring their copious streams into the entrance of Loch Carron.

Then he 'embarked in a boat to make the cruise of Loch Carron', and added:

This loch is equal in beauty to any that I had yet seen on the west coast. The north side, which is the property of Applecross,§ abounds in people, and in cornfields that slope gently towards the water. About two-thirds from the entrance on the north side is Slumbay, with good anchorage but open to the north-east. Near this place are a church, manse, school, public house and corn-mill.

Mention was made of the road and population through Glen Carron:

From the head of the loch, there is a road to Inverness, at a distance of 60 miles, of which the first nine miles run through a populous glen. The number of people, from the entrance of the loch to the extremity of this glen, is calculated at 1,000.

---

* The first Lord MacDonald of Sleat, pronounced 'Slate'.
† The full name was the *British Society for extending the Fisheries and improving the Sea Coasts of this Kingdom*.
# pronounced 'Ray'.
§ i.e. Captain John MacKenzie of Applecross.

Knox also commented favourably on the district of New Kelso, at the head of Loch Carron, and he explained the origin of the name:

> Many years ago, the Board of Trustees at Edinburgh purchased several acres of land at the head of the loch, and sent Mr Jeffries of Kelso to instruct the inhabitants in spinning, weaving, etc. Many small houses were built, and a number of people were collected together, which gave the place an appearance of a populous, though detached, village. The trustees built a house and ware-rooms for Mr Jeffries; but the design failed after a great sum of money had been expended in the experiment. This country is, however, greatly indebted to Mr Jeffries for the example he has shown, and the improvements he has made in agriculture, gardening, draining, planting of trees and hedges.
> The spot on which he resides, and to which he has given the name of New Kelso, was composed of heath and bog; it is now divided by hedges into square fields, and produces excellent crops which are beheld with admiration by the ignorant neighbourhood. So averse were the people to innovations and to instruction that Mr Jeffries was forced to hire soldiers from the barracks of Bernera* for the purpose of digging, planting and trenching. Many thousands of improvable land lie still buried under a bed of moss which Mr Jeffries or his son would bring into agriculture if they had the land upon a lease of two or three lives.

From New Kelso, he 'crossed the hills to Loch Kishorn, a good fishing-station'; but he thought that Plockton, too, was suitable as a new station:

> The bay of Plock is a commodious, safe harbour for small vessels, and has good anchoring ground; it lies at the entrance of Loch Kishorn and Loch Carron; and here, several busses were at anchor, from whence they sent their boats to the fishery in Kishorn. From the great number of people that inhabit Loch Alsh, Loch Carron, Loch Kishorn and the opposite coast of Skye, a town on some of these shores seems indispensibly necessary. The station last described is the most central to all these places for the purpose of fisheries, and is nearly in the general track of shipping.

In 1803, James Hogg, the 'Ettrick Shepherd', poet and friend of Walter Scott, the writer, left his Border country on foot 'with a view of traversing the West Highlands, at least as far as the Isle of Skye', and he provided an account of his tour in a series of letters to Scott. From Lochaber, he walked through Glen Shiel and eventually arrived in Lochalsh, where he obtained accommodation at Ardhill, the manse of the Lochalsh parish minister. Leaving there and 'climbing the mountains towards the country of Loch Carron', he reached the Strome ferry, where he found that to cross to the opposite shore was more demanding than he had anticipated:

> I came in upon Loch Carron at the narrowest place, nigh where it opens to the sea, when there was a boat just coming to land, freighted from a house several miles up on the other side of the loch by some people bound to the place from whence I came. I waited their arrival, thinking it a good chance, but in this I was mistaken. No arguments would persuade them to take me along with them. They alleged that it was depriving the ferryman of his right. But effectually to remove this impediment, I offered them triple freight, but they dared not to trust themselves with such a sum, for they actually rowed off and left me standing on the rocks, where I was obliged to bellow and wave my hat for no small space of time. The ferryman charged me sixpence and *a dram of whisky*. I then kept the north-west side of the loch, which stretcheth about 10 miles into the country, following a kind of formed road, but on which a wheeled carriage seemed never to have gone, nor had the makers ever intended that it should.

On this side of Loch Carron was the fishing village of Jeantown:†

---

* At Glenelg and now long in ruins.
† Now called Lochcarron, Jeantown was named after the daughter of MacKenzie of Applecross.

I was exceedingly gratified at here meeting with a long, straggling village, consisting wholly of neat, modern, commodious houses. Having never heard of it, I made enquiry concerning its erection, and was informed that it had lately arisen under the auspices of MacKenzie of Applecross, who had let it off in feus* to the fishermen, and such as chose to settle there. This is a most laudable example set by this gentleman, an example of which every reflecting mind must approve, and which can never be too much encouraged, either by individuals or by public bodies of men.

This spot, pitched on by Applecross for so beneficial a purpose, is not so commodious in every respect as it might be wished that it were; but perhaps Applecross had no better. In this spot, it is impossible to unite utility with compactness and elegance, for there being no valley, the houses are drawn out in an irregular line along the side of the loch, and however well situated for taking advantage of trade and fishing, it is a very untoward field for improvements in agriculture.

Passing on, I went past the church and through a carse, reaching New Kelso to my breakfast, a distance of nearly 20 miles from Ardhill. This is a spacious house, with a well-stocked garden for such a soil. It stands in the middle of a large, coarse plain, a great part of which is uncultivated and which could only be cultivated with much labour. The history of the erection of this place by Mr Jeffries, and for what purpose, is too well known to need recapitulation here.

The Ettrick Shepherd did not cross to Skye, but he did ultimately go further. He continued north-eastwards, up the valley of the River Carron for eight miles to the inn at Craig, where he experienced one of the difficulties faced by any stranger in the 'foreign' country of the West Highlands.

At the inn, he was able to obtain whisky, but not meat because the two serving girls there, in speaking only Gaelic, did not understand, amid his remonstrations, that he also wanted this. He sprang into a rage as a result of the girls' laughter, but his anger soon subsided into regret, and he was on his way again. He headed over the hills to Kinlochewe, Letterewe, Strathnasheallag, Dundonnell and then to Loch Broom, where he secured a passage to Stornoway.

The early travellers encountered difficulties in trekking across the West Highlands and islands because of poor or non-existent roads there. In Skye, for the first decade of the 19th century, there was no proper road anywhere, other than the old, rough drove-tracks which had been marked out by the passage of the many herds of black cattle on their way to the large markets at Muir of Ord, Crieff and Falkirk. From various parts of the island, the drovers sent the cattle up Glen Arroch and the Udal Pass, at 900 feet, and then steeply down to the crossing at Kyle Rhea. Cattle from the Outer Hebrides, having been landed at the northern sea lochs of Skye, were also routed across the tracks towards Kyle Rhea. The animals, made to swim the ⅓-mile narrows to the Glenelg side, were then driven over the steep Mam Ratagan Pass, thereafter to head through Glen Affric for Muir of Ord, or Glen Shiel for Crieff and Falkirk. It was estimated that from 5,000 to 8,000 cattle annually were sent across Kyle Rhea.

During the first two decades of the 19th century, road conditions in the Highlands attained a significant improvement, even in the West, including Skye. With the passing of the Highland Roads and Bridges Act, which brought into effect the Commission for Highland Roads and Bridges, the Government had finally taken an interest in the communications of the Highlands. Appropriately, Thomas Telford, the experienced Scottish civil engineer - then familiar with the Highlands in his capacity of surveyor to the British Fisheries Society† - had been appointed engineer to the commission, with the aim of making surveys wherever new roads were requested. The Government had decided that the cost of the roads would be borne jointly by the Treasury and by the local

---

* Feu: Scottish alternative for 'tenure'. Pronounced as 'few'.

† For convenience, the British Society for extending the Fisheries became known as the British Fisheries Society.

proprietors and authorities. Due to the exertions of Telford and the encouragement of the commission, many Highland roads were constructed or improved, so that much of the remote North and West was now opened up, in some degree, to progress from the South. Thus, in 1816, Telford was able to state, in a general sense, that 'the whole of Scotland, from its southern boundary near Carlisle to the northern extremity of Caithness, had been intersected with roads'.

Skye greatly felt the benefits of this new era of communication because, prior to the roads' formation, the quickest and easiest way to travel from one part of the island to another had been by rowing or sailing round the coast or across the sea lochs. The first road, from Dunvegan to Portree, being a principal cattle-drove, had been completed in 1811, to be followed, in 1812, by the route from Broadford to Ardvasar. Then, in 1813, had come the road from Kyle Rhea to Sconser, although this was not in good condition. The stretch from Sligachan to Portree was finished in 1816, but its continuation to Uig was not in operation until 1819. The only proposed but incomplete sections at this time were from Sligachan over the west route through Bracadale to Dunvegan and the short distance from Sligachan to Sconser.

Robert Southey, a renowned English poet, made a three-months' tour of the Highlands in 1819 - he was Poet Laureate at the time - and his itinerary included a run over the 'Loch Carron road' from Dingwall through Achnasheen and Jeantown to the Strome ferry. He came to Scotland with his friend, John Rickman, who was secretary of the Commission for Highland Roads and Bridges, and with Rickman's wife and two children. Rickman was also a friend of Thomas Telford, and it was arranged that the party should accompany Telford on an inspection of the various works under his charge. They proceeded by carriage on an extensive jaunt of the Highlands that allowed the opportunity to see the progress of Telford's immense undertaking, the Caledonian Canal, still in course of construction from its commencement in 1803.

The Loch Carron road over which Southey, Rickman and Telford travelled had only just reached its completion. Having been commenced as far back as 1809 by Telford as part of the work of the Commission for Highland Roads and Bridges, this coast-to-coast route had suffered many contractual problems; but 10 years later, it was effectively finished from Contin to Strome, thus providing a good road from Inverness, by way of Dingwall and Strathpeffer, to the West. However, Southey did record that there were still some workers on the road to Achanalt, as he described what was seen in this locality:

There are some fine rapids on the way, and we observed the stumps of several large oaks, apparently the remains of a forest. The only man whom we saw in a philibeg during the day's journey was a poor idiot who ran after the chaise, not to beg, but with an idiotic delight at seeing it. The road lies sometimes near and sometimes along a chain of small lakes, or broads, as some of them might properly be called. The workmen were finishing this division of the road, under the inspection of Mr Christie, the contractor: their tents, which had been purchased from the military stores, were pitched by the wayside, and they had made a hut with boughs for their kitchen - more picturesque accompaniments to so wild a scene could not have been devised. In a country like this, where there is little use of wheel-carriages, the road is constructed wholly of gravel, and all the stones are picked out and thrown aside.

Southey was dissatisfied with the state of the inn at Achanalt - 'a miserable place' and 'wretched as it was', he wrote - although he was pleased with the liquid refreshments that were served. Beyond Achnasheen, they stopped at another inn, at Luib, 'a house one degree better than the hovel at Achanalt'. They spent the night at Jeantown, and the poet noted:

Jeantown, the capital of Applecross's country and the largest place in the west of Ross-shire, is a straggling but populous village, chiefly or wholly inhabited by fishermen. A few of the huts on the shore are contiguous, the much greater number stand separately on the hillside.

The next morning, the travellers headed the short distance south to the Strome ferry in order to cross Loch Carron - 'but not without a suspicion', Southey declared, 'that we might find it necessary to return, for want of a boat capable of carrying the chaise and horses'. This turned out to be the case:

Piers on both sides have been built by the commissioners; and Applecross, to whom the ferry belongs, had long promised to provide a boat. This work, from want of interest on his part and inactivity in those whom he employed, had been delayed at first, and then slowly carried on, till the expected arrival of Rickman and Telford made him eager to have it finished . . . But when we arrived at the ferry, the boat was not there.

Nevertheless, they were able to be ferried, minus their conveyance and horses:

We ourselves crossed to see the farther shore. Loch Carron is a beautiful inlet. A tongue of land runs out on the north side and forms a natural pier, protecting the bay where Jeantown stands. The pier at Strome Ferry is sheltered by a smaller neck of land. The loch is enclosed by mountains on three sides, and on the fourth, the mountains in the Isle of Skye are seen at no great distance.

Southey was pleased to record: 'Ours was the first carriage which had ever reached the ferry; and the road on the southern shore, up which we walked, had never yet been travelled by one'.* He then led to a brief explanation of how the road construction in Skye and the West Highlands had benefited the local proprietors, whereby they had only to contribute half the cost of each road that was required while the Government, through the work of Telford and the commissioners, had provided the other half:

We went up the hill so as to command the descent along which it inclines toward Lochalsh - a district, not a lake - and communicates by Kyle Haken† Ferry with the Isle of Skye, where a hundred miles of road have been made by the commissioners. To hear of such roads in such a country, and to find them in the wild, western Highlands is so surprising, everything else being in so rude a state, that their utility, or at least their necessity, might be doubted, if half the expense were not raised by voluntary taxation. The lairds indeed have one inducement for entering largely into the scheme, which explains what might otherwise seem, on their part, a lavish expenditure on such improvements. Large arrears of rent were due to them, which there was no chance of their ever recovering in money; but the tenants were willing to work for them and so discharge the debt. When, therefore, the estimated expense of a road was £5,000, they received from Government £2,500, and the tenants did for them £5,000's worth of labour; thus, they were clear gainers by all which they received and by the improved value of their estates.

Having had 'a pleasant walk and a view into the wilds leading to Loch Alsh', Southey, Rickman and Telford recrossed Loch Carron to their carriage. It had been their intention to return to Inverness by way of Kintail, Glen Shiel, Glen Moriston and the Great Glen, but the lack of the suitable ferry-boat forced them to make their way back by the route that they had come, and then to head southwards through the Great Glen.

In the early years of the 19th century, another possible way to reach Skye was by the crossing at its southern end, which was much wider than Kyle Rhea and Kyle Akin. A

---

* This road, which had been completed in 1813 by the Commission for Highland Roads and Bridges, wound through the eastern and southern portions of the Lochalsh peninsula, by way of the villages or hamlets of Achmore, Auchtertyre, Kirkton, Balmacara, Erbusaig and Badicaul, to connect the Strome ferry with the Kyle Akin ferry at the hamlet of Kyle.
† Kyle Akin, pronounced '*Ah*-kin', was named after the 13th-century King Haakon of Norway.

ferry-boat sometimes plied from Traigh,* two miles north of Arisaig on the Morar coast, across the Sound of Sleat to Ardvasar on Skye, a distance of eight miles. In 1812, the Commission for Highland Roads and Bridges had completed a road from Fort William to Arisaig, but there was no road from Arisaig to Traigh, and passengers had to make their own way along the shore. One man who experienced difficulty in trying to use this ferry was Dr John MacCulloch, who was born in Guernsey and was a surgeon and geologist. He spent some time every year from 1811 to 1821 in the Highlands and islands in the study of the rocks, and he provided an account of his impressions in a long series of letters to Sir Walter Scott, which were published in four volumes in 1824. Of the Traigh-Ardvasar ferry, MacCulloch wrote:

> I had been directed to Skye by this route as the best and the most commodious, and as there was, at Arisaig, the best of all ferry-boats. But when the inquiry came to be made, nobody knew anything about a ferry-boat. There might be one, or not: if there was, it was uncertain if it would carry a horse; whether it was on this side of the water or the other; whether it would choose to go; whether there was a ferryman; whether the wind would allow it to go; whether the tide would suffer it. The Arisaig road had been made on account of the ferry, or the ferry on account of the road; and though a carriage-ferry and a horse-ferry, there was no boat that could hold a carriage, and no horse had ever dared to cross. Furthermore, the ferry-boat, if there really was one, was two miles from Arisaig, somewhere among some rocks; and there was no road to it, nor any pier.

It was two days later that MacCulloch was able to be taken across, where he 'was landed, very much like a buccaneer, on some rocks; which proved, in the end, to be Skye'. He had more positive words regarding the crossing at Kyle Akin:

> There is now an admirable ferry at Kyle Haken, which conducts the Inverness road by Loch Alsh to Skye, and nearly supersedes that of the Kyle Rhea. A road also communicates with Broadford. The air of life given by the ferry houses, and by the boats and vessels perpetually navigating this strait, adds much to the natural beauty of the scenery, which is also further enhanced by the ruins of Kyle Haken or Moil† Castle, as it is sometimes called.

He also managed to obtain a sail into Loch Carron and he commented on the settlements of Plockton, firstly, and then Jeantown:

> The entrance to the anchorage of Loch Carron is rendered difficult by rocks, and it was not without striking twice that we got into it. I was somewhat surprised to find that we were near a considerable village, as Highland villages are; expecting to see nothing but scattered houses along the northern shore, just as from the Mull of Kintyre to Glenelg. But so little is known of this remote country beyond its immediate limits that a distant visitor need not be much mortified at his ignorance: its pains, also, will be generally compensated by its pleasures. If he runs himself into dangers by attempting a harbour of which he is ignorant, he will make up for it on some other occasion by discovering one that is unknown; and if, trusting to the map and expecting a town, he only finds half a dozen black houses, he will sometimes meet a real village, as on the present occasion, where he expected nothing but barren hills and a deserted, rocky coast. It is almost ludicrous to reflect that a voyage through these western seas - the seas of Britain, maritime Britain, the queen of the ocean - should so often resemble an expedition of discovery on the coasts of New Holland or northern Asia.
>
> You must excuse me if I cannot give an account of the foundation, the police, the politics, or the scandal of Plockton. It would be fully as easy to acquire such information in Congo or Ashantee, and there would be less danger of detection in case of error. I can only conclude, from the number of fishing-boats, that the inhabitants are active fishermen, and, from the surrounding cultivation, that, as usual, they combine fishing with agriculture. The presence of some slated houses appeared to indicate a state of comparative wealth not often found along these shores.

*Pronounced 'Try', meaning 'sands'.
† Alternatively spelt as Maol, meaning 'headland'.

The following morning was dedicated to the circumnavigation of Loch Carron; a wide and spacious inlet, bounded on all hands by mountains, but not affording any striking scenery. The shores are generally low; and though there is a good deal of cultivation, there is no wood; or, at least, not enough to produce any effect in the landscape. There is a considerable village on the northern shore, called Jeantown; newly built, and consisting of good, slated houses. It appeared populous, and, being clean and orderly, is probably a thriving and useful establishment. The difficulty of forming towns or villages in the Highlands would render it desirable to trace the origin and history of the whole of these, since useful hints might be derived from those which appear to have succeeded. But the inhabitants can give no information; they are not mentioned in books; the proprietors are rarely accessible to a casual traveller; and mere conjecture can serve little purpose. This one, which belongs to Applecross, seemed to be arranged under a system of leases and an extent of tenements larger than is usual in this country. When the herrings frequented this coast, all the villages of this description had probably been comparatively opulent; and I believe I am correct in stating that this circumstance was the origin of the whole. With the desertion of this fish, they have evidently declined; but such are its caprices, that they may again, in no time, recover their former value.

In 1841, Lord Henry Thomas Cockburn, an eminent Scottish judge, reached Skye by carriage as part of a travelling holiday with his wife and family. Having surmounted the Mam Ratagan Pass - 'which is as long a steep pull as I have seen', wrote the judge - they arrived at Kyle Rhea, and he was far from impressed with the ferry and its operators:

This ferry, though boasted as the best in Skye, is detestable, at least for carriages, and is as ill-conducted as possible. But what can a ferry be for carriages where ours is only the third that has passed this year* and the object of the landlord of the ferry-house on each side is to detain instead of advancing the passenger, and where, when at last it is seen that they can carry it on no longer, the only machinery for putting the vehicle on board consists of dozens of lazy and very awkward Highlanders, all scolding in Erset, who almost lift it and throw it into the groaning boat.

Cockburn was pleased to record that they had set foot on the 'misty isle' - 'Here we are in Skye, as proud as Columbus when he first landed in America' - and he provided a glimpse of the country over the route from the ferry, up the Udal Pass, to the village of Broadford:

The first six miles or so of the 12 miles to this are a continuance of the same striking, mountain scenery. There is a still-worse ascent immediately after leaving this side of the ferry. It is a worse road, rises as high, or nearly so, and is, in one place, steeper, altogether more formidable. We hired two leaders for it, and without them, our making it out would have been very doubtful. So far as we have gone, these two hills and the ascent up Glencoe (which, however, we came down) are the only three places where there can be any pretence for putting more than two horses to a light chariot with six people, besides the driver, and all their indispensable luggage.

The last six miles next this open and descend into a commonplace, pastoral country. But (observe this 'but') there is, from that descent, a good view of the landlocked sea, ending with the Bay of Broadford, and bounded on all sides, except round its upper end, with good, stern hills. This (the upper) end, or head of the bay, is flat and mean. But all below is beautiful. Perfectly treeless, hard-looking and bare, but still capable of all the beauty that a bright sun can bestow on calm water, and on silent, massive hills.

Their return to the mainland was by Kyle Akin, and Cockburn summarised the strait, Kyleakin# village on Skye, the ferry, and then Skye itself:

The inn at this kyle seems excellent, and the kyle itself is beautiful. I mean its position, placed

---

* This was at the beginning of September.
† i.e. Gaelic.
# Pronounced as Kyle Akin.

as it is at the junction of Loch Carron and Loch Alsh, and not far from the opening into Loch Alsh of Loch Duich; made respectable by the old fragment of Castle Moil and gay by fishing-boats. It was intended, it seems, to have been a small metropolis, but like other over-grand building plans, has stuck at about a dozen of two-storied houses. The ferry is ill-provided with a boat and machinery for carriages, but hands, and the hope of whisky, did the business, though certainly their knocks and jolts, if survived, are the coach-maker's triumph.

We said farewell to Skye from one of the heights on this side. We had seen little of it, but quite enough to give us an idea of the whole. The sun, if the wind keeps quiet, makes anything pleasing. We have seen this island rose-coloured. But its prevailing state is marked by features that cannot be mistaken. The cold, cheerless rocks; the treeless desolation; the perpetual tendency of the clouds to rest, as if it was their home, on the tops of the hills; the great corries into which the weather has hollowed one side of most of the mountains; the utter want of natural verdure; the grey, benty colour of the always-drenched pasture; the absence of villages and of all human appearance - these things mark Skye as the asylum of dreariness.

Then they headed for the crossing at Strome:

The stage to Strome Ferry (12 miles) is very hilly, and few of the hills have much to recommend them. But it was a beautiful drive because much of it lay along Loch Alsh and Loch Carron. Wood returned to us, and the day has been fine. Strome Ferry is like the rest - picturesque - (and for this, the worse conducted, the better) and as well managed as mere hands, without proper boats, piers or any apparatus, can ever manage a ferry. When our ferrymen were loitering on the south side, it was curious to hear them excited to activity by the mail-horn on the other. I had forgot, in these solitudes, that there was a post.

Another traveller, Robert Somers, from his 'Tour of Inquiry in the Highlands' in 1847, supplied more details of the social conditions because this was his specific aim. In Ireland in 1845, there began the failure of the potato crop - the result of a killer fungus - and this soon spread over the country to produce famine. By the following year, the potato disease had reached the West Highlands, causing the same scenes of misery there as in Ireland. Somers' accounts of the state of the Highlands, due to the blight, originally appeared as a long series of 'letters' or articles in the Glasgow newspaper, the *North British Daily Mail*, and they were subsequently published in book form. He travelled from Easter Ross to Wester Ross, as far as the head of Loch Carron, in a public vehicle belonging to a well-known resident of Skye, and a general description of the intermediate country was provided:

Thanks to MacLeod of MacLeod,* the journey from the east to the west coast, through the moors and mountains of Ross-shire, is much easier and more expeditious than the porer over maps and guide-books could anticipate. This gentleman runs a handsome stagecoach, three times a week, from Inverness to the gates of his own castle at Dunvegan; and, except when boisterous weather obstructs the passage of the ferries between Skye and the mainland,† this long journey of 144½ miles is accomplished in little more than 20 hours. Taking a seat at Dingwall in this admirable conveyance, I was carried with unexpected rapidity to what, properly speaking, are the distressed districts of the Highlands. Our route lay through Strathpeffer, famous for its mineral waters; and Strathgarve and Strathbran, remarkable for nothing that I could learn, save the bleakness of their scenery and the scantiness of their population. As you approach the west coast, the aspect of the country becomes more thoroughly Highland. The valleys grow narrower and deeper - the mountains higher, rounder and more verdant. Wide-sweeping corries, the misty recesses of which are the homes of the red deer; straggling remains of pine forests; trackless ravines, worn in the mountain's side by the rain and the tempest; and watercourses innumerable, that alternately dwindle into rills and swell into cataracts, are the principal characteristics of this Alpine scenery.

---

* MacLeod had made commendable efforts at great personal expense, leading almost to financial ruin, to alleviate the distress of his many crofters during the potato famine.
† MacLeod's coach crossed by the Kyle Akin ferry.

Part of the village of Erbusaig, looking east from the curved embankment or causeway of the railway. This view was taken by Duncan Macpherson, the well-known pharmacist of Kyle, in 1913, but it is also representative of how the crofting and fishing houses of the area appeared at and before the time of the Kyle Extension.

R. Charnley

Somers' description of Jeantown - or Janetown, as he called it - clearly illustrated the poor state of the place and its inhabitants as a result of the potato failure:

Janetown consists of a single row, fully a mile long, of mean-looking cottages. A large inn, bearing the MacKenzie arms and having for its boniface the biggest and jolliest Highlandman I have ever seen, is apt to give you an inflated opinion of the comfort and importance of the city into which you have entered; but, walking a few paces round the corner, that long monotony of miserable hovels speedily informs you of your whereabouts. One or two houses, occupied as shops, and a few cottages with larger windows and whiter and higher walls than the rest, bespeak a degree of tolerable comfort; but, with these exceptions, the entire village presents the same low level of poverty and wretchedness. And the tattered garments and wan faces of the children that dabble about the shore, and of the women that cast half-frightened glances at you past the dirty rags stuffed in the broken windows, are quite in keeping with the miserable aspect of the dwellings. You are at no loss to perceive that famine has been at work upon those shrivelled forms, and that the life to which they have been doomed is one of hardship and privation, even at the best.

From Jeantown, he 'passed over to Plockton' which, with over 500 people, was 'the principal seat of population in the parish of Lochalsh':

The houses, of which several are two storeys high and slated, are erected behind a craggy promontory that runs out into the loch, answering all the purposes of a breakwater pier and forming a natural harbour in which the small fishing-vessels of the villagers ride in perfect security from storms. Plockton seems well adapted by its position for a fishing-station, and the population has made some slight advances to a state of trading activity.

The village and the parish were fortunate because the resident proprietor of Lochalsh - Isaac Lillingston of Balmacara, an Englishman - had shown concern for the people; and Somers acknowledged the support that had been given by this gentleman. Thus, in addition to helping the Plockton fishermen to purchase their boats,

Mr Lillingston manifested the utmost anxiety for the people during the recent distress, and did all in his power, both by employment and gratuitous assistance, to alleviate the calamities of the crisis. He sent large supplies of turnips to Plockton and other places, by means of which the injurious effects of the perpetual meal diet distributed by the Relief Board* were counteracted, and the people saved from the disease which broke out in other districts.

Unfortunately, as at Jeantown to the north-east, conditions were more deplorable only a few miles to the south-east, in the parish of Kintail:

A ferry over a narrow arm of the sea, called Loch Long, connects Lochalsh with Kintail. On both sides of the loch, there is a collection of wretched-looking huts, inhabited by poor cottars and fishermen. On the Lochalsh side,† the cottages are scattered irregularly along the shore, and back over a tract of swampy ground, on which all the evils of subdivision and squatting run riot. On the Kintail side, the houses are more numerous and concentrated, forming two goodly-sized villages, called Dornie and Bundalloch. The former has a few substantial, slated houses, but the general aspect of the place is one of poverty and wretchedness. When I reached the ferry, the dropping rain, and the black clouds rolling wildly in the wind, gave indication of a wet and stormy night. A few minutes placed me on the small quay of Dornie. About a dozen stout men were standing against a corner, crouching together in the rain and cold, and looking wistfully down on the rising turmoil of the fickle waves. A bad herring-fishing was written legibly in the long, grave faces of the poor fellows . . .
It would be tedious repetition to describe, minutely, the resources and condition of Dornie and

* i.e. the Central Relief Board, the full title of which was the Central Board of Management of the Fund for the Relief of the Destitute Inhabitants of the Highlands.
† At the village of Ardelve.

Bundalloch. The fishing villages of the west coast are too much alike to admit of separate detail. Some are wretched in the positive; some in the comparative; and some in the superlative degree; but all are wretched. Dornie is, if possible, more miserable than either Janetown or Plockton. One-half the people here have no land, and the other half have, on an average, about an acre each. The failure of the potatoes last year, coupled with the low price of herrings, plunged the village into extreme distress. Some idea may be formed of the extent of the pressure, as well as the uniform poverty of the people, from the fact that, out of a population of 690,* only 10 individuals were exempted from the relief list.

Similar poverty was conspicuous in Skye:

Crossing the ferry of Kyle Rhea, I found myself safely landed on a district of the Isle of Skye, belonging to Lord MacDonald. Here, I was at once introduced to a scene of misery which gave me an ominous foresight of the degradation and wretchedness that awaited me in other parts of the island. About a score of huts are scattered irregularly over a piece of mossy ground, at a little distance from the shore. These habitations bear every indication of extreme discomfort; and the narrow patches of soil to which they are attached speak in palpable terms of the slender resources and the scanty food of the inmates.

And in the parish of Bracadale, the property of MacLeod of MacLeod:

The clothing, furniture and hovels of the people bear every mark of extreme poverty; the children are pale and emaciated; and the dirty and slovenly habits which characterise many of the women serve to aggravate the discomforts entailed by narrow means. Domestic order, economy and cleanliness are ideas which seem never to have entered into the minds of a large proportion of the female population. To boil a pot of potatoes, or mix a brose of meal and water, is their highest attainment in the art of cookery; and you can see, from their dirty and ragged clothing, that, in the operations of washing, dressing and mending, they are equally deficient. A few pieces of cast-off dress are dabbled occasionally in the nearest stream, and spread out on the green bank, with a heavy stone on the top of each to prevent them from being lifted by the wind, and there left to bleach and dry, and sometimes to rot, as the natural changes of the weather may dictate. Of the interior of the cottages, it is needless to speak, so long as these consist, for the most part, of only one apartment, in which the family and the cattle find the same accommodation.

Having recorded the destitution in Skye, Somers sailed from the capital, Portree, 'by one of the Glasgow steamers', to the mainland at Arisaig. This was the start of the era of steamers regularly serving the West Highlands and islands, with Oban having become the crossroads for this new enterprise in sea transport, which was bringing tourists instead of 'explorers'. Steamboats had made their appearance in the Hebridean waters by 1820, but for much of the ensuing decade, they were largely employed for pleasure voyages. During the 1830s, sailing-boats were still outnumbering them for scheduled services, and by sail, the journey between Glasgow and Skye would take from 10 to 15 days, with numerous intermediate places having to be served. Steam navigation began to take over from sail for the Skye passage in the late 1830s, and, by the early 1840s, steamboats were regularly plying the route, greatly reducing the voyage to two days. It was as part of such a service that Somers completed his Highland tour, from the Isle of Mull by the *Tartar* steamer, owned by the Glasgow firm of Thomson and MacConnell. The *Tartar* sailed weekly between Glasgow and Portree, calling at the following ports: Oban; Craignure on Mull; Lochaline in Morvern; Salen and Tobermory on Mull; Armadale and Isleornsay on Skye; Glenelg; Balmacara; Kyleakin; and Broadford.

---

* At Dornie, Bundalloch and Ardelve.

Chapter Two

Planning the Skye Railway

By the time of the start of another new transport era in the Highlands - that of the railway - the ravages of the potato famine in the West had relented, although the effects were still evident. The railway age began in the Highlands with the opening of a line from Inverness to Nairn on 6th November, 1855. The 15 miles-long Inverness and Nairn Railway was created by Joseph Mitchell of Inverness, a civil engineer of great foresight who was to revolutionise the transport needs of the Highlands with the building of more lines. Mitchell had served as an apprentice of Thomas Telford on the Caledonian Canal; he had succeeded his father as Chief Inspector and Superintendent of Highland Roads and Bridges; and, as engineer to the Scottish Fisheries Board, he had planned or improved many harbours. With railway engineering having taken his interest, Mitchell had devoted much of his spirit to a project that had resulted in a serious and unprecedented proposal, in 1845, for a line from Inverness over the Grampian Mountains to Perth, but this ambitious scheme had turned out to be ahead of its time. After his success with the line to Nairn, he extended the system eastwards, in stages, through Forres and Elgin, to reach Keith, 55 miles from Inverness, on 18th August, 1858. All of this became constituted under the Inverness and Aberdeen Junction Railway, which, at Keith, joined the Aberdeen-based Great North of Scotland Railway and provided rail communication between Inverness and Aberdeen. Since there was already a railway from Aberdeen via Forfar and Perth to Stirling, and then to Glasgow and Edinburgh, this meant that, by 1858, Inverness had been connected by rail - albeit circuitously - with the South.

Joseph Mitchell, though, was still only at the early stages of his railway building. Having created a line east of Inverness, he next had to try to conquer the North, and for this direction, he found a particularly encouraging ally, without whose exertions and financial support the railway would not have proceeded there as early as it did. This help came from Alexander Matheson of Ardross Castle, near Alness, in Easter Ross. Matheson, who was MP for the Inverness District of Burghs, was a very wealthy businessman and great landowner. His Ardross estate amounted to 60,000 acres, and he had also acquired various large properties extending as far as Loch Alsh and Loch Duich in South-West Ross-shire. He had been involved in the promotion of the railways from Inverness to Keith, and now he was interested in seeing a line built north from Inverness. His enthusiasm and enterprise for such a line resulted in the passing of an Act of Parliament on 3rd July, 1860 for the Inverness and Ross-shire Railway, of which he was Chairman. The line, engineered by Joseph Mitchell, was opened over the 18½ miles from Inverness to Dingwall on 11th June, 1862, and from Dingwall to Invergordon, 12¾ miles, on 23rd March, 1863. The latter section was completed as part of the Inverness and Aberdeen Junction Railway, since this had incorporated the Ross-shire line on 30th June, 1862, with Alexander Matheson remaining Chairman.

On 9th September, 1863, Joseph Mitchell's dream for two decades finally came into operation, when the Inverness and Perth Junction Railway was opened throughout from Forres, on the Inverness and Aberdeen Junction line, to Dunkeld in Perthshire, where there were existing rails to Perth. It was a monumental undertaking, running for 104 miles and crossing the Grampians at almost 1,500 feet at Drumochter Pass, to give Inverness a much more direct rail connection with the South than by way of Aberdeen. The new line, via Grantown, Aviemore and Pitlochry, passed through much desolate and sparsely-inhabited country, and there were no large towns; but it was all the more

The view looking east from near Plockton towards Duncraig Castle and the towering crags of Creag an Duilisg in the late 1860s. Duncraig was the residence in Lochalsh of Alexander Matheson, the chief promoter of the Dingwall and Skye Railway of 1864, and the route of the line was to proceed along the edge of the coast and through a large cutting below the castle.

Drawing by Aurore McConnell

remarkable because, due to Mitchell's expertise, the whole length had been built in only 23 months. It was also Mitchell's railway in the sense that he had always believed, when others had been sceptical, that such a line could be accomplished - a magnificent achievement by this skilled and determined engineer, whose name was synonymous with railways in the Highlands by the early 1860s.

While Mitchell was forging further northwards during the second half of 1863 and the early part of 1864 with the Inverness and Aberdeen Junction Railway's Bonar Bridge Extension, which would take the railway 58 miles from the Highland capital, he may have had some thoughts about the possibility of being able to construct yet another line. From Inverness, there were railways proceeding in three directions: eastwards to Aberdeen; southwards to Perth; and northwards to Bonar Bridge, with the aim of reaching Wick and Thurso. However, except as far as Dingwall, there was no line heading westwards, intent on linking Inverness with the beautiful, rugged, isolated and extensive coastline and the islands beyond. Fortunately, Mitchell was soon to obtain the opportunity to try to expand the system in this fourth direction when a railway from Dingwall towards Skye was promoted during the spring of 1864. The idea was that the line, which would terminate on the west coast at a newly-created port, would provide the quickest and most modern means of transport for the people and commodities of the West Highlands and islands, with Portree, the capital of Skye, and Stornoway, the capital of Lewis, being of particular importance.

The Skye Railway as the new scheme was initially called, received serious consideration when a number of Highland landowners, including Alexander Matheson, who were deeply interested in the formation of such a line, met in London on 26th and 28th April, 1864. On the first of these dates, Joseph Mitchell reported that he had made a trial survey of a line, from which he was able to state that the cost of construction would not exceed £350,000, or £5,500 per mile. The gentlemen present resolved to bring the proposed line before the public in order to ascertain the amount of local support which might be relied upon; and, with this in view, a Prospectus was to be prepared and a provisional committee constituted to promote the undertaking. The scheme was warmly received by everyone in attendance, and letters were read from others along the proposed route, regretting their inability to attend but promising their support. A large sum, approaching £40,000, was subscribed at the meeting, with £10,000 having been offered by Alex Matheson who, in addition, agreed to take stock for the 24 miles of his land through which the 63 miles-long railway would pass, and thereby substantially increasing his contribution to about £20,000. Two days later, at the second meeting, it was agreed to change the name of the proposed line to the Dingwall & Skye Railway, and to appoint Messrs Joseph Mitchell and Company as the engineers.

Joseph Mitchell was the obvious choice as Engineer, with his experience in railway-making and his knowledge of the country; and, having been requested to determine the best route, he had readily decided upon the most natural one from Dingwall to the west coast. This was along the valley of the River Peffery, towards the spa village of Strathpeffer, and then by the hamlet of Contin, and the Black Water, along the western shore of Loch Garve and the northern shore of Loch Luichart.* From there, the line would proceed up Strath Bran to the old staging post of Achnasheen, down Glen Carron and along the southern shore of Loch Carron and the sea, by way of the fishing village of Plockton, to terminate at the hamlet of Kyle, beside the Kyle Akin strait and opposite Kyleakin village in Skye.

It was thus intended that Kyle, with its scattering of less than half a dozen houses and its little passenger ferry was to become the new port and railhead for the West

---

* Pronounced 'Loy-chart' ('ch' as in 'loch').

Highlands and islands, and Mitchell's reason in making the terminus here - at 'Kyleakin' or 'Kyleakin Ferry', as he and others referred to it - was because of its advantageous position in allowing the railway to compete with the existing steamers passing along the narrows of Kyle Akin. Although the country through which the line would pass was sparsely populated, Mitchell was impressed by the potential offered, particularly with traffic in the form of fish, but also in tourists because of the splendid scenery. The Dingwall and Skye promoters, too, were fully aware of how the line would revolutionise the transport facilities west of Inverness. Since there was no railway in the whole of the West Highlands, the plentiful supplies of fish caught around the Hebrides had to be conveyed either to the Firth of Clyde or round to North-East Scotland in order to reach

DINGWALL AND SKYE RAILWAY

CAPITAL, £350,000; IN SHARES OF £10 EACH.
DEPOSIT, £1. 10s. PER SHARE.

PROVISIONAL COMMITTEE.

MACLEOD OF MACLEOD, *Chairman and Convener.*
The Right Hon. Earl of Listowel, Curator for Lord
  Macdonald.
The Viscount Hill.
The Lord Lovat.
The Lord Middleton.
The Master of Lovat.
Hon. Rowland Clegg Hill.
Vice-Chancellor Sir John Stuart.
Sir Jas. Matheson, of Achany and the Lews, Bart., M.P.
Sir Kenneth Smith Mackenzie, Bart.
Sir William Mackenzie, of Coul, Bart.
Sir John P. Ord, of North Uist, Bart.
Evan Baillie, Esq. of Dochfour and Glenelg.
Meyrick Bankes, Esq. of Letterewe.
John Binning, Esq., Brae, Dingwall.
Donald Colin Cameron, Esq., Talisker.
Duncan Davidson, Esq. of Tulloch.
John Finlayson, Esq., Balmacara, Factor for Lochalsh.
Captain Fraser, of Culbockie.
Thomas Fraser, Esq., Sheriff-Substitute, Portree.
George Loch, Esq., 12 Albemarle Street, London.
Colin Lyon-Mackenzie, Esq., Provost of Inverness.
Dr Martin, of Husabost.
Alexander Matheson, Esq. of Ardross, M.P.
Hugh M. Matheson, Esq. of Elsick.
Æneas R. Macdonell, Esq. of Morar.
Thomas Mackenzie, Esq. of Ord.
Alexander Macdonald, Esq. of Lyndale.
H. Macdonald, Esq. of Trieslan.
A. K. Mackinnon, Esq., Corry.
J. M. Macleod, Esq. of St Kilda.
Kenneth Macleod, Esq., of Grishernish.
Donald Macleod, Esq., Scorrybreck.
Hector Munro, Esq., Provost of Dingwall.
Laurence Skene, Esq., Banker, Portree.
Andrew Smith, Esq., Factor for Coul.
Charles Waterston, Esq., Banker Inverness.
  (With power to add to their number.)
Engineers—Messrs J. Mitchell & Co., Inverness.
Bankers.
Caledonian Bank. | Commercial Bank,
  National Bank.
Solicitors.
Messrs Stewart & Rule, Inverness.
Messrs H. & A. Inglis, W.S., Edinburgh.
Parliamentary Agents.
Messrs Martin & Leslie, 27 Abingdon Street, Westminster.
Interim Secretary.—Mr Andrew Dougall, Inverness.
The proposed undertaking will connect an extensive and important district of country on the West Coast of Scotland, together with a large group of Islands, comprehending Skye, the Lews, Harris, North and South Uist, &c., with the Rail-

ports from where it could be forwarded by rail to the large markets, especially London. Such a lengthy detour in each case meant that the fish could not reach the markets fresh and so could not obtain the best prices.

Similarly, the new line would enable the sheep and cattle of the West Highlands and islands to be carried to the markets of central Scotland swiftly and in good condition, which would be in striking contrast to the way in which the animals had made their journeys of four to six weeks on foot over the drove roads, prior to the railway era in the Highlands. This had resulted in them arriving in poor condition and, consequently, with a reduced value at the markets. And passengers would also be important to the new railway: tourists would be able to see with ease the unspoilt beauty of Wester Ross and the Hebrides, while the people from these parts would be afforded a convenient connection with Inverness and elsewhere in the country.

Mitchell and the promoters were confident that the new line would be profitable, and, based upon the survey of the great engineer, the Prospectus of the Dingwall and Skye Railway was issued in early July 1864, as follows:

> The proposed undertaking will connect an extensive and important district of country on the west coast of Scotland, together with a large group of islands, comprehending Skye, the Lews, Harris, North and South Uist, etc., with the railway system at Dingwall, and enable a passenger to travel from Kyleakin, the western terminus of the proposed line, to Inverness in three hours, to Edinburgh and Glasgow in 10 hours, and to London in 21 hours, without change of carriage.
>
> The importance of this line of railway for local purposes, and also as placing the whole west coast of Inverness-shire, Ross-shire and Sutherlandshire, extending to upwards of 150 miles of seaboard, and the numerous islands adjoining the mainland, in direct connection with the railway system of the kingdom, will be obvious to all who are acquainted with the country; and the successful completion, in the autumn of 1863, of the great Highland line from Inverness to Perth not only indicates that the time has arrived for making a vigorous movement on the subject, but affords the certainty of a remunerative return, owing to the stream of traffic which will flow to and from the west coast via the great central direct route thus established to the South.
>
> Kyleakin stands on the western shore of Ross-shire, from which a ferry, half a mile in breadth, takes the passenger to the island of Skye. All the steamers to and from Glasgow, as well as the whole shipping on the west coast, pass and re-pass it. There is an excellent harbour, with deep water close in to the shore, and, at a moderate outlay, a pier may be constructed, which can be rendered accessible at all states of the tide for vessels of even 1,000 tons burden, and this, from its position, will form the point on which the whole traffic of the western Highlands and islands must concentrate.
>
> In addition to the local traffic of the agricultural and pastoral districts which the line will command, it will have a valuable and lucrative traffic with Strathpeffer, famous for its mineral waters, and, likewise, a large tourist traffic throughout its entire length during the summer and autumn months. This will be brought, on the one hand, by the Glasgow and other steamers to Kyleakin, to be conveyed via Dingwall and Inverness to the South; and, on the other, by the direct Inverness and Perth line, from the great cities and towns throughout the kingdom to Dingwall, to make the return journey via Kyleakin. The scenery through which it passes and to which it leads, including Loch Maree, Loch Coruisk and Loch Duich, is well known to be unsurpassed by any in the north of Scotland. The country abounds in sheep and cattle, reared for the markets of the South. Important fisheries, which, for their development, only want means of rapid transit to the great centres of population, exist along the whole coasts and islands of the West, and will furnish a large and profitable source of revenue.
>
> The proposed line will be 63 miles in length, and will leave the Inverness and Aberdeen Junction Railway at the town of Dingwall, pass westwards through Strathpeffer, and thereafter follow pretty nearly the course of the present road to the west coast, forming a junction with the Ullapool road at Garve, and with the Gairloch and Loch Maree road at Achnasheen. It will then take the south side of Loch Carron, and terminate at Kyleakin.
>
> A preliminary survey has been made, and it has been ascertained that the line can be constructed for £5,500 per mile, including land, with good gradients for its whole distance.

Estimates of the traffic have been carefully compiled from returns made up from actual local enquiry and observation, which fully bear out the conviction of the promoters, that a remunerative return on the capital may be relied on.

The proposed line is approved and will be supported by all the leading proprietors whose property is traversed.

The capital of the new company was to be £350,000 in 35,000 shares of £10. The promoters had formed a large provisional committee, totalling 37, to advance the scheme, and among the list of names was a number of the most influential landowners of North-West Scotland. Included were some of those who had been present at the initial London meetings back in April, such as Alex Matheson; Vice-Chancellor Sir John Stuart of Lochcarron; Sir James Matheson, MP, of Achany and the Lews, who was Alex Matheson's uncle; and a gentleman called Norman MacLeod, who was better known by the old clan-chief name of MacLeod of MacLeod,* whose ancestral home was Dunvegan Castle. Other titled members of the provisional committee were the Earl of Listowel, who was the curator for Lord MacDonald of Sleat;† Viscount Hill of Achnashellach; Lord Middleton of Applecross; and Lord Lovat# and his son, the Master of Lovat, of Beaufort Castle, near Beauly. The promotion was therefore being launched under excellent auspices. The Prospectus stated the Engineers as 'Messrs Joseph Mitchell and Co., Inverness', which meant Mitchell and his partners, William and Murdoch Paterson; while the Interim Secretary was Andrew Dougall, who was the Secretary of the Inverness and Aberdeen Junction Railway. MacLeod of MacLeod was the Chairman and Convener of the provisional committee.

'It is a great undertaking', commented the *Inverness Advertiser*, in referring to the ambitious Dingwall and Skye Railway, 'but we cannot doubt that it will be successfully pushed through, if the northern public generally can be made to perceive the immense importance of the enterprise.' In order to introduce the scheme to the public and to appeal for subscriptions, with the aim of obtaining an Act of Parliament for authorising the construction, a meeting of 'landed proprietors, tenants and others interested in the formation of a line of railway between Dingwall and Kyleakin' was arranged to take place in the Caledonian Hotel, Inverness, on 15th July, 1864. The provisional committee had selected this date - the Friday of the bustling week-long sheep and wool market that was held annually in the Highland capital, with its population of 16,000 - as being best calculated to bring the attention of their railway proposals before the northern people.

A full attendance had been requested, and that was what turned up; the room was crowded, and many influential gentlemen were present, eagerly interested to hear about this new railway. MacLeod of MacLeod, the Chairman and principal speaker, having enumerated the advantages that the line would bring, drew attention to a certain lack of direct communication:

> You are all aware of the very little communication which exists betwixt the west coast and the town of Inverness. This town is undoubtedly the county town, but, at present, I call Glasgow my county town because I go there for everything I want by means of the steamers. I need not say that I should prefer coming to my proper county town, and that I should undoubtedly do so if we had a line of railway. This is a very important matter, and it is also important that gentlemen living and trading in Inverness should have pointed out to them the advantages which would accrue from the country between this and Skye being opened-up, and from the circumstance of Inverness again becoming the great centre of trade and commerce in the North.

* The same MacLeod who had operated the public coach between Inverness and Dunvegan, and who had provided assistance during the potato famine.

† The fifth Lord MacDonald.

Of clan name Fraser, with the ancestral Lovats having been the chiefs of the clan.

With reference to the anticipated success of the new railway, MacLeod stressed the question 'Can we make it?' - and then answered it by urging what would be required:

> In the first place, I must tell you that it requires the co-operation of every individual interested in the country through which the line must pass. The requisite sum of money, although not a *very* large one, is still large, unless, indeed, the matter is taken up by the whole community, and it seems to me that the whole community ought to take it up . . .
>
> But what I want to impress earnestly upon you is this - that the proposed railway cannot be made unless all come forward strenuously to aid us . . .
>
> You cannot get the public to subscribe towards the construction of a railway unless they are interested in it, and then they come forward and show their interest in it by subscribing largely. We require a large sum for the formation of our line, and I hope the result of this meeting will be that you will feel the necessity of taking shares to the utmost of your ability.

MacLeod, nevertheless, felt sure that, as long as not too much money was spent on preliminaries, the line would pay well; and he announced the result of the subscriptions that had been promised at the London meetings in April. The Duke of Sutherland had agreed to take stock to the value of £5,000; Sir John Stuart, £2,500; Alex Matheson, £10,000; MacLeod himself, £7,000; Ewan Baillie of Dochfour, near Inverness, £5,000; Sir James Matheson £3,000; and others, bringing the total amount close to £40,000.

Alex Matheson, who was received with much applause, also referred to how the line would benefit the West Highlands and Inverness. At present, he said, the large traffic from the west coast went by steamers to Glasgow, and this would certainly be secured by the railway and come to Inverness. If the northern people could obtain all their necessities from Inverness as cheaply as from Glasgow, they would not go to the latter place, which involved considerable loss of time. Thus, when they could transact their business and return home from Inverness the same evening, they would never think of making a two-days' voyage to Glasgow and run the risk of seasickness - a comment that raised laughter among the large audience.

One of the resolutions proposed at the meeting summed up the great need for the new line, stating:

> That the northern counties having now been opened up by the successful completion of the railway system to the county of Sutherland, the time has arrived when the wants of the important districts to the west, including the islands of Skye, Lewis and others, call for the benefit of railway communication.

while agreement in the choice of the terminus was shown by another resolution, this being:

> That the proposed line from Dingwall, where it will be connected with the railway system of the kingdom, to Kyleakin, the nearest point of the mainland on the west to Skye, and distant only about half a mile from that island, is, in the opinion of the meeting, the best calculated to supply this want.

Following the encouraging Inverness meeting, others were arranged elsewhere, during the late summer of 1864, to promote the Skye railway. The first of these was held on 29th July at Dingwall; and there was one on 17th August at Portree, the principal port of Skye; while another occurred on 20th August at Stornoway, the largest port of Lewis. These meetings were well attended, with various resolutions carried in favour of the new line; and at all three, the provisional committee was represented by Andrew Dougall and by Charles Stewart of Inverness, who was one of the solicitors for the scheme. MacLeod of MacLeod chaired the Portree meeting, by the end of which the

Skye subscriptions had amounted to over £16,000. A considerable number of shares was also subscribed at the Dingwall and Stornoway meetings. A resolution carried at Stornoway illustrated the importance of the railway to the town and the outer isles, stating:

> That the meeting, being alive to the great inconvenience entailed on this community by the want of a regular and speedy communication with the southern portions of the kingdom, hail with much satisfaction the announcement of a railway from Kyleakin to Dingwall; there uniting with the whole railway system of the country, and that the said scheme will, in the opinion of this meeting, form the route best calculated to meet the wants of the Lews and the Outer Hebrides.

Two further meetings took place on 23rd August. The *Inverness Courier* and the *Inverness Advertiser* provided a summary of these, as follows:

> *Dingwall and Skye Railway.* Public meetings in support of this undertaking were held at Lochalsh and Lochcarron, and were influentially attended. Vice-Chancellor Sir John Stuart presided at the Lochalsh meeting and Lord Middleton at the meeting in Jeantown. Resolutions approving of the scheme were passed with acclamation, and at each meeting, a large number of shares was subscribed for by those present at the conclusion of the business.

Finally, a second 'large and influential meeting' was held at Inverness - this time in the Station Hotel - on 28th September for the purpose of considering what further steps were to be taken in the promotion of the railway. MacLeod of MacLeod was again Chairman, and he addressed the meeting by summarising the scheme's popularity and progress:

> It will be in the recollection of many present that a meeting took place in Inverness in July last, at which a very favourable opinion was expressed with reference to a line of railway between Dingwall and Kyleakin. Since that time, great exertions have been made in order to ascertain what the feeling is throughout the country, and I am glad to say that, at every meeting which has taken place on the subject, the proposal has been most favourably received. I presided over one meeting at Portree, and there was a very strong feeling shown in favour of the line, for it was seen that its construction would not only be advantageous to Skye, where most of those present resided, but that it would also be a paying line. And, gentlemen, I think that the inhabitants of the Isle of Skye are fairly entitled to offer an opinion on that point, inasmuch as there are among them many men of ability, industry and enterprise, and who know what the capabilities of the country are.
>
> We have met today for the purpose of considering the subscription list, and I am glad to say that the subscriptions which have been obtained are quite as satisfactory as we anticipated; and they are still coming in every day. Since I came to Inverness, I have learned that, already, the subscriptions are such as would almost enable us to go to Parliament for the necessary powers, and I look to the present meeting to add to the amount. Many persons naturally desire to see in what spirit a proposal of this kind is taken up by those more immediately interested and through whose estates the line is proposed to pass, because these persons are better qualified than others to decide upon the value of the undertaking, and to judge of the nature of the results to be expected from it. I therefore hope that, after seeing what has already been done, a large number of shares will be taken up in this room.

At the meeting, another important consideration was discussed, involving the possibility of a change of starting point for the line. There had been serious talk to the effect that some doubt existed in regard to Dingwall being the junction, and that Muir of Ord, about six miles south of Dingwall, had been proposed, with the intention that the deviation should meet the original route somewhere near the Falls of Rogie, on the Black Water. One reason given in favour of the suggested change was that the grounds of an influential gentleman, Sir William MacKenzie of Coul, near Contin, would be affected by the original line, although the aim was to do as little damage as possible to his land. Another reason was that engineering problems were said to exist between Strathpeffer and the Falls of Rogie, but Joseph Mitchell explained at the proceedings that this was not the case. The only difficulty, he added, was in how to construct the line so that it would not interfere with MacKenzie's estate. However, the meeting was firmly of the view that Dingwall should be retained as the starting point. Dingwall, with a population of 2,000, was the county town of Ross-shire, and other people who resided in its neighbourhood, through which the line was initially proposed to pass, had a necessary connection with the town. If the original intentions of the promoters were to be changed, the Dingwall subscriptions would be withdrawn. Shares to the value of £4,000 had been subscribed by the town when only £3,000 had been expected, and with the neighbourhood included, the total was about £10,000. The meeting, therefore, unanimously resolved that the line would be carried from Dingwall.

At the first meeting of the provisional committee of the Dingwall and Skye Railway Company, held at Inverness on 6th October, 1864, a list of the subscriptions that had been promised up to this date, was placed before those present by Andrew Dougall. Exclusive of the value of land to be given in exchange for stock, there was a satisfactory potential sum of just over £101,000. Alex Matheson also reported that the Boards of the Inverness and Aberdeen Junction and the Inverness and Perth Junction railways had agreed to recommend to their shareholders that each company should subscribe £25,000 towards the Dingwall and Skye line. As MacLeod of MacLeod had intimated to the large Inverness meeting in September, the provisional committee was in a position to proceed with its efforts to obtain an Act of Parliament.

In November 1864 the required notices for Parliament were issued, giving details of the Bill to be applied for in the session of 1865, which was intended to incorporate the Dingwall and Skye Railway Company with the following powers; principally:

> To make and maintain a railway, with all proper works, approaches, stations and conveniences connected therewith, commencing by a junction with the Inverness and Aberdeen Junction Railway, at or near the Dingwall station of that railway, and terminating at Kyle of Lochalsh, in the parish of Lochalsh, at or near the, sea, at or near a point 210 yards or thereabouts south-eastward of Kyle Inn, in a field occupied by Mrs MacLennan, widow; and which railway will be situate in, or pass from, in, through or into the several parishes, townships, burghs and places following (that is to say) - the royal burgh of Dingwall, the parishes of Dingwall, Contin, Lochcarron and Lochalsh, all in the county of Ross, and the parish of Fodderty, partly in the county of Ross, and partly in that part of the county of Cromarty which is locally situate in the county of Ross.
>
> To authorise the company to construct and maintain a pier, with all proper wharves, landing-places, works and conveniences connected therewith, at or near the terminus of the intended railway at Kyle of Lochalsh, in the parish of Lochalsh and county of Ross, and the soil or bed of the sea in or adjacent thereto, or one of them; and to lay down and maintain upon the said pier and wharves all such rails, sidings, cranes, sheds and other conveniences as may be necessary for the accommodation of traffic in connection with the said railway.

It was also proposed by the same Bill to confer upon the company a number of other powers; essentially these: to work steam vessels to carry passengers, animals and goods between Kyle of Lochalsh and the Western Isles and the northern coasts; to acquire the rights of the ferry between Kyle of Lochalsh and Kyleakin; to erect a hotel at or near the terminus of the railway at Kyle of Lochalsh; to acquire, by compulsory purchase, lands, houses and other property for the use of the intended railway and pier; to enter into arrangements with the Inverness and Aberdeen Junction Railway for the working and use of the intended railway and pier, and for the joint-use of Dingwall station; and to enter into arrangements with other railway companies, including the Inverness and Aberdeen Junction and the Inverness and Perth Junction railways, to contribute capital towards, and hold shares in, the proposed undertaking.

The application to Parliament in the session of 1865 for the Dingwall and Skye Railway was opposed by a few landowners, and the provisional committee, in consequence, was put to considerable expense. The Bill struggled through Parliament, but, since such a railway in the West Highlands was desperately needed, failure to provide it on this occasion might reduce the chances of any other similar scheme materialising in the future. Success was ultimately achieved with the passing of an Act of Parliament on 5th July, 1865, authorising the line's construction: An Act for Making a Railway from Dingwall to Kyle of Lochalsh, to be Called the Dingwall and Skye Railway; and for Other Purposes. The shortened title was the Dingwall and Skye Railway Act, 1865, and the Act allowed five years for the completion of the line.

Objections to the railway had been registered by proprietors along the route who professed to be supporters of the scheme in general, having only opposed the respective portion of it which affected each of them. Thus, Lord Hill of Achnashellach had contested the Bill because the line was planned to pass too close to the front or south side of the lodge; while Duncan Davidson of Tulloch Castle, north of Dingwall, had fought to have the line turning south of the Dingwall Canal instead of to the north, so that it would avoid his land. Both men's names had appeared on the Dingwall and Skye Prospectus, as members of the provisional committee. The most stringent opponent, however, was Sir William MacKenzie of Coul, whose name, most ironically, had been on the Prospectus as a committee member. At the initial gathering in Inverness back in July 1864, it was communicated that MacKenzie was prepared to do all that he could to assist with the promotion; while at the second Inverness meeting in September 1864, he was reported as not being opposed to the undertaking, although he was anxious that the line should pass through his estate with the least possible damage to it. Unfortunately, his subsequent attitude showed little concern for the interests of the railway, and it was indeed to cause considerable anxiety to the Dingwall and Skye company, who had won the Parliamentary battle, but at a price.

The Act had to take account of MacKenzie's demands. The railway was to come through Strathpeffer on the slopes of its southern side, turning westwards and then north-westwards, and in so doing, running north of Coul and the Black Water towards the Falls of Rogie. Because it was to pass within a ¼ mile of Coul House, the line would, at MacKenzie's insistence, have to be carried under a 510 yds-long, landscaped tunnel, which was needless and costly as far as the company was concerned, but essential from MacKenzie's viewpoint - in the literal sense, in order to keep the railway concealed from his house. The expense of the tunnel, including the associated landscaping and all the maintenance, was to be borne by the company. Not only had the company been forced to waste some of its financial resources in combating MacKenzie and the other complaining proprietors, but it would have to pay still more for the superfluous tunnel and earthworks at Coul. MacKenzie's action was certainly far removed from his intention of doing everything to assist the promoters.

Meanwhile, over the preceding year, other railway enterprises had become established in the Highlands. The railway system, again with Joseph Mitchell's endeavours, had expanded northwards from Invergordon, having been opened to Ardgay* in north-east Ross-shire on 1st October, 1864, with the station there named Bonar Bridge. The third Duke of Sutherland, with his developing interest in railways for opening up the northern Highlands, had contributed generously to this scheme, known

---

* Ardgay, pronounced 'Ardguy', is now within Sutherland District.

as the Ross-shire Extension, so that it was virtually on the border of his county; and, with his great wealth, he was planning to continue the line from Bonar Bridge. Thus, on 29th June, 1865, the Sutherland Railway had been authorised over a distance of 33 miles, inland by way of Lairg, to Brora, on the east coast. On the same day, another railway company had been sanctioned by an Act of Parliament. This occurred as a result of the amalgamation, on 1st February, 1865, of the Inverness and Aberdeen Junction and the Inverness and Perth Junction lines, and the large, new concern was known as the Highland Railway, which was, therefore, in possession of the lines from Inverness north to Bonar Bridge, east to Keith, and south to Perth. The Chairman of the Highland Railway was Alex Matheson and the General Manager and Secretary was Andrew Dougall.

The first general meeting of the shareholders of the Dingwall and Skye Railway Company was held in the Boardroom of the Highland Railway in the Station Hotel, Inverness, on 28th October, 1865. It was unanimously agreed that the following gentlemen be elected Directors of the company for the ensuing year: Alex Matheson, Chairman; MacLeod of MacLeod, Deputy Chairman; the Master of Lovat, who was a Director of the Highland Railway; the Honourable Thomas Charles Bruce, Deputy Chairman of the Highland; Colonel William Fraser-Tytler of Aldourie, near Inverness, and Eneas William Mackintosh of Raigmore, Inverness, who were Highland Directors; Alexander Dallas of Dochfour, near Inverness; and Captain William Fraser of Kilmuir, Skye. A disheartening statement, resulting from the lack of further advancement by this time, was read by Andrew Dougall, the Secretary:

The Directors have to state that the Bill for incorporating the company passed through Parliament under considerable opposition from landowners, and received the Royal Assent on 5th July last. In consequence of unforeseen difficulties, which have arisen in arranging with certain landowners on the line, no progress has been made with the works, and the Directors think it right to state at once to the shareholders that no steps will be taken until the difficulties are removed.

Alex Matheson expressed his regret to the meeting that the Directors had been obliged not to proceed with the railway at present, although he was glad to say that Lord Hill 'had completely given in', having made 'a very satisfactory arrangement' with the company; while it was also believed that Davidson of Tulloch was prepared to be reasonable with his land. 'Sir William MacKenzie, however, was as obstinate as ever', he had to add, since he had tried everything in dealing with MacKenzie, but without success; and it remained to be seen what they were to do in regard to the line passing through Coul.

Thus, as was concluded at the meeting, the company was left with no option than to postpone matters for another year. The *Inverness Courier* briefly explained the position:

The Skye railway, we regret to say, has been temporarily abandoned. The Directors have met so much opposition at the hands of the landowners along the line that time and money have been lost in the attempt to conciliate them. Sir William MacKenzie still holds out, and it is apparently on his account chiefly that the execution of this great public undertaking, fraught with such vast benefit to the West Highlands, is now delayed.

Nevertheless, the Skye railway had been warmly talked about by the public because the West of Scotland was in great need of the line. In this respect, the proposed scheme formed a short dialogue in a book about Skye which was published in 1865. This was *A Summer in Skye* by Alexander Smith, a poet and essayist who was born in Kilmarnock, Ayrshire, and the contents were based on his annual visits, since 1857, to the island. He had married a Skye woman called Flora MacDonald, from Ord in Sleat, who was a descendant of her famous namesake of Bonnie Prince Charlie connection. The conversation about the railway took place between two of his friends, one known as 'Pen' and the other as 'the Landlord'; and Smith noted that 'Pen and the Landlord had drifted away to the subject of the Skye railway - this summer and the last, a favourite subject of discussion in the island':

'You are a great friend of the railway?'

'Of course I am', said the Landlord. 'I consider the locomotive the good wizard of our modern day. Its whistle scares away filth, mendicancy and unthrift; ignorance and laziness perish in the glare of its red eyes. I have seen what it has done for the Hindoo, and I know what it will do for the islesman. We hold India by our railways today, rather than by our laws or our armies. The swart face of the stoker is the first sign of the golden age that has become visible in my time.'

'What benefits do you expect the railway will bring with it to Skye?'

'It will bring us in closer contact with the South. By the aid of the railway, we shall be enabled to send our stock to the southern markets more rapidly, more cheaply, and in better condition, and, as a consequence, we will obtain better prices. By the aid of the railway, the islands will be opened up; our mineral treasures will be laid bare; our marbles will find a market; the Skye apple and the Skye strawberry will be known in Covent Garden; our fisheries will flourish as they have never flourished before. The railway will bring southern capital to us, and humane southern influences. The railway will send an electric shock through the entire island. Everybody's pulse will be quickened; the turf-hut will disappear; and the Skyeman will no longer be considered a lazy creature: which he is not - he only seems so because he has never found a proper field for the display of his activities. There are ten chances to one that your Skye lad, if left in Skye, will remain a fisherman or a shepherd; but transport him to Glasgow, Liverpool or London, and he not infrequently blossoms into a merchant prince. There were quick and nimble brains under the shock heads of the lads you saw at my school the other day, and to each of these lads, the railway will open a career, great or small, or, at all events, the chance of one.'

Smith also related the difficulties that he and another friend had encountered in reaching Skye from Jeantown, and his story further illustrated the remoteness of the area:

Late in the afternoon, we reached Jeantown, on the shores of Loch Carron. 'Tis a tarry, scaly village, with a most ancient and fish-like smell . . . We had tea at the primeval inn, and on intimating to the landlord that we wished to proceed to Broadford, he went off to engage a boat and crew. In a short time, an old sea dog, red with the keen breeze and redolent of the fishy brine, entered the apartment with the information that everything was ready. We embarked at once, a sail was hoisted, and on the vacillating puff of evening, we dropped gently down the loch.

About ten, we passed the rocky portals of the loch on the last sigh of evening, and stood for the open sea . . . The coast on our left had lost form and outline, withdrawing itself into an undistinguishable mass of gloom, when suddenly the lights of a village broke clear upon it like a bank of glow-worms. I inquired its name, and was answered, 'Plockton'. In half an hour, the scattered lights became massed into one; soon, that died out in the distance. Eleven o'clock!

The boat was caught in a squally shower, and after it had died down, Smith noted:

It is plain our fellows are somewhat tired of the voyage. They cannot depend upon a wind; it will either be a puff, dying as soon as born, or a squall roaring down on the sea, through the long funnels of the glens; and to pull all the way is a dreary affair. The matter is before us - the voices of the crew are loud for our return. They will put us ashore at Plockton - they will take us across in the morning. A cloud has again blotted the stars, and we consent. Our course is altered; the oars are pulled with redoubled vigour; soon, the long, dim line of coast rises before us, but the lights have burned out now, and the Plocktonites are asleep. On we go; the boat shoots into a 'midnight cove', and we leap out upon masses of slippery seaweed. The craft is safely moored. Two of the men seize our luggage, and we go stumbling over rocks, until the road is reached. A short walk brings us to the inn, or, rather, public house, which is, however, closed for the night. After some knocking, we were admitted, wet as Newfoundlands from the lake.

Smith explained that the owner of the boat had insisted on being paid at Jeantown for the full journey to Skye, and then on another payment for he and his companions to stay overnight at Plockton. The boatman was supposed to waken Smith and his friend shortly after dawn, but he did not keep to his word:

No information could be procured; nobody had seen our crew. After a while, a fisherman sauntered in, and, in consideration of certain stimulants to be supplied by us, admitted that our fellows were acquaintances of his own; that they had started at day-break, and would now be far on their way to Jeantown. The scoundrels; so overpaid too.

Nevertheless, there was still hope for them to make their destination:

With some difficulty, we gathered from our friend that a ferry from the mainland to Skye existed at some inconceivable distance across the hills, and that a boat perhaps might be had there. But how was the ferry to be reached? No conveyance could be had at the inn. We instantly dispatched scouts to every point of the compass to hunt for a wheeled vehicle. At the height of noon, our messengers returned with the information that neither gig, cart nor wheelbarrow could be had on any terms. What *was* to be done?

Happily for the travellers, they discovered a former fellow-student of Smith who was now a minister in Plockton, and Smith continued:

I told him our adventure with the Jeantown boatmen and our consequent helplessness; at which he laughed and offered his cart to convey ourselves and luggage to Kyleakin ferry, which turned out to be only six miles off . . . It was a wild, picturesque road along which we moved; sometimes comparatively smooth, but more frequently rough and stony, as the dry torrent's bed. Black, dreary wastes spread around. Here and there, we passed a colony of turf-huts, out of which wild, ragged children, tawny as Indians, came trooping, to stare at us as we passed. But the journey was attractive enough; for before us rose a permanent vision of mighty hills, with their burdens of cloudy rack; and every now and then, from an eminence, we could mark against the land, the blue of the sea flowing in, bright with sunlight. We were once more on our way; the minister's mare went merrily; the breeze came keen and fresh against us; and in less than a couple of hours, we reached Kyleakin.
The ferry is a narrow passage between the mainland and Skye; the current is powerful there, difficult to pull-against on gusty days; and the ferrymen are loath to make the attempt unless well remunerated. When we arrived, we found four passengers waiting to cross; and as their appearance gave prospect of an insufficient supply of coin, they were left sitting on the bleak, windy rocks until some others should come up. It was as easy to pull across for ten shillings as for two!

Unfortunately, all the benefits to be derived from the Skye railway would have to incur a delay, because of Sir William MacKenzie. No progress whatsoever had been made, or seemed likely to be made, with MacKenzie, who had argued about the route, the line's conditions of passing, and the purchase of his land. The Directors had become intolerant of his demands, and, in spite of their agreement at the shareholders' meeting to do nothing for another year, they felt that they had to try something else, perhaps in desperation. Thus, as quickly as the end of January 1866, arrangements were complete for surveying a new route which would avoid Coul. At a meeting of the Directors on 30th January, their impatience was in evidence when they resolved 'to instruct the engineers to make this survey without delay'. The alternative route, surveyed in early February, was to take the line from south of Conon Bridge along the northern side of the

River Conon and through the Brahan estate towards Kinnahaird, crossing the Black Water and proceeding on its southern side by Contin to a point west of the Falls of Rogie, where it would meet the Parliamentary line. The diversion was almost entirely level, with a possible short-term saving of several thousand pounds; but the long-term drawback was that it by-passed Dingwall as well as Strathpeffer, and, hence, the plan failed to materialise.

The Directors were back in a familiar situation. Throughout 1866, there was still no sign of a tangible railway, and this was reflected in the short report to the shareholders at the annual general meeting in Inverness on 30th October of that year:

> The Directors have to report that, chiefly in consequence of the state of the money market during the last twelve months, the works have not been commenced, and they regret to say that the difficulties in arranging with certain landowners on the line, alluded to in the last report, still exist.

Alex Matheson had nothing in particular to add to what had been stated, but he mentioned that there were to be certain deviations in the line, which would require them to go to Parliament before any work could be commenced. They did not intend to go in the session of 1867, but he hoped that they would be able to do so in 1868, after which they could proceed with the building of the line.

The stubborn opposition to the railway had been an expensive affair for the company, but there was also some difficulty with the subscription list, which was not increasing in the anticipated manner. The company were disappointed in the lack of assistance from the large railway companies in the South of the country, who had been willing to help at first. Perhaps, to them, the Skye railway scheme looked too ambitious ever to be accomplished, just as this seemed to be the reason why many individuals had contributed little or nothing. While various landowners from the districts in and nearby the route of the line had purchased shares to large amounts, the financial support of the public, generally, was not very extensive. There had been many enthusiastic applicants for shares, but, subsequently, when the time came for paying their instalments, these subscribers were not very forthcoming, either for long or at all. It was not that they had lost interest in the new scheme; it was just that, after their initial enthusiasm, they later realised that they could not afford to help to pay for it. Thus, the company had to depend on further help from some of the more able subscribers, especially Alex Matheson.

With the finances having been determined almost exclusively by local, in the sense of Highland, subscriptions, the consequence was that there were insufficient funds to enable the project to be carried out all the way to the point originally proposed, at Kyle of Lochalsh; but during the summer and autumn of 1867, there were new hopes for a Dingwall and Skye Railway over a reduced length. This was specially discussed and encouraged at a meeting of four shareholders, in the presence of Andrew Dougall, which took place at Jeantown on 5th September, 1867. The four gentlemen were Lord Middleton, who chaired the meeting; Sir John Stuart of Lochcarron, and his son, John Stuart of Kishorn; and Alex Matheson. They held the view that the line should be made from Dingwall to a point on Loch Carron where there was deep water suitable for steamers, and to which the capital that was likely to be available would take the line. After consideration and an examination of the Admiralty chart, it was resolved 'to recommend to the Directors not to undertake the construction of the line beyond Attadale to begin with, the expense of which will be £220,000 or thereby'.

The four shareholders also discussed the list of new subscriptions, which had resulted from an appeal by the Directors during the summer. It was found that £24,160 of new shares had been received, while Lord Middleton announced that he would take an additional £2,000, making his total £5,000. An outline of the subscriptions read like this:

Original subscription list, £103,000, of which probably only £91,000 can be relied on	£91,000
New list laid before the meeting, including Lord Middleton	£26,160
Value of land which it is expected will be taken in shares of the company, 30 miles, estimated at an average of £200 per mile	£6,000
Contributions from other railways, assumed	£30,000

These figures added up to £153,160, 'thus bringing the sum, with £60,000 of debentures, within £7,000 of what is required to proceed with the undertaking'. The four gentlemen agreed to make vigorous efforts to have the deficiency subscribed, so that the company could go to Parliament in the ensuing session.

Attadale, which, appropriately, was the birthplace of Alex Matheson, was two miles south of the head of Loch Carron on its eastern shore, and it was considered a satisfactory location for the terminus. The original intention of taking the line all the way to Kyle had been because the communication to and from the West could be conveniently carried on by trains and steamers running in conjunction; but this, it was now believed, could also be done effectively at Attadale, which, although inland from Kyle, was still on the coast. It was felt that a port at Attadale would be little further from Portree and Stornoway than would a port at Kyle. With the limited funds of the company, but with sufficient expected to be found to make the line to Attadale, the Directors readily agreed to the abandonment of virtually all of the sea portion of the original line. This meant that 15 miles of railway-making would be saved, and most of this length would have required engineering of a difficult and expensive nature through hard rock along the coast, which would have been much too costly for the company in its present financial state.

During the summer of 1867, the Directors had been considering other changes to the route, such that they had had the line re-examined with the aim of making deviations which would allow the scheme to proceed and avoid objections from landowners. The principal alteration, due to the continuing obstinacy of Sir William MacKenzie, involved the railway being diverted away from Strathpeffer, Coul, Contin and the Falls of Rogie; and, instead, it was to take a more northerly course, by which means the expense that would have resulted from MacKenzie's stipulations would be saved. The other important diversion was at Achnashellach, where, in order to fulfil the agreement with Lord Hill, the company would run the line behind the lodge instead of in front of it. These changes were discussed at a Board meeting on 19th September, 1867, when the Directors agreed to have a survey carried out in preparation for going to Parliament in the session of 1868.

The autumn of 1867 heralded yet another change for the Dingwall and Skye Railway. Since the line's inception in 1864, the chief Engineer had been Joseph Mitchell, who, having trained William and Murdoch Paterson, had taken the two brothers into partnership with him in 1862. William began business on his own in 1866, while Murdoch, who was the younger, continued working with the great engineer. However, it was in 1867 that Mitchell decided that it was time to retire, on account of his declining health. He had suffered a paralytic illness in 1862, from which he had generally recovered; but now, five years later, his stamina was diminished. The partnership was dissolved, and it was the end of a highly distinguished career in civil engineering for a well-respected gentleman. Joseph Mitchell was to play no further part in the making of the Skye railway, but his legacy would remain by virtue of the company's choice of successor. At the Board meeting of 19th September, the Directors

The view from the northern end of Strathpeffer village, in the late 1860s, looking north-east to the Ben Wyvis Hotel and the 700 ft-high Knockfarrel hill. *Drawing by Aurore McConnell*

Strathpeffer village from the south in the late 1860s, looking north to the slopes above Achterneed. The Dingwall and Skye Railway ascended from the low ground of Strath Peffer, on the right of the view, through the valley in the background, and behind the hill on the left, to continue climbing the deviation towards Raven Rock. *Drawing by Aurore McConnell*

. . . considered arrangements for carrying on the engineering department, and were of opinion that, in the financial circumstances of the company, and the absolute necessity there exists for exercising economy in every department, it is expedient to place the engineering of the line and the carrying-on of the works under the charge of an Engineer to be paid a fixed annual salary, whose whole time and services shall be exclusively devoted to the company's business; and the meeting resolved to offer the appointment to Mr Murdoch Paterson, civil engineer, Inverness, at a salary of £500 per annum, provided he can undertake the duties at once.

Murdoch Paterson was well acquainted with Joseph Mitchell's plans for the Dingwall and Skye Railway, and having learned his profession with such a renowned engineer, he was the ideal choice of the Directors. He accepted the company's terms and was thereby appointed Engineer, with the arrangement being approved at a Board meeting on 29th October, 1867.

The next day was the annual general meeting of the shareholders, and on this occasion, Andrew Dougall was pleased to be able to read a report of genuine optimism:

The Directors have to state that, during the past summer, they had the whole route of the line carefully examined and partially re-surveyed, with the view of reducing the expense, and they are glad to say the result has been satisfactory. By effecting alterations and deviations in several parts of the line, there will not only be a great saving in the cost, but the route will be unobjectionable to those landowners who felt themselves compelled to oppose the original scheme. On 29th July last, the Directors issued a circular to the shareholders, giving full details of the proposed alterations and modifications, and requesting additional subscriptions. Since that time, replies have been received by which nearly £40,000 of new capital has been taken, and this, with the sum originally subscribed, will admit of the line being made from Dingwall to Loch Carron, a distance of 50 miles or thereby, as a commencement. In these circumstances, the Directors propose to apply to Parliament in the ensuing session for a Bill to authorise the deviations referred to. Landowners along 30 miles of the route have agreed to take shares of the company in payment of the value of their land.

Since the last annual general meeting, certain changes had occurred in the Board. Captain Fraser of Kilmuir had resigned as a Director, and Sir John Stuart of Lochcarron had been elected to fill the vacancy. The latter had, additionally, taken over as Deputy Chairman in place of MacLeod of MacLeod, who had resigned from that position in September, but who still remained a Director. Lord Middleton of Applecross had also joined the Board.

Having moved the adoption of the report, Alex Matheson spoke of the company's new progress and expectations:

The Directors have of late caused the whole of the line to be carefully examined by practical men, with the view of ascertaining what reduction could be made in the cost of the works; as it was manifest to the Directors that, unless a saving of expense could be effected, the scheme would have to be abandoned. I am glad to say that the result is most satisfactory. Not only can the cost of the works be reduced at many points, but a new route through Strath Peffer has been found, which is quite practicable, and by the adoption of which a large saving will be effected, while we shall have a line unobjectionable to the landowners.

By considerable exertions, we have raised nearly £40,000 of additional capital, and we are in hopes of receiving further subscriptions. In the meantime, we propose to go to Parliament in the ensuing session for a Bill to authorise the deviations, and to regulate the capital of the company. If all goes well, and we meet with no opposition, I hope the Directors will find themselves in a position early next summer to contract for such a portion of the works as will bring us to the first deep water in Loch Carron. I trust, therefore, that, in three years from this date, we may hope to see passengers from Edinburgh and Glasgow reach Portree, the capital of Skye, in about 13 hours; and passengers from Inverness in about six hours, at very moderate fares. I need not add that we rely on being supported by the people of the North-West Highlands and islands in carrying through this great scheme, which is calculated to confer so much benefit on these remote districts, and that, instead of throwing difficulties in the way, all will lend a helping hand in bringing the Skye railway to a satisfactory termination.

Matheson appeared enthusiastic about the 'new route through Strath Peffer', but there were disadvantages which were not stated amid the optimism. From Dingwall, the railway would head westwards along the low ground of the valley of the River Peffery for just over two miles, as originally planned; but thereafter, it was to turn sharply north and then west again, all the while rising quickly, to pass on the northern side of Fodderty and continue on a heavy ascent towards the small village of Achterneed. From here, the course was still steep, through the narrow glen of the Peffery, with the line attaining a summit of about 450 feet at Raven Rock, 6½ miles from Dingwall; and then it would descend, at first steeply, to the southern shore of Loch Garve, where it would meet the original line. Thus, the new route would not only avoid the heart of Strathpeffer Spa, but, in so doing, it would have to contend with more severe gradients, at 1 in 50, than on the initial route, at 1 in 75, and there was hardly any population along the way.

Although the deviation would be cheaper - in the sense that there was no Sir William MacKenzie to deal with - the great loss to the railway was Strathpeffer. It was an attractive village in a pleasant, fertile valley below the 3,400 ft-high Ben Wyvis, and its fame had resulted from the medicinal value of the mineral waters found there. Their healing powers had transformed Strathpeffer from a hamlet of thatched cottages into a fashionable spa-resort, and many visitors, in search of cures for various ailments, arrived from all over Britain and from abroad 'to try the waters'. With its splendid, though limited accommodation facilities, and fine tourist potential, together with its half-dozen shops and little market also serving the surrounding communities, Strathpeffer would have been the principal intermediate stop for the Dingwall and Skye trains. It was undoubtedly a pity that, because of the attitude of one man, the Directors were forced into taking their railway along the course to the north, out of reach of the village. The nearest that the line would come to Strathpeffer was an inconvenient 1½ miles away, on a considerably higher level, at Achterneed.

Based on the plans of Murdoch Paterson, the Parliamentary notices, issued in November 1867, announced the company's intention of proceeding in the session of 1868 to authorise the deviations by-passing Strathpeffer and running behind Achnashellach Lodge. The same Bill proposed to allow the construction of a pier and associated works at Attadale, and to abandon as much of the original line as would be rendered unnecessary by the alterations. Seven months later, the company's proposals were sanctioned by Parliament, when the Bill received Royal Assent on 29th May, 1868: An Act to Enable the Dingwall and Skye Railway Company to Make Deviations of Their Authorised Line of Railway; and for Other Purposes. One of the powers of the Dingwall and Skye Railway (Deviations) Act, 1868 was an extension of three years, from the passing of the Act, for the completion of the line. This was essential because three years had elapsed out of the original five allowed for completion, from the passing of the Act of 1865, without any work having taken place.

Chapter Three

Building the Line to Strome

At last, the way was clear for the construction of the Dingwall and Skye Railway. Tenders for building the 48 miles-long line, which was to consist of two sections, had been requested from contractors who would take at least £2,500 of the company's stock, and those received were considered at a Board meeting on 5th August, 1868. Four days later, the selections were made, and these were: the eastern contract, from Dingwall to Achanalt, 21 miles, and referred to as the 'Dingwall contract', to be let for £63,584 16s. 3d. to J. and A. Granger of Perth, who had built the line from Invergordon to Bonar Bridge; and the western contract, from Achanalt to Attadale, 27 miles, and known as the 'Loch Carron contract', to be let for £62,798 to A. and K. MacDonald of Glasgow, who were constructing a new harbour at Wick. The date fixed for the opening of the railway was 1st July, 1870.

The Directors did not have all their own way in regard to the amount of shares to be taken by the contractors as part-payment. At a Board meeting on 18th September, Andrew Dougall reported that he could not induce Messrs Granger and MacDonald to take more than £1,500 and £2,000 of stock respectively, and this situation, which the company had to concede, was thereby approved. At the same meeting, the tenders for the pier at Attadale were discussed, and it was resolved to accept that of Donald MacGregor and Co. of Dingwall, at £4,840 14s. 4d. MacGregor was engaged in the construction of a new Free Church at Dingwall, and he had been the contractor for a large portion of the masonry work on the Ross-shire line. During October, the plans for a proposed hotel at Attadale were considered, and it was agreed to erect the hotel on a terrace 20 feet above the railway. The architect was to be Alexander Ross of Inverness.

Operations for the building of the railway had commenced on 2nd September, 1868 with the Dingwall contract, and it was on 9th October that work began on the Loch Carron contract. For the former, the first priority had been in proceeding with the construction of a large embankment near Fodderty, which was necessary for carrying the line across the valley, together with the bridging of the road and river, for the start of the deviation on its climb towards Achterneed. During the first four months on the Loch Carron contract, to which everything had to be conveyed by sea, there were many problems because of stormy weather and the consequent delays of the steamers in bringing the plant for the works and also the materials for the navvies' huts. Thus, a proper start was not able to be made here until February 1869, by which time the Dingwall contract was well under way, due to the equipment being transported easily by land.

Back in August 1868, the Dingwall and Skye company had obtained a new Director. He was John Fowler, a Yorkshireman, who was a renowned civil engineer with much experience in railway-building, and who had purchased the estate of Braemore, south of Ullapool. His railway-engineering ability made it natural for him to have ideas of his own about aspects of the making of the Dingwall and Skye line; and earlier, as a shareholder, he had disagreed with Joseph Mitchell on some matters. One of these had been the suggestion by Fowler of a narrow-gauge track of 3 ft 6 in. for the line, with Mitchell having rejected this because of the heavy traffic of cattle, sheep and fish that would be carried, and because of the inconvenience of a change from the standard gauge of 4 ft 8½ in. at Dingwall. Another difference of opinion had occurred in regard to the deviation away from Strathpeffer, with Fowler having given his approval in opposition to Mitchell's view that the company should not have surrendered the original route through the Spa.

However, a recommendation by Fowler, after he had become a Director, was responsible for the further progress of the railway in distance. He rejected Attadale as a terminus and, instead, wanted the line to be extended down Loch Carron. The other Directors disagreed, but they subsequently decided, on 4th January, 1869, that they would not fix the western terminus of the line until Fowler had returned from abroad, in March. In the intervening period, an extension to Strome Ferry was seriously discussed, with Murdoch Paterson carrying out a survey of the five extra miles. Thus, by the time of a Board meeting, held on 23rd March at 'Mr Fowler's chambers, Westminster', a final decision was to be made. Murdoch Paterson read his report, from which it was found that the additional expense of carrying the line to Strome would be £5,232 4s. 10d. It was then resolved 'to proceed at once with the extension to Strome, and offer the works to Messrs A. and K. MacDonald, contractors for the Loch Carron contract, at their present schedule of prices, provided they take £2,000 of the stock of the company in part-payment'.

The name Strome Ferry did not strictly refer to a place, but, instead, was the little ferry which had long plied the half-mile stretch between the northern and southern shores of Loch Carron, near its narrows. A few houses and an inn had been built on both sides of the loch near the ferry-crossing. The remote Strome ferry had originally served mainly a scattered, local population, until the much-delayed completion of the coast-to-coast road by Achnasheen, along the northern shore of Loch Carron through Jeantown. This road, established by the Commission for Highland Roads and Bridges, had been used, while still unfinished, by the mail-gig; and its opening, in 1819, allowed travellers a stagecoach connection between Skye, Lochalsh, Jeantown, Achnasheen, Contin and Inverness. The road, in transforming the northern side of the loch, was also responsible for quickly tripling the size of Jeantown from a small settlement; and by the middle of the 19th century, the population had further increased to 600, such that the village became the second largest in Wester Ross, after Ullapool. The southern point of the ferry, which was what the Dingwall and Skye Directors referred to as 'Strome Ferry', lay below the steep and winding road that, proceeding over the Lochalsh hills by Auchtertyre, Balmacara and Erbusaig, connected with the Kyle Akin ferry. The southern shore of Loch Carron was now to be revolutionised by the Dingwall and Skye Railway, with its new terminus and port at Strome Ferry.

The Strome Ferry extension was let and begun in April 1869, the contractors being A. and K. MacDonald, as intended. On 4th June the Board confirmed an arrangement made with Messrs MacDonald for the works, but under which the latter had agreed to take only £400 of the company's stock in part-payment of the cost, instead of the £2,000 as previously resolved upon at the Board meeting back in March. Murdoch Paterson had arranged with Donald MacGregor, whose tender had been accepted for the pier at Attadale, to build, instead, a timber pier at Strome Ferry for £3,500; but his report also stated that 'the works of the Strome extension will cost about £2,000 more than the original estimate of £5,300'. In response to this, it was 'resolved to inform Mr Paterson that savings to that extent must be effected and that the Board rely on his not exceeding the £5,300'.

The works on the whole line generally progressed well during the summer of 1869. In early July, the *Inverness Advertiser* carried an account referring to Strathpeffer waking up for the summer season, and part of this briefly described the scene of the railway taking shape in the vicinity of Loch Garve:

> The line of the Skye railway emerges from the mountains shortly after passing the Falls of Rogie, and skirts Loch Garve near the roadway in curiously serpentine fashion all the way to Garve Inn, where it makes an easy ascent to the hillside. Over all the lochside portion of the railway, the rails

appear to be permanently laid, and it is a wonderful sight to see this lately unbroken mountain solitude dotted all over with navvies and their wooden dwelling places - with, more singular still, a real locomotive flying backwards and forwards on the line in aid of human and horse labour. Strathpeffer will, we dare say, not experience much benefit from the formation of the railway, considering the route its promoters were compelled to follow - a route nearly altogether ignoring the famous glen as a place of residence - yet no art of man can destroy a place so full of interest and romantic beauty, and it is quite possible that its absolute secludedness may, in the eyes of many, confer on it an additional charm.

Nevertheless, the Directors were showing some displeasure about one important aspect of the works on the Loch Carron contract. Based upon a report by Murdoch Paterson, they were concerned that 'the masonry on Messrs MacDonald's contract is proceeding very slowly, and that, unless greater energy is used, the line cannot be completed in time for opening on 1st July next'. With this in mind, a committee of the Directors were to 'proceed on an early day to examine the works, and to confer with Mr MacDonald on the spot, with the view of expediting what remains to be done'. An examination of the whole line took place in the first week of August, when Alex Matheson, Sir John Stuart and Alex Dallas, accompanied by Murdoch Paterson and Andrew Dougall, visited the works. Two days were devoted to the inspection, with the first ending at Achnasheen and the second at Strome Ferry. It was reported that the Directors had found the works to be in a very advanced state and that they were well satisfied with what had occurred, which, apparently, included the masonry on the Loch Carron contract.

Overall, the earthworks had made great progress. On the Dingwall contract, the foundations had been secured and were above the high-water marks, while eight miles of the permanent way had been laid and were ready for the locomotive. On the Loch Carron contract, now reaching to Strome Ferry, the permanent way had been laid for over 13 miles, nine of which extended continuously from Craig to Attadale. A locomotive was constantly running on this portion, conveying rails, sleepers and stones from Loch Carron to the interior, and this was of great service in pushing on the works here. The masonry, admittedly, was not as far advanced as on the Dingwall contract, but this had partly arisen because of an absence of suitable stone along the Loch Carron contract. Thus, it was acknowledged as a remarkable circumstance that, in the country between Dingwall and the watershed, which was four miles south-west of Achnasheen and ¾ mile south-west of Luib Inn, an ample supply of fine building stone had been found adjoining every bridge to be made, but when the summit was passed, no stone worth quarrying was discovered all the way to Strome Ferry. The consequence of this was that Messrs MacDonald had to take all their stone from Applecross, where it was quarried, and transport it by a special steamer to the head of Loch Carron, after which it was sent inland by the railway as far as its progress eastwards.

Over the 53 miles of the line from Dingwall to Strome Ferry, there were to be six stations, called Strathpeffer, Garve, Achanalt, Achnasheen, New Kelso and Strome Ferry. The Directors inspected the sites of these and decided upon the positions of the platforms and station-houses, etc. Actively engaged on the works of the whole line were about 2,500 men, 300 horses and four locomotives, and it was believed that the line would be opened to the public early in the following summer.

The Dingwall and Skye Railway was unusual in the sense that all its stations would represent communities in the neighbourhood which were villages or hamlets, and even its western terminus contained few houses; but the line would be advantageous in serving places further afield, especially the fishing villages west and north. Thus, Garve was also intended to be the station for the districts around Ullapool; Achnasheen would be for those in the vicinity of Gairloch and Poolewe; while New Kelso would be for

Jeantown, the largest community between Dingwall and Skye, being four miles from the station, which would also serve the small settlements of the Applecross peninsula. Achanalt station was the exception in this respect, accommodating the adjacent hamlet but no other communities, near or far. The name 'Strathpeffer' was to be given to the station which, because of Sir William MacKenzie who was now deceased, would not be in the village but situated 1½ miles to the north, and on the hillside, at Achterneed. In being an inconvenient location for Strathpeffer, it was, nevertheless, the nearest point that allowed the Spa access to the railway, considering the unreasonable deviation. In August 1869, the *Invergordon Times* reproduced an account from the *Liverpool Mail*, entitled 'Hints as to Home Spas', which, in describing Strathpeffer as 'the most efficacious spa in the three kingdoms', included a reference to the route of the line:

> It is to be regretted that the railway from Dingwall to Skye will not pass any nearer to Strathpeffer than the hamlet of Achterneed, fully a mile and a half distant. Owing chiefly to the pertinacious opposition of the late Sir William MacKenzie of Coul, the railway will have to make a detour until it falls in again to the old Skye road, about three miles beyond that favourite resort of anglers, Achilty Inn; and the line thence passes on to Attadale, opposite Jeantown on Loch Carron.

However, the Skye railway would have much to offer the many prospective tourists. 'The scenery along the line deserves a chapter to itself', commented the *Inverness Courier*, 'and this we must devote to it at a future time'; but the paper did immediately add something about the scenery:

> It gradually changes character as the line advances from the fine wheatfields of Strath Peffer through Strath Garve, Strath Bran and the valley of the Carron to the terminus at Strome, when the traveller is introduced at once to the full majesty of the Atlantic coast. There are not many finer hills than those of Applecross and Kishorn on the right, or those of Lochalsh on the left; but if there be any, they are those of the Cuillin range in Skye, which rise almost sheer out of the ocean at a distance of only a few miles in front of the terminus. Steaming out of the bay of Loch Carron towards Skye and the islands of the far West is one of the pleasures that will be reckoned hereafter among the greatest of a Highland tour.

Mention was then made about much-needed accommodation facilities for tourists along the route:

> Meantime, let us stick to what is practical, in considering the progress of the railway works, and give a hint to proprietors upon a matter of essential importance. The British tourist has wants and ways of his own; he refuses to admire even the Cuillin Hills after a sleepless night, or upon an empty stomach. Now, it is hopeless to expect that the small, old-fashioned, fusty inns of by-gone days will suit the requirements of modern travel, either in point of extent or comfort, and we think not a day should be lost in supplying the deficiency. It will well repay the cost - as witness Oban, Banavie and other places which could be named. Mr Matheson, MP, is immediately to extend the accommodation at Strome Ferry Inn, and to erect a new house at New Kelso station, which will suit the Applecross district. Captain Fraser of Kilmuir has also done a good deal in the same direction during the last year; and we hope others will promptly follow the example.

During August 1869, the contract for the timber pier at Strome Ferry, and the other works connected with the terminus, proceeded well, and the *Inverness Advertiser* was 'glad to understand that should any delay occur in the opening of the line at the period proposed, it cannot possibly originate at this important point'. About 40 men were daily employed under the active superintendence of Donald MacGregor. Fortunately, a good clay foundation had been available for the pier, with hardly any obstruction to the pile-driving. The pier would be extensive and would afford accommodation for large vessels at all states of the tide. At low water, there would be a depth of 12 feet at the head of the pier, and this, with a further rise of 18 feet at high tide, would allow a total depth of 30 feet.

For much of October, the western end of the line was subjected to meteorological conditions which were far from ideal for railway-building. 'The weather here is terrible', conveyed a report from Lochcarron to the *Inverness Advertiser* in the middle of the month, while adding: 'The hills are covered with snow, and for the last week, constant rain, hail and wind has prevailed'; but in spite of this, 'great progress has been made by Messrs MacDonald on the Attadale side of the Skye line', and it was believed that the distance from there to Strome Ferry would be finished by the end of December, or sooner if good weather was to set in.

The same report from Lochcarron made it known that great inconvenience was felt about the 'day coach being withdrawn from Strome Ferry to Dingwall', and that a requisition had been sent from the most influential people in the area to Mr MacIver of Achnasheen* for him 'to put a conveyance on the road'. Such a circumstance provided one more example of the need for a railway in the area; but another note from Lochcarron, later that month for the same paper, outlined an improvement that was demanded in regard to the Western Isles' steamers:

> It will be a great blessing to travellers visiting these islands, either on business or pleasure, when the Skye line is opened, and more especially if steam communication be in connection with the railway direct to Portree and the Lews. There is no regularity whatever kept by the present steamers; they come and go to places at all hours of the night . . . It is hoped that the energetic Directors of the Skye line will put their shoulders to the wheel and have their line in working order before the fishing season commences.

The annual general meeting of the shareholders was held on 29th October, 1869. The Directors at this time and for the succeeding year were: Alex Matheson, Chairman; Sir John Stuart, Deputy Chairman; Lord Middleton; MacLeod of MacLeod; Eneas Mackintosh; the Master of Lovat; John Fowler; and Alex Dallas. The report of the Directors and a detailed report by Murdoch Paterson on the progress of the works were presented to the shareholders. The former read as follows:

> The Directors are glad to be able to state that the works of the whole line from Dingwall to Strome Ferry, including the pier there, have made satisfactory progress during the past year. The foundations of all the important bridges have been secured, and the earthworks are in a very advanced state. The Directors, therefore, entertain no doubt that the line will be opened for public traffic about 1st July next. From additional information received during the last few months and inquiries made on the spot by some of the Directors respecting the probable traffic, they feel confident that previous estimates will be amply borne out by the result.

Alex Matheson, in moving the adoption of the report, had some additional words, particularly in relation to the anticipated traffic:

> The works along the whole line have made very satisfactory progress during the past year, and we have every reason to expect that it will be ready for opening at the time specified - viz., 1st July, 1870. We are fortunate in having such good contractors as Messrs Granger and Messrs MacDonald, who are most active and energetic in pushing on the works. The pier at Strome Ferry - the contractor for which is Mr MacGregor - is also in a very advanced state and will, in all probability, be completed in April next. The Directors are fully alive to the importance of having the line opened in time to secure next season's traffic, and a deputation of their number go over the works every month in order to satisfy themselves of the progress made.

---

* Murdo MacIver, the respected landlord of Achnasheen Hotel, also operated the mail- and passenger-coaches between Achnasheen, Gairloch, Poolewe and Aultbea.

It must be recollected that the Skye line is no mere branch line running into a Highland district where there is a limited population and a sparse traffic. On the contrary, it is a main trunk-line traversing the country from east to west, connecting important parts of the country to the north and south of the line with the east and west coasts. During winter, there are no fewer than four steamers each way weekly between Glasgow and the west coast, while in summer, there are as many as five and six steamers each way weekly, engaged in this traffic; and I believe it is no exaggeration to say that they all have as much as they can carry, and are doing well. We, of course, expect, with the accelerated service which we will be able to give, and the facilities which a railway can afford, to secure a fair share of that through traffic, which I know, from observation and experience, to be very large.

With regard to steamers, it is obvious that our success in carrying the traffic will depend very much on the regular and expeditious service which is given between the western terminus at Strome Ferry and the islands and coasts of the West. The Directors, therefore, have it in contemplation to enter into arrangements with steamboat owners, whereby steamers will ply in connection with the trains to and from Inverness and all parts of the South. This is a question of great importance, and the Directors are giving their best attention to it, in order that everything may be ready on the opening of the line.

I refer you, with pleasure, to the elaborate report of Mr Paterson, the Engineer, on the progress of the works, which you will find annexed to the report of the Directors; and I hope that when we hold our next annual meeting, we shall be able to congratulate ourselves on the completion and successful opening of the line.

Then came Murdoch Paterson's account to the Directors on the state of the line's construction:

I have to report, for your information, that the works on the Dingwall and Skye Railway are, on the whole, progressing satisfactorily. The weather during last winter was unprecedentedly fine, and the works were prosecuted without intermission, except for about ten days during a snowstorm at the end of February.

On the Dingwall contract, extending from Dingwall to Achanalt Inn - 21½ miles - Messrs Granger broke ground on 2nd September of last year, since which time they have pushed forward the works with very great energy. I am of opinion that, by the end of this year, weather permitting, all the earthworks and rock-cutting, and all the masonry and ironworks of the viaducts and bridges will be completed over the whole of this contract; and that the permanent way, fencing, station works and general finishing will occupy about five months thereafter. Of the permanent way, 11½ miles have already been laid down and half-ballasted, and one third of the fencing has been erected.

On the Loch Carron contract, extending from Achanalt to Attadale - 27½ miles - the contractors, Messrs A. and K. MacDonald, broke ground on 9th October of last year. During the first four months, very great difficulty was experienced in getting forward materials for building huts for the workmen and plant to carry on the work with, as these had all to be conveyed by sea, and most of the vessels were detained by adverse winds and otherwise for from three to seven weeks. It was not, therefore, until February that a fair start was made. Since February, however, very fair progress has been made. The portions farthest behind are between Achanalt and Achnasheen - 6½ miles - and from Achnasheen to the crossing of the River Carron - eight miles. On the former, about one half of the earthworks and masonry, and on the latter, about two thirds of the earthworks and one third of the masonry have been completed. From the crossing of the Carron to Craig Inn, a distance of two miles, the line is nearly all formed and a considerable stretch of the permanent way laid. The earthworks on these portions are light, and could, with good weather and an ordinary force of men, be overcome in three months. The foundations of the river and burn bridges, where any difficulty was anticipated, have been got in and secured against floods. From Craig Inn to Attadale, a distance of 11 miles, the line, with the exception of 1½ miles, is all formed and the permanent way laid, and for the greater part ballasted. The bridges over the rivers Carron and Taodail are all but ready for the iron girders, and only three small bridges remain to be built. As regards the Loch Carron contract generally, I am of opinion that, if the contractors manage to keep even an ordinary force of men - say, from 350 to 400 - in the upper district - viz., from Achanalt to the Carron — and are favoured with an open winter, the line can easily be got ready by 1st July next.

The extension of the line from Attadale to Strome Ferry - 4¼ miles - was, as you are aware, let to Messrs MacDonald in April last, and they have pushed forward the works vigorously. Large squads of men have all along been employed on it; the result is that, in about two months hence, all will have been finished, with the exception of the permanent way, fencing and some protection from the sea. This extension runs close to the shore for nearly its whole length, and on the first mile and a half from Attadale, the high precipices of rock, and loose rocks and boulders on the slopes on the one side, and the sea - in many parts very deep close inshore - on the other, made the works necessary for a line of railway look very formidable. These difficulties, I am glad to say, have been successfully overcome. All the loose rocks and boulders on the upper slopes have been removed, and the embankments made secure against the sea.

Mr MacGregor has pushed forward the works of the timber pier at the terminus at Strome Ferry in a very creditable manner. He has now merely to put on the vertical planking and embank the interior of the pier, and these works are in progress. The works of the pier will be complete before the time specified, which is 1st April next.

The station-houses at Garve and New Kelso have been begun; and at Strome Ferry, the agent's house has been begun, and the porters' houses are ready for roofing. The contractors are also preparing for the engine shed, etc. at Dingwall, and for the station buildings at Strathpeffer and Achnasheen. I hope to have all those buildings complete early in summer.

I have the honour to be, gentlemen, your obedient servant, - Murdoch Paterson, Engineer.

However, in spite of the generally good progress, the Board were still unhappy with part of the Loch Carron contract, and their disapproval was expressed in this manner:

The Directors regret to observe from the report of the Engineer that the works of Messrs MacDonald between Achanalt and the crossing of the Carron above Craig are not making the satisfactory progress which is indispensable to ensure the timeous opening of the line, and while they are persuaded that the contractors must be sincerely desirous that the expectations of the shareholders and the public, as to the time of opening, shall not be disappointed, the Board desire to convey to Messrs MacDonald that, in their opinion, more strenuous efforts on their part are required, and they hope that the intimation of this opinion will have the effect of at once stimulating the efforts of the contractors, who are, of course, responsible that the contract shall be duly implemented. And the meeting instructed the Engineer to report to the next meeting of the Board what shall have to be done by Messrs MacDonald to carry out these views.

Over the next few months, extending into the spring of 1870, the railway took shape to a significant degree. 'Quietly but surely, during the long and dreary winter which we have just passed through', recorded the *Inverness Courier* in April, 'have the works of this great undertaking been making steady progress towards completion'; although perhaps too much optimism prevailed when the paper added that 'the Skye railway is now so far advanced that its opening to the public on 1st July next may be looked upon as a certainty'. The progress on the Dingwall contract was such that an engine with a first-class carriage was able to run over the whole of the 21 miles from Dingwall to Achanalt. On board the train, which made stops at the stations of Strathpeffer and Garve, were Alex Matheson and his son, Kenneth; Murdoch Paterson, Andrew Dougall, and J. and A. Granger, the contractors. The inspection trip was said to be 'in every way successful', with the works found to be 'highly satisfactory, while the new views opened up by the line, particularly at Strathpeffer, Raven Rock, Loch Garve, Loch Luichart and Loch a' Chuilinn surpass anything which can be conceived when travelling along the old coach road'. The party then examined the works on Messrs MacDonald's contract, over which they were conveyed by locomotive on 23 of the 32 miles from Achanalt to Strome Ferry which had been laid with the permanent way. Whereas the Dingwall contract was well forward, a good deal still remained to be done on some parts of the Loch Carron contract, especially between Achanalt and Achnasheen, and in Glen Carron between Loch Sgamhain and the crossing of the river at the newly-constructed Glencarron Lodge, two miles north-east of Craig.   On 16th April, Sir John Stuart, accompanied by John Stuart junior, Murdoch Paterson, Andrew Dougall and Kenneth MacDonald, contractor, made a journey from Achanalt to Dingwall, when, 'the day being fine, the country was seen to great advantage, and everyone was charmed with the splendid scenery which abounds along the entire route'.

The pier at Strome Ferry was now complete and was ready to be used by the steamers. 'At Strome terminus, all is bustle and activity, and already the hill-side is well covered with houses, stores and buildings of various kinds, in anticipation of the opening of the line'.   Alex Matheson was making a large addition to the inn at Strome, to include bedrooms, sitting-rooms and a coffee-room, and he was building a 'commodious inn', entirely of concrete, at Strathcarron station - this name replacing the originally-proposed one of New Kelso.   The station-houses along the line were well advanced and were expected to be ready in good time for the opening.   It was also in April that consideration was being given for honouring Alex Matheson and the other Directors by having a grand banquet at Strome on the opening day.   The engine shed was intended to be the setting, with many invited guests who would arrive by special train from Inverness. 'We have no doubt the movement will be eagerly and heartily supported in the North', the *Inverness Courier* further added, 'and we hope to see deputations sent from the public bodies in Inverness, Dingwall and other districts to testify, by their presence, the appreciation they feel towards those who, in the face of great difficulties, have successfully carried through an undertaking calculated to confer great and lasting benefits on the North-West Highlands and islands of Scotland'.

However, there was a significant amount of work to be done before the opening, especially on the Loch Carron contract, which was still causing the Directors anxiety.   At a Board meeting on 12th May, at John Fowler's chambers in Westminster, reports were read from Murdoch Paterson on the progress of the works.   From the content of these, Andrew Dougall was instructed to write to Paterson, 'expressing the disappointment of the Board with the rate of progress made by Messrs MacDonald on the Loch Carron contract, and ordering him to put the powers of the contract immediately in force, and to employ whatever men are necessary to ensure the opening of the line on 1st July, as provided by the contract'.   In its issue for 19th May, the *Inverness Courier*, in noting that the works were being pushed forward with much activity and with an additional large force of men, had reason to believe that the original opening date would be adhered to; but the *Inverness Advertiser*, on 20th May, contained other information: 'We regret to learn, from a perfectly trustworthy source, that the Skye railway will not be opened for a considerable time after 1st July'.   At another Board meeting on 30th May, a further report by Paterson was read on the progress, which the Directors considered unsatisfactory, as it stated that the line would not be ready for the government inspection until 15th July.

Towards the end of June, while most of the Dingwall contract had been complete for some time, much of the Loch Carron contract was still unfinished.   From Strome Ferry to Glencarron Lodge the permanent way was laid, but in the long section between the latter and Achanalt the rails were not ballasted and some sleepers were not secured. Small engines were running along the line, bringing materials for the bridges and carrying the men to and from their work.   Messrs MacDonald now had about 1,000 men in their employment, with the operations going on day and night, weather permitting.

A picture of the hardy navvies on the Skye line was provided by a correspondent for the *Inverness Courier*, who walked the route in late June.   His descriptions referred mainly to the workers on the Loch Carron contract, due to the virtual completion of the Dingwall contract, but they were also representative of those on the latter. The writer had reached Garve after a pay day for the workmen, who 'were enjoying themselves in a somewhat noisy manner', and he was heading further west:

Having mentioned my intention of walking to Achanalt the same evening, a friend tried to dissuade me from the journey. 'You are not safe with the navvies; they would not think anything of attacking you'. And on starting, the speaker added, 'I wish you safe at Achanalt'. Surely the navvies did not deserve this suspicion! At any rate, they were respectful enough, and the most ferocious animal I met on the journey was a Highland bull that seemed strongly inclined to try the effect of a charge with his long horns!

The correspondent outlined the character and life of the navvies:

Wandering along the railway route at present, the traveller observes numerous bodies of workmen busily engaged in their employment, or lying during meal hours half-torpid in the sunshine. The natives of different districts meet and mingle here, and exhibit their various characteristics. The western Celts are numerous, stolid in feature, and disposed to take things easy; the eastern Scot, open-faced, with his broad accent - a striking contrast to the Gaelic - is a trifle more active; the bluff, hearty Englishman, with his southern dialect, is also represented; and, no doubt, the Irishman is also here, rich in brogue, if not in purse. These men, labouring hard from day to day, are crowded at night in their small huts, and experience little relaxation in their life of toil, except what the wet weather affords. Once a month, as they receive their pay, a large proportion enjoy a holiday - such enjoyment as it is; but, can you wonder, after all though, they vary the dull round of their existence with an occasional 'spree'? The cause of this periodical outburst lies very much in the fact that they have no entertainment beyond what is obtained in mere animal excitement. It is difficult, of course, on a line of railway to make any provision for mental recreation; but it might be arranged, at least, that the men should not be paid in the immediate neighbourhood of a public house. A few squads could also have their small newsroom, with papers and periodicals. I happened to meet the 'tommy' cart on the road, and it was very interesting to see many of the old weather-beaten men gathered round it, with letters just received from home, the contents of which they were slowly spelling out. The contractors, it is right to observe, are careful of their men, and attentive to their wants; the accidents on the Loch Carron contract have been comparatively few.

Knowing the importance of retaining a strong force of men to the end, Messrs MacDonald were endeavouring to keep on all hands to push the work rapidly forward. Against this principle were some of the workers who wanted to leave the railway works for employment with the fishing. The correspondent continued:

Some of those who go to the east coast fishing are now desirous to get away - not that their services are just immediately required, but they would like a short holiday, with its usual boisterous accompaniments, before entering on a new engagement. At Craig, I witnessed a rather singular scene. A number of men were anxious to get paid, and about 300 were gathered in the neighbourhood of the office, basking on the hill-side in the rays of the afternoon sun. Any quantity of 'lines' - that is, certificates for food from the shops about - were forthcoming, but no money was to be had. The men waited patiently, keeping the office in a state of siege, and thirsting sorely for the supplies of a neighbouring inn; but, in the evening, one of the contractors came upon the ground, and we believe they were satisfied by his explanations and promises. Payment signified the departure of some hands, and loss of time in the beginning of the week; so it was considered best to retain the money and pay in a lump at the close. Many of the men, however, were determined to leave, and I hear that they have been paid, and that 50 or 60 have departed for the fishing. Of these, a considerable proportion were good, steady workmen. Should a large number of the men leave, it will hardly be possible to have the line opened on 15th July, as was contemplated.

The delay in finishing the Loch Carron contract was attributed to unfavourable weather for much of the time, including during the summer. While the eastern side of the country had recently enjoyed fine, warm weather, with farmers beginning to complain of drought, it was a different matter in the West. The correspondent explained something about the western weather:

> The wet character of the west coast has become proverbial, but our Inverness friends would be slow to believe that, during the last five weeks, the workmen on this railway have lost about a fortnight in enforced idleness. That, however, was the case, and the industrious portion of the men were lamenting the interruption as well as the discomfort. No reliance can be placed upon the weather in this humid climate. A bright, promising morning may be followed by a pouring afternoon; though more frequently, the morning is wet and the afternoon fair. Within the short period of three days, I have experienced something of the changeable climate. On my starting from Achanalt about seven o'clock am, the rain was falling in torrents and the clouds lying so low that there seemed little hope of the sky clearing up. Most of the workmen who had quitted their huts returned to their shelter, and my companion was deploring another lost day. About eleven o'clock, however, the clouds cleared off, the sun shone out, and hardly a drop of rain fell during the afternoon. Yesterday, rain was falling from early morning till five or six o'clock in the evening, and today, the weather is the finest that could be desired.

Although great efforts were made to have the line ready for the Inverness Sheep and Wool Market traffic of mid-July, there was more disappointment when the *Inverness Advertiser* reported, in the second week of that month, that the opening would not, after all, take place until the first week in August. However, before the end of July, the Loch Carron contract was finished at last, and the Dingwall and Skye Railway was complete.

Now that this was so, the line could be seen in terms of its principal engineering features. Crossing the fertile valley of the River Peffery, near Fodderty, was the curved and inclined embankment which had been formed to take the line from the low ground towards the higher level by Achterneed on a steep gradient of 1 in 50, and this rise was to stretch for four miles, so that it was the most severe on the whole route. The embankment was pierced by two arched bridges, one of 22 ft span over the Dingwall and Strathpeffer road, and the other of 32 ft span over the Peffery. But, commented the *Invergordon Times*,

> . . . although the strath is a beautiful sight from the railway, the railway is not a beautiful sight in the strath. What was formerly a fine view of the entire vale, from either the Spa on the one hand or Dingwall on the other, is interrupted by the high gravel bank which bisects it.

From Achterneed, the line cut through the glen of the Peffery, at 1 in 50, to lead to a summit of 458 feet, lying below the striking Raven Rock, which, in legend, was the gathering place of the ravens, where they held their annual ball. It was said that, from time immemorial, there had been a raven's nest upon it until the building of the railway, when the birds deserted the rock, never to be seen on it again. It was also sometimes referred to as the 'Echo Rock'. A heavy cutting, through 20,000 cubic yards of gneiss and slate, was mainly carried out on the northern face of the glen, while Raven Rock was on the southern side, rising perpendicularly as an overhanging precipice to a height of 250 feet above the railway.

Having descended, partly at 1 in 50, through the Rogie glen towards Loch Garve, the line crossed the Black Water at the eastern extremity of the loch by an iron girder bridge of three spans, one of 60 ft and two of 40 ft; and then it squeezed along the whole length of the southern shore, with the road and steep-sided hills on the other side. From Garve, again by a 1 in 50 gradient, another summit, of 492 ft, was reached at Corriemoillie; and after running along the northern shore of Loch Luichart, the railway, east of Grudie, crossed the junction or mouth of the River Bran and the River Grudie - forming the start of the River Conon - on a lattice girder bridge of 100 ft span. A little further, into Strath Bran, was a skewed girder bridge, 200 ft long, of four spans of 50 ft, taking the line from the southern side of Loch a' Chuilinn to the northern side of Loch Achanalt.

Through Strath Bran, the railway, ascending amid the more hilly and bleak country, followed the River Bran to the old staging post of Achnasheen, and immediately beyond the station, it crossed the Bran on a lattice girder bridge of 80 ft span. Four miles later was the summit of the whole line, of 646 ft, at Luib, and then it was downhill through narrow Glen Carron, where the gradient was 1 in 50 between Glencarron Lodge and Craig. At Achnashellach, with its verdant and partly-forested hill-slopes, the River Lair was bridged by a central arch of 50 ft span and two side arches of six feet; while two miles south of the hamlet of Balnacra, the line was carried over the River Carron on a skew of iron girders of 140 ft span. Then there were two 60 ft girder bridges, one over the River Taodail at Achintee, and the other over the River Attadale at its mouth.

From Attadale to Strome Ferry, the route followed the winding southern shore of Loch Carron, and it was along these five miles that the heaviest work on the line had occurred. This stretch had tested Murdoch Paterson's engineering ability most severely. The rocks projected very close to, and rose abruptly from, the water, which, in some places, was many fathoms deep near the edge. Parts of the rock had to be cut away, and there were many loose, falling boulders to contend with; while the creeks of the loch had to be bridged and embanked, so that the railway could be brought along the narrow coastline. As the correspondent of the *Inverness Courier* had recorded during his walk over the route in late June:

> The passenger steaming along will be surprised to find himself on a narrow strip of land, bounded on one side by rock, and on the opposite side by the firth. The first journey on this coast must give rise to somewhat novel sensations . . . It would be worthwhile for a stranger to walk along the railway from Attadale to Strome Ferry to observe the engineering skill which Mr Paterson has brought to bear on this portion of the route. The pathway formed between the hills and the sea is unparalleled, so far as I am aware, on any railway in the country.

Except for these last few miles, the construction of the line had, in general, not been very difficult, considering that the route was partly through wild, hilly terrain; and except for the rock cuttings in the glen of the Peffery, the course was chiefly through moss, gravel or clay, with gravel frequently underlying the moss. The whole works had comprised 800,000 cubic yards of earth and rock excavation. Across districts watered by numerous streams, it was inevitable that a large number of bridges would have been necessary, and the total was over 140. Great economy had always been essential to the company in building the line, and this had been achieved initially because of the skill in the surveying of the ground by Murdoch Paterson. He had taken every opportunity to avoid the worst obstacles in order to secure the easiest permissible route for the line, which had become the first to be constructed by him on his own. The cost of the works was at the low average rate of £4,300 per mile, which, with an additional £200 per mile for the acquisition of the land, made the total for the 53 miles about £240,000. It was said to be the cheapest per mile in Britain - 'a miracle of cheapness', said the correspondent of the *Inverness Courier* - and, again, this was all the more surprising in view of the nature of the country. In comparison, the Ross-shire Extension, from Invergordon to Bonar Bridge, over an easier course than the Skye line, had averaged £5,900 per mile, inclusive of land; while the expense of the Inverness and Perth Junction Railway, with its heavier works through the Grampians, had been £8,900 per mile.

DINGWALL AND SKYE RAILWAY.

OPENING OF LINE POSTPONED.

The Public are informed, that in consequence of the FAILURE of the CONTRACTORS to COMPLETE the FENCING at the period agreed on,

THE OPENING OF THE LINE

FOR PASSENGER TRAFFIC IS POSTPONED

FOR A FEW DAYS,

But GOODS TRAINS will be run daily.

Further notice will be given when the Line is ready for Passenger Traffic.

By order.

AND. DOUGALL, Secretary.

Railway Office,
Inverness, 8th August, 1870.

SALE OF PERISHABLE ARTICLES.

OWING to SKYE RAILWAY BANQUET being POSTPONED, the PERISHABLE ARTICLES prepared for it, will be Sold at the "PEACOCK," TO-DAY and TO-MORROW at extremely Moderate Prices.

N.B.—The Articles are all prepared in the usual First-class Style.

Inverness Advertiser, 9th August, 1870.　　　　　　　　*Inverness Public Library*

Inverness Advertiser, 19th August, 1870.　　　　　　　*Inverness Public Library*

LOCAL AND DISTRICT NEWS.

OPENING OF THE SKYE RAILWAY.—We are glad to be able to announce that the Board of Trade yesterday authorised the opening of this railway for passenger traffic, Mr Paterson, the engineer of the line, having telegraphed on Wednesday to Captain Tyler, R.E., that the fencing had now been completed, and that the line was in every respect ready for opening. The formal announcement of the opening and the times of the different trains will be seen from our advertising columns. The steamer arrangements between Strome and the outer islands have also been re-arranged and materially improved.

Chapter Four
The Opening

On the evening of Wednesday, 27th July, 1870, the first locomotive to travel the whole line from Dingwall arrived at Strome Ferry, having brought 13 wagons over the 32 miles of the Loch Carron contract from Achanalt in an hour and a half. On the train were most of the contractors, sub-contractors and other builders who had been connected with the construction of the contract. 'The driver of the engine, Mr Ramsay, an old and experienced hand', added the *Inverness Advertiser*,

expressed himself as thoroughly satisfied with the road, found the locomotive going smoothly and well, with full command of the rails, and experienced not the slightest difficulty or inconvenience during the journey. During the different stoppages, there was, as usual in such circumstances, a numerous gathering of people belonging to the different districts passed through - all of them anxious to be initiated into the mysteries connected with the 'iron horse'. The natural curiosity, particularly of the ladies, was not to be overcome, and every possible facility was afforded nearly all and sundry of inspecting the mysterious and powerful stranger who had made his appearance in their midst, and is expected to effect so many wonderful changes in the country. On the party landing at Strome, they went over in detail the various buildings required for the station and terminus, which appear to be ample and satisfactory for the efficient working of both passenger and goods traffic. A number of persons awaited their arrival, and the whole proceeded to the pier to drink success to the new railway, at the kind invitation of Mr Kenneth MacDonald, jun., who has had the practical management of the western contract and has carried out the work with the greatest credit and satisfaction for the firm of Messrs A. and K. MacDonald, with which he is connected.

On Thursday, 28th July, Captain Tyler, of the Board of Trade, arrived at Dingwall in connection with the official inspection of the line. On Friday morning, he began his examination, accompanied by Eneas Mackintosh, Alex Dallas, Murdoch Paterson and Andrew Dougall. The contract of Messrs Granger was covered that day and much of Saturday, when Achanalt was reached in the evening. The inspection continued over Messrs MacDonald's contract as far as Achnasheen on Monday, 1st August, which was 'a day of thunder, lightning and rain in the West, as we learned by telegram - the first telegraphic news we have heard from Strome Ferry!', exclaimed the *Invergordon Times*. By Tuesday evening, Captain Tyler had completed his work over the remainder of the line to Strome. The outcome of his inspection would be eagerly awaited, with the hope that he would readily pass the line fit to be opened to the public.

The Dingwall and Skye Railway Company was not to possess and run its own trains, for the line would be worked by the Highland Railway using its own locomotives and rolling stock. Back in October 1868, at the half-yearly meeting of the Highland shareholders, a special session had been devoted to considering the terms of an agreement proposed to be entered into for the working of the Skye line. At that time, it was realised that, like the Sutherland Railway which had opened from Bonar Bridge to Golspie on 13th April, 1868, the Dingwall and Skye line would be built not with any contribution from the Highland but by individuals interested in the districts through which the line was to pass. Nevertheless, the Highland company was in a position to be able to help the Dingwall and Skye company in regard to operating the line, because the former, with its large resources and experience, could do so more economically. The proposed agreement between the two companies had been brought before the meeting at such an early stage in the development of the Skye line because the Dingwall and Skye company, having secured its capital, had wished to be assured then of the terms on which its railway would be worked. As read to the meeting by Andrew Dougall, the Secretary of both companies, the principle of the agreement was that 'the Highland company work and maintain the Skye line for a period of 10 years, at 2s. per train mile for two trains each way daily, and 1s. 10d. per train mile for any trains beyond two'. The Dingwall and Skye company was also to pay the Highland company a rental of £200 per year for the use of Dingwall station. In relation to the train agreement, there was the following arrangement, as read by the Hon. Thomas Bruce, the Highland's Vice-Chairman:

> The Dingwall and Skye company should determine the number of trains to be run daily on their railway, but the Highland company were to decide the time at which the trains should run, their speed, the loads they should carry, etc. Thus, the Dingwall and Skye company could not call upon them to carry more than the Highland company thought proper; and if there was more traffic, more trains would thus have to be paid for.

Some members of the Highland Board and shareholders were not in favour of their company working the new railway because of doubts about the revenue to be obtained from it, compared to the costs of operation; but, ultimately, by a majority, the agreement was sanctioned. In general, the Highland company was confident of the success of the Dingwall and Skye Railway. At the Highland shareholders' meeting in October 1869, when reference was made to the great progress in the construction of the Skye line and the expected opening in the following summer, it was added, with approval, that 'the result cannot fail to be beneficial to the Highland line'.

Just as the Dingwall and Skye line was intended to be worked by the Highland Railway, the Directors of the former had anticipated that a separate company would operate the steamboat services between Strome, Portree and Stornoway. They had had in mind the experienced firm of David Hutcheson and Co. of Glasgow, who had been in the steamboat business, serving the West Highlands and islands, since 1851. Hutcheson's steamers, in connecting Portree and Stornoway with Glasgow, sailed past the narrows of Kyle Akin and would have found a new port of call at Kyle to be ideal - if the railway had been able to reach there. Unfortunately, the Skye railway, having its terminus at Strome Ferry, was no incentive for these steamers to connect with the trains. With the additional distance up Loch Carron to Strome and back amounting to over 20 miles, it was too much of a detour in the opposite direction to the steamers' usual route. Consequently, Hutcheson had shown no interest in Strome Ferry, and the Dingwall and Skye Directors, not being able to find any other operator, were left with no alternative than to run their own steamer service. Thus, in May 1870, two 'large and handsome iron screw steamers' had been purchased and these vessels reached Strome at the end of July. They were the *Oscar* and the *Jura*, both of which had previously been employed carrying passengers and goods on the Glasgow and Bristol route. The *Oscar* was to ply daily between Strome and Portree, and the *Jura* three times weekly between Strome and Stornoway.

At the beginning of August, some details were communicated about the proposed grand banquet at Strome, which was planned for 10th August. The cost of the dinner and the special-train journey from Inverness to Strome and back was to be a moderate 12s. 6d. and this would include a 'sail in one of the company's steamers down Loch Carron, far enough to show the Cuillin Hills of Skye, the shores of Applecross and the new house of Mr Matheson, MP, at Duncraig'. The train was to leave Inverness at 8 am and arrive at Strome at 11.30, and, with two hours allowed for the sail, the banquet would begin at 2 pm. A very large number of guests had agreed to attend the celebrations in honour of the Directors and the opening of the line, and the provisions for the gathering were to be supplied by an establishment called 'The Peacock', of Inverness.

For the morning of Thursday, 4th August, with the verdict of Captain Tyler, regarding the opening of the line, still to be received, a train of several carriages had been organised to make a trip from Dingwall to Strome Ferry. This train was to convey the station officials to their posts, and also on board were Alex Matheson and his son, Kenneth; Captain Tyler, Murdoch Paterson, Alex Dallas and a number of other guests, including a representative of the *Invergordon Times*. This privileged correspondent, having travelled from his home town by the service train to Dingwall to meet the special train, had noticed a few other passengers there from his train who, on discovering the special for Strome, wished to take advantage of it, because they were heading in that direction:

There were some passengers by the south-bound train for the West, and they appealed to get by this train, some by words and some by looks. Of course, they could not be taken for money, but they could for love, as the Board of Trade does not enter the latter province, which ends oftenest with the control department. They made no objections to the new condition, and some got forward. The whistle sounded a little after eleven, and we moved out of the station.

The correspondent commented on Dingwall station and its station master:

Dingwall - by the way, its name now and hereafter, in railway records, is not Dingwall, but Dingwall Junction - is rather ill-off for platform and crossing accommodation, and the inconvenience is felt when there is a crowd. But the station master, Mr Paterson, is an active and obliging official, who shows himself willing to do anything for your travelling welfare, and is quite cheerful when no more than six at a time din him with questions.

It took a leisurely four hours to reach Strome, and the correspondent outlined the scene at the new terminus:

The train by which we went, owing to its principal purpose, had pretty long delays at some stations, and it was past three o'clock before it finished the journey. It was a pleasant journey. All our expected sensations were realised . . . The formerly quiet little spot of South Strome has now an altered appearance. A large new pier, rectangular in form, and built on wooden piles, runs out into the sea near the railway station for the convenience of the steamers to work the traffic with the islands. It looks a very substantial and efficient piece of work. The steamers are already on the spot waiting the opening - the *Oscar* and the *Jura* - smart-looking screws brought from the Clyde. The station premises on the spot are necessarily extensive, and the passenger station is covered-in, as at Invergordon.

Reference was made to the heaviest engineering, between Attadale and Strome, and commendation was given to those who had built the line:

The rocks run close-in upon the water, and there had to be hard scarping of them for forming the embankment most of the way. On the one side of the train, the rocks are seen towering-up perpendicularly, while on the other, there is the sea pushing its little waves close up to the foot of the high embankment, and there is plenty of sharp curving. The line, however, gets the credit from all competent to judge of being an exceedingly well-engineered one.
We have said that the engineer's part gets high praise. This applies to it over the whole line. The contractors also have made very satisfactory work. Messrs Granger, although not old men, are veterans in railway-making, and were finished with their portion some months ago. Messrs MacDonald also have done excellent work, and have been popular with their men and all others.

As the correspondent had declared at the beginning of his report:

Thursday last deserves to be hereafter specially noted in the history of the Highlands; for then the first railway train in the way of ordinary traffic passed from the shores of the German Ocean to those of the Atlantic. The line is the only one as yet constructed from sea to sea north of the Forth, and its importance to the country, and especially to the parts which more immediately it connects and will serve, cannot well be overestimated.

In regard to how Captain Tyler had viewed the state of the line during his four-days' inspection, it had been reported that the works appeared to be 'quite satisfactory' and even 'highly satisfactory', with only a few slight improvements suggested in regard to the fencing and ballasting. The impression then was that, if these were attended to quickly, the line would be opened for goods on Friday, 5th August, and for passengers on Tuesday, 9th, while the grand banquet to the Directors would be held on Wednesday, 10th. Unfortunately, the fencing was not so satisfactory for Captain Tyler to sanction the line for passenger traffic, and, to everyone's surprise, he failed it for this reason. Due to the hurry in trying to finish the Loch Carron contract, the fencing here was incomplete, with more sections still to be erected than the inspector would allow, and it was said that the deficiencies in the fencing were not only on this contract but also at several places on the Dingwall contract. There were rumours, too, that more than the fencing had been condemned - such as earthworks and bridges - but these were untrue, having possibly originated from the disbelief that the fencing alone could have prevented the line's approval. Captain Tyler ordered the fencing to be completed before he would pass the line, and this he would do on Monday, 8th August, if the various parts were remedied by then. On the Monday, however, he found that much had still not been erected, and he insisted on this being done prior to classifying the line as satisfactory. Thus, the *Invergordon Times* reported, amid disappointment, that the following circular, based on word received from Andrew Dougall, had been issued on Monday evening:

Dingwall, 8th August 1870, 9.30 pm. - Sir, - I regret to learn from a telegram, just received from the manager of the Dingwall and Skye Railway, that, in consequence of the non-completion of part of the fencing of the line, the opening of it has been postponed for eight days; and that the banquet must also be postponed. Early intimation of the opening, and of renewed arrangements for holding the banquet, shall be given. I am, sir, your obedient servant, - Andrew Smith, Hon. Secretary.

The fencing seemed to have been unaccountably neglected, and the Directors held both firms of contractors responsible, but no one had looked upon this aspect as sufficient to stop the line from opening as planned. The most strenuous efforts now had to be made to have the remaining fencing erected, but, because of the delay, passenger traffic was being lost at the best time of the year. However, goods trains had been allowed to run a day earlier than originally anticipated on the basis of Captain Tyler's inspection. They had commenced on Thursday, 4th August, which was the same day as the special train had travelled the line to Strome. The steamers between Strome and Portree and between Strome and Stornoway had also run to the originally-planned timetable, in spite of having no passenger-train connections, and they were said to have been keeping time 'very exactly' since the opening for goods. It was confidently expected that the line would soon be in full operation, but the banquet had had to be postponed until another suitable date could be found.

The fencing was finally completed on 17th August, and a message that the line was now ready in every respect was at once telegraphed by Murdoch Paterson to the Board of Trade, who replied on the 18th, sanctioning the opening of the line. On the following day - Friday 19th August, 1870 - the Dingwall and Skye Railway was, at last, opened for passenger traffic. There was no ceremony: there had been no time for one, as the company had been determined to open as soon as they could after the Board of Trade's permission, but the banquet would still take place. As the *Invergordon Times*, of 24th August, commented:

Advertisement from the *Inverness Advertiser.*   *British Library Newspaper Library, Colindale*

Above: Advertisement from the *Inverness Advertiser.*
    British Library Newspaper Library,
                   Colindale

Right: Advertisement from the *Inverness Advertiser.*
    British Library Newspaper Library,
                   Colindale

It is a pleasure to say that the Dingwall and Skye Railway is now carrying on its traffic in all departments. We are happy further to hear that the banquet to the Directors is still to come off - the day arranged being 7th September, this day fortnight.

The paper was certain that the banquet would still be a hearty and successful one, as the northern public would not be discouraged by the delay. Three days later, the *Inverness Advertiser* briefly reported on the line's initial success:

We are glad to learn that there is a good tourist traffic on the line, and that the daily average number of passengers is very fair indeed. The goods traffic has made a favourable start for this season of the year, but much of it yet has still to be developed by the company.

After the opening for goods traffic in early August, the *Illustrated London News* had sent a correspondent to provide an account of the new line, and, not surprisingly, he was impressed. His report was published in the magazine's issue for 20th August:

A line has this week been opened for traffic which carries the system of railway communication more than fifty miles further into the heart of the Highlands. The gauge is the same as that used generally in England, so that, the line being unbroken, it is practicable to travel from Euston Square or King's Cross to Strome Ferry without change of carriage, and at so little cost of time that one may dine late in London today, and tomorrow sup in full view of the islands of the Hebrides. The journey is one of infinite variety, and the last part of it, just opened, possesses many remarkable features, surpassing all other railway routes that we have seen in Britain, in splendour of mountain landscape combined with lake and ocean scenery.

He referred to the line's importance in respect of trade, particularly to the Outer Hebrides:

Of late years, the traffic has been limited to a few coaches in summer and a carrier's cart from Lochcarron once or twice a week. But it is expected that the railway will bring back to Dingwall and Inverness all the commerce of the Hebrides, which now finds its way by means of steamers to Glasgow. The Isle of Skye, with about 25,000 inhabitants and an annual rental of £35,000, derived chiefly from pastoral cultivation, is within easy reach of the terminus, by means of the steamers which the railway company have placed on the route. But of much greater consequence are the island of Lews and the adjoining islands of the Outer Hebrides, which possess resources in fish, cattle, sheep and agricultural produce, and a demand for shipping requirements and general merchandise, which it is believed will increase enormously when facilities are given for developing the capacities of the district by means of a railway within a few hours' sail.

However, in addition to the potential offered by the new line, the correspondent observed a certain dispassionate attitude in the local population, and he explained the reason for this:

A railway from Inverness to the Atlantic is really about the greatest event that could possibly happen to that part of the country; but the people had been gradually educated to the puffing of engines and the appearance of trains, even composed of trucks; and when the first legitimate train for the conveyance of goods passed over the line, there was hardly a bonnet doffed or a handkerchief waved in honour of the occasion. The popular enthusiasm was put off till it should air itself at a promised banquet to be given when the line was opened for passenger traffic. The goods carried by the first train were of the most ordinary and miscellaneous description - trucks of wood, wagons of hay, luggage and furniture; while such lighter gear as fishing-baskets, gun-cases, an occasional box of books from Edmonston and Douglas's reading-club, reminded one how, at the very first, the railway began to contribute to the comforts and graces, as well as the material prosperity, of the country.

Scenery on the Dingwall and Skye Railway, as portrayed by an artist of the *Illustrated London News* in 1870. *Above*: Loch Luichart, *below*: Achnashellach. These drawings, and two others on page 52, appeared in two successive issues of the journal in conjunction with an account of the opening of the line to Strome Ferry, and although they exaggerate the height and steepness of the hills, they do not over-dramatise the quality of the scenery.

British Library Newspaper Library, Colindale

The reason for the railway avoiding Strathpeffer village was also outlined, and then there was the following comment on the unsuitable location of the Spa's station:

The access from Strathpeffer to the station at Achterneed is most inconvenient. No one who can help it will ever venture up such an ascent by road.

From Achterneed, the railway headed towards what he described as 'the gorge known as the Raven Rock':

This is a narrow pass at the base of a lofty crag which seems to rise up sheer from the line of rails. One would think that if a sharp touch of frost got into the rock and dislodged some of the topmost fragments, they would inevitably fall with a crash upon the rails; but in this, we are told, the eye is deceived. The abruptness of the precipice is the safety of the line, for, though it looks so imminent, there is, in reality, a considerable space between the precipice and the rails; and if some masses were dislodged from the giddy height above, they would fall harmless, as there are no projections in the descent against which they could strike and rebound outwards. There is plenty of time to see the Raven Rock if one happens to be seated in a coupé with glass in front. The ascent, from the time of leaving the old avenue of Dochmaluag in the valley, has been at the rate of 1 in 50, up which the engines snort and pant as if they positively felt the drag of the train.

The correspondent also referred briefly to the effects of a thunderstorm:

When we were at Garve, the country was only beginning to breathe again after the alarm caused by a terrific thunderstorm. Twenty or thirty of the telegraph-posts were stripped and splintered by lightning, while the wires were twisted into extraordinary convolutions. So terrible was the storm that it was remarked by one of the squads of men at work that their 'ganger' had not uttered an oath for full twenty minutes!

Of Strath Bran, he recorded, with particular attention to an indigenous insect, that the plain

. . . is so flat that the river meanders through it in the most tortuous manner; in flood, it overspreads a great part of the land, forming great marshes that are the fertile origin of myriads of midges, as aggravating, if not as painful, as mosquitoes in Norway. The persistency of these gnats is dreadful. It happened repeatedly during the formation of the railway that the navvies had to drop work, being ignorant of the local custom, on days when the atmosphere is favourable to the lively labours of the midges, of veiling the neck and face, leaving only small loop-holes from which to look out. We are glad to see large squads of men at work, raising embankments and constructing drains along the riverside. These, we trust, will have the effect of diminishing the pest of midges, which, at present, is positively a curse on the country.

Regarding the western portion of the line, the verdant nature of the country and the final distance along the sea were remarked upon:

The west-coast influence is perceived immediately in the character of the vegetation. Even the most rugged of the hills betrays a tendency to put on a coating of green, while in the valleys, the brawling streams that come tumbling down the gorges are fringed to the edge with luxuriant vegetation. Even the bothies erected for the workmen, when the line was in course of construction, have a rich coating of fresh grass growing upon the turf of which the walls are made. The descent to the sea is much more rapid than on the other side, but is characterised, like it, by a succession of lakes connected by streams that flow, at last, into the sea at Loch Carron. The last few miles of the journey are literally on the water's brink - space to lay the rails has been scarped out of the rock, and from the carriage window, we look down into fathoms of the most exquisite green, in which long masses of sea-ware swing from the side with every motion of the water.

Drawings from the *Illustrated London News* in 1870 (*see also page 50*). *Above*: 'Strath Carron with Loch Carron in the distance', *below*: 'Opening of the Skye Railway: Strome Ferry, the terminus', as the original captions read. *British Library Newspaper Library, Colindale*

For working the new Dingwall and Skye Railway, the Highland Railway had assigned two engines which were not new. These were 2-4-0s, built in 1858 by Hawthorn and Co. of Leith, and they had initially been used for goods traffic on the Inverness and Aberdeen Junction Railway. Over the 53 miles between Dingwall and Strome Ferry, the service consisted of two trains in each direction per day, except Sundays, calling at all the stations, and with the journeys timed at three hours exactly; while over the 4½ miles between Dingwall and Strathpeffer station at Achterneed, there were two additional trains each way. The first timetable, with the Inverness, Portree and Stornoway connections, read as follows:

	am	am	pm	pm
Inverness d.		9.15	3.10	6.50
Dingwall d.	6.30	10.15	4.15	7.55
Strathpeffer	6.43	10.26	4.28	8.08
Garve		10.45	4.49	
Achanalt		11.21	5.15	
Achnasheen		11.45	5.40	
Strathcarron		12.45 *pm*	6.44	
Strome Ferry a.		1.15	7.15	
Portree a.			*11.15*	
Stornoway a.		*10.45*		

* Tu, Th, Sat only.

	am	am	am	pm
Stornoway d.			*5.45	
Portree d.		4.15		
Strome Ferry d.		8.15	3.15 *pm*	
Strathcarron		8.45	3.45	
Achnasheen		9.45	4.50	
Achanalt		10.09	5.15	
Garve		10.45	5.40	
Strathpeffer	8.35	11.03	6.02	8.30
Dingwall a.	8.48	11.15	6.15	8.43
Inverness a.		12.15 *pm*	7.30	

* M, W, F only.

The originally decided sailing schedules had been daily, except Sundays, for the *Oscar* to and from Portree, together with Tuesdays, Thursdays and Saturdays for the *Jura* to Stornoway, and Mondays, Wednesdays and Fridays from Stornoway. However, these had been very quickly changed - as early as the third working day after the opening of the line to passengers - although the train times had remained the same. From 22nd August, the sailings of the *Oscar* had still been daily but retimed, with calls also made at Kyleakin and Broadford; while those of the *Jura* had been reduced to two per week, being Mondays and Thursdays from Stornoway, and Tuesdays and Saturdays to Stornoway. The changes meant that, on these days, the Portree and Stornoway passengers travelled on the same connecting trains, which were the 1.15 pm arrival at Strome and the 3.15 pm departure from Strome. The rescheduled Strome-Portree and Strome-Stornoway timetable was now this:

	pm			am	
Strome Ferry a.	1.15		Stornoway d.	4.00	(M)
Portree a.	8.00	(daily)		6.00	(Th)
Stornoway a.	10.00	(Tu, Sa)	Portree d.	8.30	(daily)
			Strome Ferry d.	3.15 *pm*	

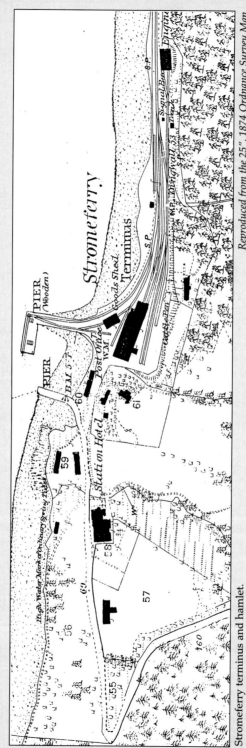

Stromeferry terminus and hamlet.

Reproduced from the 25", 1874 Ordnance Survey Map

The rearranged date for the grand banquet was Wednesday, 7th September. On the following day, the *Inverness Courier*, in recalling the reason for the event being held later than expected, explained that the success of the proceedings had not been affected:

The delay that took place, quite unexpectedly, last month, in the opening of the Skye railway caused great disappointment in the Highlands. The cause - insufficient fencing - aggravated the disappointment. People were quite prepared to believe that the inspector for the Board of Trade would be scrupulous in passing the works of a line made through a difficult country, in which steep gradients were inevitable, and under circumstances which obliged the Directors to count every shilling that was expended, but they did not anticipate a revival of the objection made to the first railway that was ever constructed. 'Suppose', said the counsel in that case, 'that a cow were to stray upon the line. Would not that be very awkward?' 'Yes', said the witness, George Stephenson, 'very awkward - very awkward indeed, for the coo!' Experience has, however, taught that a cow straying upon a line of railway may be very awkward for passengers as well as for cattle, and the fencing on the Skye line having been inadequate at the time the government inspector was asked to approve of the railway for passenger traffic, the opening was delayed till the defect was remedied.

One consequence of this was that the banquet, which the northern public had resolved to hold at the terminus in honour of the Directors, had to be postponed. So many people arranged to attend the gathering at Strome that the disappointment was very great and very general; but there is this comfort in the altered circumstances under which the banquet was yesterday held: that while the gratitude of the public is unabated, they have now had some experience of the vast benefit which the Skye railway will confer upon the important district which it brings into direct communication with the South. Day after day, since the opening of the line, passengers and goods have pressed upon the resources of the company for accommodation beyond the most sanguine expectations of the promoters; and if we could only anticipate a continuance of the present rate of business, the shareholders would indeed be most fortunate. This, however, is hardly to be looked for. Happily, the cost of the line is, on the whole, so moderate that even a partial diversion of the trade of the West will suffice to pay at least the working expenses of the railway, and those who know the country best are the most sanguine that, in a very few years, the resources of the West Highlands and islands will develop a large and remunerative traffic.

It was hardly possible that the banquet should go off with the same enthusiasm that might have been expected had it not 'hung fire'. The novelty of the situation had ceased; many of those who were present had already traversed the line, and the people along the route were no longer excited by the passing of a huge passenger train, such as that of yesterday. The universal feeling of satisfaction with the accomplishment of this great work was, however, too strong not too find hearty expression, even at a postponed banquet, and the Directors of the Skye railway must have been deeply gratified by the cordial thanks accorded to them yesterday, not only at the banquet but on every platform between Dingwall and Strome. An undertaking of great magnitude has been accomplished, the social advantages of which, to a large district of the Highlands, it is hardly possible to exaggerate.

According to previous arrangements, a special train, having between 20 and 30 carriages, and hauled by two engines, left Inverness at eight o'clock in the morning of the 7th, to call at all the stations on the way to Strome Ferry. Passengers from the North arrived at Dingwall by the 6 am service train from Golspie a little before nine o'clock to meet the special train, which left Dingwall at 9.10 to traverse the new line. The morning was sunny and clear, which added to the enjoyment of everyone on board, allowing them to appreciate fully the route and the splendid scenery of Ross-shire. It was not until the train had reached Strathcarron station, two hours after leaving Dingwall, that any symbolic indication of the rejoicing of the occasion was visible. A large flag was flying, bearing the design of a locomotive and the inscription 'Welcome to Lochcarron'. The train made a stop at Strathcarron so that tickets could be collected, and some of the passengers took the opportunity of inspecting the new but unfinished hotel, built close

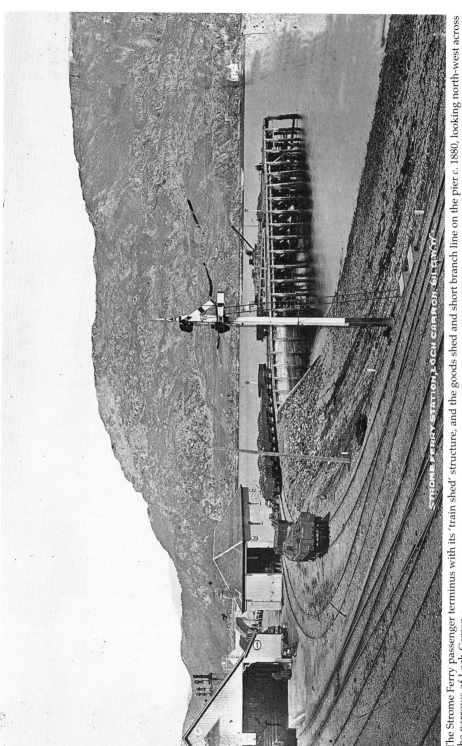

STROME FERRY STATION, LOCH CARRON, SKYE RLY.

The Strome Ferry passenger terminus with its 'train shed' structure, and the goods shed and short branch line on the pier *c.* 1880, looking north-west across the narrows of Loch Carron.

Aberdeen University Library

to the station by Alex Matheson. The hotel was unusual in being formed of concrete, which was cheaper than masonry. Good building stone was scarce in the district, and that which did exist was of a porous kind, making it difficult to build houses free of dampness. Concrete had recently come into popular use in England, and Matheson had decided to have the new hotel constructed in that fashion. The walls were 18 inches thick, consisting of a series of large, stone slabs, made up of cement and the small shingle of the local shore. The building was said to have a very clean and neat appearance, and would be of great benefit to the area. Matheson had realised the importance of good, modern accommodation for tourists to the West by way of the railway.

As the long train proceeded from Strathcarron along the shore of Loch Carron, it was further welcomed in the form of a gun salute by the Lochcarron Artillery Volunteers from the opposite shore at Jeantown. The sound of the gunfire across the two miles could not be heard by the railway travellers, due to the noise of the train, but the flashes and the resulting volume of smoke were readily visible as an acknowledgement from Jeantown. The train completed its final few miles to Strome by the narrow, twisting sea coast of Loch Carron, and over this portion, recalled the *Invergordon Times*, 'is the most difficult engineering work of the line to be seen':

> The rocks, for a considerable part of the distance, advance boldly upon the water's edge, and here, the engineer had to cut and form his way as best he could. The passenger finds himself sharp over the sea on one side, and on the other, sharp to the side of enormous precipices - the water-runs from which, in many places, toss themselves over the top, to be broken into spray by catching projections here and there on the way down, and, as he almost imagines, drenching the train in which he sits.

The new railway terminus and port at the hamlet of Strome Ferry - it was hardly a village - was reached 2½ hours after leaving Dingwall, and it had been well prepared for the day's celebrations. 'Strome was resplendent with flags, and from all the sheds and station offices, banners were flying', reported the *Inverness Advertiser*, and there were also decorations of evergreens. The *Invergordon Times* noted that 'when the long line of carriages had themselves emptied of their occupants, there was quite a large gathering of respectably-dressed gentlemen about the spot'. Everyone headed for the pier and looked for the steamer from Portree that was to take them for the sail, but it had not yet arrived. However, a little over an hour later, it was seen approaching, and before one o'clock, the *Jura* was alongside the new pier. On board was a considerable number of Skye gentlemen for the banquet, and many cordial greetings and congratulations were expressed at the crowded pier. The *Invergordon Times* added:

> One could hardly help now contemplating the genuinely-Highland gathering with peculiar interest. It was perhaps the largest ever held on the shores of the Atlantic. Had Prince Charlie as influential a one as to landownership when he hoisted his standard at Glenfinnan, he had not probably so soon been wandering among the hills not far away, with only half a kilt and entirely shoeless. By themselves, or members of their families, or their factors,* the owners of nine-tenths of the soil of Ross-shire were present or represented, as were those of more than half of Inverness-shire. The gentlemen present, in whose honour the meeting was held, comprised almost all those who used the exertion and largely bore the burden in giving railway communication to the Highlands, from Perth and Keith to Sutherland and Skye - about 300 miles, at a cost of between two and three million pounds.

Almost everyone who came by train boarded the *Jura*, which, with its many passengers, left the pier shortly after one o'clock. However, owing to the departure time being later than planned, the distance for the sail had to be shortened, and it was confined to the vicinity of Plockton. On the vessel passing the large, castellated mansion

* Factor: Scottish alternative for 'estate manager'.

STROME FERRY STATION (LOCH CARRON. 610. G.W.W.

The original station building at Strome Ferry c. 1880, from the north, showing the short branch line on the pier. The goods shed is on the left, and the station master's house is on the right. The station building was accidentally destroyed by fire in 1891 and was replaced by a similar structure.

Aberdeen University Library

of Duncraig on the hill above the bay across from Plockton - this residence being the property of Alex Matheson - three cheers were given in honour of the Chairman of the Dingwall and Skye Railway, without whose generosity and enterprise in bringing the line to the West Highlands, the day's celebrations would not be taking place.

The steamer arrived back at Strome about half-past two, after which there was a rush towards the place where the banquet was to be held - in the large, wooden engine shed to the east of the station, which was considered extremely suitable for such a numerous gathering. The passengers who had made the trip by the steamer were augmented at the banquet by other guests from places east of Inverness, who had not been able to make the sail because they had travelled on the 9.15 am service train from Inverness. The *Inverness Courier* described the setting inside the shed:

Messrs MacDonald of The Peacock, Inverness, were purveyors for the banquet, and all the arrangements were of the most complete character. The decorations were very neat, though not profuse; at the upper end, evergreens were wreathed in appropriate festoons; and at the back of the Chairman's seat, devices were wrought into a pointed arch, intermixed with flowers. Along the other sides of the shed, birch twigs were wreathed at intervals from roof to floor, surmounted by a border of the same pleasant green. Flags hung at different points gave variety to the scene. Four tables ran along the length of the shed, with a transverse table at the upper end for the Chairman and his supporters. The decorations of flowers and ferns on these tables were exceedingly pretty. The courses were all excellent and well served, and included fine salmon caught in the Tweed on Monday, some of which weighed from 18 to 20 pounds. Covers were laid for 470. The militia band attended from Inverness, conducted by Mr MacGillivray, and played appropriate airs between the toasts.

Six of the eight Directors of the Dingwall and Skye Railway were present. They were Alex Matheson, Sir John Stuart, MacLeod of MacLeod, Alex Dallas, the Master of Lovat and Eneas Mackintosh. Lord Middleton and John Fowler were unable to attend. Alex Matheson, who was received with loud and repeated cheering, outlined the history of the railway to the near-500 audience; and then he expressed the Directors' particular appreciation to two members of the Board:

First of all, to MacLeod of MacLeod, who, at the outset of the undertaking, took much personal trouble in presiding at meetings in various parts of the country, successfully recommending the scheme to public support.

And then:

We are also under the very greatest obligations to Mr Fowler of Braemore, who, as well before as since he joined our Board, has at all times given us the gratuitous benefit of his eminent scientific skill; and to his judicious suggestions, we are in no small degree indebted for having constructed the line at the comparatively-small cost of £4,500 per mile - being, I believe, the cheapest line yet constructed in Britain, and entirely at the cost of the landowners and others connected with the district.

Also praised was 'Mr Murdo Paterson, our Engineer, who never missed an opportunity of saving expense, when such was possible, consistent with efficiency'; as were the contractors 'for the substantial manner in which they executed the works entrusted to them'. Having presented figures of revenue, inclusive of the steamboat operations, which showed that the traffic had commenced most satisfactorily,* Matheson referred to the company's steamers and he explained why they were not as prestigious as those of David Hutcheson, such as the *Clansman* on the Glasgow-Stornoway run:

* Matheson reported: 'For the eight days from the opening of the line till the 28th ultimo, the traffic amounted to £527 3s. 7d. for passengers; £130 18s. 4d. for goods; £14 3s. for livestock; and £46 15s. 9d. for parcels, carriages, horses and dogs - being £719 1s. 2d. in all'; to which there was cheering.

STATION HOTEL, STROME FERRY, LOCH CARRON. 1547. G.W.W.

Strome Ferry *c.* 1880, looking east from beside the Station Hotel. The roof of the station master's house is visible immediately left of the hotel, with the goods shed and engine shed in the distance.

Aberdeen University Library

An enlargement of part of the previous photograph which shows the goods shed (*left*) and the engine shed in the background. The signal box is behind one of the chimneys of the original station building, and the water tower is to the right. The engine shed is not the original structure that held the opening day banquet in 1870, for that was destroyed by fire in 1872.

Aberdeen University Library

Disappointment has been expressed by many parties that splendid, large steamers, like those employed by Messrs Hutcheson and Co., have not been provided by us. But, in the first place, our boats have not, like Hutcheson's, to encounter the heavy sea round the point of Ardnamurchan and the Mull of Kintyre. We have only to navigate what may be called comparatively inland waters, and as we try to confine their voyages to daylight, sleeping accommodation is not required. Hitherto, our boats have done their work most satisfactorily. They are strong, excellent sea-boats, and in good order, and are commanded by skilful captains. I have no doubt they will continue to give satisfaction. And, secondly, having been purchased at a moderate price, their earnings will, we expect, leave a surplus after paying all expenses; whereas, if we had the means, and had purchased vessels like the *Clansman* for carrying on our traffic, I am confident that the result would have been most serious loss. With the boats we have, we shall be able to accommodate the traffic from Ardnamurchan northwards to Cape Wrath, and that is all we aim at. The traffic south of Ardnamurchan, we leave to Messrs Hutcheson.

In recalling the poor, but subsequently-improved, road transport earlier in the century, he concluded his speech by stating the land-value potential offered by the railway:

I am old enough to remember the time when there was not even a driving road from Loch Carron to Contin. The first journey I made to school - I think in 1819 - was on horseback, and it took me two days to travel from Loch Carron to Dingwall. We have seen what an effect the opening of the roads had in improving the West Highlands, and it cannot be doubted that the opening of the railway will have far more important results. I have in my possession, in the handwriting of a gentleman of this country - the father of Sir Roderick Murchison - a paper, in which the rental of Kintail, Glenshiel and Lochalsh in 1787 is stated at £1,761 6s. The present rental of these three parishes is now little short of £15,000 a year. This great rise in the value of property was, no doubt, very much owing to the construction of the roads. What the further increase of value may be from the opening of the railway, I shall not venture to predict.

There was an instance, though, when the potential of the new line was not realised at
first, but a little explanation soon clarified otherwise. At the banquet, the sheriff of Portree
recounted a conversation that he had heard of between two gentlemen having shares in
the Dingwall and Skye Railway. One of them, having invested £400 and looking very
doubtful about the prospect of a dividend, was asked by his optimistic companion:

> 'You sometimes go to Inverness, do you not?'
> 'Yes'
> 'And what does it cost you?'
> 'I cannot very well get there for less than £3, and it costs the same coming back.'
> 'And how do you travel?'
> 'On the top of the mail gig, exposed to all the sky and other influences.'

Then the pessimistic shareholder was informed: 'With the railway, you will get from
Portree to Inverness and back for £2, so that you will save £4 on every journey - a sum
equal to one per cent of your shares, besides the greater comfort of travelling.'

Laughter and cheering rang out from the audience upon this convincing reasoning -
and the dialogue had taken no account of the saving in time.

The banquet was a success and formally represented the completion of the Dingwall
and Skye Railway; but back in August, prior to the opening to the public, the
correspondent of the *Invergordon Times* had already paid tribute to the line's principal
motivator, Alex Matheson:

> Only twenty years ago, the idea of seeing a railway to the west coast of Ross-shire would have
> been heartily laughed at, had it been mooted - for we do not suppose any mortal man did moot
> it. But then, so almost was the idea of having a railway into the Highlands at all. There was
> perhaps just a possibility of seeing a line to Inverness by Aberdeen; but bowling in a coupé over
> Drumochter, and continuing therein to Lairg and Golspie - no, no; not in our day; you may speak
> of it as you please! As to a line to Loch Carron, there was neither speaking nor dreaming in the
> matter. The direct Perth and Ross-shire lines, however, came to be made, and then there did come
> across the minds of many the thought that connecting the West with the railway system was a
> thing most desirable and worth making an effort for. The thought resulted in a movement, chiefly
> among the proprietors and others having important interests on that side and along the route; and
> at its head was Mr Matheson, MP - himself the largest proprietor in Ross-shire, west and east.
>
> To the northern landowners, it is but fair to remember, the country is, for the most part, indebted
> for the benefits of railway communication in the Highlands, and Mr Matheson's name and
> services in connection with it can never be forgotten. This, as regards him, is now said and
> reiterated so often that, to some, it may, and we daresay it does to himself, sound as *ad nauseam*;
> but it is sober truth, whenever our railway-making is at all spoken of, that calls for it. Others may
> have done as much or more in the way of money-giving, just as in war, some leading officers may
> have given as much individual exertion to secure victory as the commander-in-chief has done; but
> the commander-in-chief, it is to whom the splendid conceptions are due, who has the qualification
> to inspire confidence in others, who knows how to organise and direct movements to practical
> results, who can quietly stand or beat a retreat when necessary, and then lead on the phalanx to
> overpower the adversary - himself all the while taking his full share of the personal exertion and
> risk. These traits, Mr Matheson has exhibited conspicuously in his railway campaigning for the
> Highlands - he has been a combined Napoleon and Wellington in it. He is now Alexander the
> Great, having nothing more to conquer, and he will perhaps treat himself to a weep in
> consequence. The ocean stops him - he can extend his road of iron no further.

Chapter Five

Early Operations and Occurrences and the Strathpeffer Branch

It was unfortunate that Alex Matheson's road of iron, in running through districts with little in the way of a population, had, of necessity, to by-pass the two largest villages between Dingwall and Skye. The correspondent of the *Inverness Courier*, in his walk over the line in June, had described both of them - Jeantown and Strathpeffer. In regard to the sizeable fishing community of Jeantown, which lay four miles from Strathcarron station, he had noted the following:

> The line takes the shore opposite to Jeantown, or Lochcarron (it goes by either name), and this may possibly diminish the trade of the place. The village consists of a row of houses overlooking the loch, some of them poor enough, but others very neat and respectable. There is one good shop, and an excellent bank - a branch of the Caledonian - of which Mr Simon Fraser is agent. Being situated at the entrance of an important district, the bank is of much use, and transacts a good deal of business.

In referring to the Spa, the correspondent had highlighted the amenities of this special place:

> During the present summer, visitors have come early to Strathpeffer, attracted by the genial weather which the east coast has enjoyed. Apart altogether from the medicinal properties of the waters, the Strath is one of the most pleasant summer resorts that can be found anywhere. The natural scenery is splendid, and many of the prettiest spots are quite accessible. Something has also been done by art. There are quiet, secluded enclosures, laid out like pleasure-grounds; these have recently been improved, and part of them set aside entirely as a promenade for ladies. The walks are kept in good repair, and the whole place is neat and tidy. The Spa Hotel and the Strathpeffer Hotel are both excellent houses, and a commodious Temperance Hotel has also been erected, which adds materially to the accommodation for strangers. Besides these, lodging-houses are built in the neighbourhood, and the Duchess of Sutherland, who owns the property, encourages feuing for the erection of neat and comfortable dwellings. Among the recent improvements at the Wells is the fitting-up of excellent bathrooms, where baths of mineral water are supplied. Enamelled tile is used in these rooms, as the water would soon destroy other substances. The pump-room is large and convenient, and outside, there are open verandahs, with seats in front; also a bowling-green and a croquet-green. Mr Fraser, who is lessee of the Wells, is attentive and obliging, anxious to enhance the comfort of visitors.

It was also a pity that the Dingwall and Skye company had insufficient financial resources to be able to take their line just six miles further west to the fishing village of Plockton. A number of people on the west coast and in the islands had strongly urged the company to extend the line more towards the open sea, to a point nearer the route of the passing steamers, such that good access would be available to shipping by day and at night. The recommended spot for the terminus was on the west side of the Plockton peninsula, a mile beyond the village, at An Dubh-aird, or Duart, and it was said to possess better facilities for a harbour than Strome. The coastline from Strome to Plockton had already been examined by Murdoch Paterson who estimated the cost of the extension, including a pier, at £40,000. Continuing the line to Plockton, it was believed, would lead to a considerable increase of traffic and repay the expense; but since it would be Skye and the other islands that would benefit most by the extra miles, the company was hoping that the island proprietors would come forward with a substantial subscription list. If this was to be the case, it was expected that those

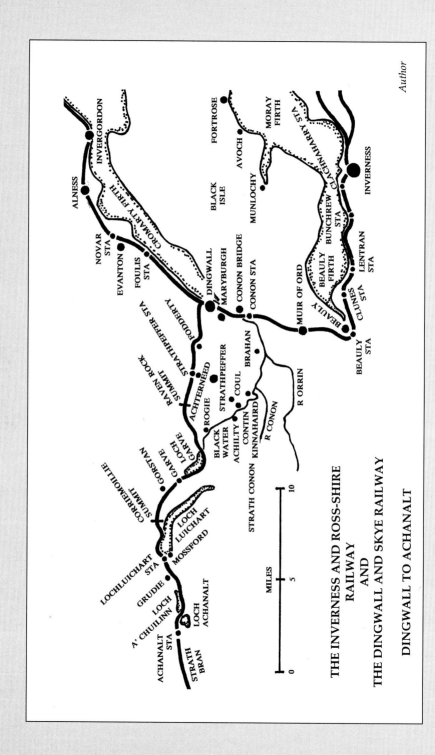

THE INVERNESS AND ROSS-SHIRE
RAILWAY
AND
THE DINGWALL AND SKYE RAILWAY

DINGWALL TO ACHANALT

Author

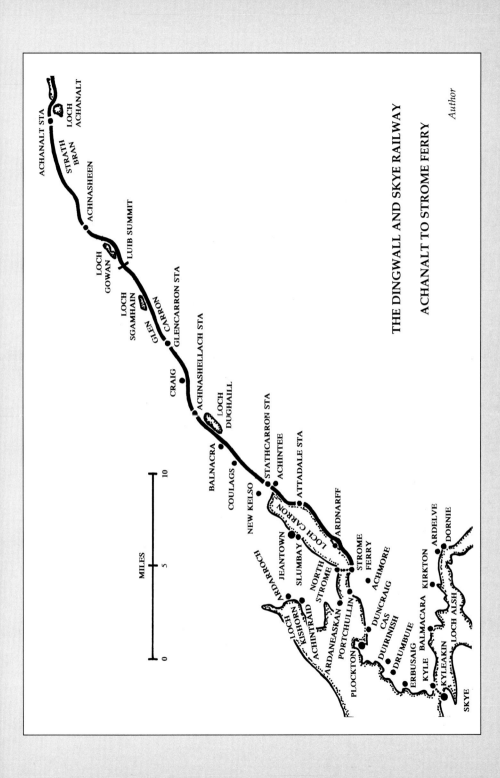

THE DINGWALL AND SKYE RAILWAY

ACHANALT TO STROME FERRY

Author

interested on the mainland would contribute their share and Alex Matheson was ready to add a fair proportion - but the first moves towards this capital had to come from further west.

Six weeks after the opening, the Dingwall and Skye Railway received the honour of a special guest at the invitation of a landowner along the route. Their Royal Highnesses Prince Christian and Princes Alexandra, the Prince and Princess of Wales, had been staying at Dunrobin Castle as guests of the Duke and Duchess of Sutherland, and on Tuesday, 4th October, the Prince, accompanied by the Duke and several other influential gentlemen, left Dunrobin with the aim of making a trip over the Skye line, together with a day's deer-hunting in Ross-shire. The invitation had come from Captain John Robert Tennant of Achnashellach, a Yorkshireman who was now the owner of the estate, and he had arranged for the accommodation of the Prince at his residence. 'Achnashellach' said the *Inverness Courier* in reporting on the visit, 'till very lately a secluded spot at the foot of Strath Carron, has now become more accessible and familiar by the opening of the Dingwall and Skye Railway. The lodge was built by Lord Hill and sold by him to Lord Elphinstone, from whom it was purchased, along with the property, by Mr Tennant a few years ago'.

Departing by the 3.30 pm service train from Golspie, to which the royal saloon carriage was attached, the party reached Dingwall at 6.40, where a very large gathering of the townspeople had turned out to give a hearty cheer to the Prince. A special train was in waiting and the royal carriage was coupled to this, which was in the charge of Andrew Dougall, accompanied by Alex Dallas, along with David Jones, the Highland Railway's Locomotive Superintendent, and Peter Wilson, the Highland's Resident Engineer. The Inverness newspapers briefly described the setting as the Prince journeyed over the line. In the words of the *Inverness Advertiser*:

> No stoppage was made until the platform at Achnashellach was reached, but at all the intervening stations - Strathpeffer, Garve, Achanalt and Achnasheen - crowds of people had gathered to see the royal train pass. The shades of evening had set in before the train left Dingwall and, thus, the run was made to Achnashellach without the Prince being able to see the wild and picturesque country through which he was passing, excepting in so far as the pale moonlight brought out the more prominent features of the landscape. Captain Tennant was in waiting at Achnashellach to welcome the Prince, and conducted the party to the lodge, which adjoins the railway.

And as the *Inverness Courier* observed:

> It was dusk when the special left Dingwall, and a smart run was made to Achnashellach without stopping. The evening was beautiful, though somewhat chilly; the moon shone brightly in a clear sky; and mountain, lake and valley were seen in its silvery radiance. Loch Luichart, Loch Achanalt and other lakes looked extremely pretty in the pale moonlight. The train arrived at its destination at 8.10 pm, the journey from Dingwall having been performed with great expedition. Captain Tennant received his guests at the station and conducted them to the house, where dinner was served.

Achnashellach station, which was a private platform for the use of the lodge, had resulted from the fulfilment of an agreement between the Dingwall and Skye company and Lord Hill when he was the owner of the estate. The platform was close to the lodge, but it was believed that, if a certain potential transaction in connection with the Prince was to materialise, the convenience of this would become a disadvantage. There were reports that the Prince had the intention of purchasing a Highland residence and that he was looking favourably at Achnashellach. 'Than that of Achnashellach', added the *Inverness Advertiser*, there is no prettier shooting-lodge in the Highlands, situated as it is in the midst of magnificent mountain and lake scenery, and surrounded by grounds artistically and beautifully laid out. The only possible objection to it - so far as privacy is concerned - is the proximity of the railway and public road, both of which are within a stone's throw; but in the event of the place becoming a royal residence, as has been rumoured, slight deviations in either case could no doubt easily be made.

Among those present at the dinner were four of the Dingwall and Skye Directors - Sir John Stuart, the Master of Lovat, Lord Middleton and John Fowler. On the following day, the Prince, the Duke, John Fowler and Captain Tennant, with a large party of gentlemen, enjoyed their deer-hunt in the well-stocked Achnashellach Forest to the east of the lodge. Then, on the day after that - Thursday, 6th - the Prince, the Duke and some of the guests were taken by special train along the rest of the Skye line to Strome Ferry. The train, of which Andrew Dougall was again in charge, left Achnashellach at 11 am and reached Strome at noon; and, on the way, as it had made its appearance on the south side of Loch Carron, a royal salute of 21 guns was fired by the Lochcarron Artillery Volunteers on the north side at Jeantown. At Strome, the Prince was greeted with frequent and enthusiastic cheering from the assembled multitude who had come from near and far to offer their Highland welcome, and it was here that he met Alex Matheson.

At the pier, the Prince and his party boarded John Fowler's awaiting steam yacht and set sail amid renewed cheering from the crowd. The privileged passengers were taken outward to a distance of two miles, obtaining a sea view of the surrounding picturesque scenery and being within sight of Alex Matheson's residence of Duncraig Castle. The return of the yacht signalled further cheers from the increased number of spectators, and after a brief inspection of the station, the guests were ready to depart. As the special train pulled out, there was a last, long cheer from the local people who, as a result of seeing the Prince among them, had treated the occasion as a gala day. Meanwhile, the Lochcarron Artillery Volunteers had made a speedy journey by conveyances to Strathcarron station to form a guard-of-honour there for the passing train. Achnashellach was reached at 1.30 pm, with a stop made here for lunch, after which the journey was resumed to Dingwall, where the royal saloon was attached to the mail train for the North to return to Dunrobin.

Regret was expressed all round that the Princess had not been able to make the trip to receive an ovation from the people of the West, and there was another aspect of disappointment that was stated by the Lochalsh correspondent of the *Inverness Courier*, who was saddened that there was no official recognition of the event at Strome:

Beyond a hearty cheer, there was no attempt at making a demonstration, but that was owing to the ignorance of the people regarding the visit of his Royal Highness. The station was not even made the most of - a union jack and two tricolours (!) represented the bunting; and as to floral or other emblems of welcome, there was none. However, we'll do better next time. Captain Ferguson's artillery volunteer corps at Jeantown fired a royal salute, and did it well too; but we should like to have seen a detachment of the brave fellows acting as a guard-of-honour at Strome as well as Strathcarron.

The rapid communications offered by the Skye line were of immense advantage to the West Highlands and islands, and to other parts of the country in connection with the West. Individuals everywhere benefited, and an example of this was illustrated by part of a letter, in October 1870, from a large sheep-farmer in Skye:

What a comfort the railway is. Having breakfasted yesterday at Inverness, I was comfortably here (in the north part of Skye) the same evening at seven o'clock. Our lambs went *safely* from hence

(Skye) to my own farm (in Easter Ross) *in 10 hours*, in place of 14 days, hashed and lame, and several deaths.

The importance of the line for this kind of farming was also illustrated by the fact that on one occasion - the same day as the Prince's visit to Achnashellach - the Highland Railway had dispatched 60 wagons to Garve for the conveyance of sheep to the Lowlands. Other new forms of traffic were able to be developed because they could now be taken quickly to the markets by train. An example of this effect was contained in some notes from the Isle of Harris that appeared in the *Inverness Courier* in October:

> Great preparations are being made by the lobster dealers for the transit of that fish to the English markets. The facilities offered by the Dingwall and Skye Railway for the speedy conveyance of lobsters to the large towns in England has induced the dealers to construct boxes specially for the purpose. In this line, the *Jura* may expect a good deal of traffic, providing that her charges are reasonable.

The Dingwall and Skye Railway had a good first autumn. At the shareholders' yearly meeting on 28th October, the Directors were pleased to state that the revenue had more than realised their expectations. However, matters were different by the early winter when there was no longer any tourist traffic, although this was anticipated for a line that would depend so much upon seasonal visitors. From late October, the steamer sailings were reduced to four per week in each direction between Strome and Portree, calling at Broadford; and to one per week each way between Strome and Stornoway, calling at Applecross 'when there are passengers or cargo to land, and by signal when there are passengers or cargo to take on board'. On 9th November, the company suffered misfortune when the *Oscar* was wrecked near Applecross, having intended to call there on the weekly run from Strome to Stornoway. As evening fell, there was a heavy snow-storm which reduced the visibility to a few yards, and the vessel ran against a submerged rock in the full tide. By means of the ship's small-boats and by other boats that had set out from the shore, the 12 passengers and 12 crew members, together with a portion of the cargo, were safely landed. The Stornoway sailing was thereafter abandoned, with the *Jura*, which was to have been laid up all winter, taking over on the Portree run. There were now only three sailings per week each way between Strome and Portree, but one of these connected at Portree with Hutcheson's Stornoway steamer, *Clansman*, so that the Dingwall and Skye Railway was still carrying some Stornoway passengers and cargo. From 1st December, the train service was reduced to one per day in each direction between Dingwall and Strome. The 8.15 am up train from Strome and the 4.15 pm down train from Dingwall were discontinued, leaving the 10.12 am down, arriving at Strome at 1.15 pm, and the 3.15 pm up, arriving at Dingwall at 6.31 pm, to deal adequately with the limited traffic during the winter.

In January 1871, the Dingwall and Skye Board were of the view that a single steamer - a smaller and more economical one - would be sufficient for their requirements. At this time, the large Edinburgh-based North British Railway wanted to part with its steamer, *Carham*, which had been plying the Firth of Clyde between Dunoon, Helensburgh and the Gare Loch, and this little vessel seemed ideal to the Dingwall and Skye Directors. In May, *Carham* was purchased for £3,000, with the aim of it eventually succeeding *Jura* on the Portree run. At this time, there were still three sailings each way per week between Strome and Portree, with the connection at Portree for Stornoway on Friday evenings and from Stornoway on Tuesday mornings. An announcement had been incorporated into the Highland Railway timetable, thus:

On and after 1st May the Dingwall and Skye company's steamship, *Jura*, or other steamer, will sail as under - weather, etc., permitting; viz.:

Leave Portree for Strome Ferry every Tuesday, Thursday and Saturday at 9 am, calling at Broadford, and arriving at Strome Ferry in time for train to the South.

Leave Strome Ferry for Portree every Tuesday, Friday and Saturday, as soon after arrival of first train from the South as passengers and cargo are on board. Will call at Broadford, and arrive at Portree about 6.30 pm.

Passengers and cargo from Stornoway and other ports north of Portree, to be forwarded by rail from Strome Ferry, will be booked through as formerly, and will be received from Messrs David Hutcheson and Co. at Portree every Tuesday morning.

Passengers and cargo for Stornoway and other northern ports will also be booked through and delivered to Messrs David Hutcheson and Co. at Portree every Friday evening.

When, from any cause, the steamers do not reach Strome Ferry in time for the connecting train, the passengers will be forwarded by first train after arrival.

Note No. 1 - The company do not guarantee time being kept by the steamers; and they reserve the power to call at intermediate places to suit the requirements of the traffic.

Note No. 2 - Tickets for the steamer must be taken out before going on board at Strome Ferry.

From 1st June, the steamer timetable continued similarly, except that there were now two connecting services per week between Strome and Stornoway - these being from Stornoway on Tuesday and Thursday mornings and to Stornoway on Tuesday and Friday evenings.

Also from 1st May, the train that had ceased to operate from December had been restored for the summer, with the times of the two daily services in each direction remaining the same as from the opening. The station at Achnashellach had now been included for the use of the public, and the entire timetable - this time, having no extra services between Dingwall and Strathpeffer - comprised as follows:

	am	*pm*		*am*	*am*
Inverness d.	9.15	3.10	*Portree d.*		9.00 †
Dingwall d.	10.12	4.15	Strome Ferry d.	8.15	3.15 *pm*
Strathpeffer	10.26	4.23	Strathcarron	8.45	3.45
Garve	10.45	4.49	Achnashellach	9.03	4.03
Achanalt	11.21	5.15	Achnasheen	9.45	4.50
Achnasheen	11.45	5.40	Achanalt	10.09	5.15
Achnashellach	12.27 *pm*	6.26	Garve	10.45	5.40
Strathcarron	12.45	6.44	Strathpeffer	11.03	6.02
Strome Ferry a.	1.15	7.15	Dingwall a.	11.15	6.15
Portree a.		6.30 *	*Inverness a.*	12.15 *pm*	7.30

* Tu, F, Sat.   † Tu, Th, Sat.

The statement regarding the steamers not reaching Strome in time was strange for two reasons. Firstly, if the steamer failed to arrive by the 3.15 pm departure time of the connecting train from Strome, there was no other train that day, and a sufficiently-late steamer on a Saturday meant that there was no other train until Monday. Secondly, it was ironical that the connecting train would not wait for a late steamer, when the purpose of the Skye railway was to serve that island and further west. Since most of the railway's eastbound passenger traffic originated at Strome by way of the steamers, there were few people elsewhere along the route who had to be accommodated by the train running to time, in priority to it being held back to await the steamer.

Another public station was brought into use in the summer of 1871. At or soon after the opening of the line, there had been, as at Achnashellach, a private platform at

Lochluichart. This was for Lady Louisa Ashburton of Lochluichart Lodge. At a meeting of the Dingwall and Skye Directors on 16th August, 1870, 'with respect to a platform at Lochluichart', it had been 'resolved to stop the trains for Lady Ashburton personally, on proper intimation being given to the company's officials'. On 26th January, 1871, the Directors had discussed a petition, signed by the residents in the Lochluichart district, requesting them 'to establish a permanent station at the Mossford road, a little west of Lochluichart Lodge'. The Directors were also in receipt of a letter stating that, in the event of this being done, Lady Ashburton would dispense with the platform already erected for her use in the private grounds; and they had recommended that, whatever accommodation was given, it should be made available to the public.

Further to this request, at a Board meeting on 10th February, a correspondence had been read to the effect that, if the company established a regular station at the Mossford road, Lady Ashburton would give the necessary land on her property free of charge, contribute £100 towards the expense, and give up the platform in the grounds. It had then been 'resolved to give the station on these terms, and to put in a siding for carriages, wagons, etc., if her ladyship agrees to contribute an additional £100'. The *Inverness Courier* of 29th June and the *Inverness Advertiser* of 30th June were able to report, with reference to the immediate Saturday: 'On 1st July, a station will be opened at Lochluichart, on the Dingwall and Skye Railway'. The attitude of Lady Ashburton, in contrast to that of Sir William MacKenzie several years previously, was indeed commendable, and this was especially so in her consideration of the facts that there were few people in the vicinity - Mossford itself being only a hamlet - and that a public station at the Mossford road, in replacing her private one, would be much less convenient for her. The new station lay a mile to the south-west of the lodge.

Soon after the opening of the Skye line in 1870, there had been various recurring problems with the two Hawthorns 2-4-0 engines, due to their wheelbase being too rigid for the sharply-curved route, but the Highland managed to persevere with them, and with others of the same class, because there was nothing better. David Jones, the Locomotive Superintendent, suggested that a more flexible, or 'bogie', type of engine should be designed specially for the line, to provide sufficient lateral motion to combat the sharp curves. The Board responded negatively to a new engine because of the expense, but, in October 1871, authorisation was given for an old engine to be modified. Ultimately, in 1873, at the Highland's Lochgorm Works at Inverness, Jones converted one of the original 2-4-0s of the Skye line - HR No. 10 - into a 4-4-0 bogie; and then, in 1875, the other principal Skye-line engine - HR No. 7 - into a 4-4-0. For their use on the Skye line, Nos. 7 and 10 were given the names *Dingwall* and *Duncraig*, and they were successful in overcoming the problems that had been inherent with their previous 2-4-0 wheel arrangement.

For the Dingwall and Skye Railway's steamer operations, *Carham*, in suceeding *Jura*, had plied between Strome and Portree from 1871 until 1873, while also having made special sailings to ports further north, such as Gairloch, Poolewe and Ullapool; and from January 1872, the Strome-Portree service had included Plockton. This fishing village with its line of cottages and its picturesque bay, had no pier at which steamers could dock, but a substitute solution was presented. At a Board meeting on 2nd January, 1872, the Dingwall and Skye Directors

... resolved that the steamer *Carham* call at Plockton in going to and from Portree, commencing on the 15th inst, and to accept the offer of Kenneth MacKenzie and Roderick MacRae to furnish boats and keep them in repair, for the purpose of landing goods and passengers, at a charge to the company of £10 for the first six months. Each passenger to pay 3*d*. for landing.

One of the two original engines of the Dingwall and Skye Railway after its 1875 conversion from a 2-4-0 to a 4-4-0 bogie, to cope with the sharp curves of the line. This was HR No. 7, the second locomotive to be converted by David Jones. The first was HR No. 10 in 1873.　　*J.L. Stevenson*

During 1873, the vessel's boiler was causing trouble, and yet another new steamer was found to be necessary. A larger replacement was agreed upon, and this was the *Ferret*, which, having been bought from the steamboat operators G. and J. Burns of Glasgow for £15,000, arrived at Strome in January 1874. *Ferret* took over as the principal vessel in conjunction with the regular railway traffic, while *Carham* was kept mainly for special sailings to other places in the West.

One scheme which the Dingwall and Skye company had planned during the railway's construction stage in 1869 was not to materialise. The Directors, in appreciating the significance of the fishing trade to the line, were then not only giving great consideration to the conveyance of that commodity over their rails, but they also had the idea that their trains could transport some of the vessels that would catch the fish. The number of fishing-boats heading from eastern Scotland to the west-coast fishing grounds was about 800, and, in making the voyage once a year, they had to take a route either through the Caledonian Canal or round the Pentland Firth. The journey took about 10 days in good weather and sometimes up to three weeks in stormy conditions; but if the boats were able to be carried over the railway, they would undergo only three hours in safe transit, to the immense advantage of the fishermen who would have an extra ten days or a fortnight at the fishing or at home.

The aim of the new scheme was to make use of the whole length of the Skye line by lifting the fishing-boats from the Dingwall Canal, just north of the station, by means of a crane, onto specially-constructed wagons on the railway. They would then be conveyed to Strome Ferry pier, where they would be lifted from the wagons onto the water. The ¾ mile-long Dingwall Canal, having been sanctioned by the terms of the Highland Roads and Bridges Act of 1803, had opened in 1817, running from the north side of the town along the course of the River Peffery to the Cromarty Firth. With the clearing of the silt from the river over this distance, the canal allowed cargo boats to sail into the county town, instead of having to beach on the sands of the firth. Although it was of limited success, due originally to the continued problems of the silting of the river, and latterly in having to endure competition when the railway reached Dingwall from Inverness in 1862, the canal was still in use at the time of the proposal for it to be worked in conjunction with the Skye line. Detailed plans had been prepared during the summer of 1869, and these, in taking account of the width of the boats, had led to increasing the distance separating the tracks at the station crossing-loops; while the bridge that carried the road over the railway at Garve - being the only road overbridge on the entire line - had been built wider than what would normally have been required. Unfortunately, the incentive had been lost by the spring of 1870, with the company realising that the delay to the opening of the line meant that the boats could not be carried in time for the fishing season. Strangely, in spite of the modifications having been made to the line to accommodate the boats, and of some boats having been conveyed at the end of the season in the autumn of 1870, the ambitious but feasible project, which would have stimulated the Dingwall Canal, was not revived.

The shipping exploits of the Dingwall and Skye Railway, though of great benefit to the population, were financially unsuccessful, but the company was ultimately to be relieved of this burden. The Highland Railway, still intent on expanding its enterprise, felt confident that it could succeed with the steamboat operations where the Dingwall and Skye company had not. Thus, subsequent to an agreement between the two companies, an Act was passed on 24th April, 1877 which conferred powers upon the Highland Railway to own and operate steamboats to and from Strome Ferry. The Highland Railway (Steam Vessels) Act, 1877 allowed the Highland company to raise half a million pounds for the purpose of developing steamer services, and this meant that substantial capital was now to be applied to the shipping interests at Strome. On 7th August, 1877, the Dingwall and Skye and the Highland Directors resolved that *Ferret* and *Carham* be transferred from the former to the latter company. The Highland paid the Dingwall and Skye £9,850 for *Ferret* and £3,000 for *Carham*, and the Strome ferry-boat was also purchased for £130. The Highland steamboat operations commenced on 1st September, 1877.

It was in the autumn of 1877 that another royal visit took place on the Skye line, when Queen Victoria travelled to Loch Maree. The outward railway journey began at 10 am on Wednesday, 12th September from Ballater on Deeside, with the Great North of Scotland Railway controlling the royal saloon carriage as far as Keith, where the Highland Railway took over, under the charge of Andrew Dougall. There was no stop until Dingwall, which was reached just after 3.30 pm, amid a large crowd on the platform; and here the train was joined by Alex Matheson and Sir Kenneth MacKenzie of Gairloch, who was Convener of Ross and Cromarty. Then, as stated in the Inverness newspapers, 'Strathpeffer and Garve were swept past at a high rate of speed which, however, was diminished at Achanalt, as there, the royal train had to cross the 3.10 pm from Strome'. It arrived at Achnasheen exactly at the scheduled time of 4.50. The station was attractively decorated with bunting, tartans and stags' heads - the tartans being of the Royal Stuart and Hunting Stuart designs - while the portion of the platform over which the Queen had to walk was carpeted with Hunting Stuart tartan. There were inscriptions on the walls of the station and the adjoining hotel, such as 'God save the Queen' and 'A thousand welcomes to your Highlands'. Prior to the arrival of the train, a large number of the people of the surrounding districts - from Lochcarron, Gairloch, etc. - had gathered outside the station. The carpeting was continued outside the station to the awaiting royal carriage for the Queen and Princess Beatrice, and on their departure for the Loch Maree Hotel, 18 miles distant, cheers were given by the onlookers. The Queen expressed her delight at having witnessed the wild and romantic scenery of the Dingwall and Skye Railway.

Having spent five whole days in the neighbourhood of Loch Maree, Gairloch and Torridon, Queen Victoria left the hotel on the wet morning of Tuesday, 18th September for the start of her return rail journey from Achnasheen. The station and hotel were again well decorated. At the entrance, there was an arch of evergreens and heather, surmounted by a large star and flags, and coloured flags were hung in front of the premises. In the presence of a crowd that had collected outside the station, Alex Matheson conversed with the Queen, who told him of her delight with the scenery of Ross-shire and of her regret that she had not time to see more of it. The special train did not stop until Dingwall.

On the evening of Sunday, 14th October, 1877, a short stretch of the Skye line suffered considerable damage as a result of an exceptionally-severe storm that crossed the Highlands. Two miles east of Achnashellach station, near Craig, the railway and its gravel embankment were swept away for a distance of 30 yards by the torrential flood water from the streams of steeply-sided Glen Carron. Being Sunday, there were no trains, but details of the damage were able to be reported to Inverness, and arrangements were made for carrying on Monday's traffic by the transfer of passengers from one train to another at the separated location, although this was not attempted for the early-morning service from Strome Ferry. Gangs of workmen proceeded to repair the damage, and working through Monday night, they completed their task on Tuesday morning. The line would have been reopened that day but for an unfortunate occurrence. An engine was sent over the repaired section in the morning, but it went off the rails because the trackbed was not fully secure. The crane from Inverness was sent to return the engine to the rails, but this was not accomplished until the evening, when the line was reopened.

It was not only the Dingwall and Skye company's steamboat endeavours that had been uneconomic since the railway's opening. The train services, too, had suffered continuous losses due to the low passenger and goods traffic for much of the year and to the limited funds injected into the company because of shareholders not contributing as expected. By the end of the decade, it was acknowledged that the only way for the Skye line to survive lay in it becoming incorporated in the Highland Railway. Such a merger was to the Highland's advantage because, apart from directly extending its territory, it would be better able to counteract some of the opposition that would result from the impending opening of the railway to Oban - a line that would especially be a rival for the west coast fish traffic. The Callander and Oban Railway had received Parliamentary authorisation in 1865 - on 8th July, which was three days after that for the Dingwall and Skye line - but it was only in the summer of 1880 that it was finally to reach Oban.* In being the second railway to serve the West Highlands, this line, worked by the Caledonian Railway, based in Glasgow, had rendered the situation vital to the Highland company that it should retain full control of the first railway, by which their share of the traffic of the West would be maintained.

While the Highland Railway had worked the Dingwall and Skye line, it had initially made no contributions towards the line; but back in 1872, the Highland Board had resolved to take £35,000 of Dingwall and Skye stock, provided that the Dingwall and Skye company placed two of the Highland Directors on its Board. This had helped the Skye line to some extent amid the escalating debts; but now in 1880, the Highland Railway was to rescue the Skye line by absorbing liabilities of £74,000 in the incorporation. On 2nd August, 1880, an Act sanctioned the merging of the two companies and, thus, the ending of the Dingwall and Skye Railway in name, 16½ years after its origin and 10 years after its opening: An Act to Amalgamate the Undertakings of the Highland and Dingwall and Skye Railway Companies; and for Other Purposes. However, little difference was made to the life of the line by the Highland and Dingwall and Skye Railways (Amalgamation) Act, 1880. The Highland trains still covered the

---

* The line to Oban was opened on 12th June for goods, and on 1st July for passengers, with a ceremonial opening on 30th June.

Strome Ferry *c*. 1880, from the east, with the large building of the Station Hotel overlooking the original station terminus.   *G.E. Langmuir*

Strome Ferry pier *c*. 1880, looking north-east along Loch Carron. The end of the station terminus is on the right, and the station master's house is on the left.   *G.E. Langmuir*

miles of the Skye line, with the same railwaymen along the way, and the same Chairman, Alex Matheson, and General Manager, Andrew Dougall, to see to the running of what was now the Strome Ferry branch of the Highland Railway.

The year 1880 had earlier been of significance in another way for the Highland Railway in regard to its Dingwall and Skye operations. This was when the company's shipping venture ended, having been no more prosperous than the exertions of the Dingwall and Skye company; but the demise was of no detriment, either to the Highland or to the travelling public, because the service had been revolutionised from elsewhere. The firm of David Hutcheson and Co., formed in 1851, had consisted of the partnership of David and Alexander Hutcheson along with David MacBrayne. After Messrs Hutcheson had retired, in 1876 and 1878 respectively, David MacBrayne operated the business himself under his own name from 1879; and it was by an agreement between the Highland Railway and MacBrayne that the new successor had provided regular steamboat connections at Strome Ferry from 19th April, 1880. With services between Strome, Plockton, Broadford, Raasay, Portree, Stornoway and other northern and western ports, the steamers running in conjunction with the Skye railway had now been taken over by an experienced operator - at long last.

From the promotion of the Dingwall and Skye Railway in 1864, Alex Matheson had done a great deal to ensure that it would become a reality, and no one had given as much as he had towards that vital line. While his enthusiastic efforts and large financial support were being assigned in that direction, another wealthy gentleman - more so than Matheson - had been providing the means to extend the railway system to the North. He was George Granville William Sutherland-Leveson-Gower,* who was better known as the third Duke of Sutherland. His estates totalled nearly 1,400,000 acres in Sutherland, which was almost the whole of the county, and his Highland residence was the splendid Dunrobin Castle, near Golspie, on the route of the Sutherland Railway. The Duke, who had contributed to the Dingwall and Skye line, was the principal shareholder, by far, of the Sutherland Railway, which had opened from Bonar Bridge to Golspie on 13th April, 1868; and in November of that year, he announced that he was prepared to extend the Sutherland Railway from Golspie to Helmsdale, a distance of 17 miles, *all at his own expense*. In carrying out this plan, the Duke would be creating railway history, because no one had ever attempted to finance a railway entirely on his own, although he had already come close with the initial Sutherland line. The Duke of Sutherland's Railway was opened as part of the Highland Railway's system on 19th June, 1871.

Having reached Helmsdale, 101 miles from Inverness, the railway was destined to be extended to the Caithness towns of Wick and Thurso. With the difficulties of the route having been resolved in 1870, due to the intervention of the Duke, who would again supply much of the capital, the two northern towns were to receive a long-awaited railway communication. Thus, in 1871, the Sutherland and Caithness Railway was promoted by the Duke, and among the provisional committee for the new company were Alex Matheson and John Fowler. Due to the precipitous nature of the coast, the route had to proceed on a circuitous inland detour through the Strath of Kildonan and the bleak and virtually-uninhabited country that extended for many miles on either side of the County March or boundary between Sutherland and Caithness. William Baxter of Brora, who had engineered part of the Sutherland Railway before continuing with the Duke's own line, was responsible for the 28 miles from Helmsdale to a point on the County March four miles east of Forsinard, and Murdoch Paterson completed the 38 miles from there to the two termini. The Sutherland and Caithness Railway was opened on 28th July, 1874, making Thurso 154 and Wick 161 miles from Inverness.

* Pronounced 'Looson-Gore'.

Strome Ferry from North Strome *c.* 1880. The station and pier are in the centre, with the engine shed on the left and the Station Hotel at the right, on the slope.   *G.E. Langmuir*

Strome Ferry pier *c.* 1890, showing two steam cranes, with the ferry slipway for North Strome in the foreground.   *G.E. Langmuir*

Highland Railway steamer ticket.   *I. Wilks*

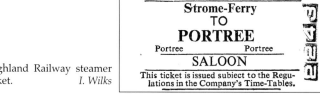

The third Duke of Sutherland's eagerness to develop the far north of Scotland by means of the railway had resulted in a unique munificence by him which consisted of the following individual contributions: £42,500 to the Ross-shire sections; £116,000 to the Sutherland line; £60,000 to his own extension of the Sutherland line; and £60,000 to the Sutherland and Caithness line. The whole of the railway system from Inverness to Wick and Thurso was worked and maintained by the Highland Railway on the same terms as the Dingwall and Skye line.

Three years after the Highland Railway had acquired full control of the Skye line, it was confronted with an astonishing climax to a controversy that had emerged in the days of the Dingwall and Skye company. The Skye line was an important route, carrying tourists in summer, if not in winter; but of greater value was its traffic in fish, and it was the Sunday conveyance of the fish that culminated in the Strome Ferry riot of 1883. This most unusual disturbance, which almost ended in serious bloodshed, took place on the pier of the secluded and normally quiet western terminus. It resulted from the religious fervour of the people of the parishes of Lochcarron and Lochalsh being in conflict with the Highland Railway's operations of transporting the fish on Sundays from Strome to London.

By the summer of 1883, the transfer of fish from steamers to trains at Strome on the Sabbath was nothing new. It had been carried on for several years, much to the displeasure of the local Presbyterian population who were of the Free Church - having separated from the established Church of Scotland in 1843 - and who were not only against the employment of labour on the Sabbath but were deeply offended by its occurrence. It was during the 1883 herring-fishing season that the Sabbatarians resolved that they would somehow have to put an end to what they believed was a desecration of the Sabbath.

The Free Presbytery of Lochcarron had made numerous protests over the years, initially to the Dingwall and Skye company and latterly to the Highland company, which the respective Boards had not heeded. In 1882, the Highland Directors were once more approached on the subject by some of the local church representatives, but the latter were again not to be satisfied with the railway company's response. The Highland reiterated that it was vital to forward the fish traffic whenever it was available, and this, necessarily, included Sundays.

Fish caught in the Minches and beyond on a Friday evening or a Saturday morning, and cured at Stornoway, would arrive at Strome Ferry late on the Saturday evening or early on the Sunday morning; and in either case, it would usually be sent over the railway on the Sunday quickly after its arrival at Strome. The Stornoway curers had an arrangement with the Highland Railway that the fish was to be unloaded from the steamers, loaded onto the railway wagons, and dispatched speedily to enable the fish to reach London's Billingsgate market early on the Monday morning. Sometimes, the steamers would arrive at Strome early on the Saturday evening, in which case all the work could be completed that evening; but at other times, owing to the later arrival of the steamers, it was found necessary to continue or commence the work in the early hours of the Sunday morning. It was against this background that the Strome Ferry riot occurred.

With the herring season of 1883 having started in May, the local people were on the alert for a repetition of the 'Sabbath-breaking' of the previous years, and, this time, they were set on taking action. Heavy fish trains had begun to be dispatched from Strome on the Sabbath, and it was expected that they would continue. On Sunday, 27th May, there was, as usual, a brisk morning's work at Strome Ferry pier. In addition to a large cargo of herrings being unshipped, various other goods, such as boxes, timber and even a boat, were consigned with the fish, so that, in the opinion of the local people, a portion of the cargo, at least, was decidedly unnecessary. Their indignation was aggravated; but, in reality, the carrying of this additional traffic was irrelevant because it was the Sunday labour resulting from the principal traffic which they intended not to tolerate in future. In an attempt to stop any further Sabbath desecration, a number of local men took an active part in encouraging the population on both sides of Loch Carron to unite on the following Sunday of 3rd June. This meant that an organised invasion of Strome Ferry was agreed upon, in the event of the fish arriving there when its transfer from ship was to take place on the Sunday.

It became known to the locals that two steamers, the *Harold* and the *Lochiel*, which were chartered by the Highland Railway for the fish cargoes, would arrive at Strome from Stornoway either late on the Saturday night or early on the Sunday morning with fresh fish for the London market. The appearance of a steamer in the distance was to be the signal for the aggrieved population to gather at Strome pier to make their demonstration to the railway company. At 11 o'clock in the Saturday evening twilight, a steamer, approaching from the distance of the Inner Sound, was seen by the people of Ardaneaskan. With great haste, they manned their small craft, headed for Strome, and spread the word to their brethren in the other townships - who were already prepared - that they should come to Strome to stand together in their cause. The *Harold* was the steamer, and by midnight, it had docked at Strome, but by then, the Ardaneaskan men and others were at the pier with the aim of preventing the unloading of the fish taking place. At first, the railway employees treated the demands of the locals with derision because the former were slightly greater in number at 20, and they set to work to unload the fish by means of the steam crane on the pier. For some time, they paid little heed to the demonstrators, but Sabbatarian reinforcements, armed with sticks, arrived to increase their number to 50. A more aggressive attitude was now adopted by the locals, who pushed away the wagon that was receiving the fish. The railway workers pushed it back into place, but it was again forced aside, and for a time, the scene represented a novel tug of war, with a wagon instead of a rope. Ultimately, the ever-increasing crofters and fishermen were much too strong for the railway workers, and the man in charge of the crane was seized and dragged from his position. The employees still bravely persisted and began to land the fish without the aid of the crane, but as soon as the boxes were deposited onto the pier, they were thrown back onto the steamer by the crowd, who were uttering threats of violence.

New arrivals kept strengthening the Sabbatarians, and at one o'clock, by which time the second steamer, the *Lochiel*, had reached the pier, there were over 100 protesting. They originated from several of the villages and hamlets in the neighbourhood, many having come in small boats. All the while, the ringleaders made it clear to the workmen that they were determined not to have the Sabbath desecrated, as it had been for some time, and that such violations of the Fourth Commandment would not be permitted to continue for fear of a judgement from heaven. The railwaymen explained that they had to do their duty, since it was essential that the fish should reach Inverness in time to overtake the 10.10 am 'limited mail' for London, as otherwise, there would be a great loss. However, these words were answered by cries about Sabbath-breaking and further shouts to the effect that, until the expiry of the Sabbath, not a stroke of work would be allowed to be done.

The hopelessness of struggling against the continually-growing and almost-violent crowd meant that the employees finally had to cease their efforts of trying to unload the fish, and they were pushed back from the pier and along the short branch railway towards the station. It was then that the station master decided that he had no alternative than to report the remarkable occurrence by telegraph to the night superintendent at Inverness station, telling him that a large number of men had taken possession of the pier, and that, unless a strong body of police could be sent, nothing could be done by the staff until Monday morning. The superintendent quickly arranged for an engine to be forwarded from Inverness to Dingwall for the purpose of opening the office there, and to communicate the affair to the Sheriff and to the Procurator-Fiscal of Ross-shire. They were informed that the Highland Railway's property at Strome Ferry had been taken possession of by an enraged mob and was in danger. Police protection was requested, and after consultation between the Sheriff, the Procurator-Fiscal and the Chief Constable of Ross-shire, Donald Munro of Dingwall, who received word of the trouble at 5.30 am, it was decided that a police force should leave for the scene. A special train was placed at the disposal of the force, which, of necessity, at such short notice, could only be small to meet so formidable a number of protesters. Chief Constable Munro, three other constables from Dingwall, the Chief Constable of Sutherland from Dornoch, and a sergeant from Conon Bridge left Dingwall at eight o'clock, and on the way, the train picked up two more policemen, these being the constable for Strathpeffer and the sergeant for Jeantown.

Arriving at Strome at 11 o'clock, the eight policeman, by their appearance alone, added to the anger of the crowd, still on the pier after their long vigil, and now numbering upwards of 150. Chief Constable Munro tried to reason with them, but they refused to yield their place, and so he was obliged, firstly, to warn them and, secondly, due to their stand, to take action. With the aim of clearing the pier, he ordered the small force to charge the crowd, but they were attacked with sticks and stones, to be driven back against shouts of 'Push the policemen to the sea!' Hard blows were exchanged, in which the batons of the police were freely used in combating the weapons of the rioters, but the overpowering strength of the latter forced the officers back from the pier and beyond the branch line towards a corner of the station. The police, who were bravely supported by the workmen, charged again and again, making six unsuccessful attempts, and, not surprisingly, injuries occurred on both sides. At one point, the crowd threatened to board the steamers, but the crews warned that they had prepared hoses for the application of boiling water, while they also presented iron bars and spikes, and these measures compelled the agitated locals to stay on the pier. Another time, the railway workers managed to reach the pier and the steam crane, but they were depending on the police to keep back the mob. Unfortunately, the police were not able to do so, and the workers were eventually pushed towards the station. In the end, the police, defeated and dejected, had no option but to stand away from the pier and be spectators to the crowd's aggression.

A representation of the Strome Ferry riot of 1883. *D.C. Thomson & Co. Ltd*

During the afternoon, the anger subsided as the locals realised their triumph, but they still had no intention of giving up the pier. They were now being relieved by others who arrived in small boats, and they continued to ensure that no further attempts would be made to discharge the fish, although the railwaymen had received instructions to make no more efforts to do so. However, the crowd were also quiet because a different enactment had commenced in the afternoon - one that contrasted markedly with the ferocity of what had gone before. This was that outdoor religious services were now in process, being conducted by an elder of the Free Church in the district. Prayer, praise, scriptural readings, and addresses on the necessity of preserving the sanctity of the Sabbath were engaged in, with most of the people congregated on the pier, while some paraded the branch line, daring anyone to approach and interfere with the devotions.

In the late afternoon, Chief Constable Munro, on seeing that his force was unable to do any more, even with the scene now quiet, withdrew the men, and he and four other officers returned to Dingwall by the special train, leaving the remaining three at Strome to keep watch. The railway employees were advised to obtain sleep so that they would be ready to resume the work at midnight, on the assumption that the crowd would then relinquish their possession of the pier.

Throughout the evening, a second session of praises and singing was held, but everything was subdued. At 10.30 pm, a message by telegraph to Inverness read as follows: '200 men still here. They are engaged in prayer. No women here, nor have there been women all day.' At 11 o'clock, the railwaymen attempted to reach the pier to light the fire of the engine that worked the crane, so that the steam would be at full force by midnight, but they were forbidden to do this by the crowd, as not the slightest act of work would be permitted. At half-past eleven, the number of people on the pier was about 250, and they continued their services with much fervour almost to the decisive hour. A few minutes before the new day, the last prayer finished, and then the whole crowd, as one body, moved in the direction of the station. The railway workers were thrown into a state of alarm by the onrush, and, thinking that the building was to be taken by force, they massed together in order to defend themselves; but the crowd proceeded peacefully in their aim, which was to ascertain the exact time from the station clock. When the hands pointed at midnight, the shout of 'Twelve o'clock' twice rang out in a stentorian tone. Having satisfied themselves that it was now Monday, the Sabbatarians left the station and dispersed in various directions to head home. They had accomplished their purpose, which was the prevention of work on the Sabbath.

At two minutes past midnight, a communication received at Inverness read: 'Men are all away. Will proceed as quickly as possible.' Strome Ferry, which, throughout the preceding 24 hours, had been subjected to such an alien aspect, returned to its quietude; only the splashing of the oars of the locals' boats, gradually becoming fainter, now broke the stillness of the midnight twilight. With the siege ended, the railway employees resumed the work of unloading the fish from the two steamers and loading it onto the two waiting trains, 24 hours later than they had intended. The first fish train departed at 4.30 am, followed by the 5.30 passenger and goods service.

A large amount of fish - about 80 tons and equivalent to a train of 20 wagons - had been delayed. The *Harold* had contained 5,000 boxes of kippered herrings and 20 boxes of fresh herrings, while the *Lochiel* had brought 1,700 boxes of kippers and 100 boxes of fresh herrings. The value of the cargoes was estimated at £1,750, with a loss of somewhere between £100 and £200 because of the delay.

The authorities did not overlook the occurrence at Strome Ferry. The names of 10 men - the alleged ringleaders - had been noted and, with warrants issued for mobbing and rioting, their apprehension ultimately took place. The 10 were: Roderick Finlayson and

Alexander Finlayson, brothers, from Ardnarff; John MacRae from Portchullin; Finlay MacKenzie, North Strome; Alexander MacKay, Jeantown; Roderick Gillies, Ardaneaskan; Donald MacRae, Ardaneaskan; Donald Matheson, Ardaneaskan; John MacKenzie, Slumbay; and Alexander Gollen, Slumbay. Their trial was held at the High Court of Justiciary in Edinburgh on 23rd July, 1883 before Lord Justice-Clerk Moncrieff and a jury of 15 men in a court room crowded with eager spectators for this unique case. When all the evidence had been heard, the counsels for the prosecution and the defence addressed the court.

Mr Brand, Advocate-Depute on behalf of the Crown, asserted that the prisoners were the chief offenders in conducting the riot and the obstruction, and the fact that many were there to prevent the Highland Railway from unloading the vessels constituted mobbing and rioting, according to the law. They could have used other means to impress the railway company and the public of their views, and they had no right to use that which they did, which was unlawful. The railway company, in utilising the hours between midnight and six o'clock on Sunday morning, had not attempted to forward the fish in the hours of church service; and had they been allowed to go unhindered with their work, the fish would have been dispatched by six o'clock. The accused, however, were determined that the work should not be done at all on Sunday, and there were not only threats from them but assaults and the defiance of authority. The occurrence at Strome Ferry, said Mr Brand in conclusion, was not the outcome of a rash impulse, but was premeditated with some degree of organisation.

The Dean of Faculty, Mr MacDonald, speaking on behalf of the prisoners, stressed that the men had no selfish motive in their hearts in whatever they were alleged to have done. Their only desire was that of sentiment arising from their belief in the law against working on Sunday, which had been taught at their mother's knee, and which was being outraged. They looked upon this outrage to their feelings as not being directed against the law of man but against a much higher law, which every man had the duty to support to his utmost, which had been handed down from the earliest times, and which was a divine precept. He contended that it was still the law of the land that men should not carry on their ordinary business on the Lord's day, and that the railway companies were breaking this law, while the police were assisting them. The prisoners were charged with being 'riotous and evilly-disposed', which he said was an abuse of terms, but nothing had been disclosed in the evidence further than the fact that, without intending to do harm to anyone, they had prevented that which was wrong. He asked the jury to decide the matter in the only way that it ought to be decided, and that was by dismissing the men.

Lord Moncrieff, in addressing the jury, said that the only question for them to consider was whether the prisoners were entitled to take the law into their own hands. He ruled that they were not, and added that the law was open to everyone for redress. The representatives of the law were violently prevented from doing their duty, and this was a matter not to be lightly passed over. Upon the whole question, he strongly advised the jury to consider how far the accused were guilty on the facts and not on whether Sunday traffic was authorised by law. There might be strong and difficult religious opinions regarding the Sabbath, but it was impossible to permit any party to force their opinions on others. Of course, they would have a feeling for the accused, who were respectable men and who thought that they were doing good service, but that did not justify them doing what they did.

It took the jury half an hour to reach their decision, and the following verdict was read: 'The jury find the accused unanimously guilty of mobbing and rioting, but recommend them to the utmost leniency of the court on account of their ignorance of the law and the strong religious convictions they hold against Sabbath desecration.' Lord Moncrieff fully concurred with the verdict, but on the following day, he nevertheless pronounced what was generally felt to be a severe sentence of four months' imprisonment at Calton Jail in Edinburgh. However, in early September, as a result of pressure mainly from the Free Church presbyteries throughout Scotland and from Members of Parliament for the Highlands, the Home Secretary, Sir William Harcourt, agreed to discuss the matter of mitigation with Lord Moncrieff; and the happy outcome for the men and their supporters was that they were released on 21st September, which was three days before the expiry of half their period of imprisonment.

The view held by the Free Church that the Sunday fish traffic was against the law was disputed by the Highland and other railway companies, and the reason was by virtue of such a law becoming inoperative by desuetude, which meant that it had passed into disuse. In Scottish law, statutes could become inoperative by desuetude, losing their power by changes of circumstances and attitudes. If the breaking of a law had been occurring without objection for many years, then that law would eventually cease to have any value and would thereby, in practice, no longer be a law. Although railways had been in use for over half a century, no prosecution for Sabbath-breaking had ever been attempted, so that there was, against the application of any statute of profaneness, a long period of consuetude, or custom having legal standing. The Highland Railway Company had this measure on its side in defence of the working of the Sunday fish traffic, but the Highland Railway had not been on trial.

The fish traffic was lucrative business for the Highland Railway, which intended that it should remain so. For example, on Wednesday, 20th June, 1883, upwards of 150 tons of herrings, from Stornoway via Strome, were carried over the company's rails for the English markets. Three special trains were run from Strome to Inverness, and two from Inverness to Perth. The railway system had greatly increased the English demand for both fresh and kippered herrings, and the value of the west-coast fisheries had consequently been enhanced by this consumption, in addition to the large quantities still sent overseas to places such as Hamburg, Riga and St Petersburg.

The year of the Strome Ferry riot was also the year of the death of the man who had pioneered the route of the Skye railway two decades previously. Joseph Mitchell, the great engineer, died in London on 26th November, 1883, at the age of 80. For a number of years, he had spent the larger part of his time at his residence in London, passing only two or three of the summer months at his villa in Inverness. His recent health had not been satisfactory; but, nevertheless, in 1883, he made his annual visit, returning to London in October and expressing doubt as to visiting Inverness again. Throughout his life, over most of which he had transformed the facilities of communication in the Highlands, he had enjoyed good health. However, in 1862, he suffered a stroke of paralysis, and, having recovered from this, he was unfortunate to receive a second, though less severe attack; but his vitality and mental vigour remained unaffected, and up to within a few days of his death, he was able to transact some business. Such was the strength of this highly-respected, hospitable and agreeable man. However, a feature of his strong character was that he did not easily tolerate others' differences of opinion within his professional capacity.

Born in Forres, Morayshire, in 1803, Joseph Mitchell came to Inverness at an early age with his father, John, who was employed by the renowned Thomas Telford as Chief Inspector and Superintendent of Highland Roads and Bridges. Joseph, on completing his education, served his apprenticeship as a mason on the Caledonian Canal, after which he was sent to Telford's office in London, where his great master soon noticed his interest and ability for engineering. Joseph received expert training and guidance from Telford, and with the death of John Mitchell in 1824, he was appointed his father's successor.

Thus, at the age of only 21, Joseph Mitchell held a prestigious position in engineering, and he continued in this post for 38 years, until 1862; while, from 1828 to 1850, he was also engineer to the Scottish Fisheries Board, planning or improving harbours.

It was when Mitchell was in his prime that the railway movement commenced in the Highlands, in which he played such a vital part. The Highland railway system, in its various sections, developed on the basis of the engineering skill and enterprise of Joseph Mitchell. He carried out surveys north, south, east and west of Inverness, and he either completed the stretches of line or laid out the plans that he, himself, was not able to finish. In his railway endeavours, he was well assisted by William and Murdoch Paterson, who, under his excellent training, became his partners in 1862, with Murdoch remaining in the firm after the elder brother had left to pursue an independent career. Joseph Mitchell and Co. had planned all, and built some, of the sections of the railway that was gradually stretching northwards from Inverness; but, having commenced the engineering works of the Sutherland Railway in 1865, Mitchell withdrew his firm's services in 1867, after disagreements with the Duke of Sutherland on matters of economy. John Fowler had convinced the Duke that Mitchell was extravagant in his designs, as in building bridges that were unnecessarily ornate, which Mitchell had denied. In referring to Joseph Mitchell and Murdoch Paterson at the opening of the Inverness and Perth Junction Railway in 1863, Eneas MacKintosh, when proposing the health of the engineers, added that 'not a sportsman or poacher in the country knew every corrie and glen in the Highlands so well as Mr Mitchell and Mr Paterson'.

Joseph Mitchell was an active-minded man who found various other outlets for his energy, especially in those that would benefit Inverness. He served for more than one period as a member of the town council and he was once proposed for provost. He assisted in enhancing the town, such as in the laying-out and bridging of the islands on the River Ness. Being a warm benefactor, he presented £500 to the town council in 1873 for the purpose of establishing a public library, and the money was left to accumulate, amounting to £600 by the time that the construction was started. He was also one of the originators of the Caledonian Bank and one of its first Directors.

During his long life, Mitchell witnessed numerous significant changes in the Highlands - many of them due to himself - and in his later years, he passed some of his leisure time by writing about his experiences. The material was to fill two volumes, and at his death, one volume had been published, but only in a private form for limited circulation, while the second volume was ready for the printers. In *Reminiscences of My Life in the Highlands*, Joseph Mitchell outlined the formation of the Dingwall and Skye Railway Company, under the heading of 'Survey and Construction of the Skye Railway'. He viewed the route from Dingwall as being the only acceptable way to the West:

> Mr Hope Scott, the eminent parliamentary barrister, had purchased a Highland estate on Loch Shiel, near Fort William; and having advocated many a wild railway scheme in Parliament, he did not hesitate to suggest and countenance a line from Kingussie along Loch Laggan side and thence to Fort William, a distance of 45 miles. He thought that this line, while convenient for himself, might become a valuable communication to the west coast of Inverness-shire and the Hebrides; and my friend, Mr Bouch,* CE, was induced to make a flying survey, and held several meetings at Kingussie and Fort William, with the view of promoting the scheme.
>
> Knowing the country intimately for many years, I could not resist stating in a letter to the *Inverness Courier* how delusive and visionary was Mr Bouch's proposal, from its pastoral character and from the utter desolation of the country as far as regards population. I indicated the proper route to Skye and the Hebrides was a line from Dingwall to Kyleakin Ferry. This line would be the most direct and nearest route south from the west coast of the counties of Inverness and Ross, as well as Skye

---

* Sir Thomas Bouch, the famous but unfortunate English civil engineer who designed the Tay railway bridge, which collapsed in 1879, and who died in 1880.

and the other islands of the Hebrides, and I had no doubt that a line in this direction would ultimately be made. Thereafter, we heard no more of the Kingussie and Fort William railway.

My letter, however, seemed to have had some influence with the gentlemen of the west coast of Ross-shire and the Hebrides, for in 1864, they formed themselves into a committee for promoting the Skye project, and, accordingly, in the summer* of that year, I received instructions from them to survey and lay out the line. Although the population was sparse, the district to be served was vast; the resources of the country were wholly undeveloped, particularly the fisheries, which were inexhaustible; and as the scenery along this route was unsurpassed in Scotland for beauty, variety and grandeur, it was thought that a cheap line in this direction would be fairly remunerative. Mr Matheson, the Chairman of the Highland Railway, possessed the large property of Lochalsh, and property elsewhere in this locality, and he became an active promoter. The other Highland lairds, and those in the Hebrides, fully appreciated the advantage of the line, but they were generally too poor to contribute liberal subscriptions. Through Mr Matheson's exertions, however, we were enabled to go to Parliament in November 1864, and the Bill passed in July 1865, after a vigorous opposition from Sir William MacKenzie of Coul.

The line, extending from Dingwall to Kyleakin Ferry, was 67 miles† - Kyleakin Ferry, half a mile wide, opposite Skye, being the point where Hutcheson's steamers daily passed to and from Glasgow to the Hebrides. The railway, however, hung fire for want of funds, although the company had obtained their Bill. There was great anxiety afterwards with the parties interested to have the line made; and Mr Fowler, CE, who had acquired a large property at Lochbroom, recommended a narrow gauge of 3 ft 6 in.; but as the traffic would necessarily be cattle, sheep, fish and other heavy commodities, a break of gauge was rejected by the Directors, as the saving, with inferior works, on full investigation, amounted to only £50,000.

Mitchell referred to the two principal alterations that occurred to the originally-planned route:

First, a change in the direction of the line, avoiding Strathpeffer Spa and the village of Contin, connecting Strath Conon and passing the beautiful Falls of Rogie. The second alteration was fixing the western terminus at Strome Ferry instead of Kyleakin Ferry, the original terminus.

The alteration of stopping at Strome saved 14 miles of very expensive railway-making, but it was an unfortunate necessity. For the Hutcheson steamers passing to and from Glasgow daily at this point,# passengers taking the railway here would thus reach Glasgow and Edinburgh in 15 hours, instead of occupying two days in sailing in the steamers by Oban and the Clyde. My calculation in making Kyleakin the terminus was that the railway could have advantageously competed with Hutcheson's steamers for goods and cattle - particularly for fish. This latter plan, however advantageous, had to be abandoned.

The first alteration, however, avoiding Strathpeffer, was a serious mistake. It saved of capital, no doubt, £15,000 to £18,000, the cost of the works; but Strathpeffer is the Harrogate of the North, rapidly increasing. The coaches yielded a traffic of £3,000 or £4,000 per annum before the railways were made. This traffic, I have no doubt - had the railway passed by the original route - would, by this time, have amounted to £8,000 per annum. Mr Fowler, being a Director, was consulted, and, in his ignorance of the country, approved of this alteration, and his opinion was held omnipotent.

The result of these changes has been that the Skye railway has hitherto been unremunerative. The Directors, having failed to come to an understanding with Messrs Hutcheson and Co., have been obliged to establish steamers of their own to Skye and the Lews, and these running in opposition to those of that company have hitherto been an annoyance and unprofitable expense, an expenditure, in fact, which would have constructed the line to Kyleakin.

A Bill was obtained by the company to authorise these changes in 1868, and as my partnership with Mr Murdoch Paterson had then expired, and as I had, from failing health, arranged to retire from my profession, the Directors secured Mr Paterson's services, and the works of this important railway have been successfully carried out and completed by him, and, with the exception above alluded to, in accordance with the plans of J. Mitchell and Co.

---

* Mitchell's survey was carried out in the spring.
† The line was 63 miles long.
# i.e. at Kyleakin Ferry or, more correctly, Kyle.

Finally, he briefly remarked on the potential of the railway:

There is, as I have said, a vast district to be served. The scenery along the whole line and in Skye is unsurpassed in beauty and grandeur, and is already attracting thousands of tourists, who are annually increasing. Besides, the fisheries on the coast and round the Hebrides are inexhaustible; and as the railway is the shortest route to the southern markets, several steamers are now bringing cargoes of fish to the railway. When this traffic is developed, even this article alone will prove a considerable source of revenue.

Within three years of the death of Joseph Mitchell, the life of the Dingwall and Skye Railway's great promoter, Alex Matheson, came to an end. Sir Alexander Matheson - having been knighted in 1882 - died at his London residence on 27th July, 1886, and the Highlands, and the railway interests there, lost a valued friend. Like Mitchell, Alex Matheson, with his strong constitution, attained a good old age, having completed his 81st year; and although it was known that his health was a little precarious, the news of his death was unexpected. He had spent much of the preceding winter at Ardross Castle, leaving for London in May, with intention of returning to his native Ross-shire in the autumn.

Alex Matheson was born in 1805 at Attadale, the little estate that had been in the possession of his ancestors since the beginning of the previous century. His father, however, was not successful in business, and, in 1825, the family were forced to part with the last heritable Matheson property by the sale of Attadale. With the death of his father the following year, he had to make his own way in life; but, fortunately for him, his uncle, the late Sir James Matheson of the Lews, had achieved great success in commerce, trading in opium from India and tea from China, and he found a suitable opening for his nephew in his firm of Jardine, Matheson and Company. Alex Matheson went out East in that connection, and after a few years, his talent for business yielded him much financial reward. He founded his own firm in London - Matheson and Co. - from which various branches in India and China also emerged.

In 1840, having returned home with a fortune, he began his aim of devoting it to the purchase of the lands in Ross-shire that had formerly been held by his ancestors. In that year, he bought the estates of Letterfearn, on the south shore of Loch Duich, and Ardintoul, on the south shore of Loch Alsh, at a combined cost of £15,500. In 1844, he obtained the lands of Inverinate, on the north shore of Loch Duich, for £30,000; in 1851, he acquired the estate of Balmacara, in Lochalsh, for £120,000; and in 1857, he became the owner of Strath Bran and of Ledgowan, by Achnasheen, for £32,000 together. It was in 1861 that he reclaimed his childhood home of Attadale, for £14,500. In 1866, he bought New Kelso and Strathcarron for £26,000, and by this time, he had also spent £50,000 on completing the impressive, baronial-styled and turreted castle at Duncraig in Lochalsh. Including £70,000 on improvements, his extensive properties in Wester Ross, covering 115,000 acres, had cost him a total of £358,000. During the years of accumulating his territory in the West, Matheson had similarly been acquiring lands in Easter Ross, and the sum for these properties had amounted to £185,000, while the outlays for improvements had reached a further £230,000. His entire possessions in Ross-shire had extended to more than 220,000 acres at a total cost of £773,000, and he was also the owner of several properties in the town of Inverness.

The history of Alex Matheson's middle life, like that of Joseph Mitchell, was, to a large degree, illustrative of the development of railway extension in the Highlands. Although the first line there - the Inverness and Nairn Railway - was not made under his promotion, he provided assistance by taking shares to the value of £1,000; and from that time, his attention turned in the direction of railway affairs, ultimately leading to his association with the Highland Railway. 'When the various schemes were amalgamated

to form one Highland Railway, stretching between Bonar Bridge, Keith and Perth, Mr
Matheson was appointed Chairman of the united company', the *Inverness Courier*
recollected on his death:

> At this time, again his great financial experience was called into service. For a time, the
> undertaking was not particularly prosperous, and a large amount of stock remained unissued.
> Then Mr Matheson and his fellow-Directors took a very bold step - they interposed their personal
> security for advances of money, which amounted in the aggregate to nearly a million sterling. As
> the affairs of the company improved, the shares moved off, and the Directors were relieved of this
> enormous liability; but it should not be forgotten that, unless the Directors had been men of
> exceptional firmness and exceptional wealth, the results might have been serious, not so much for
> the railway itself as for the community through which it passes. In such trying times, the sagacity
> and financial credit of the Chairman were of the very highest importance, and were fully
> appreciated by the shareholders, who stood by him with the utmost loyalty. As a mark of their
> esteem, they asked him to sit for his portrait, which, painted by an eminent artist, now hangs in
> the board-room at Inverness.

The fact that he had also been the chief promoter of the Dingwall and Skye Railway was
well known in the Highlands. He was the first shareholder to double his already-large
subscription when the company needed financial help most, and, without his enterprise,
the Skye railway would not have been built. There was no doubt that the railway system
had expanded in the Highlands principally due to the enthusiasm and financial support
of two gentlemen: the Duke of Sutherland and Alex Matheson.

Having established himself as a Highland proprietor, Matheson became a suitable
candidate for a constituency there. He became a Member of Parliament in 1847,
representing, as a Liberal, the Inverness District of Burghs until 1868, when, in
succeeding his uncle, Sir James Matheson, who had just retired, he stood for his own
Ross and Cromarty. He remained the county's Parliamentary representative until health
forced his retirement in August 1884; and it was in October of that year that he stepped
down as Chairman of the Highland Railway. Back in 1882, his public services had been
acknowledged by the Crown when he was created a baronet. Although he had been
known for many years as 'Alexander Matheson of Ardross', he chose Lochalsh as the
title of his baronetcy, preferring 'Sir Alexander Matheson of Lochalsh' because it linked
the present to the past in his name. He was also a Justice of the Peace and a Deputy-
Lieutenant for Ross and Cromarty, Inverness and London; a Commissioner of
Lieutenancy for London; and a Director of the Bank of England. In tribute, the
Invergordon Times summarised: 'Sir Alexander Matheson was one of nature's noblemen;
one who, on coming to man's estate, determined - as his works show - to leave the world
a little better than he found it.'

Joseph Mitchell, in his memoirs, expressed displeasure at the Dingwall and Skye line
by-passing Strathpeffer Spa. However, shortly before his death, he may have known
that there were plans for a direct railway connection with the village, because, earlier in
November 1883, the Highland Railway supplied the Parliamentary notices of its
intention to proceed in the session of 1884 for this purpose. The Spa had increased in
popularity, and a railway into the village was imperative to allow easy access for the
large number of visitors. Since the opening of the Skye line in 1870, horse-drawn
coaches had connected with the trains at the station on the hill at Achterneed and at
Dingwall station; but both of these were inconvenient for the Spa, being especially so for
the many guests who were older and in poor health or who were invalids. The Highland
Railway wisely accorded to the demand by agreeing to make a 2½ miles-long branch
from the Skye line at Fodderty.

The popularity of Strathpeffer had long been foretold by Kenneth MacKenzie or Coinneach Odhar, the seer, who said of the settlement that: 'Uninviting and disagreeable as it now is, with its thick-crusted surface and unpleasant smell, the day will come when it shall be under lock and key, and crowds of pleasure- and health-seekers shall be seen thronging its portals, in their eagerness to get a draught of its waters'. The curative properties of the mineral springs in the valley of the Peffery were ascertained by the local people early in the 18th century, and it was around 1750 that the waters began to attract the attention of the medical fraternity. The first published account of the qualities of the 'Castle Leod waters' - named from the residence of the Earls of Cromartie at Achterneed - was produced in 1772 for the Royal Society in London by Dr Donald Munro of the city's St George's Hospital. In 1777, the factor of the Cromartie estate, who was Revd Colin MacKenzie, the parish minister, submitted a memorial to the Commissioners of Forfeited Estates - the Cromartie lands having been one of many confiscated in the Highlands after the 1745-46 Jacobite rebellion - and with this memorial, his intention was to publicise 'a fine mineral well' that had been discovered at Strathpeffer. He explained that some of the country people had drunk from this spring and had found that it cured them of their ailments. He suggested, from the lack of accommodation near the well, that it would be 'proper, for the ladies and gentlemen resorting to the well, to build a good house, kitchen and stable', which, he added would also benefit the 'whole barony of Strathpeffer' because it would offer a ready market for the local people's produce. 'Nor is it impossible', he believed of Strathpeffer, 'that, in time, this place might become a thriving village'. He further recommended that a proper building should be erected to provide protection for the well.

There was sufficient interest in the memorial to lead to the discovery of other springs; but even by the end of the century, Strathpeffer had only become a spa of local importance, although it was recorded that 'great numbers of the lower class of people were going to the Strath to take the water for all kinds of disorders, without exception'. However, it was not until 1818 that Strathpeffer's healing waters, of mainly sulphur salts, were prominently publicised. This was due to Dr Thomas Morrison of Elsick in Aberdeenshire, who had suffered from arthritis for 15 years and had visited the spas of England in search of a cure, without success. He turned to Strathpeffer and a great improvement soon occurred, after which he took up residence there, to promote the health-restoring properties of the valley. He advocated these, with much enthusiasm, in the Scottish and English newspapers and in the medical journals, where he urged the leading practitioners to encourage the establishment of Strathpeffer as a watering place. He was responsible for the building of a pump-room in 1819, at which the visitors could conveniently drink the waters; and from that time, the popularity of Strathpeffer steadily increased, such that, ultimately, it became a fashionable spa-resort.

Much of the later development and design of Strathpeffer resulted from the enterprise of Anne Hay-MacKenzie, Countess of Cromartie, and, later, Duchess of Sutherland by marrying the third Duke in 1849. She had great enthusiasm for Strathpeffer Spa, and, having visited spas on the Continent, she was able to use her knowledge of them and appoint architects from London to improve the village with buildings of character and charm. A new pump-room of stone was erected to replace the original wooden one; a pavilion in the form of a concert-hall was established to cater for entertainment; while outdoor leisure and recreation facilities were provided by attractive footpaths, gardens, and greens for bowling, tennis and croquet. Large hotels - the Spa Hotel, the Strathpeffer Hotel and the Ben Wyvis Hotel - were built to meet the growing demand for accommodation, and villas began to appear for the same reason.

Improved railway communication would next be of benefit to the potential of the Spa.

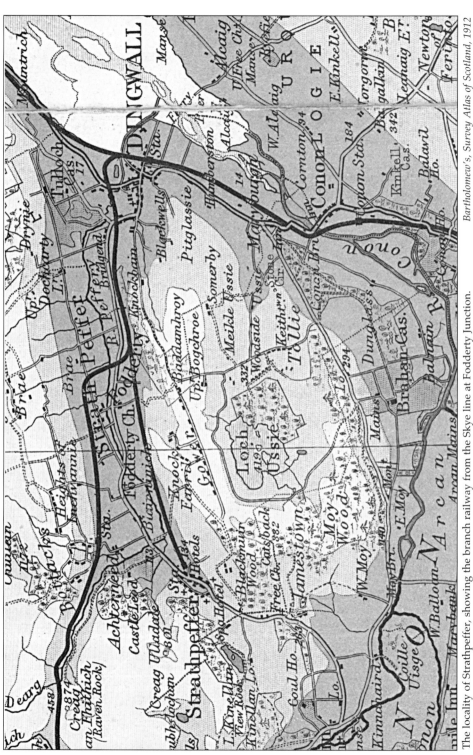

The locality of Strathpeffer, showing the branch railway from the Skye line at Fodderty Junction.

Bartholomew's, Survey Atlas of Scotland, 1912

The Strathpeffer railway was authorised by Parliament on 28th July, 1884, and ten months later, its leisurely construction allowed it to be virtually finished in time for the Spa's summer season. According to the *Inverness Courier* towards the end of May 1885:

> The new railway line to Strathpeffer, which is expected to be open for traffic early in June, is now practically complete. The route chosen by the company is one which, but for circumstances over which they had no control, would have been selected by them when the line was formed to the West fifteen years ago. Beginning at the Dingwall end of the line, we find that the train to Strathpeffer will be run for a short distance over the main line to Strome. At the point, however, where the main line curves towards the northern side of the valley, and crosses to it by the stone bridge over the high road, the new line to Strathpeffer begins, proceeding, with only one or two almost imperceptible deviations, in a straight line to the Spa. From a hurried walk over the route, we should judge that the whole of the works will be finished immediately.

The laying of the short line was not a heavy undertaking. The soils were easily worked in forming the trackbed, while suitable ballast was obtained from a piece of waste ground at Fodderty. Murdoch Paterson was the Engineer; Messrs Granger and Son of Perth were the contractors for the railway; and Messrs Robertson and Gillies of Inverness were the contractors for Strathpeffer station. The steepest gradient on the 2½ miles of the branch, which left the Skye line at Fodderty Junction, was just 1 in 100, and the cost of construction was a low £3,500 per mile, or about £9,000 in total. It was a small expense to provide a much-needed railway into the popular Highland resort. There were no significant engineering features on the line, but the terminus was impressive, and the *Inverness Courier* briefly described it and its location, thus:

> Strathpeffer station itself is a neat structure, being formed of a stone base, and above that, of wood. The other necessary erections are the station master's house and the pointsman's box, the latter being very similar to that built at Fodderty Junction. The platform is a covered one along the entire length of the station frontage, while the promenade is extended for a distance at either end. The station, situated as it is immediately below the Ben Wyvis Hotel, will be found a great convenience, being only one minute's walk from the pump-room and pavilion, and within a reasonable distance of some of the more distant parts of the Strath.

The single platform was sheltered by a glass-roofed canopy, made up of a series of 11 gables which were supported by 12 ornate cast-iron pillars. The Highland Railway had decided, rightly, that such an attractively-designed station was appropriate for the importance and the setting of the Spa.

On Tuesday 2nd June, 1885, the line was formally inspected by Major Marindin, on behalf of the Board of Trade. He was accompanied by several representatives of the Highland Railway, including Lord Lovat, Eneas Mackintosh, Andrew Dougall, Murdoch Paterson, and David Jones, the Locomotive Superintendent; while also present were Messrs Granger and Robertson, the railway and station contractors. Having arrived at Dingwall by the two-o'clock train from Inverness, the party left by a special train, composed of two saloon carriages and a brake van. At Fodderty Junction, a halt was made when Major Marindin examined the signal box and the signalling apparatus; and then, together with Messrs Jones and Robertson, he took up position on a special construction which had been fitted up at the front of the train, so that the permanent way of the new line was able to be suitably studied. At each of the five small bridges, a thorough investigation was carried out, with the train being made to run over the bridges several times while the inspector was underneath them, taking measurements of the vibrations. Finally, at Strathpeffer, the inspection was completed by a survey of the station building. The outcome was that Major Marindin expressed himself highly pleased with the construction of the branch, and he

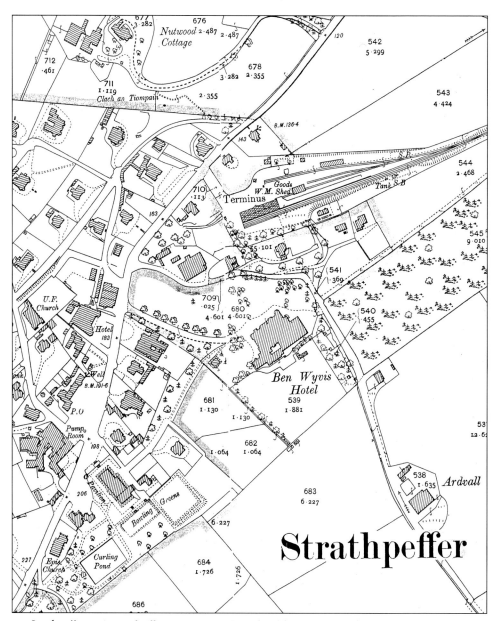

Strathpeffer station and village.   *Reproduced from the 25″, 1904 Ordnances Survey Map*

authorised the traffic to begin. At the conclusion of the inspection, as reported by the *Inverness Advertiser*, the gentlemen involved in the day's work

> . . . dined together in the Ben Wyvis Hotel, under the genial presidency of Lord Lovat. The workmen and others employed at the station buildings - upwards of 20 in number - were also entertained to dinner in another part of the hotel, the company being presided over by Mr George Robertson. At both entertainments, every success was wished to the new line. The bills of fare and service on both occasions amply sustained the well-earned reputation of the Ben Wyvis, which, under the efficient management of Mrs Mackintosh, continues to offer the very best of creature comforts and accommodation to visitors to this favourite summer resort. The new railway station stands almost within a stone's throw of the hotel, but in order to further shorten the distance, we understand that it is intended to construct a footpath direct through the wood leading from the station to the hotel.

On the following day - Wednesday, 3rd June - the Strathpeffer branch was opened to the public, with a service of six trains daily, except Sundays, in each direction over the 4¾ miles between Dingwall and Strathpeffer. The times were: from Dingwall at 7.10, 10.15 and 11.40 am, 2.40, 3.50 and 8.30 pm; and from Strathpeffer at 8.15 and 10.35 am, 2.15, 3.25, 5.40 and 8.55 pm. There were connections at Dingwall with the trains for Inverness and the South and for the North. The *Inverness Advertiser* summarised the success on the first day:

> On Wednesday, the passenger traffic on the new line was considerable, and highly encouraging for so early in the season. Every train each way was well-filled, the midday train particularly being even crowded. This is not to be wondered at, when it is considered the run is now made from Strathpeffer to Dingwall and vice versa in ten minutes, which is even less than the time taken to walk from Strathpeffer to the old and now effete station at Achterneed. The additional facilities thus offered to visitors to the Strath will be thoroughly appreciated not only by that class but by the local residents, and is sure to give an impetus to the rapidly-increasing popularity of the place. During the opening day, the traffic was worked very smoothly and successfully, not a single hitch occurring, for which thanks are due to the different officials concerned, and particularly to the Strathpeffer station master, Mr Cameron, whose attention and courtesy were all that could be desired.

The *Ross-shire Journal*, which was published in Dingwall, recorded that, on the opening day, 'a large number of passengers took advantage of the new railway service, notwithstanding the inclemency of the weather', while adding that:

> On Thursday, the number of passengers was quite as large as on the preceding day, and we are informed that over 200 tickets have been issued for the opening two days. We have no doubt that, during the ensuing season, the line will be greatly taken advantage of by visitors to the famous Strathpeffer Spa.

In its issue a week later, for 12th June, the *Ross-shire Journal* described the growth of Strathpeffer and the importance of the new railway to the Spa:

> The season at Strathpeffer Spa is just opening with great promise. The past few bright and warm days, and the opening of the new Dingwall and Strathpeffer railway, have been bringing visitors by every train. We, this week, begin the publication of our list of visitors, and it will be seen that already a goodly number of health- and pleasure-seekers have arrived. The Spa promises to become, under the admirable and fostering care of Mr Gunn, the resident factor, increasingly popular. Its fame as a health resort and its attractions as a place of restful enjoyment are already widely known, but the more extensively they become known, the greater does the annual influx of visitors grow. And what is pleasing is that the provision made for the accommodation and recreation of visitors is becoming commensurate with the demand - a constantly-increasing quantity.

Strathpeffer Branch and Strome Ferry Services
July 1885

		am	am	am	pm	pm	pm	pm	pm
Inverness	d.			9.00		*12.10*		*3.15*	
Dingwall	d.	7.10	10.15	10.20	12.50	12.55	4.15	4.20	8.30
Strathpeffer	a.	7.20	10.25	-	1.00	-	4.25	-	8.40
Achterneed				10.35		1.13		4.33	
Garve				11.00		1.38		4.53	
Lochluichart				11.20		1.48		5.05	
Achanalt				11.35		2.02		5.18	
Achnasheen				12.10 *pm*		2.20		5.35	
Glencarron Plat.				*		*		*	
Achnashellach				12.45		2.50		6.10	
Strathcarron				1.00		3.05		6.25	
Attadale				1.07		3.12		6.32	
Strome Ferry	a.			1.25		3.30		6.50	
Portree	a.					*7.00*			
Stornoway	a.					*11.00*			

		am	am	am	pm	am	pm	pm	pm
Stornoway	d.					*3.00*			
Portree	d.					*7.00*			
Strome Ferry	d.		5.45			11.00		2.40	
Attadale			6.03			*		2.58	
Strathcarron			6.10			11.25		3.05	
Achnashellach			6.25			11.38		3.20	
Glencarron Plat.			*			*		*	
Achnasheen			6.55			12.10 *pm*		3.55	
Achanalt			7.15			12.28		4.15	
Lochluichart			7.30			12.40		4.30	
Garve			7.45			12.55		4.53	
Achterneed			8.07			1.13		5.17	
Strathpeffer	d.	8.05	-	10.35	1.25	-	5.10	-	8.55
Dingwall	a.	8.15	8.30	10.45	1.35	1 45	5.20	5.35	9.05
Inverness	a.		*9.40*			*2.30*		*6.40*	

* Request stop.

Strathpeffer Spa in the early 1900s, looking west from the side of Knockfarrel hill and showing the position of the station relative to the village, the centre of which is hidden by the trees on the left.

J.L. Stevenson

This year, the great novelty is the new railway, and the railway company, though they have not yet granted the boon of a passenger platform at the west-end of Dingwall, cannot be said to be stingy in the way of railway communication to Strathpeffer. Six trains running to and from Strathpeffer daily in connection with the main-line trains is a liberal service, and there are indications that, during the season, this service will be sufficiently remunerative.

At Strathpeffer itself, buildings continue to grow apace. There are, of course, the railway station and the officials' houses, but besides these, we may note an exceedingly-massive, three-storied building, to have accommodation on the ground floor for three shops. There is also an excellent villa, to be known as 'Richmond House', almost completed, on the northern slope of the valley, belonging to Mr Beaton, postmaster; and also a commodious building - 'Seafield Villa' - erected and already occupied by Mrs Grant, also on the same slope. Preparations are being made, too, for the erection of at least one other large house, and probably before next season, several more will be in progress.

Similarly, the *Inverness Courier* had briefly remarked on the influence of railway communication to the Spa:

Since the advent of the railway in the district, even with the station about a mile distant, Strathpeffer has increased in size and importance by rapid strides. The demand for accommodation during the summer months has been such that the erection of new villas has become an annual necessity, and there can be no doubt that, with this new development of the Highland Railway system, Strathpeffer has an important future before it.

On the day that the Strathpeffer branch opened, the original Strathpeffer station on the hillside was renamed 'Achterneed', which was more appropriate to its location; and this station was still of use to Strathpeffer for anyone wishing to travel between there and Strome Ferry. The Spa now, effectively, had two stations; and, strangely, it had taken 21 years from the origin of the Dingwall and Skye Railway, and 15 years from its opening, for Strathpeffer to have its own line and station, although the distance was only 2½ miles from the track of the Skye line at Fodderty.

The *Ross-shire Journal* had been impressed by the frequency of the service on the branch because Strathpeffer had previously been served in a more limited way and at a distance by the Skye-line trains. Now, at last, the Spa had a service that was independent of the Skye line, and it was ironical, but not surprising, that the Strathpeffer line, in being classed as the branch, contained a more frequent service than the main line to Strome. However, for the summer timetable from 1st July, 1885, there was one train less in each direction on the Strathpeffer branch, while the trains on the Skye line were increased to three daily each way, with a timetable that included the most recent stations of Glencarron Platform and Attadale, although these halts, as they were, had now been open for a number of years. Where no time was given for these in the timetable, the asterisk indicated that the trains would stop 'by signal to pick up, and, by parties giving notice at the previous stopping station, to set down passengers'.

The Highland Railway provided the Strathpeffer branch with its own locomotive, named *Strathpeffer*. This was a 2-2-2 tank-engine, built in 1862 by Hawthorn and Co. of Leith for the Inverness and Ross-shire Railway, and given the name *Belladrum* and the number 12. It was one of a pair of twin engines - the other being No. 13, *Lovat* - to have been constructed with a cab in an era when there was generally no protection from the weather for the enginemen. In 1871, it was converted into a side-tank and, renamed *Breadalbane*, was used on the Highland's branch from Ballinluig to Aberfeldy in Perthshire. Further alterations were made in 1885, when it was reconditioned and renamed again, as *Strathpeffer*, in time for the opening of the branch to the Spa.

A very dark photograph of the first *Strathpeffer* engine, 2-2-2 HR No. 12, formerly *Breadalbane* and *Belladrum*, which worked the branch from its opening in 1885 until 1890.
G.E. Langmuir

Fodderty Junction and its signal box which was very similar to the cabin at Strathpeffer. The branch can been seen running straight on, while the Skye line curves to the right, onto the Fodderty embankment in this poor quality view. *A.J. Lambert*

The *Strathpeffer* railway employees beside the branch train at the Spa terminus in the 1890s. The engine is the second *Strathpeffer*, 0-4-4 saddle-tank HR No. 13. The station master's house is on the right, and the roof of the signal box is visible above the carriages at the left.

Railway Magazine

Strathpeffer station in the 1890s. The engine, once again, is No. 13, the second *Strathpeffer*, which stands with a train for Dingwall. On the slopes are some of the villas that were built to accommodate the numerous visitors to the Spa.

D. St John Thomas

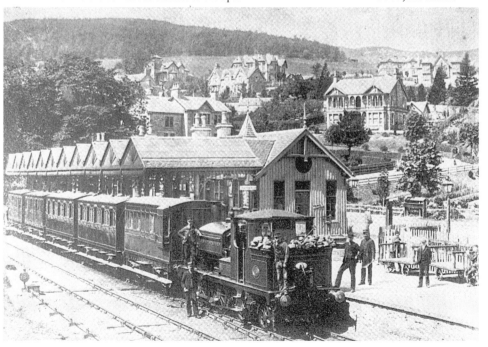

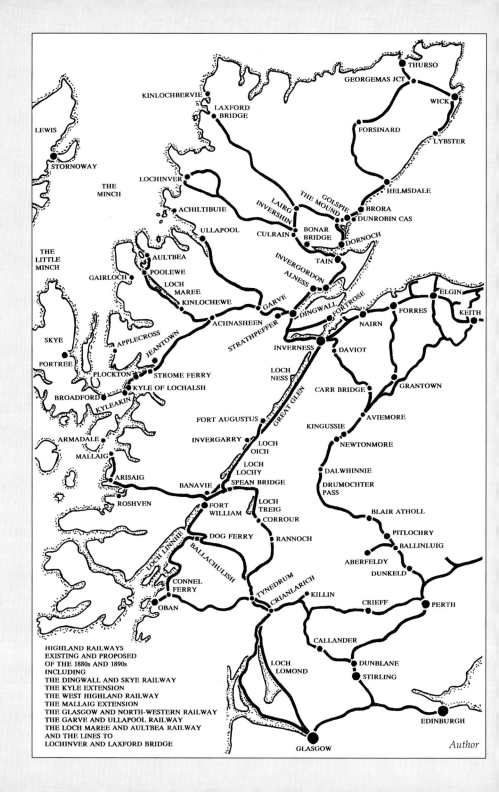

HIGHLAND RAILWAYS
EXISTING AND PROPOSED
OF THE 1880s AND 1890s
INCLUDING
THE DINGWALL AND SKYE RAILWAY
THE KYLE EXTENSION
THE WEST HIGHLAND RAILWAY
THE MALLAIG EXTENSION
THE GLASGOW AND NORTH-WESTERN RAILWAY
THE GARVE AND ULLAPOOL RAILWAY
THE LOCH MAREE AND AULTBEA RAILWAY
AND THE LINES TO
LOCHINVER AND LAXFORD BRIDGE

Author

Chapter Six
More Rails to the West Highlands

The notorious Highland Clearances, which encompassed the period from the mid-18th to mid-19th centuries, formed a disgraceful and terrible episode in the history of the Highlands, when the landowners heartlessly evicted their tenantry of farming families - later called crofters - to reap the financial rewards of leasing the land to sheep-farmers of the Border country.

Many of the people had to leave their beloved Highlands forever, to try to make a new life in the industrial Lowlands or in the 'New World' of North America. However, there was still a large population who had no option but to remain on their landowner's estate, and these families were forced to resettle, generally without compensation, help or even sympathy, in other parts with inferior land. For this, they had to pay excessive rents, and they were treated with contempt and often victimised by the factors of the landowners. The already-poor conditions of the tenants were made appalling by the potato famine of 1846, but even then, there were landowners who showed no concern and would not expend their money on the starving people.

For most of the period of the clearances, the Highland people, who were largely of the Presbyterian faith, had counted upon the spiritual support of the Church of Scotland; but, in general, the ministers had not criticised - at least, openly - the immorality of the evictions. This was due to the influence of the landowners, for they appointed the ministers, and the churches were on their property. However, in 1843, some of the ministers agreed that they would no longer tolerate this state of affairs, and the outcome was the 'Disruption of the Church of Scotland', when there was an exodus of over a third of the 1,200 ministers. They formed the Free Church of Scotland, which, in being free from the influence of the landowners, provided solace and self-respect for the tenants, who now had a genuine spiritual ally amid the continuing oppression.

Clearances still occurred after 1850, especially in the Western Isles, where the southern sheep arrived later than on the mainland; but, during the 1850s and 1860s, there was a decline in sheep-farming in the Highlands, because of the import of cheaper wool and mutton - especially from Australia and New Zealand, which, ironically, were countries that had latterly received Highland emigrants. Deer-hunting then became popular in the Highlands, and many of the landowners converted the sheep-walks into sporting estates and leased them to the wealthy Englishmen who indulged in shooting deer. Since there was less profit from deer than from sheep, the landowners charged their tenants higher rents, by resorting to rack-renting to a greater extent than previously.

For over a century, the powerless tenant families had generally suffered the clearances and the consequent oppression without significant resistance; but, by the 1870s, the gradual emergence of a new strength and anger within the crofters had produced a change in their attitude to the treatment that they received from the landowners. Thoughts of rebellion had originated from the growing number of courageous land-reform activists, within and beyond the Highlands, who, in having nothing material to gain for themselves, encouraged the crofters to demand their basic right of fair treatment, together with the restoration of the land that had been taken from them.*
Much encouragement for the Highlanders had also come from Ireland - that other country of clearances oppression and rack-renting - where the people's fightback, with

---

* One of the most notable and determined activists was the radical John Murdoch, a former exciseman from near Nairn, who, in detesting landlordism, formed the Inverness-published *Highlander* newspaper in 1873 as a means of publicising and counteracting the crofters' oppression.

99

the formation of an Irish land league in 1879, had led to concessions by the Liberal Government of Prime Minister William Gladstone. The Irish Land Act, 1881, in lessening the power of the landowners, introduced important rights and security of tenure to the Irish tenant farmers. This was a significant victory for the people against authority, and it acted as an inspiration for the Highland crofters to unite with the aim of obtaining the same rights.

Indeed, the crofters or their allies had already begun to act, and were continuing to do so. In 1874, a minor riot had occurred in connection with the crofters of the island of Great Bernera, which, in lying off the west coast of Lewis, was part of the land of Sir James Matheson. The crofters' victory was the restoration of land that had been taken from them. In 1880, at Leckmelm on the eastern shore of Loch Broom, the new owner of the estate - Alexander Pirie, a paper manufacturer from Aberdeen - seized all of the good and hard-won land of his crofters for himself, and forced the occupants to become his menial employees, or face eviction. The selfish manipulation of this case produced widespread condemnation and bad publicity for the landowners in general.

However, it was in Skye that the strongest resistance was encountered. Firstly, in 1881, on the Kilmuir estate of Captain William Fraser - the former Director of the Dingwall and Skye Railway, and one of the worst offenders of rack-renting - the crofters were eventually given a rent reduction after they had refused to pay their increased rents from the time of implementation back in 1877. Then came two events of physical retaliation in Skye in 1882 that brought the crofters' plight to national attention. In both cases, the crofters stood firm in keeping their livestock on forbidden land and in refusing to pay their rent. In February, at Glendale, in the north-west of the island - an estate that was controlled by the trustees of the recently-deceased owner, Sir John MacPherson MacLeod - the local people rallied to the extent of 500 and chased away, with sticks, forks and scythes, a small police force and the sheriff officer with the summonses of eviction, such that a government gunboat, HMS Jackal, had to be dispatched to restore order. A similar but even more eventful resistance occurred in April in the district to the south of Portree, known as The Braes, on the lands of the 6th Lord MacDonald. The sheriff officer and his two assistants were accosted by many of the people from the townships, and, with their summonses being burned, the action later led to the 'Battle of the Braes'. This was fought between a large contingent of policemen, mostly drafted from Glasgow, and the men, women and children of the Braes, who stoned and assaulted their outnumbered opponents of authority.

With such lawlessness in Skye, and with growing dissent and unrest in the Highlands generally, the Government had to take notice of what was wrong in this distant part of the nation. In February 1883, a Highland land league - the Highland Land League Reform Association - was formed to add further strength to the crofters' fight, and at the end of the same month, the Government finally agreed, after much persuasion, to set up a royal commission 'to inquire into the condition of the crofters and cottars in the Highlands and islands of Scotland, and all matters affecting the same, or relating thereto'. Named after the chairman, the all-Scottish Napier Commission of seven members* collected evidence directly from the crofters, by visiting 61 places in the

---

* The members were: Lord Napier and Ettrick, whose estate was at Selkirk and who was the only non-Highlander; Sir Kenneth MacKenzie of Gairloch, who owned 164,000 acres in Wester Ross; Donald Cameron of Lochiel, Conservative MP for Inverness-shire and the owner of 110,000 acres in the county; Charles Fraser-Mackintosh, Liberal MP for the Inverness Burghs and a strong activist for the crofters' rights; Alexander Nicolson, Sheriff-Substitute of Kirkcudbright and a native of Skye; Donald MacKinnon of Colonsay, who was the recently-appointed first Professor of Celtic at Edinburgh University; and Malcolm MacNeill as secretary, who was chairman of the Board of Supervision for the Relief of the Poor and whose father was the owner of Colonsay.

Highlands and islands from May until October 1883. Their report, published in April 1884, acknowledged the Highland people's sufferings and also their land rights in a moral, if not legal, sense. The findings led the way for the passing of the Crofters' Holdings (Scotland) Act, 1886, under Gladstone's Liberal Government, and it was legislation that permitted the Highlanders the same rights and security of tenure as their Irish brethren. While the outcome could not redress the injustices of everyone, the subject of the social aspect of the Highlands was given a prominence that had never been presented before.

The Highland people's resistances and uprisings of the 1870s and 1880s, having continued in Lewis until 1888, and having been referred to as the 'crofters' war', had drawn much public attention and sympathy, and, of greater importance, much governmental concern to the dreadful social circumstances of the West Highlands that had resulted from the clearances. Even before the investigation by the Napier Commission, it was evident that a principal cause of the backwardness of the West Highlands was the inadequate communication with the rest of the country; and the Napier Commission did recognise this adverse effect by recommending the improvement of postal and telegraphic facilities and the construction of new harbours and railways. The isolation was such that over the whole coastal stretch of the West Highlands, there were only two railheads - at Strome Ferry and Oban - and these were insufficient to handle the social and economic requirements, especially in regard to the large fish traffic. Thus, in consequence of the crofters' war - of the people taking up their own cause to obtain fair treatment - Parliament had been awakened further to the urgency of new communications for the West Highlands.

Back in 1882, an ambitious railway scheme had been promoted that would have opened up part of the interior of the West Highlands and would have offered the potential for railway progress further westwards to the coast. This was the Glasgow and North-Western Railway, which was to run for a distance of over 160 miles from the city via Loch Lomond, Glen Coe, Fort William and the Great Glen to Inverness. The line was to commence at Maryhill, on the North British Railway's Helensburgh route and run, generally northwards, through Strath Blane towards the south-eastern corner of Loch Lomond and along the whole of the eastern shore of the loch, to ascend Glen Falloch and reach Crianlarich. From there, it was to climb Strath Fillan to Tynedrum, and then continue on a stretch that rose steeply at 1 in 50, to pass Loch Tulla on its western side and attain a summit of 1,077 feet at Black Mount, on the edge of Rannoch Moor. Then the route became westerly, down Glen Coe on steep gradients of 1 in 53 and 1 in 50 for 11 miles to Ballachulish, where an eastwards turn was made to head along the southern shore of Loch Leven, and to cross by a bridge at the Dog Ferry, the narrowest part. Continuing on the northern shore of the loch, the railway followed the sea round Loch Linnhe, to arrive at Fort William. There were a further 60 miles to Inverness, and the route through the Great Glen was on the eastern side of the three lochs of Lochy, Oich and Ness, with the line running partly on a causeway that would be built along the shore of Loch Ness.

The Glasgow and North-Western Railway, which was expected to be worked by the North British company, was to have its own station on the southern side of Inverness, and a connecting line was to be made with the Highland Railway. The whole undertaking was to cost £1,500,000. Unfortunately, in spite of the immense benefit that it would have been to the West Highlands, as well as reducing the distance between Glasgow and Inverness by nearly 50 miles, the grand scheme had too many powerful opponents. The Highland Railway constituted the greatest of these, because the Glasgow and North-Western was seen as a rival line to the Highland's Perth-Inverness route. Moreover, the Highland did not want its southern adversary, the North British, to reach Inverness. The Highland's ally, the Caledonian Railway, was also against the Glasgow and North-Western because of the influence that it would have on the trade of the Callander and Oban line that was operated by the Caledonian. Other opposition, by reason of competition, came from the Loch Lomond Steamboat Company, the Caledonian Canal Commissioners, and David MacBrayne, whose steamer services included Glasgow to Inverness via the Great Glen; and some landowners were against the railway because of its intrusion on their estates. In contrast, the people of the West Highlands in general, and of Fort William in particular, were very much in favour of the Glasgow and North-Western, since, to them, there was an urgent need for it.

The Bill for the line was considered in the 1883 session of Parliament, when the opposition was presented; but the argument of the Highland Railway in submitting that there was not enough traffic for two railways between Glasgow and Inverness, while adding that lost revenue due to another line would dissuade it from building any extensions of its own system in the Highlands, was the principal reason that the preamble of the Bill was defeated in Parliament. Further to the latter part of its assertion, the Highland announced that it was intending to prepare a Bill for a direct line from Aviemore through Carr Bridge to Inverness that would save about 25 miles.

Thus, the Glasgow and North-Western Railway was not to materialise, and, for the time being, there would be no railway in the area of the West Highlands between the Skye and the Oban lines.

In Parliament, the barrister acting for the Glasgow and North-Western had stressed that, if the Bill was rejected, the decision would have been made that the West Highlands would be without another railway for the next generation. However, by as early as the end of the decade, this prediction was in process of being proved wrong, because two railway schemes had been initiated in different parts of the West Highlands.

The first of these lines was a partial alternative to the Glasgow and North-Western, called the West Highland Railway, which, in connecting Glasgow and Fort William, was to begin at Craigendoran, near Helensburgh, and run above Gare Loch, Loch Long and Loch Lomond, and then follow a similar route to its predecessor as far as Loch Tulla; but, on passing east of the loch, the West Highland was to head north-eastwards to cross the desolate Rannoch Moor and north-westwards to a summit of 1,347 feet at a point on the Corrour estate, some two miles south-east of Loch Treig. The northwards descent down the lochside led into Glen Spean, where there was a westwards turn to Spean Bridge, followed by a south-westwards run to Fort William. The proposed capital for the 100 miles from Craigendoran to Fort William was £720,000. The original plan had included continuing the line 30 miles west of Fort William, to terminate on the coast at Roshven, by Loch Ailort, but strong opposition by a landowner there - Professor Blackburn, a retired mathematician of Glasgow University - had forced the extension to be abandoned. The Highland Railway again opposed the new scheme because of the possibility of the West Highland later attempting to reach Inverness; but with the Bill having made no mention of this aim, the Highland had no justification for objecting. Having obtained the support of the North British, the West Highland Railway Act received Royal Assent on 12th August, 1889, and the first sod of the line was cut at Fort William on 23rd October of that year.

Then, to the north, was the second of the two lines to be planned for the West Highlands before the end of the 1880s. In January 1889, a petition, signed by 1,020 men of Lochbroom in Ross-shire and of Assynt in Sutherland, was sent to the Highland Railway to appeal for the making of a railway from Garve, on the Skye line, to the fishing port of Ullapool, near the mouth of Loch Broom. In early March, a well-attended meeting was held at Ullapool to discuss the promotion of the railway in regard to the Highland's response. The outcome was that, while the Highland would not construct such a line, it agreed to work it 'on the most reasonable terms', if the promoters were able to build it with their own capital. Even this was considered satisfactory to the enthusiastic committee that had quickly formed for what was referred to generally as the Ullapool and Garve Railway.

The neatly-built settlement of Ullapool, where there had previously been only a farm of the same name, was established in 1788 by the British Fisheries Society as a station for the herring-fishing of the north-western seas at a time when the herring was also abundant in Loch Broom. In 1792, the construction of a road, with the support of the government, was commenced between Ullapool and Contin so that the village would have a communication with Dingwall and Inverness. Unfortunately, by the time of the road's completion in 1797, when the population of the village had grown to 700, the herring had begun to desert the west-coast waters to spread towards the east coast, although there were still shoals in the Minches; but, in general, it meant that the fishermen had to take their boats further away, and this led to the decline of Ullapool as a centre for the fisheries. Early in the 19th century, the reason of Ullapool's origin ceased to apply and a serious depression followed. A later description of the village was provided in the 1842 edition of a book called *Guide to the Highlands* by brothers George and Peter Anderson of Inverness:

Ullapool . . . stands on a fine, terraced, gravelly promontory . . . and it exhibits several parallel lines of houses; most of them whitewashed and slated or tiled; the church, manse, the principal inn and the residence of the Fishery Society's agent being the most conspicuous . . . the post-office and all the principal shops and houses being arranged along the beach, looking southwards and extending along its whole length. The village was founded by the British Fishery Society about 60 years ago when the herring trade was at its height, and was intended to be a beautiful town on a spacious and regular plan; but the herring shoals having for many years abandoned the adjoining loch, the prosperity of the place has been sealed up . . . The population of Ullapool is between 700 and 800 inhabitants. They hold their tenements of the Fishery Society, who feu the ground from Mr Hay-MacKenzie of Cromartie. There are two inns in the place, but as travellers' visits are 'few and far between', of course the accommodation for them is necessarily of an inferior kind.

In 1847, amid the potato famine of the Highlands, the British Fisheries Society finally parted with their failure of Ullapool when it was sold to James Matheson of Achany and the Lews.

Over 40 years later, in the new transport era, came the railway plans that would, it was hoped, help to revitalise the already-improved state of the fishing industry at Ullapool. In connection with the meeting in the village in March 1889 for the promotion of the railway, there had been mention of 'the enormous quantity of unused fish which is available, which is becoming an increasingly-demanded article of food among the working classes all over England, and how wrong it is not to provide proper conveyance for it, since it would be the most remunerative employment for our people'. A railway was also important because of the nature of the existing road - in reality, a track - between Ullapool and Garve; but even more significantly, the new line was seen by many as being able to advance the trade, communications and social conditions of the whole of the North-West Highlands.

In regard to the recommendations of the Crofters' Commission, the Ullapool and Garve Railway was honoured by the support of a number of prominent, radical Liberal Unionist MPs - including their leader, Joseph Chamberlain - who were concerned about the plight of the Highlands; and one of them, James Caldwell, MP for the St Rollox district of Glasgow, arrived in Ullapool on 16th April, 1889 as part of the line's promotion. He was accompanied by his daughter and by Murdoch Paterson. Having left Inverness by the 9 am train to Strome Ferry, the guests alighted at Garve, where a carriage was in readiness for the road journey to Ullapool. They were met by Revd MacDonald of the Church of Scotland, who was the convener of the railway committee, and Mr P. Campbell Ross, the secretary; and both gentlemen explained the object of the promoters and the expected route of the line. The visit of Messrs Caldwell and Paterson had been eagerly awaited by the people of the district, who turned out in large numbers to welcome them to the capital of Lochbroom, which was decked with flags in honour of the occasion. On arriving at six o'clock, they were warmly welcomed with cheers and a procession, after which the MP was presented with the reading of an address on behalf of the people of Lochbroom, and the beginning of this illustrated the necessity of providing assistance to the Highlands in general:

To James Caldwell, Esq, MP

Dear Sir:
We desire most heartily to welcome you to Lochbroom. We do so looking upon you as one to whom we are under lasting obligations. We recognise in you almost the first Member of Parliament who took sufficient interest in the people of the Highlands and islands to induce him, in the face of grave discouragements, to declare in his place in the House of Commons that Highlanders had long been labouring under great disadvantages, and would continue to do so until such time as the Government should awake to a sense of its duty in this matter, and give its support to improve their condition - until, in short, the authorities of the country should come to realise that the widespread poverty under which the Highland people were labouring was the result of economic changes over which they had no control . . .

And, said the address:

We thank you with all our heart for your unwearied diligence on our behalf with a view to put an end to our distressing state of severe isolation - a condition which, we hope, will not continue long. We look hopefully to your reporting in favour of the Ullapool and Garve Railway as a means of opening up this quarter of the North-West Highlands, and of extending its fishing and other industries. We feel sure that you will recommend the construction of harbours and quays where required, and we beg to assure you that, wherever you may be, our best wishes and our gratitude will be with you.

Caldwell assured the people of Ullapool and Lochbroom that the Liberal Unionist Party was much in favour of the proposed railway for opening up the communications of the North-West Highlands, and that Chamberlain had given him the most encouraging words in connection with it.

Murdoch Paterson had explained to the people the direction that the Ullapool and Garve Railway would take, as far as then ascertained, but it was in the summer of 1889 that a survey allowed the exact route to be designated. The survey was carried out on behalf of Paterson by C.R. Manners, a civil engineer who had practised in Inverness since 1869. The steeply-graded, 33 miles-long line would commence at a junction immediately south of Garve station and run parallel to the Skye line for ¾ mile before heading up Strath Garve, initially at 1 in 40 for a mile, and the valley of the Black Water, following the old coach road past the lonely Aultguish Inn; then ascending the bleak Strath Dirrie, to reach a summit of 903 feet, 15 miles from Garve, on the eastern end of Loch Droma. Passing the loch on its southern side, the railway would descend Dirrie

More, at first gently and then rapidly, towards the spectacular Corrieshalloch Gorge, which was 12 miles from Ullapool.

Overcoming the gorge - being a mile long, 200 ft deep and 100 ft wide, with the River Droma plunging 150 ft at the Falls of Measach - was the most serious engineering aspect of the whole line; but Paterson, while having acknowledged that there would be considerable difficulty, believed it not insurmountable. This was to be achieved by adopting an unusual U-shaped course, with the line skirting the southern side of the ravine and, at its western end, curving southwards round the hillside to head along Gleann Mor for ¾ mile. Then it would curve even more sharply, to cross the narrow valley and cut through part of the terrain on the opposite side by a 590 yards-long, curved tunnel, from which it would proceed by the western slopes. Additionally, during the U-shaped passage around Gleann Mor, and through the tunnel, the line would descend steeply, with a gradient of 1 in 40 for a continuous distance of 2½ miles.

Difficulties were also evident along the shore of Loch Broom due to the precipitous nature of the hills there, and further steep gradients of 1 in 40 were necessary over parts of this stretch and into Ullapool where the line would descend to the seafront, with the terminus adjacent to the pier. Nevertheless, even with the obstacles or construction, Paterson thought that the railway could be commenced in 1890 and opened in 1892.

There were great hopes for the proposed railway. It was said that it would serve the district from Cape Wrath in the north to Gairloch in the south, containing a population of over 40,000; and that it would afford exceptional facilities for the speedy transit of fresh fish and agricultural produce from Lochbroom, Assynt, and Lewis and Harris. It was anticipated that Ullapool, owing to its sheltered situation on Loch Broom, would become, in conjunction with the proposed railway, the port for the Stornoway steamer. The distance and direction of Strome Ferry from Stornoway was 75 miles southwards, which, with the general direction of the wind being from the south-west, involved seven hours of sailing; while Ullapool, at 50 miles south-eastwards from Stornoway, could, it was asserted, be reached in about half that time. The railway would bring Ullapool within three hours of Inverness, and it was expected that this would encourage tourists to the area, such that people from the Highland capital, who went to the Moray Firth coast during the summer, would then go to Ullapool and Loch Broom to enjoy the milder climate of the West and the good bathing beaches along the loch; while the fine scenery of the route, especially from Corrieshalloch to Ullapool, would also provide the opportunity for a tourist invasion soon after the line's opening.

The railway had the support of all the landowners along the route. Among them was John Fowler of Braemore, whose residence lay at the northern end of the Corrieshalloch Gorge. He was now the celebrated Sir John Fowler, having been knighted in 1885 in recognition of his engineering services to the Government in regard to Egypt. In 1889, his world-famous masterpiece of construction was nearing completion - this being the magnificent Forth railway bridge, which he had designed with his colleague, Benjamin Baker. Fowler, who was greatly in favour of the Ullapool and Garve Railway, was not able to devote much time to it because of his other commitments; but his son, John Arthur Fowler, was one of the members of the committee for promoting the line, and he had made spirited efforts to try to ensure its accomplishment. Seven miles north of Braemore, at Leckmelm on Loch Broom, Alexander Pirie was also in favour, although he was doubtful of the promoters obtaining sufficient capital for the project.

In general, the people of Stornoway were favourable to the Ullapool scheme, but this was not the case with some of the fish curers and merchants there, who expressed fear that the line would be detrimental to their livelihood. They believed that the fish from the Minches would supposedly be dispatched directly from Ullapool to the South instead of going via Stornoway and Strome Ferry, such that the whole fish trade, being the principal source of income of Lewis, would be transferred to Ullapool, leaving a problem of unemployment for the large population of the island. Thus, they wanted their railhead to continue to be Strome Ferry. The view in Ullapool was that these fears would not materialise, and the following considerations were made known in response: that a vast quantity of fish was lost to the fishermen every season through their inability to reach a port with the fish in good condition; that the bulk of the fish was caught on the mainland side of the Minch; that many thousands of consumers in the South, who would be in receipt of cheap, wholesome food, were ignored; and that there would be the advantage of a daily steamer between Ullapool and Stornoway.

To the north of Ullapool, there was support for the line from the people of Assynt in Sutherland. In May 1889, an enthusiastic meeting, held at the fishing village of Lochinver, recorded that:

> We, the inhabitants of Assynt, hereby resolve cordially to support the movement for the construction of a line of railway between Garve and Ullapool, as being the most central place proposed for developing the fishing industry on the west coast of Sutherland and Ross, as well as the island of Lewis, and for benefiting the crofter population of these districts. We further resolve to give our support to this movement on the understanding that a daily steamer will run from the Ullapool terminus along the west coast of Sutherland.

Not everyone, however, was happy at the thought of a railway in that direction. The people in the country south-west of Ullapool wanted a line in their district; and thus, also in May, at a meeting held at the village of Shieldaig, by Applecross, in support of another proposed line, from Achnasheen to Loch Ewe, the following resolutions were unanimously agreed:

> That it is of the first importance to the West Highlands that the Government should carry out the recommendation of the Royal Crofters Commission as to increased railway communication, deemed by them to be the principal requirement of the fishing and crofting population of the west coast.
> That a railway from Achnasheen to Loch Ewe would most materially benefit the large population in the district of Shieldaig, Torridon and the north coast of Applecross.
> That Loch Ewe is a most suitable place for landing fish caught between Lochmaddy and Stornoway.

It was strange that the Shieldaig people were so much in support of this line. By it, in being able to have their rail connection at the village of Kinlochewe, they would indeed be nearer a railway there, compared to the extra nine miles between Kinlochewe and Achnasheen, but they would still have to traverse the same distance of 18 miles by road to Kinlochewe as by road through Jeantown to their connection with the Skye line at Strathcarron station. Also, contrary to what was stated in one of the resolutions, there was not a large population in the 'district of Shieldaig, Torridon and the north coast of Applecross'.

The outlook of Stornoway's apprehensive fish dealers apart, some antagonism had developed in regard to whether a railway should come to Loch Broom or Loch Ewe. An example of this was illustrated by a letter of response, dated 11th June, 1889, that was sent to the editor of the *Inverness Courier* from a respected landowner, Duncan Darroch of Torridon:

> Sir:
> I observed a letter in the *Courier* of the 4th, dated Torridon and signed 'A Torridon Fisherman', in which the writer assures the Lochbroom fishermen *that the majority of the Torridon people are in*

favour of the Garve and Ullapool line. We have this day forwarded to the Loch Ewe committee our petition in favour of their line, and it is signed by every Torridon male, over the age of 14, as far as we can ascertain. Your correspondent's assertion as to *the majority of Torridon people* is therefore ludicrously inaccurate. But further, if the anonymous *Torridon fisherman* hailing from *Torridon* is what he pretends to be, what are we to think of his being one of these who have signed the Loch Ewe petition? And if he is not the genuine article, how has he obtained a place in your columns? The real Torridon fishermen are very indignant at his misrepresentation of them; they understand clearly what a blessing such a railway would be to them, and are determined to give all the support they can to the Loch Ewe proposals, in accordance with the resolutions of their public meeting published in the *Courier* of 10th May.

In contrast, expressing favour for the Ullapool line, there was the following letter, also dated 11th June, to the same paper from the 'Schoolhouse of Scoraig, Little Loch Broom':

Sir:
   In the name of common sense, let this unseemly railway war between neighbours now cease, for there is no doubt both sides have done more harm than good to their cause, on account of their jealous and selfish rivalry; but especially as Lord Lothian's investigation tour* to the North will ere long decide whether Ullapool or Poolewe or Gairloch is the most convenient and suitable railway connection within the Lews. Allow me, however, to notice one important hint. A correspondent, *Veritas*, in your impression of the 4th inst says: 'I am requested by one who knows to ask how many curers have come there to prosecute their avocations within the last dozen years?'
   My answer is that scores of curers have come to Loch Broom to prosecute their avocations within that interval, and that, too, with marked success. Between the end of August 1879 and the beginning of January 1880, one of the heaviest and most successful fishings in the history of Loch Broom was prosecuted here by thousands of fishermen from the east coast, the Lews, Gairloch, Assynt, etc., not to speak of our own native fishermen. During these four months, scores of curers resorted to this locality from all parts of the United Kingdom - viz., Macombie and Co. from Aberdeen; James Loudon and Co. from Fraserburgh; Mr Smith and Simon MacKenzie from Stornoway; and Thomas MacLeod from Inverness, etc., besides a fleet of fast sailing-steamers that plied incessantly day and night among the fishing-boats, purchasing fresh herrings for the southern markets. In that year, more than one correspondent of your valuable paper - myself included - wrote several letters to the *Courier* relative to this almost-unprecedentedly-heavy fishing. An old Gairloch fisherman, at present employed at the Scoraig salmon-fishings, has told me today that, in the year referred to, he, along with scores of his neighbours from Gairloch and both sides of Loch Ewe, did catch more herrings and pocket more money in Loch Broom than what they had done in Gairloch and Loch Ewe from the first day they went to sea in pursuit of herrings down to this date.

The exertions of the Ullapool railway committee resulted in a Parliamentary Bill being drawn up, in late 1889, for the purpose of proceeding in the session of 1890, to obtain authorisation for what was, with a reversal of the place names in the title, the Garve and Ullapool Railway, as it came to be known. It was for 'a railway, 33 miles, five furlongs, four chains and 50 links in length,† commencing at or near Garve station of the Highland Railway, and terminating at or near the north end of the steamboat pier, near the junction of Quay Street with Shore Street, Ullapool'. The capital of the company was to be £240,000 in 24,000 shares of £10, with power to borrow a further £80,000. Among the Directors were John Arthur Fowler and Lady Matheson of Achany and the Lews, who was the widow of Sir James Matheson and whose residence was Stornoway Castle. The engineers were Murdoch Paterson and C.R. Manners, with Sir John Fowler as consulting engineer.

---

* This tour, by the Marquis of Lothian, who was the Secretary for Scotland, had commenced on 7th June at Oban.
† One furlong = ⅛ mile = 220 yards; one chain = ⅒ furlong = 22 yards; and one link = ⅟₁₀₀ chain = 7.92 inches.

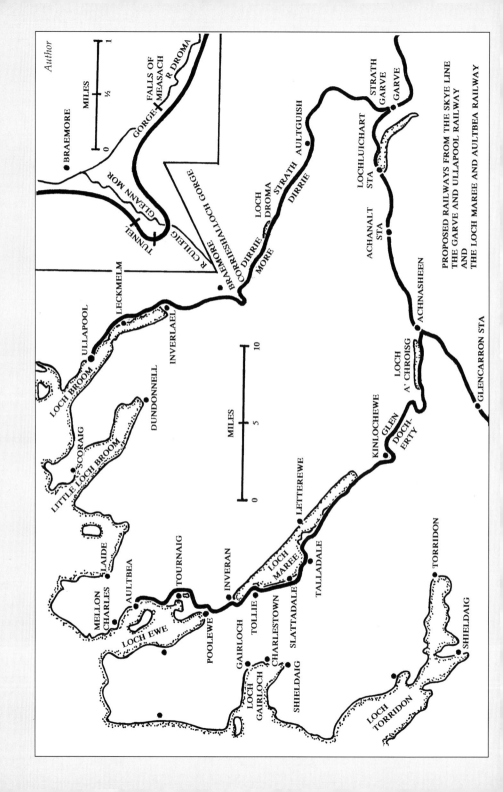

PROPOSED RAILWAYS FROM THE SKYE LINE
THE GARVE AND ULLAPOOL RAILWAY
AND
THE LOCH MAREE AND AULTBEA RAILWAY

Chapter Seven

The Report of the
West Highland Royal Commission

Back in April 1889, Sir John Fowler had returned from India to a welcoming address of praise from two dozen members of the Garve and Ullapool railway committee. This address said part of the way through: 'Sir, - Lochbroom men, in the ages to come, will speak with fervour and elation of the great engineer of that world's wonder, the Forth Bridge, and the lustre his connection with it will shed on their native parish - glorious Lochbroom - which you have improved and beautified so admirably'. And then, with reference to the Garve and Ullapool Railway, the address continued:

> We consider it a happy omen to have Mr Chamberlain, the most brilliant statesman of Great Britain, co-operating with the most eminent living engineer in an undertaking which will, as we think, permanently relieve the widespread poverty which exists more or less among a population of over 40,000 souls. It is a noble work, worthy of two such noble men.

Joseph Chamberlain, leader of the Liberal Unionists, with his deep interest in Highland matters, had done much to draw the attention of Parliament to the problems of the crofters, and he had seen these for himself in 1887 in a tour of the North-West Highlands. During 1889, he was delighted to hear of the progress of the Garve and Ullapool Railway in attempting to open up the communications, and he agreed that the scheme was well worthy of support from the public funds; but he was not able to commit himself to any specific railway, for there were others that had recently been proposed for the West Highlands. In 1886, the Conservative Party, led by Robert Gascoyne-Cecil, who was the Marquis of Salisbury, had won power from William Gladstone's Liberals, and, due largely to Chamberlain and his Liberal Unionists, the Conservatives were continually made aware of the Highland situation. This caused the Marquis of Lothian, as Secretary for Scotland, to make a tour of the North-West Highlands in the summer of 1889 and recommend that the Treasury should spend not less than £150,000 on the development of fisheries, harbours and railways there.

The consequence of all this was the proposed visit of another royal commission, which was appointed by Lord Lothian at the end of December 1889, 'to inquire into certain matters affecting the interests of the population of the western Highlands and islands of Scotland'. There were six members of the West Highland Royal Commission, its chairman being Spencer H. Walpole, who was Lieutenant-Governor of the Isle of Man, and also included was Malcolm MacNeill, who had served as the secretary of the Napier Commission. Among their tasks, they were to investigate which railway, out of six that had been proposed, would best meet the needs of the West Highlands and islands, and would, therefore, receive financial assistance from the Government. These railways to the west coast were: from Garve to Ullapool, 33 miles; from Achnasheen to Aultbea on Loch Ewe, 40 miles; from the West Highland Railway's intended Banavie branch, near Fort William, to Mallaig, 40 miles; from Strome Ferry to Kyle of Lochalsh, 10½ miles; from Culrain, on the Sutherland Railway, to Lochinver, 42 miles; and from Lairg to Loch Laxford, 37 miles.

The commission had its first meeting in private at Edinburgh on 9th January, 1890, and this involved the preparation of questions for sending to everyone interested in the matter, so that the necessary replies would be ready by April, when the tour would commence. The six gentlemen arrived at Inverness on Thursday, 3rd April, 1890 and they had an interview with Andrew Dougall of the Highland Railway which, in one way or another, would play a vital part in the decision of which line was to be made. The tour of inquiry was to start on the 4th, and the issue of the *Inverness Courier* for that day reported:

> The proceedings of the commission which begins its inquiry at Ullapool today will be closely followed by all interested in the development of the resources of the Highlands and islands. The agitation which, in 1883, led to the appointment of the Crofters Commission has, in recent years, assumed a new form, and from all parts, petitions are being sent up to the House of Commons praying for increased harbour and railway facilities . . . The commissioners will enter upon their labours today by going over the route of the proposed new line of railway from Garve to Ullapool.

They left Inverness by the morning Skye-line train as far as Garve, accompanied by Mr Manners and Mr Fowler junior, and, from the road to Ullapool, they saw the route of the intended railway without having to leave their carriages. At Braemore, they were met by a number of the railway-committee members, and at Ullapool, where flags were displayed, they were given a good welcome by a large crowd for the start of their investigation. In the evening, a deputation of the railway committee stated the merits of the line and of Ullapool as a good harbour to the commission, which then questioned the committee on various aspects of the enterprise, including the traffic potential, especially of fish.

On the following day - Saturday, 5th - the commission was to inspect the proposed railway from Achnasheen along the southern shore of Loch Maree to the small village of Poolewe and then by the edge of Loch Ewe to the small terminus of Aultbea. Because of the difficulties of travel within the West Highlands, the commission had obtained the services of the gunboat *HMS Jackal*. This took them, firstly, from Ullapool to Aultbea. As there was no pier at Aultbea, the *Jackal* dropped anchor in Loch Ewe and the commission was landed by boat onto the shore, where a large gathering of the local people, led by the Free Church minister, welcomed the members with cheers. They were met by a gentleman who was very knowledgeable in local matters. He was John H. Dixon of Inveran, near Poolewe, who was the author of a detailed book called *Gairloch, and Guide to Loch Maree*, published in 1886. He pointed out the site for a proposed pier and railway station, and then there was a meeting in the Free Church, which was crowded with fishermen and crofters, at which Dixon and the other advocates of the Aultbea route supplied the commission with information on the subject.

Dixon stated that the reason why a railway had been suggested to Aultbea was to improve the condition of the crofting and fishing population of the islands and the west mainland. He considered that the best means of raising the fishermen from their present condition might be achieved by providing them with employment at all seasons and by having a railway terminus to which they could readily bring their fish. The region that the railway would benefit was all of the west coast north of Strome Ferry, having a population of 15,000, and there was Lewis and Harris with 30,000. He then proceeded to show the supposed superiority of Aultbea over Ullapool, Lochinver and Loch Laxford as a railway terminus, with the principal point being that it lay nearer to Stornoway, where he believed the most valuable part of the fisheries must go. The anchorage of Loch Ewe was also excellent, and it was well known as a harbour of refuge. According to a survey that had just been made by Murdoch Paterson, the estimated cost of the railway was £290,000; but, added Dixon, while this was a large sum, Paterson had gone conscientiously into the question and, in allowing for extras, had called the total cost £300,000. Some information about the tourist traffic was provided by Duncan Darroch, who said that 40,000 tourists were landed every year at Gairloch from the steamers, and that, if they could go beyond Gairloch by the Highland Railway, their number would be much increased.

After the proceedings, the members of the commission were driven from Aultbea to Poolewe and shown the proposed railway route as far as it could be seen from the road. They went along the short River Ewe for its full distance of 1¾ miles to John Dixon's residence at Inveran, at the northern extremity of Loch Maree. As the railway was not to follow the Gairloch road westwards, where the gradients were too steep, but, instead, was to run by the southern shore of Loch Maree, the commission was conveyed along the loch in boats that were placed at its disposal by Dixon. The members stayed the night at the Loch Maree Hotel, where they had arranged to spend the Sunday.

However, the Aultbea scheme was not the choice of everyone in that vicinity. The *Scotsman* newspaper, published in Edinburgh, recorded that the fishermen around Gairloch were not as much in favour of having a railway terminus at Aultbea as some of the promoters had claimed. There was an important fishing community at Gairloch who wanted the terminus to be there. One of the fishermen, in conversation with a *Scotsman* reporter, declared that, if the railway was taken to Aultbea, it would still be more suitable for the Gairloch men to send their fish to Strome Ferry. They had supported the Aultbea scheme at first, he said, but after a while, they had seen that it would not do them any good. This fisherman had been entrusted with a petition for the Aultbea route, but, having obtained more than a score of names, he had put the petition in his pocket.

On Monday, 7th April, the commission left from Gairloch by the *Jackal* and crossed the Minch in a north-westerly gale to Stornoway. Several hundred of the townspeople and fishermen had gathered on the pier to witness its arrival, and soon after landing, a public meeting was held, which was attended by delegates from all parts of the island. The chairman of the commission, Spencer Walpole, explained the subject that had brought them all together that day:

In doing so, as this is the first meeting - the first formal meeting - which has been attended by this commission, I do not think I can do better than read a short extract from the instructions which my colleagues and I have received from Her Majesty's Government. We are instructed, then, to inquire: firstly, 'whether adequate evidence can be adduced of the existence of a sufficient quantity of fish in the sea adjacent to the islands to employ, remuneratively, a materially-larger proportion of the population than are now engaged in the fishing industry'; secondly, 'what steps can be taken to develop the industry, either by affording further assistance in obtaining suitable boats and tackle, additional or improved harbour accommodation, piers, landing-places, lighthouses and beacons, greater facilities for transport to the southern markets, whether by land or sea carriage, increased telegraphic and postal communication, or in any other way'; and thirdly, 'how far these objects require to be carried out or assisted by grants from the public funds, and what co-operation may be looked for from local sources'.

Now perhaps, in reference to these instructions, it may be convenient that I should add a very few words, both in respect to Her Majesty's Government and to ourselves. So far as Her Majesty's Government are concerned, we have reason to believe that they desire to consider chiefly those schemes which may be directed to permanent rather than temporary improvement, which may be calculated to encourage and promote, instead of competing with, private industry, and which may afford a fair prospect within a reasonable period of being self-supporting. So far as we ourselves are concerned, I hope that it is unnecessary for me to add that it is our desire to carry out these instructions in the spirit in which we understand them to have been framed, and to afford you all every opportunity in our power for laying before us your views regarding those schemes which you desire to lay before us. But then, I think I ought also to remind you that, in your turn, you must be good enough to recollect that we are bound to act in accordance with the instructions which we have received from Her Majesty's Government, and that, however much we may sympathise with your position, we may be reluctantly compelled to select only a portion of the numerous proposals which we understand are likely to be laid before us, or even only a portion of those which consist most closely with instructions under which we are acting, and no one would wish more.

As this is the first of many meetings which I hope it will be our duty to attend, as the words which I am uttering today may possibly travel beyond the limits of this room, I should like if you would allow me to remind you that, whatever recommendations we may agree upon, and whatever measures Her Majesty's Government may ultimately take, those recommendations and those measures will be alike purposeless if they are not seconded by your individual efforts and your individual exertions. It is true of all of us, in whatever position we occupy in this world, that we may recognise the force of the old adage that providence best helps those who help themselves.

The commission was informed of the importance to Lewis of its extensive fishing area and of Stornoway's central position and numerous fish factories that rendered the town 'unquestionably the greatest kipper emporium in the world'. Places for new harbours in Lewis were suggested to the commission, as were the most suitable routes for railways to transport the fish across the island. A system of lines was envisaged that would run from Stornoway to Barvas and Ness in the north and to Garynahine and Carloway in the west. On the subject of the mainland railway, a number of arguments were put forward for the Aultbea scheme, and it was said that 'the businessmen of Stornoway, as well as the great bulk of the fishermen', were in favour of this. However, in contradiction, it was also asserted that 'the crofter-fisher population had agreed by triumphant majorities' to support the Garve-Ullapool scheme, the stated reasons in its favour being the proximity of Ullapool to the fishing banks and the ease of access of Loch Broom.

And so, the commission continued its tour of the West Highlands during the spring and summer of 1890. Included in its itinerary was a visit to Lochalsh where, at Balmacara on 20th May, it was given the views of delegates from this district, with gentlemen from Plockton in attendance. The line that the meeting wanted was, not surprisingly, the Highland Railway's extension of the Skye line from Strome Ferry along the coast, and the only difference of opinion that existed was in regard to what would be the most suitable place for it to terminate. The Plockton men were anxious that the commission should be impressed with the amenities of their village as a terminus, while the representatives from Balmacara declared Kyle Akin to be the only place to which it would be advisable to bring the railway. Overall, the prevalent opinion was in favour of Kyle Akin, with two of the Plockton delegates admitting that, for the whole countryside, Kyle Akin would be the best place. Piers at both places were submitted as part of the scheme, and there was much enthusiasm and hopefulness about the amount of traffic that would spring up and render the extension of the Skye line a remunerative speculation.

The Highland Railway was interested in continuing the line beyond Strome Ferry. At a Board meeting on 4th June, the Directors

... considered the probability of the West Highland Commission visiting Inverness on their way south, for the purpose of ascertaining the views of the Highland company regarding various schemes which have been suggested for carrying additional railway communication to the west coast; and authorised the manager to give evidence, if desired, and to offer to extend the line from Strome Ferry to Kyle, and to construct a suitable pier there, for the sum of £120,000, and to maintain and work the extension thereafter without any charge to the Government.

This led to Andrew Dougall meeting the commissioners at Glasgow on 16th June, and the next Board meeting, on 2nd July, recorded that he 'was examined at considerable length regarding the various railway schemes projected in the West and in the islands of Lewis and Skye, as well as other questions'; and, as authorised, he had 'offered on behalf of the Highland company to extend the line from Strome Ferry to Kyle, and erect a suitable pier there, for £120,000'.

In its progress through the West Highlands and islands, the commission held 28 meetings to hear the views of the people. The extent of the country that it visited stretched from Portnahaven in the west of Islay to Talmine on the northern coast of Sutherland. Its report of 25 pages, which described the state of the inhabitants, with the suggested steps that were likely to improve their circumstances, was made available in the second half of August 1890. The *Northern Chronicle*, which was published in Inverness, provided a detailed representation of the contents in its issue of 20th August. 'The early pages of the report', the paper summarised,

> are devoted to a description of the conditions under which the population exists; and, though full of interest, cannot be said to do more than confirm the impressions which are already familiar. The crofter has advantages - as compared with the peasantry of other districts - in that he has security of tenure, a low rent and some grazing facilities. Few signs of destitution are visible, but among thousands, the house is kept in such a condition as to be scarcely compatible with self-respect, and open to condemnation by any sanitary authority. The absence of destitution depends, however, on the season, and when this is unfavourable, starvation or sale of livestock must ensue, and the consequences are necessarily deplorable. The commissioners recur again and again to what seems to have forced itself very prominently on their notice - the disinclination on the part of many of those with whom they came in contact to work. This is urged in no unkindly spirit; excuse and explanation are found in the absence at home of regular employment, in the distance from the markets and the uncertainty of remuneration after the expense of the carriage of fish has been met, and in the existence of a system of barter between the curer and the fisherman; but the 'reluctance', as it is described, 'of the people to help themselves' has created a deep impression, and it is necessary thoroughly to appreciate this view in order to judge fairly of the conclusions with which the report terminates.

Resulting from these considerations, the commission established two principal conclusions. These were that 'the number of people is, in many places, and especially in the Lews, in excess of that which the area on which they live can properly maintain', and that 'the only industry which appears capable of development is that of fishing'. But, with a discouraging lack of enterprise, even the fishing was prosecuted in what the commission described as a 'perfunctory manner', adding that 'though adverse circumstances may partly excuse, they do not wholly account for, the want of energy which we both notice and deplore'. The obstacles to the enlarged use of the fishing grounds were stated to be: the stormy character of the sea; the distance from the markets; the want of postal and telegraphic information; and the low prices of fish. The commissioners then made suggestions for securing better transport facilities to the southern markets by means of trains and steamers.

The six advocated railway schemes that had been examined by the commission were, as depicted in the *Northern Chronicle*:

No. 1   An extension of the West Highland Railway, now under construction, for a distance of 40 miles from Banavie to Mallaig, at the southern end of the Sound of Skye. This is estimated to cost £285,000, and the report recommends that the assistance asked by the promoters - viz., 2½ per cent on this sum - should be guaranteed by the Government for four years and a grant of £15,000 given for the construction of a harbour.

No. 2   An extension of the Highland line from its present terminus to Kyle Akin, on the Sound of Skye. The distance is 10½ miles and the cost stated at £115,000. The commissioners regard the request that has been made to them on the part of the Highland Railway that the Government should find the whole of this sum as 'quite inadmissible', but they are prepared to advise the same advantages being extended to the Highland company, should they proceed with this undertaking, as they propose for the Mallaig railway.

No. 3   A railway from Achnasheen, past Loch Maree, to Aultbea. The distance is 40 miles and the estimated cost £293,000.

No. 4   A railway from Garve to Ullapool, on Loch Broom; distance 33 miles and estimated at £195,000.

These proposed lines are regarded as competitive and entitled only to alternative assistance. Of the two, the commissioners are disposed to favour the first - that to Aultbea. They point out that, passing by Loch Maree, the traffic would be more easy of development, while the Ullapool terminus cannot, owing to its distance from the open sea, 'be recommended as one accommodating fishing requirements'. Intimation has been made that the promoters of the Aultbea line think they would be able to construct it if a grant of £40,000 were given in aid of the undertaking. Should the promoters of the Ullapool line be prepared to extend the railway six or seven miles so as to reach the open sea, and to construct the whole line on the same terms as that proposed in the case of Aultbea, the commissioners recommend that 'a grant of the above amount, payable on the opening of the line, should be made . . . to whichever of the two schemes Parliament should see fit to sanction'.

No. 5 would run over 42 miles of country from Invershin to Lochinver.

No. 6 . From Lairg to Loch Laxford, a distance of 37 miles.

No surveys have been made in either of the last two cases, but the probable cost is approximately given as £260,000 and £220,000 respectively. No definite assurance has been given of the willingness of any responsible person to contribute anything to the cost of construction, but should corresponding proposals be made on behalf of either of these railways to that put forward in the case of Aultbea, assistance in similar measure should be afforded to one or other of these lines.

'To sum up', said the commission,

. . . the most advantageous arrangement for the development of this district - i.e. nearly 2,500 square miles within the coast-line from Strome Ferry to Thurso - would, in our opinion, be to construct two lines of railway: one running to Loch Laxford or some point near the angle of the coast-line at Cape Wrath, so as to serve the north as well as the west coast; the other running to Loch Ewe or some point on Loch Broom nearer than Ullapool. If, however, only one line be financially practicable, Lochinver, lying about midway between Loch Laxford and Loch Broom, should have the preference.

The commission also considered railways for the two largest islands of the Hebrides: in Lewis, lines from Stornoway to Barvas, Carloway, Ness, Griais and Loch Erisort, amounting to a length of 101 miles; and in Skye, lines from Portree to Uig, Dunvegan, Stein and Glendale, with a length of 45 miles. The total expenditure for these was thought to be £450,000 and the working expenses £15,000 to £20,000 per year. However, wrote the commission: 'No evidence was given that the lines could be expected for many years to yield traffic sufficient to pay working expenses, or that any local body, public or private, would undertake even the cost of working them'. Thus, until the situation changed, with substantial proposals then originating from the localities, the commission had to dismiss these projects as impracticable.

Proposals were also suggested in regard to the improvement of communications by sea, which, as transcribed in the *Northern Chronicle*, 'by the establishment of five new routes, the produce of the sea might be drawn from almost every petty bay and conveyed with regularity to the nearest terminus, whether those already existing or those which, it is hoped, may be constructed'. With one of the steamer routes already in use, six were thus listed:

Route No. 1 lies to the west of Lewis, and lands the produce gathered from Carloway, Breasclete, etc., at West Loch Tarbert.

Route No. 2 performs a similar service for the east coast of Lewis, and brings to Stornoway the catch from Ness to Loch Erisort.

Route No. 3 is designed to serve the Long Island* from Barra to Tarbert in Harris, and the west coast of Skye from Dunvegan to Loch Slapin, landing goods at Oban.
Route No. 4 deals with the north coast of Skye from Portree to Dunvegan. Steamers have been plying on this route for the last two years.
Route No. 5 - The whole mainland from Loch Laxford to Strome Ferry.
Route No. 6 - The north coast from Loch Eriboll to Thurso.

The commission recommended that a subsidy of from £8,000 to £10,000 per year for four years should be given to secure the placing of competent steamers on these routes, provided, they said, that it would be 'practicable to carry out our suggestions without injuriously affecting, or with the co-operation of, the companies already working on the service'. On the question of improved harbour accommodation, piers and landing-places, the report enumerated 67 applications, though many of these were 'wholly impracticable, and in many others, the cost would be incommensurate with any benefits derivable'. The total expenditure, if all the suggestions of the report were carried out, was calculated at over £280,000, which was considered a great sum. In conclusion, were these words from the commission:

> While we have thus discharged our duty with the strongest personal desire to benefit the districts which we have visited, we wish to point out the success or failure of the measures we have recommended must mainly depend on the people themselves. In every case in which we have suggested the grant of assistance from public funds, we have endeavoured to couple with it conditions which would have the effect of stimulating local effort and encouraging local enterprise.

A summary and view of the report also appeared as an editorial in the *Inverness Courier*, as follows:

> The recommendations made by the West Highland Commission have proved more liberal than its critics anticipated. The commissioners are not altogether complimentary to the population of the western seaboard and islands; they think that the people are in the habit of doing too little and asking too much; but they recognise the difficulties of their circumstances, especially their remoteness from markets and their want of rapid means of communication.
> The commissioners go in for bold schemes of railway communication and of steamer service. Clearly, it is by such means that prosperity is to be brought to the west coast, if it is ever to be brought at all. The land capable of supporting a large population in comfort does not exist; but the sea is a source of wealth, and anything that makes the Highlands more accessible as a summer and autumn resort is for the welfare of the people. Perhaps the commission do not recommend grants sufficient to secure the extension of railways. That seems to us to be the weakness of the report from the practical point of view. A grant of 2½ per cent for four years, as proposed for two of the schemes, is not a great inducement for the investment of a large sum of money.
> When we examine the details of the report, we find that the commissioners are struck with the facilities which the western mainland offers for railway extension - if only there was an adequate return for the outlay. They recommend that the offer above-mentioned of 2½ per cent for four years should be made to encourage the extension of the West Highland Railway from Banavie to Mallaig, and of the Highland Railway from Strome Ferry to Kyle Akin. If both of these railways were made, the island of Skye and all the Outer Hebrides to the south of the Lews would be amply served. The commissioners express a preference for a railway from Achnasheen to Aultbea on the one side and from Lairg to Loch Laxford on the other; and they recommend that £40,000 should be given to each of these schemes if they can be locally undertaken. The Duke of Sutherland has not offered to assist a Laxford line but, manifestly, everything depends on him. The report says that the promoters of the Aultbea scheme think they would be able to construct their line with a grant in aid of the above amount. Mr Dixon and the friends who are associated with him have now their chance. There is much to be said in favour of a railway running along the side of Loch

---

* A name referring to the whole stretch of the Outer Hebrides.

Maree and connecting Gairloch with Achnasheen. The district is one of great beauty and interest, the tourist traffic already considerable, and in the fishing season, there would be a large amount of fish traffic. The commissioners, we regret to see, are not very favourable to the Ullapool scheme; they only propose to assist it in case the Aultbea scheme should break down; and they also make any assistance to the Ullapool contingent on the promoters agreeing to extend their line six or seven miles so as to reach the open sea. In any case, the idea of a double line - one to Aultbea or Lochbroom, and one to Loch Laxford - may be impracticable; should that be so, the commissioners recommend a single line to run from Invershin to Lochinver. This is also a very pretty route and would open up the magnificent district of Assynt, one of the finest in the whole of Scotland.

The commissioners have not listened to any projects for railways in Skye or Lewis because they have no expectation that they would pay the working expenses. But they are anxious to see a first-class steamer service provided for the whole of the Hebrides and for the mainland west and north from Strome Ferry to Thurso . . . The steamer service so mapped out is very complete and should be pressed upon the attention of the government. The commissioners further recommend grants for harbours or breakwaters at Ness, Portnaguran and Carloway in the Lews; for piers at a number of places on the mainland and in the islands; and for boat-slips at places which are ready to contribute one-fourth of the cost.

From all this, it will be seen that the commissioners have gone about their duties with great care and in a generous spirit. There are districts which will assuredly be disappointed; there are criticisms which cannot fail to be unpalatable; but, taken as a whole, the report is one for which the Highlands ought to be grateful. It recommends schemes which would prove substantial benefits if they could be accomplished and which are brought within the range of possible achievement. It remains to be seen what the government will do, and we trust they will not be illiberal - that, in some instances, they will even exceed the recommendations which the commission have offered.

At the end of 1890, there was sadness for the Highland Railway with the death of the Hon. Thomas Bruce who had been the Chairman for the previous six years and the Deputy-Chairman from the company's origin in 1865 until the retirement of Alex Matheson as Chairman in 1884. Bruce had been one of a number of titled gentlemen forming the majority of the Directors of the Highland Railway, and in 1890, the full list of the Board had read as follows: the Hon. Thomas Charles Bruce, Chairman; Eneas W. Mackintosh, Deputy-Chairman; the Most Hon., the Marquis of Breadalbane; Alexander Henderson of Stemster; His Grace, the Duke of Atholle; the Most Hon., the Marquis of Stafford;* Sir George MacPherson-Grant of Ballindalloch; James Grant-Peterkin of Grange; Edward G. Fraser-Tytler of Aldourie; the Most Hon., the Marquis of Tweeddale; His Grace, the Duke of Sutherland; the Right Hon. Lord Thurlow; His Grace, the Duke of Fife; George Kynoch, Isla Bank, Keith; the Right Hon. Lord Colville of Culross; Charles Waterston; Sir Kenneth J. Matheson of Lochalsh; and James E.B. Baillie of Dochfour.

---

* Son and heir of the Duke of Sutherland.

Chapter Eight

The Report of the
West Highland Railway Committee

Not surprisingly, the people of Ullapool were very displeased at the opinion of the commission in not having recommended their large village as a suitable terminus and, thus also, the Garve and Ullapool Railway if it was not extended six or seven miles westwards. It was an ironical state of affairs because, just prior to the commission's report having been published, the line had been sanctioned by an Act of Parliament on 14th August, 1890: 'An Act to Authorise the Construction of a Railway from Garve to Ullapool; and for Other Purposes'. The passing of the Garve and Ullapool Railway Act, 1890 meant that the line was the only one of the six schemes to have reached the stage of Parliamentary authorisation, and yet, the government commissioners had, in effect, rejected it.

The Act allowed the Garve and Ullapool company to enter into agreements with the Highland company for the 'working, use, management and maintenance' of the line by the latter; and there were provisions in regard to Leckmelm 'for the protection of the estate of Alexander George Pirie'. An Edinburgh civil engineer, Benjamin Hall Blyth, had been employed by Pirie to ensure that his demands would be carried out. These were principally that 'where the line will pass through the said estate, it shall be constructed only in the line and at the level shown on the plan and section signed by John Arthur Fowler on behalf of the company and by Benjamin Blyth Hall on behalf of the owner'; and that

the company shall not construct any public station on any part of the said estate, but they shall construct on some part of the estate in such position as may be reasonably required by the said Benjamin Blyth Hall a platform on the railway and siding therefrom for the exclusive use and accommodation of the owner, at which no train shall be stopped otherwise than with the consent of the owner, and if and when reasonably required for the purposes of the estate, any train shall be stopped at the said platform by a signal.

Meanwhile, amid all the subsequent discussions of the report of the West Highland Commission, the Highland Railway had felt increasing concern about which railway or railways might materialise with Governmental assistance and provide serious opposition to its own Strome Ferry line. Thus, at a Board meeting of the Highland company on 3rd September, 1890, it had been 'resolved to lodge a representation with the Secretary of State for Scotland and also with the Treasury against a grant of public money being devoted to the construction of a line of railway extending from Fort William to Mallaig, which would compete with the Highland company's line from Dingwall to Strome Ferry'.

Nothing further of significance occurred until the spring of 1891. In March, the subject was reintroduced when there were meetings between Andrew Dougall and the Financial Secretary to the Treasury, 'regarding an extension of the line from Strome Ferry to Kyle', and two letters from the latter to the former in that month stated that the Treasury would contribute a sum of £45,000 towards the expense. In response, on 17th April, Dougall wrote that, if the Government were to give this sum towards the extension, he would recommend the Highland Board to agree to the proposal.

Nevertheless, even with the offer of a subsidy from the Treasury having been communicated officially to the Highland Railway, the Government were of the view that the whole matter needed yet more investigation. The *Ross-shire Journal*, in its issue of

12th June, briefly explained what was to happen:

West-Coast Railway Schemes. These schemes are still engrossing the attention of Parliament, but before giving their definite and final decision, the Treasury Office have appointed a new committee of experts to advise the Government as to the respective advantages of the competing proposals for the construction of a line to the west coast, and this committee is to visit the various routes at the end of this month to make a personal survey and inquiry. Mr Dougall is at present in London in communication with this matter.

Thus, in spite of the information that had been provided by the West Highland Commission, the Government felt that they did not have sufficient judgement of the merits of the six railway schemes in question, or of the amount of the assistance that should be offered from the public funds. However, the people of South-West Ross-shire had become anxious that nothing had been decided, and in the summer of 1891, public meetings were organised for the purpose of applying pressure to the Government to initiate action in favour of the extension of the railway from Strome Ferry to Kyle Akin.

The first of these took place on 1st June when, in the words of the *Inverness Courier* - with its heading of 'Railway Development in the Highlands: Public Meeting at Kyle of Lochalsh' - 'a large and influential meeting, representative of a wide district of the west of Ross-shire and of Skye, was held at Plock of Kyle,* Lochalsh'. Presiding at the gathering, where fisherman and crofters were in evidence, was Sir Henry MacAndrew, who was the former provost of Inverness and who was now the commissioner for Sir Kenneth Matheson of Lochalsh, son of Sir Alexander. The Government, said Sir Henry, were bound by their pledges to assist in opening one line of railway to the West Highlands, and he was sure that an extension of the Skye line from Strome Ferry to Kyle Akin was the most desirable. He had the authority of Andrew Dougall for saying that the Highland Railway was in communication with the Government regarding the Kyle Akin scheme, but it was felt that the people of the area had not indicated their attitude on the subject by a public meeting. He reminded the audience that the promoters of the Dingwall and Skye Railway, having been interested in the people to be benefited by the project, had carried it out from patriotic, rather than personal, motives; and to this, there were cheers from the listeners. The assembly produced three resolutions, which were:

That this meeting are strongly of opinion that of all the proposals that have been made for facilitating by railway extension the trade of the western Highlands and islands, that which would confer the greatest amount of benefit, would be most easy of accomplishment, could be most rapidly carried out, and at least expense, would be the extension to Kyle of the Highland Railway.

That this meeting express its regret that, seeing that the extension to Kyle of the Highland Railway was favourably reported on by the West Highland Commission, no steps have yet been taken by Her Majesty's Government to carry out the recommendation, and strongly urge on the Government that this extension should be made a leading part of their plans for the amelioration of the condition of the Highlands and islands; and that they should offer such terms to the Highland Railway Company as will induce them at once to undertake and carry out the necessary work.

That a petition to Her Majesty's Secretary of State for Scotland in favour of the extension to Kyle Akin of the Highland Railway be immediately prepared, and that copies of the resolutions be sent to Lord Lothian, to Mr Chamberlain and to all the Members of the northern counties and burghs, with a request to them to use their influence in favour of the scheme.

At a large meeting of crofter-fishermen, on 11th June, at the small village of Toscaig on the south-western coast of the Applecross peninsula, similar resolutions were passed

---

* Plock, meaning 'lump', referred to the high ground immediately west of the hamlet of Kyle.

in favour of the extension to Kyle, but with the emphasis on the benefits that the line would offer Applecross. It was said that to leave the railway at Strome was virtually to lock out the inexhaustible stores of fish in the Sound of Crowlin, the Sound of Rona, Loch Duich, Loch Hourn and the Sound of Sleat. The majority of the people had so little land that they were obliged to turn to the sea as a means of livelihood, and that, unless they had facilities for sending the fish to market in a proper condition, there was no living at all. The proposed extension to Kyle would, to a great extent, remedy this. One fisherman added that, owing to the extreme difficulty of taking the fish to Strome, and to the small profits realised, he had serious doubts about whether or not to engage in the fishing that year. One of the resolutions referred to the remoteness of Applecross:

> That this parish is quite isolated from the rest of the country, having no regular communication, either by land or sea. That Strome Ferry, the nearest railway station, is upwards of 30 miles distant, and the extension, which would make the distance six miles by sea, would be of immense service to the whole community.

Then, on 30th June, at Letterfearn on the southern shore of Loch Duich, there was yet another large meeting of the crofter-fishermen of the surrounding district. One of the speakers, who had been several years at the fishing and in taking his catches to Strome Ferry for sale, complained of being detained by an adverse tide within a short distance of Strome, resulting in a serious decrease in the value of the fish. Besides, there was a loss of two nights' fishing that was caused by each journey to Strome. Another speaker stated that the proposed railway extension was the only means, except for lawlessness, of preventing dire poverty in the district, and that it was labour lost to carry on the fishing with the railway terminus at Strome. One man, who described himself as a cottar with a large family, said that he had been at the fishing year after year and he still remained in poverty. If the railway was extended to Kyle, he believed that he might yet make a comfortable living, but to continue the fishing under the present circumstances was a heart-breaking business. One of the resolutions summed up all these feelings:

> That, on account of the distance to Strome Ferry, the present terminus of the Highland Railway, it is impossible for the fishermen of this district to get their fish to market in a proper state, and they call upon the Government to assist the company to extend their line to Kyle, so as to enable a hard-working and industrious people to earn an honest livelihood.

Towards the end of June, there was an inspection of the Skye branch of the Highland Railway by a few of the officials of the company, consisting of Directors Eneas Mackintosh and James Grant-Peterkin; Andrew Dougall; Murdoch Paterson; William Garrow, the superintendent of the company's lines; and George Thomson, the goods manager. While there, according to the *Northern Chronicle*, they 'took the opportunity of making a cursory survey of the route by which it is proposed to extend the line from Strome Ferry to the Kyle':

> The proposed route, which hugs the coast and extends 10 miles or thereby, was first viewed from the sea, a trip being made by boat to the Kyle, after which the party drove across country, halting occasionally to make a more minute inspection of the ground. We believe the general conclusion arrived at was that the line would be one of very difficult and expensive construction. To the passer-by, this precipitous coast-line, and the birch-clad hills which rise abruptly behind, forms one of the prettiest bits of scenery to be met with in the West; but to the engineer, unfortunately, hills and valleys in picturesque succession mean tunnels and laborious embankments. Should the railway be constructed, the tourist will have little opportunity of enjoying the scenery which is admired so much from the steamer's deck, as there will probably be no fewer than three tunnels of considerable length.

Also in late June, it was reported that the new committee which had been appointed by the Government would soon begin its tour of the West Highlands that would decide which of the six railways was to receive financial assistance. The West Highland Railway Committee consisted of three gentlemen: Major-General C.S. Hutchinson of the Royal Engineers, who was Her Majesty's Inspector of Railways; Rear-Admiral Sir George Nares; and Mr Henry Tennant, the former General Manager of the York-based North Eastern Railway. In regard to the six projected railway schemes, the terms of instructions, in a letter dated 22nd May, 1891, from the Treasury to the committee read as follows:

The object which Her Majesty's Government have in view is to promote the interests of the crofting and fishing population in the districts concerned, including the islands, by the development of railway communication on the western seaboard of the mainland. They recognise that such a development is not likely to be initiated by private enterprise, and they are therefore prepared to recommend Parliament to contribute towards the cost constructing any one of the lines above referred to, provided that:
The remainder of the cost can be raised from other sources;
Arrangements can be made for working and maintaining the line in perpetuity when constructed;
There is a fair prospect of attaining the object which the Government have in view.
Having regard to these considerations, you are requested to inquire:
Which of the projected schemes is best calculated to promote the interests of the crofting and fishing population in the districts in question;
What amount of assistance would be required from public funds in each case to secure the construction of the line;
Which of the schemes, if any, you would recommend the Government to assist.
Definite proposals with respect to two of the schemes in question have been received and will be laid before you, but Her Majesty's Government do not wish you to limit your inquiries to these projects and they will request the persons who are understood to be interested in the other schemes to place themselves in communication with you. It will probably be necessary for you to make some local inquiry into the circumstances of the several districts affected and the routes of the projected lines, but Her Majesty's Government trust that this inquiry will not be very prolonged, as they are anxious to receive your report with as little delay as possible, so that the decision of the Government on the subject may be known to Parliament in the course of the present session.

With the view of acquiring the necessary personal knowledge of the various routes, the committee, with its secretary, Mr J.M. Nicolle of the Board of Trade, proceeded over the relevant ground of the North and West Highlands from the third week in July until early August. During this period, public meetings with the committee were held at Lairg, Kinlochbervie, Lochinver, Ullapool, Poolewe, Kyle and Arisaig; and at all these meetings, the attending parties presented information before the committee. It was midway through its tour, on 27th July, that the committee had arrived at Inverness, where a meeting was held at the Caledonian Hotel with some of the Directors of the Highland Railway. The proceedings were conducted in private, with the committee having informed the press that it did not intend to meet in public on this occasion. The Highland Directors in attendance were Eneas Mackintosh who, in April, had been elected the Chairman of the company; Lord Thurlow; Sir Kenneth Matheson; Messrs Baillie, Fraser-Tytler, Kynoch and Waterston; and also present were Andrew Dougall and Murdoch Paterson. Not able to be at the meeting was Sir George MacPherson-Grant of Ballindalloch, Strath Spey, who, also in April, had been appointed the Deputy Chairman. A general discussion took place upon the different lines, with the Highland Railway representatives impressing upon the commission the great importance of extending the line from Strome to Kyle, and promising substantial support from the company in the construction. Sir Kenneth Matheson, who owned most of the land, expressed his readiness to give facilities for commencing the line at once.

In July, there had been another instance of railway-route antagonism in the form of letters published in the *Inverness Courier*. This time, it was Mallaig versus Kyle versus Ullapool. The paper had reproduced a long letter from a Mr Alex MacDonald of Portree to the provost of Fort William, to be read at a meeting there, and in this, MacDonald asserted that the people of Skye - himself included - favoured the proposed extension of the West Highland Railway to Mallaig. He introduced a valid point against the Skye line:

> At present, as you are aware, our only railway communication with the South is by the Highland Railway via Strome Ferry. A glance at the map will show that, although the destination of goods and passengers from these parts may be the South, still we actually have to travel northwards (Inverness being north of Portree) and eastwards by steamer and rail for the first nine hours at least of the journey, and that it is only after reaching Forres that we really turn southwards! The time thus wasted implies a much greater loss than is at first apparent, seeing that it means in the case of fish and other perishable commodities coming from points west of Portree that they cannot be sent at all; whereas, if we had proper communication, they would arrive in the South in good condition and be a source of income and profit to the inhabitants. The long and fatiguing journey by the present circuitous route also prevents many people from coming to the North and West and taking up their quarters for the summer in these parts, who would otherwise, if the journey were shorter and quicker, cheerfully undertake it and spend their money among us.

MacDonald's view - and, according to him, that of the people of Skye in general - was that, 'if an endeavour be made to look at the various proposals fairly and impartially, it will be found that the line which would unquestionably bring the greatest good to the greatest number is that from Mallaig to the South, via Fort William'; and that, 'if we glance at the map, it will clearly be seen that Mallaig forms a natural centre to which the whole traffic of the west coast and islands can, with the greatest convenience and facility, be converged; while, at the same time, from that point, the communication with the South would be more direct and rapid for the whole population generally than that afforded by any of the other projected lines'. With further references to Kyle Akin and Mallaig, he continued:

> It would certainly be some advantage to the Isle of Skye, and especially to those parts in the immediate neighbourhood of the terminus, if the Highland Railway was extended to Kyle Akin from Strome Ferry; but all the disadvantages to the population on the whole of the present long and circuitous route to the South would still manifestly remain. There would still be eight or nine hours spent in going north and east before turning southwards! I wonder whether the people of the east coast, after the Mallaig line has been constructed (as it certainly will be, sooner or later), will send their traffic to the South via Strome Ferry or Kyle Akin and Mallaig, rather than by the present direct route via Perth. The proposal to send our traffic first to the east for many miles and then to turn southwards is very much the same thing, and most people who are disinterested will, I think, concur with me in thinking it unreasonable, if not absurd.
>
> On the other hand, a line from Mallaig goes direct southwards and gives shorter and more rapid communication. It would thus, on the whole, suit the crofters and fishermen of the west coast and islands generally much better than any one of the other proposed lines. Fish caught on the coasts of the Lews or in the Minch or Outer Hebrides, and in all parts of Skye, would, from the moment they were caught, go straight southwards, or nearly so (except in the case of Barra whence, however, the prevailing south-west wind would favour rapid communication with Mallaig by sea), and arrive at their destination much more quickly and, therefore, in better condition (thus securing better prices) than by any of the other routes.

MacDonald briefly mentioned Ullapool and Aultbea as a terminus, in that either 'would manifestly be of no use whatever to the people on the west coast south of Kyle Akin . . . or of the Outer Hebrides or of the Isle of Skye'. This was sufficient for P. Campbell Ross, the Secretary of the Garve and Ullapool Railway Company, to produce a response in which, firstly, he stated why he had to do so:

If Mr MacDonald had contented himself with confining his remarks to indicating the advantages of a line of railway from Fort William to Mallaig, I would not trouble you with this letter; and here, I cannot but note, by way of contrast, the wisdom of those present at the Fort William meeting, convened to promote the Mallaig project, in not attacking other schemes. Since, however, you published Mr MacDonald's letter, you will doubtless, in all fairness, permit me to call attention to some of the objections to it.

Ross then implied that, for the North-West Highlands, the Ullapool line was preferable to those of Mallaig and Kyle:

I would, point-blank, ask the public to remember the sparse population of the west coast south of Kyle Akin and contrast it with the many thousands north of it who would be left entirely railwayless, so far as a line to Mallaig would affect them. Kyle Akin is not more than 12½ miles from Strome Ferry by road. The inhabitants of it, and those of Broadford and Strath, and even those of Portree, cannot be looked on as badly-off with a daily steamer within three hours' sail of Strome Ferry; and if the Highland Railway Company act promptly and extend their line to Kyle at the expense of their own shareholders, I consider that the people of Lochalsh, Kintail, Glenelg and mid Skye to Portree would be favourably situated as regards railway facilities.

In referring to MacDonald's view that the Outer Hebrides would be suited better by the Mallaig line, Ross wrote:

Lewis is much the most important of the group and has a population of 30,000, and I find that there is practical unanimity on the part of the Lewismen that Ullapool would be the terminus of a railway most advantageous to them. Mr MacDonald either does not know how much a line to Ullapool has been petitioned for from every part of the Lews; or if he does know it, I fear he has lost sight of his usual candour in his desire to serve the cause he wishes to serve. Nothing would induce me to say anything offensive to the distinguished Skyeman, but to say that he was *misleading*, in not indicating the part of the Outer Hebrides for whose interests he was contending, is only fair. Perhaps his legal training may be responsible for it, however; and it may be sufficient on my part to say that Ullapool is midway between Cape Wrath and Strome Ferry, and it would be sheer folly to think that the Government would ignore the wishes of those who dwell north of Gairloch and favour the few inhabitants of the mainland south of Glenelg, whom the Mallaig line would help.

Among the arguments against the Mallaig line that Ross listed as being generally believed were these: that 'it would be next to impossible, if not *absolutely impossible*, to make a harbour at Mallaig', and that 'between Fort William and Mallaig, there are no people and no traffic'. Then he added:

No doubt, if the Mallaig project could be carried out, the route between the west coast of Inverness-shire and the South would be considerably shorter, but if it can be shown - proved - to the commissioners that a railway constructed at far less cost would meet the requirements of a far more numerous and more destitute population, and would secure the delivery of fresh fish in excellent order at Billingsgate, they will not repeat the mistake of last year's commission and choose to recommend schemes as to which they have not reliable information - the sole information as to which consists of the sanguine hopes of their promoters - while the Garve and Ullapool Railway promoters supply them with facts and figures which stood the test of the Parliamentary committees of Lords and Commons.

With the West Highland Railway Committee having completed its tour of inquiry in August, and with no verdict having been received from the Government by the end of November 1891, the *Inverness Courier* of 1st December offered a brief assessment of which seemed the most probable of the six projects to be approved:

We have reason to believe that the Government commission which visited the North some time ago are likely to recommend the construction of a railway from Lochinver to Culrain. This is a scheme which has not been much discussed, but by those who know the north-western Highlands, it has always been looked upon as a possible route. The line would open up the splendid tourist district of Assynt, one of the finest in the whole Highlands. At the same time, there is much regret that Gairloch and Ullapool are passed by. The decision to select Lochinver may not have been finally passed, but there is no doubt that it is in contemplation.

It was to be the following spring before the findings were made public. 'The long-expected report of the committee of experts on railway communication in the western Highlands has now been issued', recorded the *Inverness Courier* of 29th March, 1892:

It is difficult to say why its publication has been so long delayed, for it appears to have been in the hands of the Government since 28th November. Perhaps the Treasury did not wish to be asked to provide any funds out of the revenue of the year which is now closing. The report is an interesting document. The question whether it is satisfactory will be answered by different persons in different ways.

Early in its report, the committee mentioned, generally, that all of the routes presented considerable difficulties from an engineering point of view. The chief feature of the Laxford, Lochinver, Ullapool and Aultbea lines was that, for the most part, the ground was fairly well adapted for the making of railways, but that, to the coast, there were serious obstacles which would make the construction costly and which would involve very steep gradients. The report added that the Mallaig route presented much analogy in these respects and that the Kyle route, though short, had its own peculiar difficulties. The committee doubted that the estimated cost of construction of any of the lines would be less than £8,000 to £10,000 per mile. It appeared to the committee that, if the full benefit was to be conferred on the population, two railways would be necessary, as one, wherever constructed, would not meet the requirements of both of the districts lying north and south of the existing terminus of the Highland Railway at Strome Ferry.

In the case of the Laxford line, the committee was unable to ascertain that any local contributions towards the cost could be expected, other than the grant of the land at a nominal sum; but towards the Aultbea line, a sum of £12,500 had been subscribed and a large portion of the land would be given free or on favourable terms. Regarding the Ullapool line, the cost of the preliminary expenses had been found by landowners who were also prepared to give their land in exchange for shares. In addition to this, there had been a share subscription of about £2,500, and 400 labourers had agreed to co-operate by contributing, to the purchase of shares, one-sixth of the money that they would earn if employed upon the construction of the line. 'A railway from Ullapool to Garve would provide the shortest railway route through the district towards the southern markets', stated the committee positively, before continuing negatively:

But Ullapool is situated 16 statute miles up an arm of the sea, having an approach encumbered with islets and rocks, and narrowing for the last three miles to a channel two-thirds of a mile in width. For this reason, we concur in the opinion of the Highlands and Islands Commission that the locality is unfitted for a fisheries centre. Seaward of Ullapool, and at a distance of four miles, is the landlocked harbour of Isle Martin, more readily attainable by fishing-craft. This is, however, also too far from the open sea to give due promise of development for fishery purposes. Seaward of Isle Martin, apart from the difficulties and consequent expense of railway construction, there is no site suitable for the creation of a terminus which would meet fishery requirements, without a large expenditure upon a sea breakwater.

The committee agreed with the commission in thinking that Lochinver afforded the most convenient natural site for the establishment of a fishery centre and a railway terminus for the benefit of the north-western portion of the Highlands and islands. Then, soon afterwards in the report, the committee appeared to offer hope to Ullapool by the possibility of continuing the Garve and Ullapool line to Lochinver, but this it also had to dismiss:

With respect to the route for a railway, if a line could have been constructed at a moderate cost between Lochinver and Ullapool, it would, in conjunction with the line (which has already been sanctioned by Parliament) from the latter place to Garve, have afforded the best solution of the problem, providing, as it would, a convenient fishery and steamboat station at Lochinver, distant about 68 miles by rail from Dingwall, and a steamboat terminus at Ullapool, about 44 miles from the same point. But the country between Ullapool and Lochinver, which has been specially examined by one of our number, is very hilly, and there is reason to apprehend that the carrying of a railway through it would involve much expensive work and heavy gradients. Though the distance would not be more than about 24 miles, the only estimate which we have been able to obtain for the construction of a railway to, and pier at, Lochinver places the cost at £420,000. This estimate is probably a high one; but the expense of making, working and maintaining the line will, we think, be regarded as too heavy to allow of any prospect of its being undertaken. Under these circumstances, we are obliged to relinquish the idea of seeing Lochinver connected with the Highland Railway system via Ullapool, though this, as already explained, would have brought Lochinver within about 68 miles by rail of Dingwall.

Thus, a connection between Lochinver and the Highland Railway had to be sought in the direction originally contemplated, by way of Culrain. The length of such a line would be from 38 to 43 miles, according to whether the western section passed below the southern flank of the 2,400 ft-high peak of Suilven or by the northern shore of Loch Assynt, which would depend on the result of exact surveys. This would bring Lochinver within 80 or 85 miles of Dingwall; but towards the cost of construction, there had been no offer of local assistance, other than what might be contributed by landowners who would regard the scheme favourably. Nevertheless, with a railway terminus and fishery centre established at Lochinver, and extended steamboat communication provided between Lochinver and various points on the coast, the committee was 'of opinion that the pressing wants of the districts north of the island of Skye would be met'.

In acknowledging the existence of 'the Skye branch of the Highland Railway, with its terminus at Strome Ferry, which affords facilities for the population as far south as Kyle', the committee proceeded to mention something of Mallaig Bay which would 'meet the wants of the parts southward of Kyle, including the south-west coast of Skye and the neighbouring islands'. Here, it said, was 'the most suitable locality for a railway terminus and fishery port', but, again, there was pessimism:

Mallaig in itself presents the following disadvantages: that a large expenditure for a sea breakwater must be incurred, and then only the comparatively small area of about 30 acres would be sheltered from the prevailing winds. With a north wind, about half the area will be exposed to a sea strike of 11 miles; but it is proper to add that, with strong winds from this quarter, a large fishing-fleet could be accommodated within the wholly-protected area, and larger vessels - not alongside the pier - could find ample shelter in Loch Nevis, which is only four miles distant. In the face of its drawbacks, Mallaig could only be recommended for want of a more favoured position being attainable.

However, the committee was still hopeful about Mallaig and about Kyle:

It appears to us that the benefits which would accrue to the southern districts from the construction of the Mallaig-to-Banavie line, in conjunction with the making of the West Highland Railway, are so great that the scheme, whenever ripe for adoption, would be deserving of assistance from such funds as the Government might have at their disposal for the encouragement of railway development in this locality. The promoters have estimated the cost of this line at £260,000, and that of the harbour works at £45,000 - sums which we consider likely to prove inadequate. They think that if the Government would make a grant of £100,000 towards the railway, together with a contribution towards the harbour works, the remainder of the capital could probably be raised. They also inform us that the North British Railway Company would be prepared to make arrangements for working the line as an extension of the West Highland Railway. In the event of the Mallaig undertaking being aided from public funds, we concur with the suggestion of the Highlands and Islands Commission to the effect that proportionate assistance should be afforded to the Highland Railway Company for the purpose of extending their line from Strome Ferry to Kyle, should they desire to do so.

In closing the report, the committee remarked on the fact that the six proposed schemes that it had examined would have to be classed differently from other railways in respect of financial considerations:

We desire to give expression to our opinion that none of the suggested railway projects can be regarded as possessing a commercial basis or the elements of success as ordinary railway undertakings. If, therefore, the districts in question, or any of them, are to obtain the advantages of railway communication, these must be afforded on grounds other than anticipation of direct financial return.

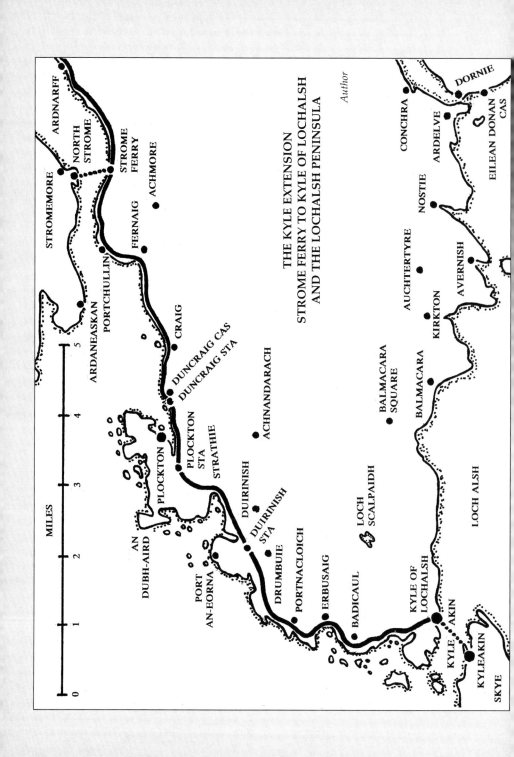

THE KYLE EXTENSION
STROME FERRY TO KYLE OF LOCHALSH
AND THE LOCHALSH PENINSULA

Author

MILES

ARDNARFF

STROMEMORE

NORTH STROME

STROME FERRY

ACHMORE

FERNAIG

ARDANEASKAN

PORTCHULLIN

CRAIG

DUNCRAIG CAS
DUNCRAIG STA

ACHNANDARACH

PLOCKTON
PLOCKTON STA

STRATHIE

AN DUBH-AIRD

DUIRINISH
DUIRINISH STA

PORT AN-EORNA

DRUMBUIE

PORTNACLOICH

ERBUSAIG

BADICAUL

LOCH SCALPAIDH

BALMACARA SQUARE

BALMACARA

AUCHTERTYRE

KIRKTON

AVERNISH

NOSTIE

CONCHRA

ARDELVE

DORNIE

EILEAN DONAN CAS

KYLE OF LOCHALSH

LOCH ALSH

KYLE AKIN

KYLEAKIN

SKYE

Chapter Nine

Authorising the Line to Kyle

At the meeting between the West Highland Railway Committee and the Highland Railway at Inverness on 27th July, 1891, the Highland company had intimated that it would be willing to enter into arrangements for constructing, working and maintaining the Culrain to Lochinver line on the same terms as would apply to the Garve and Ullapool Railway. This meant that, for either line, the Highland would be guaranteed from the Government an annual sum of £6,000 per year for 25 years if the cost of construction did not exceed £200,000, with an additional increase in the annual payment upon any cost beyond £200,000. In the case of the Lochinver line, which had been estimated at £420,000, a payment of £7,800 per annum for 25 years would be involved.

However, it was strange that the Highland had produced such a statement at the interview with the committee because the truth of the situation was that the Lochinver and Ullapool lines had never genuinely interested the company because of the responsibilities that it already had to its own Skye line, which it wished to extend to Kyle. The Highland's lack of enthusiasm for the Garve and Ullapool Railway was why the latter company, in the spring of 1891, had offered another railway company the opportunity to work its proposed line. The Great North of Scotland Railway had quickly obliged with much interest, for a line to Ullapool would allow it to expand its territory to the North-West Highlands by means of obtaining running powers over the Highland company's rails from Elgin to Garve, covering a distance of 66 miles. It was imperative to the Highland that, somehow, it would have to prevent this rival company from encroaching on what it considered was its own ground. The solution lay in persuading the Government to assist in the construction of the extension to Kyle, and this is what the Highland now intended to do.

In the summer of 1892, the Highland resolved to offer to extend the line from Strome Ferry to Kyle on condition that the Government did not subsidise any other line to the west coast and, further, that they contribute £20,000 towards the expense of erecting a suitable pier at the Kyle terminus. Then in October, it was resolved that the company would go to Parliament in 1893 for a Bill to authorise the making of the line, and in November, the required notices for this were published. The *Northern Chronicle* of 9th November drew attention to the Bill and mentioned the work that would be involved in building the scenic extension:

We publish this morning the Highland Railway Bill in which they propose in the ensuing session of Parliament to ask powers for the extension of the Skye railway to Kyle Akin, thereby bringing the Highland system almost in touch with the island of Skye and tapping the steamer route between the north and south of the west coast. Last week, the section was inspected by Mr Roberts, one of the company's engineers, who was accompanied by Mr William Burns, the legal agent for the company at Inverness. It will be a very remarkable piece of railway, on account of the difficulties of construction. Throughout nearly its entire length, it will have to be carried through rock which is, moreover, of a character very difficult to work, while the stations necessary will practically have to be excavated. The expense of these operations will be heavy; probably the cost of making the whole extension of 10½ miles will not be far short of three times the expenditure of on an ordinary section of the Aviemore line.* While that is so, it will undoubtedly prove one of the most picturesque bits of railway ever constructed in this country. Hugging the precipitous and birch-clad coast, it will pass in front of Duncraig House, the residence of Sir Kenneth J.

---

* This was the Highland Railway's new, 35 miles-long, direct line from Aviemore to Inverness, in course of construction - the first section of which had opened from Aviemore to Carr Bridge on 8th July, 1892.

Matheson; almost touch upon Plockton; cross sea-basins at Craig, Erbusaig, and terminate close to Kyle Inn. Here, it is proposed to construct a harbour and pier, which will together cost perhaps £30,000; while on the Skye side, there will be a pier of adequate dimensions to accommodate the transfer-steamers it is intended to place on the ferry. This expensive - and extensive - terminus is, of course, intended to intercept and receive the traffic of the west coast and adjacent islands, such as the Stornoway fish traffic.

The principal purposes of the Bill for the Kyle Extension were stated as follows:

To make and maintain the extension railway, pier and works hereinafter mentioned, wholly situate in the parish of Lochalsh in the county of Ross and Cromarty, and in the foreshore or bed of the sea adjacent thereto, with all necessary stations, junctions, sidings, approaches, viaducts, bridges, roads, wharves, landing-places, rails, cranes, sheds and other works and conveniences connected therewith respectively (that is to say):
A railway, commencing by a junction with the Highland Railway at or near its termination at Strome Ferry, at a point in the passenger shed there, five yards or thereabouts to the eastward of the west end of the said shed, and terminating at Kyle of Lochalsh, at a point 210 yards or thereabouts south-eastward of Kyle Inn, in a field or piece of ground occupied by Roderick Mackintosh and Malcolm Finlayson, tenants of Kyle Farm;
A pier, commencing at or near the terminus of the intended railway at Kyle of Lochalsh, above described, at a point 210 yards or thereabouts south-eastward of Kyle Inn, thence proceeding in a southerly direction for a distance of 110 yards or thereabouts, and there terminating on the bed of the sea.
To authorise the company to purchase, by compulsion or agreement, and to lease, feu or otherwise acquire for the purposes of the intended railway, pier and works, lands, houses and other property.
To authorise the company to purchase and acquire the undertaking, rights, powers and privileges of, and incident to, the ferry between Kyle of Lochalsh in the parish of Lochalsh and Kyleakin in the island of Skye, or to take a lease or leases thereof, and to make such alterations and improvements on the piers and jetties connected therewith respectively, as may be necessary for the purposes of the company, and to enable the owners and all parties for the time-being interested in the said ferry to sell and transfer or lease their undertaking, rights, powers and privileges to the company.
To confer upon the company, power to purchase, hire, work, use and let steam and other vessels of every and any description, and to carry passengers, animals, minerals and goods therein, between the several ports or places following, or some of them; that is to say: Kyle of Lochalsh and Skye, Lewis, Harris, North Uist, South Uist, Benbecula, Barra and such other ports or places in the Western Isles and on the western and northern coasts of Scotland as the company think fit, and to take and levy tolls, rates, duties and charges in respect of the use of such steam and other vessels, and to have and exercise all or any other powers in reference to such steam or other vessels which any railway company now have, or ever have had, exercised or enjoyed.

In mid-December, the Highland Railway received notification from the Treasury that they had agreed to contribute £45,000 towards the extension to Kyle. It was in 1892 that the Conservatives and Prime Minister Robert Gascoyne-Cecil had been defeated by the Liberals, so that William Gladstone was back in power at the time of the agreement for the grant - an amount that was looked upon in the Highlands as being very much insufficient for the heavy expense of the formidable project. The *Northern Chronicle* commented:

In making this concession, it is understood the Liberal Government are only carrying out what had practically been resolved upon by their predecessors when they went out of office. Considering the enormous amount of money the new line will cost - it having, as we mentioned some weeks ago, to be tunnelled out of hard and very difficult rock - the grant cannot be called an extravagant one. All it will effect will be to relieve the company of loss in abandoning the harbour at Strome, which is worth something like £20,000, and enable them to construct another at the Kyle, the expense of which will not, it is estimated, fall far short of £30,000. The whole cost of making the line itself, and erecting the stations thereon, will thus fall upon the company, including the construction of a landing-stage on the Skye side of the ferry. Approximately speaking, an average mile of the Kyle Extension is expected to cost double the money necessary for making an ordinary mile of railway on the Aviemore section, so that the scheme will not be completed many thousands under the two-hundred. Not only will the extension be an extremely difficult piece of engineering but, from a scenic point of view, it will be a bit of line unrivalled by any railway in the kingdom . . . Whatever may be thought of the various other railway schemes discussed and reported upon of late, all must concede that the extension to Kyle Akin, which formed part of the original scheme, is highly necessary, and that, in undertaking the heavy duty, the company were entitled to substantial encouragement from the Government.

And, said the *Ross-shire Journal* in regard to the communication from the Government 'which practically decides the whole question of railway extension on the west coast', the contribution of £45,000 'seems a large sum, but when the extraordinary expense of the undertaking is considered, it will be found to be comparatively insignificant'.

On 4th January 1893, a special meeting of the shareholders of the Highland Railway was held in the company's Board room at the Station Hotel, Inverness. The object of the meeting was to consider the provisions of the Bill that was to be introduced into Parliament for the Kyle Extension. An explanation was given as to why the Highland Railway needed the extra 10½ miles. It was stated that the company had found that it was impossible to develop traffic at the upper end of Loch Carron, particularly as the loch had very difficult access to vessels. One of the principal interests that had to be catered for was the Stornoway fish traffic, which was conducted by respectable firms who chartered steamers for the purpose of bringing their fish to Strome Ferry. However, the steamers could only enter the loch in the daytime, so that there was loss of time and produce. To obviate this, the Highland decided to apply for power to build a pier at Kyle which could be approached at any state of the tide and at any hour of the day or night by the steamers or the many sailing-vessels that passed Kyle Akin. Fish and goods would be able to be transferred, by the smallest-possible expenditure, to the wagons of the Highland Railway and handed over to the southern companies in a shorter time and at less expense than at present. In conclusion, it was pointed out that the Government grant of £45,000 would reduce the cost of construction from £10,000 per mile to £6,000 and that, if the Bill received Parliamentary sanction - of which the Directors did not doubt - the company would be ready at once to proceed with the undertaking.

However, in spite of the necessity of the extension to Kyle for the Highland Railway and for the localities that it would most conveniently serve, such a scheme meant nothing to the people further north, and this resulted in Ullapool and the district of Coigach* protesting about the Government's decision to ignore their area and the far North-West Highlands. At a public meeting at Ullapool on 30th December, 1892, it had been moved 'that the attention of the Government should be called to the extreme disappointment and dissatisfaction caused by the report that a sum of £45,000 was to be presented to the Highland Railway Company to aid them in extending their line 10½ miles further from the southern markets than the present terminus at Strome Ferry'. Then, on 24th February, 1893, there was a meeting of the crofters and fishermen of Achiltibuie and its neighbouring townships, at which it was resolved 'to express surprise and indignation at the proposal of the Government to grant a subsidy of £45,000 to the Highland Railway Company for the extension of their line to Kyle Akin, which extension will be of no benefit whatever to the important fishing industry of the Lews and north-west Mainland'.

* Pronounced '*Coy*-ach' ('ch' as in 'loch').

The people of Ullapool and Coigach felt that the most numerous and needy of the crofter-fishermen were in Lewis and along the opposite mainland shores of the Minch. The grant for the Kyle extension, they said, was money wasted because it would only benefit the Highland Railway Company and one of its Directors, through whose land the line would pass. The comparatively small number of inhabitants to be benefited in Lochalsh, Kyleakin and Broadford were sufficiently near the terminus at Strome Ferry and, therefore, already in possession of railway facilities, while one-third of the coast-line of the west of Scotland had been left unprovided. Why not construct the Garve and Ullapool Railway? was their plea, as it was situated about halfway between Strome Ferry and Cape Wrath.

It was to be too late, though, for the Garve and Ullapool line, as was also the case with a revived line from Achnasheen to Aultbea. In November 1892, notice had been given that a Bill would be presented to Parliament in the session of 1893 for sanctioning the Loch Maree and Aultbea Railway, which was a further attempt by those who were determined to have a line in that direction. The principal promoters were Sir Kenneth MacKenzie, MP, of Flowerdale House, Gairloch; the Right Honourable, the Earl of Lovelace of Ben-Damph House, Torridon; Paul Liot Bankes of Letterewe; Duncan Darroch of Torridon House; and John Dixon of Inveran. The route had been surveyed at the expense of the promoters by the Edinburgh engineering firm of Thomas Meik and Sons, with the line taking a similar course to that surveyed by Murdoch Paterson in 1889.

Commencing by a junction with the Highland Railway immediately south of Achnasheen station, the 39½ miles-long line was to pass along the southern shore of Loch a' Chroisg and through Glen Docherty to Kinlochewe, and then along the whole of the southern shore of Loch Maree to Poolewe. From there, the line would head north of Carn an Eich Dheirg and east of Loch nan Dailthean and Tournaig, and finally by the coast at Loch Ewe, to terminate at Aird Point, Aultbea. The estimated cost of the line was £325,000, which included £8,000 for the pier at Aultbea and four stations, necessitating a total capital of £400,000; but the promoters had been informed by Meik and Sons that, if the railway was constructed in a manner similar to those being made in Ireland, it should not cost more than £200,000. Such a line would have no station except at Aultbea, with passengers being taken up and set down at platforms adjoining the public roads that were crossed by the railway. The gauge would be the standard one, but costing less by having steeper gradients and sharper curves than usual and by the reduction in station, signalling and staff expenses.

Over the difficult, twisting route, the gradients were indeed steep. There were several at 1 in 40 and 1 in 33, the heaviest being a 3¾ miles-long ascent at 1 in 33 eastwards from Kinlochewe through Glen Docherty towards Loch a' Chroisg. The engineering aspects, which were not particularly difficult, included two short, adjacent tunnels, of 200 and 137 yards length, at the extreme north-western end of Loch Maree, about a mile south of Tollie Bay, so that the line could be taken through the hillside there.

The principle of the scheme had been approved by the Board of Trade, which was of the opinion that a railway constructed in this way was well adapted to the nature of the district that it would traverse. The promoters had had the intention of incorporating a company, with a capital of £315,000, to construct the railway on the Irish pattern, which meant that the Board of Trade would dispense with, or modify, its usual requirements for railways, provided that the speed of the locomotives did not exceed 25 miles per hour.

The Bill for the Loch Maree and Aultbea Railway was unsuccessful. It was not proved in Parliament, so that the scheme had to be withdrawn. The exertions of the promoters of the Garve and Ullapool Railway were also rendered ineffective with the passing, on

29th June, 1893, of the Act of Parliament that allowed the Highland Railway to proceed in extending the Skye railway by 10 miles, three furlongs and seven chains: 'An Act to Empower the Highland Railway Company to Construct an Extension of Their Railway from Strome Ferry to Kyle of Lochalsh; to Erect a Pier at Kyle; and for Other Purposes'. By the terms of the Highland Railway Act, 1893, the Kyle Extension and its pier had to be completed within five years from the passing of the Act.

Two months later, the Ullapool promoters officially withdrew their scheme when the Garve and Ullapool Railway (Abandonment) Act, 1893 was passed on 24th August: 'An Act to Provide for the Abandonment of the Undertaking Authorised by the Garve and Ullapool Railway Act, 1890'. Nothing material had resulted from the interest of the Great North of Scotland Railway because of the Government's subsidy to the Highland, and the wording of the Act reflected the disappointment that Ullapool felt at being deprived of their railway:

Whereas, by the Garve and Ullapool Railway Act, 1890, the Garve and Ullapool Railway Company were incorporated and authorised to construct a railway from near Garve station of the Highland Railway to Ullapool, and it was provided that the capital of the company should be £240,000 in 24,000 shares of £10 each . . .

And whereas, negotiations took place between the Directors of this company and the Treasury with respect to the grant of a subsidy in aid of the construction of the said railway . . .

And whereas, the Treasury have not assented to grant the subsidy or pecuniary aid for the construction of the said railway, and it is impossible in those circumstances that the undertaking can be carried out . . .

And whereas, no part of the capital of the company has been issued and none of the powers of the said Act with respect to the purchase of lands has been exercised . . .

And whereas, the purposes of this Act cannot be effected without the authority of Parliament . . .

. . . The time for the completion of the undertaking authorised by the Garve and Ullapool Act, 1890 shall be deemed to have been limited to the date of the passing of this Act, instead of the 14th day of August 1895, and as from the date of the passing of this Act, the undertaking shall be abandoned.

Strome Ferry section of the 1893 session Parliamentary plans for the Kyle Extension.

Duachlas Museums Service, Portree

Chapter Ten

Building the Line to Kyle
1893-1894

While the people of Ullapool and its vicinity were naturally displeased that the extension to Kyle had been decided in favour of their railway - also when Ullapool was, by far, the largest of the six proposed termini - there could be no argument over the fact that the Ullapool line, for much of its distance from Garve, passed through largely-bleak country with virtually no population.

It was true that the Skye railway passed through similar bleak and lonely country, but there were villages and hamlets along its length, with its stations serving places further afield. A short account of the last few scenic miles of the line to Strome Ferry, with a mention of the district's other transport communications, was included in the *Handbook to the Highland Railway*, published by the *Northern Chronicle* in 1890:

> At Strathcarron station, there is a good hotel, in connection with which a coach and mail-gig are run to Lochcarron (formerly known as Jeantown, 4 miles), a long and straggling but prosperous fishing village on the north shore of the loch; also to Shieldaig and Loch Torridon.
> Leaving Attadale station, situated in the midst of a fine piece of meadow ground, Attadale House (Sir K.J. Matheson) is passed on the left. Thereafter, the railway crosses a stream of the same name and, for the next four miles, follows closely the shore of the loch, at an elevation little above the tide level. This is one of the most picturesque and interesting parts of the route, and so little space is there between the rocks on the one side of the train and the sea on the other that the incautious traveller, putting his head out of the window on the left after a heavy shower, may receive a cooling from one of the many miniature waterfalls pouring over the rocks. The best view of the loch is obtained from the terminus, Strome Ferry, but the extraordinary winding nature of this part of the line may be seen by looking out of the carriage window; the train seems to wriggle along like a huge serpent - now one end visible, now the other, again neither. The ferry across Loch Carron has no connection with the railway, but formerly constituted an important link in the through-route to the North.
> There is an excellent hotel at Strome. From the pier adjoining the station, mail-steamers run daily to Portree in Skye and to Stornoway in Lewis. A mail-car runs daily from Strome to Balmacara (8 miles), where there is a good hotel and steamboat communication with Oban and Portree.

The making of the railway through the rocks to Kyle would offer a greater extent of the picturesque, coastal scenery that was already appreciated along Loch Carron; but, more importantly, there would be improved communications for the people of the West. The Kyle Extension, for most of its length, would hug the precipitous northern and western coasts of the Lochalsh peninsula and run by a succession of cuttings, embankments and ledges. One mile west of Strome Ferry, the line would pass beside the small fishing village of Portchullin and then turn southwards to cross the Allt Cadh an Eas at its mouth near Fernaig. The route continued generally westwards below the steep slopes of Creag an Duilisg and Creag nan Garadh, having also to twist below the Matheson residence of Duncraig Castle that lay between these high crags, with the village of Plockton lying across the bay. Because of geographical considerations, the station for Plockton would have to be ¾ mile south-west of the village, but this was a substantial improvement for the population, as their nearest station, Strome Ferry, was eight miles distant by road.

Having had a long history of seafaring and with a sheltered harbour that had been used by schooners participating in the export of herring to the Baltic in the 18th century, Plockton was developed in the early 19th century by Sir Hugh Innes of Lochalsh, who,

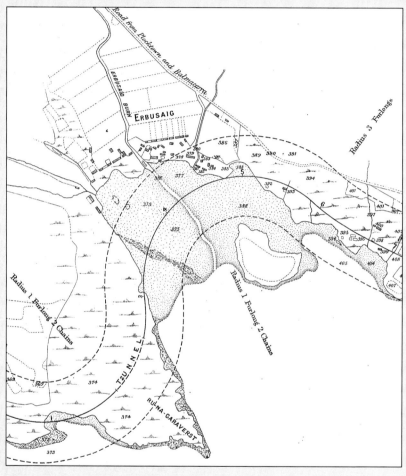

Erbusaig section of the 1893 session Parliamentary plans for the Kyle Extension.
Duachlas Museums Service, Portree

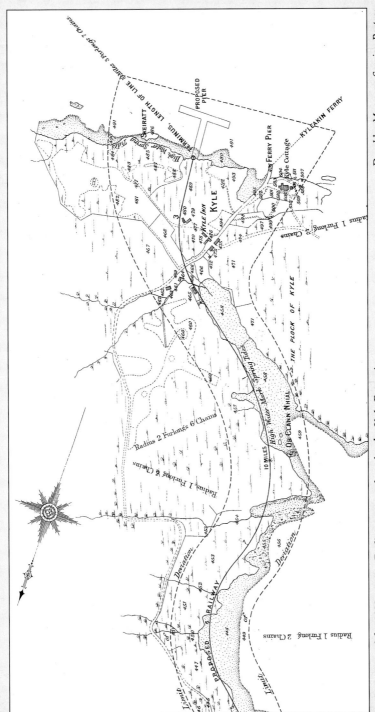

Kyle section of the 1893 session Parliamentary plans for the Kyle Extension.

having bought the land from the Mathesons, had his village designated a 'Burgh of Barony' in 1808 by a charter from King George III. Plockton, whose name originated from the Gaelic *ploc*, meaning 'lump' or 'promontory', became similar to Jeantown, Dornie and other coastal villages of the Highlands as an impoverished crofting and fishing settlement for victims of the clearances during the first half of the 19th century. Now, towards the end of the century, the extension of the railway to Kyle would, it was expected, provide the opportunity for improving the social conditions of the people of Plockton, the rest of Lochalsh, and Skye, as the line to Strome had already done for the West in general. Certainly, the extension would considerably diminish the isolation of Plockton, the largest village and port of Lochalsh, by bringing it into direct communication with Inverness and the South.

At Plockton, the railway would turn south-westwards to run, partly inland, by the crofting villages of Duirinish and Drumbuie, and then by the coastal hamlet of Portnacloich. Half a mile further south, the line was to take a sharp curve south-eastwards, to be driven through what would be the most difficult rock-cutting, and then it would sweep round Erbusaig Bay in front of the village of Erbusaig. Where the cutting was to be formed on the curve had recently been planned as a 150 yds-long tunnel by Murdoch Paterson for the Parliamentary plan of 1893, and had originally been intended as a tunnel of 250 yards on the survey of Joseph Mitchell three decades earlier. For the last two miles from Erbusaig, the line would firstly head south-westwards again, running below the hamlet of Badicaul, and then it would curve southwards to the hamlet of Kyle, where it was to terminate on a large new pier. Only half a mile across the Kyle Akin strait was the village of Kyleakin and the Isle of Skye; and, thus, pending the success of constructing the extension, the Skye railway would stretch as near as possible to the island in its name.

The name Kyle Akin - although Gaelic by reason of *Caol Acainn* or *Hacoin* - had resulted from the Norse domination of Skye and the rest of the Western Isles from the 9th to the 13th centuries. It referred to the 'Strait of Haakon', after Norway's King Haakon IV. The Viking possessions also included the islands of Shetland and Orkney, but the King of Scotland, Alexander III, was determined to have all the islands of the West and North returned to his nation. In 1262, one of Alexander's feudal lords, the Earl of Ross, invaded Skye with brutal treatment and slaughter of the inhabitants, and the Norse King of the Isles, Olav the Black, appealed to the aged Haakon to help their defenceless people.

Haakon responded in the summer of 1263 by leading the greatest-ever fleet, consisting of 120 warships, out of Norway, with the aim of not only ensuring the future safety of the islanders and maintaining the sovereignty of the islands, but also conquering all of Scotland, as had been tried unsuccessfully by his predecessors. His ships sailed through the Sound of Raasay to anchor in the narrow stretch of water between Skye and the mainland that would commemorate his name. The fleet continued southwards to the Firth of Clyde as far as Largs, where, in the autumn, a storm caused a large part of his fleet to sink and run aground. Alexander and his army were in waiting, and they forced the Vikings to retreat. Haakon, with the remnants of his fleet, headed for Norway, but in passing the winter at Kirkwall in the Orkneys, he died, and with him died the Vikings' control of the Western Isles. The Scots' victory at the Battle of Largs resulted in Norway ceding these to Scotland by the Treaty of Perth in 1266, although the Shetlands and the Orkneys, for the time being, remained under Norway.

In the early part of the 19th century, there had been a proposal for a new seaport to be built on the Skye side of Kyle Akin. This was due to the foresight of Sir Alexander Wentworth MacDonald, who was the second Lord MacDonald of Sleat, and the eldest son of the Lord MacDonald who had met Johnson and Boswell in 1773. His vision was for a 'New Liverpool' at Kyle Akin, which would stimulate the trade and industry of Skye and the west coast, and for this, he commissioned an architect, James Gillespie Graham of Dunblane in Perthshire, to draw up a plan in 1810. The design showed the town and port as triangular in overall shape, with the houses and streets laid out in a regular manner, and with two squares and a marketplace. There was a harbour along the northern shore of the peninsula directly facing Kyle Akin, together with a 'grand wet dock' that was incorporated into the narrow stretch of water, known as An t-Ob and meaning 'The Bay', on the southern shore.

The new town and port did not materialise but, instead, a village gradually developed and took its name from the narrows. Dr John MacCulloch, the surgeon and geologist, commented on Kyleakin in his four-volume work on the Highlands and islands, published in 1824:

> The town of Kyle Haken, though but just founded and therefore containing but the mere germs of Lord MacDonald's intention, is, notwithstanding, a very interesting object here; its crowded and commodious anchorage compensating, in life and bustle, for the defects of the city itself. After solitary days or weeks spent in the wild and deserted harbours of these seas, the sight of this place is like a return to life and civilisation. The situation is beautiful as well as commodious - for the buildings at least, since they have abundance of room on an extended, gravelly and dry beach. Nor is it less so for the shipping, which can lie close inshore, in excellent holding ground, and with perfect security against all weather and winds. The design also appears convenient and good, judging from the drawings; and, being in the form of a single crescent, it is picturesque and neat. The policy is another question. If an agricultural town were not, in itself, a useless, as well as an impolitic contrivance, Kyle Haken is, at any rate, unfit for one because it has not access to a sufficient tract of good land. It is impossible to discover any use for it, as a town simply. Of the usual business of towns, it can have none, because there is no demand. It is not a very good fishing-station - far from it - and if it were, there can be no fishing, on the present system, to furnish such a town with sufficient employment; while the houses, or feus, are far too expensive for the population of this country, for any population that it is ever likely to possess.

Similarly, in regard to the lack of success of Sir Alexander's plan, George and Peter Anderson wrote in their *Guide to the Highlands*, published in 1842:

> At Kyle Akin, the late Lord-MacDonald contemplated the establishment of a considerable seaport town, and had imposing and splendid plans prepared for it; but the scheme has proved quite abortive. The scale of houses fixed upon - two stories with attics - has proved beyond the means of the people, and no man of capital was got to settle in the place; and, hence, Kyleakin has never attained a greater status than what half a dozen respectable-looking houses can lay claim to, but it possesses a capital inn.

Or, in the words of Hugh Miller, the Cromarty stonemason, geologist, Free Church devotee and strong critic of the clearances, who sailed through Kyle Akin in 1844: the village 'refused to grow; and it has since become a gentleman in a small way, and does nothing'. However, he added that it formed a handsome group of houses, pleasantly situated on a flat, green tongue of land, on the Skye side, just within the opening of the kyle'.

In May 1893, at the half-yearly meeting of the shareholders of the Highland Railway, it had been stated that 'the Kyle Extension of the Skye line would be commenced as soon as Parliamentary powers were acquired'. The Directors had kept this promise, for it was in mid-August that Andrew Dougall had been able to produce an advertisement for the purpose of obtaining tenders for the building of the new railway and pier; and it read:

The Highland Railway Company - Extension of line from Strome Ferry station to the Kyle of Lochalsh - To railway and harbour contractors. The Directors invite tenders for the construction of the works on this extension of their line, as follows; viz:
    Contract No. 1, extending from Strome Ferry to the commencement of the terminal station at Kyle, and measuring 10 miles, 700 yards, comprises about 380,000 cubic yards of rock-cutting, and 120,000 cubic yards of soft or other excavations; 47 culverts and bridges for streams and roads, varying from 4 to 30 feet-span; rail-laying and ballasting, station works at Plockton, etc.
    Contract No. 2 consists of the construction of a deep-water pier for steamers, and terminal station at Kyle, and comprises about 110,000 cubic yards of rock excavation landward of, and 95,000 cubic yards of rock-filling and concrete work in, the pier; also, culvert for stream, and two over-line bridges for roads, rail-laying and ballasting, passenger platforms, loading-banks, etc.
    The drawings and specifications of these works will be seen with Murdoch Paterson, Inverness, the company's engineer, on and after Tuesday, 22nd current.
    Assistant engineers will meet contractors at Strome Ferry station at 1.30 pm on Thursday, 24th current, and accompany them over the line to Kyle on that and the following day.

It was three weeks later that the contracts were decided by the company. At a meeting on 6th September, the Directors read Murdoch Paterson's report of the previous day on the tenders that had been received, and it was then resolved to accept, for both contracts, the offers of Messrs John Best and Sons of Edinburgh. The tender for the first contract, which was for the building of the line, amounted to £83,873; while the second, being the construction of the deep-water pier and station at Kyle, was £37,099 - making a total of £120,972 to be payable to John Best for his firm and his workers. However, including the sum to be expended in the purchase of land and other outlays, the overall cost was estimated at a high £150,000 for 10½ miles of railway and the associated harbour works - towards which the government would contribute £45,000, leaving £105,000 to be provided by the shareholders. The line would, therefore, be the most expensive per mile, by far, in the British Isles - comprising almost 400,000 cubic yards of rock-cutting, 120,000 cubic yards of excavation, and 47 bridges and culverts. The deep-water pier was to be 120 yards long and 85 yards wide, and it would have a minimum depth of water of 24 feet at the lowest tide, enabling vessels to arrive and depart at any time, whatever the tidal state.
    In spite of the difficult nature of the work to be done in pushing through the new line, no apprehension was felt by the Directors in their choice of John Best, who was an experienced and extensive contractor in the construction of railways and harbours. Best ensured that no time was wasted in beginning the large undertaking. Thus, in the Highland Directors' half-yearly report, dated 4th October, 1893, to be read to the shareholders at the meeting on the 25th, it was recorded that 'the works have already been let to a contractor, who has commenced operations'. At the meeting itself, it was explained that the company proposed to expend a considerable portion of the government grant in making the pier at Kyle, which would accommodate vessels of all descriptions; while ferry-boats would ply between Skye and the mainland; and suitable vessels would collect traffic from the lochs and harbours north and south of the terminus. In this way, the extension would benefit the districts concerned and the Highland Railway.
    It was a small squad of workmen that had arrived on the scene by early October, and for the first few weeks, they were employed chiefly in clearing some of the ground for the foundations of the line and for the building of huts and stores before the arduous constructional work could begin. Most of these men - about 50 by the end of November - had been newly-hired from the surrounding districts, with only a few regular navvies from elsewhere, mainly because of the lack of accommodation until the huts were complete. There were to be six large huts between Strome and Kyle, and each of them would cater for 80 to 100 men. By early December, one hut was almost finished, while

two large stores - one for railway plant and the other for provisions - were also in progress, and a brick magazine for gunpowder was being built near Erbusaig, where a deep cutting and an embankment were to be made. Plant and materials were arriving by steamers, and one steamer was soon to be used along the coast in connection with the line's construction. The superintendence of the works was to be carried out not by John Best who had taken the contract but by his son of the same name, as part of the firm and under the consultancy of his father, who was also involved with other contracts. Best senior and junior had examined the line together at the end of November, with the former having departed on 2nd December.

A transformation would be occurring in the parish of Lochalsh. As the *Northern Chronicle* recorded in its issue of 29th November:

> The change which the railway will make on this locality will be very great indeed, and much work will be given to willing hands for a good while to come, as the construction of the railway will be a very difficult and expensive undertaking. Several deep cuttings through solid rock have to be made, while many bays and rivers have to banked and bridged.

Two days later, the *Inverness Courier* reported that 'the west coast traders are also making preparations for the reception of the men, and are looking forward to a large increase in business'. Soon, two merchants were in process of erecting wooden stores at Kyle for the sale of provisions to the large number of invaders who would build the railway. However, for much of December, the weather was extremely wet and stormy, such that, sometimes, very little progress could be made with the initial work. Nevertheless, the *Northern Chronicle* of 20th December was able to contain some remarks of success from Kyle, and of the start of the transformation there:

> Such is the wet character of our climate at present that it is almost impossible for people to do any outdoor labour, and that which is done is done imperfectly . . . The general appearance of Kyle has changed very much during the last month. Instead of being the quiet, solitary place it used to be, it more resembles a thriving village, what with its half-dozen new buildings and new population. A good deal of work is being got through, notwithstanding the unsuitable weather conditions. The principal excavations, as yet, are at the terminus. The rock seems hard, but is of a broken nature so far, and does not require the use of explosives to remove it. Another steamer arrived a few days ago with a cargo of timber and rails, so that a very large quantity of plant for the railway is now on the ground. A steam-launch is expected to arrive in a few days. It is to be used for general purposes around the coast. One large hut is now finished, and additional men are taken on at the works every day. Should the weather settle more favourable, the works will evidently be pushed forward with energy and speed.

During the first week of January 1894, better weather was in evidence when a number of dry days allowed the work to proceed much more positively. With another hut having been completed at Kyle, the number of navvies were increasing daily. It was felt that some of the local fishermen, in obtaining employment on the railway, would be kept from following their own occupation for some time to come, especially those who had lost their boats and gear in a recent gale. Blasting operations were in progress at Kyle, and a squad had begun at Craig, east of Plockton, where a steamer had brought more plant. It was expected that work would soon commence at Erbusaig, where there was to be the most difficult cutting on the line. The cutting would be nearly half a mile long and 65 ft deep, and the blasting of the solid rock, together with the embanking of the adjoining bay, would require two or three years to complete. Meanwhile, two new shops had opened at Kyle, and the new village of railway inhabitants presented a lively and busy appearance.

In early February, the appointment of arbiters was decided in connection with the compensation to the crofters for the loss of the land through which the line would pass. Donald Grant, solicitor, of Grantown, was to act for the Highland Railway, while a popular and respected local gentleman was to represent about 150 crofters, within the terms of the Crofters' Act. He was Donald MacRae of Balallan Cottage, Plockton, who was admirably suitable for this assignment because, initially, of his experience in having been an active member of the Highland Land Law Reform Association. A native of Plockton, he had been dismissed as the headmaster of a school in Alness in 1886 as a result of his land-reform efforts in that area. He had been able to continue his profession at Balallan school in Lewis, and in persisting with his pro-crofter and anti-landlord agitation, he had won much support on the island. In 1889, he had been appointed the organising secretary of the Highland Land League. On the subject of the land for the railway to Kyle, 'Balallan', as MacRae was referred to, was now to have the honour of being the crofters' representative for what the *Inverness Courier* said was 'the first occasion in which the question of the measure of interest in the land conferred on the tenants by the Crofters' Act will fall to be decided'. With this in view, he and Grant, the solicitor, traversed the line all the way from Strome to Kyle for the purpose of evaluating the land and homes that would be lost to the crofters to make way for the line.

Also in early February, operations had commenced at Strome Ferry, with a small squad of workmen having broken the ground and levelled a portion of the route below the hotel. Two more navvies' huts, at Plockton and Craig, were nearing completion, but the *Inverness Courier* of 13th February contained a criticism on another aspect: 'A considerable feeling of dissatisfaction prevails, however, as to what is considered the delay of the contractor in getting the necessary plant on the ground, large numbers of men arriving by train and steamer in search of employment and being compelled to return home, as there are no tools available'. In his efforts to do this, though, John Best junior may have been hampered by bad weather, as implied by the following meteorological remarks in the *Northern Chronicle* of 14th February, with reference to the Highlands generally: 'So far as the month of February has gone, it has proved one of the stormiest experienced for many years - wind, frost, snow and rain alternating with never-ceasing rhythm . . .' and 'from a weather point of view, 1894 has already a chequered history'. On 15th February, the *North Star* newspaper, which was published in Dingwall, reported from Lochalsh that 'owing to the extremely stormy character of the weather, progress with the new railway works has been very much retarded'; adding that 'last week, however, a steamer arrived at Kyle with tools and railway plant, and this week, a good many more men are employed'. Then, on 21st February, the *Ross-shire Journal* announced progress:

> *Kyle. Railway Notes.* Notwithstanding the very unfavourable state of the weather, a good deal of work has already been done on the Kyle Akin railway. There are now about 300 men employed between Strome Ferry and Kyle. About 200 of these are working between Erbusaig and Kyle in three sections - the largest of which is at Kyle. A good clearance has been made at the pier at Kyle, where cement and other stores are to be placed. Three lines of rails are laid, and the material quarried is embanked with the aid of wagons drawn by horses. The rock is partly hard and partly broken, and, on the whole, works well. Three large huts are now erected on the line, and at least three more will be required, besides private houses, to accommodate the workmen.

In March, there were more gales and heavy rain, with much damage done to the lands in the district, so that very little progress, once again, could be made. Nevertheless, ground had been broken by seven squads of navvies engaged in rock-cutting at different places between Strome and Kyle. It was on the last day of the month that the first notable incident of trouble among the navvies occurred, and a correspondent for the *Northern Chronicle* described it thus:

On Saturday, the 31st ult., a very foolish affray happened at Kyle railway works, and we are thankful that the results did not end more seriously. It appears that about two weeks ago, an Irishman and a Skyeman quarrelled and fought at Kyle Inn, and the Skyeman was badly beaten. To avenge this, the Skyeman formed a league and determined to have it out of the Irishman. Consequently, about 40 or 50 Highlanders, employed on the railway, joined in after the pay and arranged to see the battle on Saturday. The Irishman took refuge in the railway hut and demanded fair play, which seems to have been denied him. None of the other Irishmen (of whom there are about 40) interfered. After some slight skirmishing, Constable Matheson, Balmacara, managed to disperse the crowd and to advise them to go away quietly. Public feeling is very strong against the foolish conduct of the Highlanders over such a common affair as a slight exchange of blows between a Skyeman and an Irishman, and it is to be hoped that they will show more sense and wisdom should the same thing occur in future - otherwise the consequences may be more serious to themselves and to others. Considerable damage was done to railway tools on the same evening. Barrows, etc., were thrown into the sea and a patent smithy-bellows smashed to pieces. Mr Best, contractor, and Constable Matheson are now investigating the matter, and we have no doubt, if the depredators are brought to bay, they will deservedly meet with their reward. It is high time additional police were stationed here, or private property as well will be in danger.

At the half-yearly meeting of the Highland Railway shareholders on 25th April, 1894, Murdoch Paterson's report on the company's new lines was presented, with these words about the extension to Kyle:

The weather on the west coast, for nearly five months, was so wet and stormy that very little progress could be made; but Mr Best has now 380 men at work at rock excavations and preparing for the works of the deep-water pier at Kyle, building of bridges, etc. I quite expect that he will make a considerable impression on his contract this season.

A little more information concerning the line appeared in the newspapers during the summer and autumn of 1894. A note from Kyle in the *Northern Chronicle* of 23rd May communicated that the railway works were progressing favourably, and that for some time, the weather had been dry, with the men having little or no broken time. A steamer had also brought in more railway plant and other cargo to Kyle, where a large general store had now been erected. The *Ross-shire Journal*, two days later, reported that Sir Henry MacAndrew, commissioner for Sir Kenneth Matheson of Lochalsh; Mr Burns, solicitor for the Highland Railway; and Messrs Roberts, Pollock and Newlands, engineers for the Highland, had visited Kyle to arrange for the building of a hotel, which the company was proposing in connection with the extension. In mid-July, the same paper briefly referred to the building of the line:

East Kyleakin. The New Railway Works. Although a commencement has been made in several places between Strome Ferry and East Kyleakin, not much progress has, as yet, been made. But the difficulties are great. Surprise is, however, often expressed that more men are not employed, especially at a time when the weather is so favourable for such work.

At the end of August, the *Northern Chronicle* reported on something that was seen to be necessary in the vicinity of the railway:

Plockton. Police Station Demanded. The extension from Strome Ferry to Kyle Akin, at present in progress, has brought into the Lochalsh district a large number of navvies of various nationalities. Although, on the whole, matters have hitherto progressed smoothly, still it is felt in the district that a police station is urgently required at Plockton. Accordingly, a public meeting was held in the schoolhouse, Plockton, for the purpose of bringing this matter before the authorities.

It was then moved that 'it was necessary, in the interest of life and property, to get a police station erected at Plockton forthwith'. Finally, a further record, if rather vague, of the progress of the railway works appeared in the *Ross-shire Journal* of 21st September:

About 4½ of the ten miles of the Kyle Akin railway have now been cut. The portion traversed is the most difficult part of the route, with the exception of one point a little distance ahead, where there will be a cutting through solid rock about 70 feet deep and 100 feet long. The construction of the pier at Kyle Akin is also pretty well advanced.

For the Highland Railway's half-yearly meeting of the shareholders on 24th October, 1894, Murdoch Paterson's report on the extension read as follows:

Satisfactory progress has been made with the excavations all along the line, four-fifths of which are rock and the remainder gravel, etc. One-fourth of this rock has been excavated and put to bank. The building of bridges and culverts has been delayed from the difficulty of procuring suitable stone; but the contractor has now arranged for stone of excellent quality from the north shore of Loch Carron. The walls and hearthing of the pier at Kyle are being steadily proceeded with.

Away from the subject of the railway matters, the *Ross-shire Journal*, under the heading of 'Plucky Capture of Dishonest Navvies at Kyle Akin', related another instance of trouble, and of the courage of the local constable in dealing with it. On 22nd September,

. . . during the temporary absence of the barman from the bar in Kyle Inn, a lock-fast desk was broken and a considerable sum of money in silver and copper was abstracted. The case was at once reported to Constable Matheson of the railway police, and in a few minutes, came on two navvies at the back of the hotel in the act of dividing the stolen money. He charged them with theft and took them into custody, but, in doing so, they resisted strongly, and in this, they were assisted by two other navvies, named John Monaghan and James MacGregor - the officer being repeatedly struck with their fists and kicked. He, however, stuck pluckily to his prisoners and escorted them to the police station at Strome Ferry, 10 miles off, where he lodged them safely, and then at once returned and apprehended Monaghan and MacGregor, and brought them also to Strome Ferry; afterwards bringing his prisoners to Dingwall. In the first assault made on the constable, he received valuable assistance of Mr Thomas Brown, time-keeper, and that gentleman also came in for a somewhat rough handling on the occasion. The names of the two men charged with theft are James Summers and Roger Carn. They were brought before the sheriff and, after emitting judicial declarations, were committed for further examination. Monaghan and MacGregor were tried summarily, and pled guilty to assaulting Constable Matheson and Mr Brown. The former was fined 30 shillings or 21 days' imprisonment, and the latter 20 shillings or 14 days. They accepted the latter alternative, and the four prisoners were sent to Inverness prison the same evening, the local prison here having its full complement.

On 14th November, 1894 - over a year after the works had commenced - there was the first death on the railway. This was at a rock-cutting on the southern shore of the mouth of the Allt Cadh an Eas, by Fernaig. The *North Star* described the tragedy, with the heading of 'Man Blown into the Air at Kyle Akin', when

. . . a blasting accident occurred in connection with the railway operations carried on between Strome and Kyle Akin, which, unfortunately, was attended with fatal results. It appears that, while some of the workmen were engaged in blasting operations with gelignite, the charge exploded, and one of the men, named Michael Poiner, an Irishman, who was conducting the operation known as 'stemming' the charge, was pitched into the air and landed on the seashore some 40 yards from the seat of the accident. The body was fearfully mutilated, and death, as a matter of course, was instantaneous. The accident occurred in what is termed the 'Fernaig cutting'. Three other men, named John MacDonald, John MacLeod and Malcolm MacAulay, all from the west coast, were more or less injured, but not seriously.

Another Irish navvy was found dead on 2nd December from a different cause. This was in the locality of Plockton on a Sunday morning. On the previous day, the navvies received their fortnightly pay and there was the inevitable spree in the evening. It was supposed that the unfortunate man had been drinking heavily, and as he made his way in the dark to his hut, he stumbled and fell into a pool by the roadside and, in his drunken state, drowned in a few inches of water.

The last newspaper report of 1894 on the construction of the railway was provided by the *Northern Chronicle* in early December:

Kyle. The weather, which was for some time wet and stormy, has now taken a favourable turn. There is slight frost at night, but the days are very pleasant for work. The railway works are being vigorously pushed forward, and about four miles of the new line are finished. A new hut is built at Erbusaig village to accommodate the extra men required for Craig-an-tallan* there. This rock is the most difficult part of the line, it being in some places over 60 feet high. A pay-office is built at Erbusaig, and, henceforth, all men working at this end of the line are to be paid there, instead of Kyle as formerly. Several new houses are being built at Kyle, and this place has every appearance of very soon becoming a thriving village. There is little fishing being done around this coast, most of the people being employed on the railway works.

However, the following warning, contained in the *North Star* of 20th December, was given to those hardy souls who were physically transforming Lochalsh:

The West-Coast Navvy Nuisance. It is a well-known fact that the construction of a railway in a district brings in its train a very perceptible increase in the work of the local criminal courts. This is nowhere more noticeable than in Ross-shire at the present time, where the Highland system to Kyle Akin has led to the influx of a large number of the navvy species, a considerable proportion of whom have an unfortunate faculty for getting into trouble. Sheriff Hill, at Dingwall on Monday, took notice of this characteristic, and through an unfortunate specimen, William Mantach by name, who was charged with committing a breach of the peace at Plockton on Saturday night, he extended a warning to all and sundry that, if there was not an immediate and perceptible improvement in the conduct of the navvies, their misdemeanours would be more severely dealt with. On this occasion, Mantach was fined 10 shillings, with an alternative of five days' abstinence from railway construction.

While the work of building the extension to Kyle had proceeded satisfactorily during 1894, the construction of the other West Highland line further south had been successfully completed in the late summer. After nearly five years since the cutting of the first sod in late 1889, the West Highland Railway had reached Fort William from Glasgow, and parliamentary approval had also been obtained for its extension to the west coast. The 100 miles-long line from Craigendoran to Fort William, which was engineered by Formans and McCall of Glasgow and built by Lucas and Aird of London, was opened to the public on 7th August, 1894, with a ceremonial opening four days later at Fort William. Not opened at this time, due to difficulties with the viaduct over the River Lochy, was the 1¾ miles-long branch to Banavie, 2¾ miles from Fort William on the Caledonian Canal, with which an interchange of passenger and goods traffic was anticipated.

The line to Fort William had become the third to reach the West Highlands, after those to Strome Ferry and Oban; but Fort William, even with its population of 1,700, was not visualised as the ultimate extremity of the West Highland Railway. At the head of Loch

* The name of the headland on the north side of Erbusaig Bay through which the largest cutting on the line was to be constructed: in Gaelic, *Creagan an t-Salainn*, meaning 'salt rock'.

Linnhe, the town was too far from the open sea to be considered as a suitable terminus in the West Highlands. To be able to survive, line needed to be taken to the sea about 40 miles west of Fort William, so that, principally, it could partake in the large fish traffic from the western waters, while it would also serve some of the islands, including Skye. Thus, in November 1893, the West Highland Railway Company had given notice that it would present a Bill in the ensuing session of Parliament for the purpose of authorising the line's extension from the Banavie branch to the west coast.

It had been the intention of the Glasgow and North-Western Railway in 1883 that, if its Bill had succeeded, it would have sought Parliamentary sanction in the following session to build another line westwards from Fort William. This had also been the aim of the West Highland Railway in 1889, the extension to Roshven having had to be abandoned due to opposition. Now, a different terminus had been decided upon, which was along the same route but continuing further west to Arisaig and then north to Mallaig. Originally referred to as the Loch Eil and Mallaig Railway, the new scheme was later known as the Mallaig Extension, and from it came the West Highland Railway (Mallaig Extension) Act, which received Royal Assent on 31st July, 1894.

The Highland Railway and the Caledonian Railway had opposed the extension to Mallaig because of competitive reasons to the Skye and Oban lines, but more especially in regard to the Highland having commenced the construction of the Kyle Extension. In Parliament, Andrew Dougall had stated that the Mallaig line would divert traffic from the Highland and lessen the power of the Highland to give good service to the public; while Eneas Mackintosh had pointed out that when the line to Kyle was completed, the pier at Strome Ferry, having cost £20,000, would be abandoned, and that this fact should be kept in view in connection with the Government's grant of £45,000 for the Kyle Extension. Other witnesses had been called in support of the Highland company's opposition, and one of them, Gilbert Beith, who was MP for the Inverness Burghs, had said that he looked upon the Mallaig extension as being promoted in the interests of the landed proprietors and the North British Railway, and that he would not give public money to assist in carrying out a scheme for individuals, instead of for the people generally. Spencer H. Walpole, having been the chairman of the royal commission of 1890 and who was now Secretary to the Post Office, had also cautioned against developing further railway enterprise in the West Highlands which would interfere with the existing interests. Thus, he felt that, in the event of the Mallaig line being made, something else should be done for the Highland Railway in respect of the Kyle Extension, considering that the line from Dingwall to Strome Ferry had been built by private enterprise.

The opposition had not managed to prevent the Parliamentary authorisation of the extension to Mallaig, but the line could not be built without the passing of another Bill that would guarantee a financial grant from the Treasury. Unfortunately, for the promoters, the West Highland Railway (Guarantee) Bill had failed in the session of 1894, the outcome being that the terminus would have to remain at Fort William in the meantime. The Highland Railway was pleased at this, but there had been disappointment from one newspaper in the Highland's territory. The *North Star* had commented in 1894:

> It is difficult to understand the jubilant tone in which certain north-country papers notify the fact that the Mallaig Extension scheme of the West Highland Railway Company has been rejected by the Treasury. The Mallaig branch would confer a vast boon upon the inhabitants of the western seaboard of the Highlands and provide cheap and rapid transit from the best of our native fishing grounds to the great markets of the South. From a shareholder's point of view, the action of the Highland Railway Company in opposing the scheme may appear prudent, but there is very little

patriotism in it. The more railways that are made in the North, the more advantageous it will be to the lines already working; for the opening-up of the country and the developing of its resources will bring an ample harvest of prosperity and enable all to reap a generous share.

The Highland Railway officials were particularly distressed at the idea of the Treasury being asked to give financial assistance to the Mallaig line. If a company earning five per cent can get Government aid, as in the grant of £45,000 for the Kyle Akin extension, why should not a pioneer company, earning nothing per annum, receive reasonable assistance in their attempt to confer a great benefit upon a wide and important district? The geographical position of Mallaig renders it eminently suitable for the purposes contemplated in the Bill promoted by the West Highland Railway, and notwithstanding the selfish and unpatriotic opposition which has temporarily delayed the project, it must yet become an accomplished fact.

An illustration of one of the noteworthy improvements of the railway system to the Highlands had been provided by 'a special correspondent of the *Dundee Advertiser*', and his words were reproduced by the *Inverness Courier* of 7th December, 1894, with the heading 'The Highland Railway and the Highlands: the Change since 1855':

At recent meetings of land-reforming bodies in the Highlands, I heard the miserable state of the crofter of 10 or more years ago contrasted with his independence and prosperity today. The march of change has been rapid. I ask could it have been possible without the railway facilities in existence? The agitation which has had such beneficial results could not have been carried on with anything like the same success; indeed, the agitators would not have had the opportunities of studying the condition of those they have done so much to relieve of their burdens, without the means of transit afforded by the railway. The work of 10 years would have taken 30, and so I claim that the crofters' emancipation may be added to the other good things the railway in the Highlands has done for the people.

Workmen in the Erbusaig cutting.   *W. Ramsay*

Looking north through the 85 ft-deep and 600 yds-long Erbusaig cutting, as it would have appeared without verdure on the top, at the time of completion of the Kyle Extension.

Drawing by Aurore McConnell

Chapter Eleven
Building the Line
1895-1896

The close of 1894 was marked throughout the Highlands by the beginning of a succession of severe blizzards and deep drifts that continued into the following February, bringing many deaths in addition to great general hardship and widespread disruption to the railways and roads. The onset was on 29th December, which also heralded the first snowstorm of the winter. 'On the west coast', reported the *Ross-shire Journal*, 'the storm raged with terrific violence' and on the Dingwall and Skye line, there was heavy drift. Nevertheless, the line did not become blocked and the trains managed to run with regularity. The storm passed over Lochalsh without causing much damage, although the railway embankment at Erbusaig was demolished by the sea. A violent blizzard also occurred on Sunday, 6th January, and the *Ross-shire Journal* contained the headline of 'Another Terrific Snowstorm - Traffic Completely Paralysed - Trains Snowed-up in Ross-shire', together with the following accounts, in part:

> The storms of the past three weeks culminated on Sabbath night in one of the fiercest blizzards which the country has experienced for many years. Its severity was more or less felt all over Scotland, but in the Highlands, it was exceptionally violent. The whole of Sabbath was boisterous, with frequent showers of snow and a stiff gale from the north-east . . . The storm raged in this manner during the whole night and did not abate until between six and seven on Monday morning . . .
> *Trains Blocked for Five Hours near Dingwall.* Naturally, a storm of such violence very largely interrupted the traffic on the Highland Railway. The many cuttings on the track were completely filled-in and trains, whenever they ran, were in danger of being snowed-up . . .
> *A Hard Day's Work on the Skye Line.* On the Dingwall and Skye section, the trains and surfacemen had a hard time of it. The 5.45 morning train to Dingwall left Strome Ferry at its usual time, and during the early part of its journey, was little impeded by the snow. Westward from Achnasheen, the line was comparatively clear, owing to the direction from which the gale blew, but no sooner had the Dingwall-bound train passed Achnasheen station than it plunged into a series of heavy wreaths . . .

The *Northern Chronicle* remarked that the second storm would be remembered as one of the eventful winter incidents in the history of the Highland Railway; but-in spite of this, the same paper recorded in mid-January that the works on the Kyle extension were progressing favourably, both on the line and at the pier.

In early 1895, there occurred the death of a respected gentleman who had begun his association with the Skye railway, as one of the promoters in its year of origin in 1864. Norman MacLeod, or MacLeod of MacLeod, the 25th chief of the clan that was descended from the Norse King of the Isles, died in Paris on 5th February at the age of 83. He was born in 1812 and succeeded as chief on the death of his father in 1835, which placed him, just over a decade later, with the burden of having to support the large number of his tenantry during the extreme distress on Skye that resulted from the potato famine. His actions were admirable. In addressing his tenants by a circular in December 1846, he declared that no exertions had been, or would be, spared to alleviate their distress, and that it was his duty to ensure that they were supplied with sufficient wholesome food. He imported large quantities of meal, and by the spring of 1847, he was providing for 8,000 people, which included tenants from neighbouring estates, at a cost to himself of up to £300 per week. However, his response to his high expenditure had already been that 'ruin must be faced, rather than let the people die'.

MacLeod worked vigorously at Dunvegan Castle until 1849 in trying to ease the state of misery of his people, but the arduous task ultimately became too much for him. On the verge of financial ruin, he had to leave the castle, which was placed under trust, and his aim now, at the age of 37, was to find employment in order to recover his property. He did not consider it beneath his dignity or adaptability to accept a position of junior clerk in the Prisons Department of the Home Office in London, where he earned a poor salary until 1852; but then, his prospects began to improve when he was appointed assistant secretary in the Science and Art Department. Though he had to live in London because of his employment, he was able to visit Dunvegan in the summer. In 1874, he became the head of the department, so that there was a considerable increase in his salary, and he remained in London until his retirement in 1881, receiving a pension.

During the famine, MacLeod received praise from the government's relief officers for his efforts in helping the people. Major Haliday, who was in charge of the Portree meal depot, wrote that 'MacLeod of MacLeod is the only thoroughly active and good landlord of the larger class'; while Captain Eliot of the Central Board of Management* referred to 'the benevolent and judicious exertions of MacLeod of MacLeod', adding that: 'Alike firm and kind, he sustains and animates their spirits and exertions to struggle through the sad calamity that has overtaken them with independence; sparing neither time, trouble or expense on his own part; full of courage and good hope of the blessing of God on their efforts, he affords a beautiful representation of a good man and a good landlord'. Unfortunately, four decades later, the land reformers of the Highlands in the 1870s and 1880s did not acknowledge his unselfish endeavours, and it grieved MacLeod that he then found himself as fiercely attacked as the landlords who had done nothing for their tenants.

MacLeod was educated at Harrow, Paris and Vienna, becoming well versed in French and German, and he also studied law, though not practising it significantly. He was an excellent speaker when he chose to appear in public, which was not often; and his ability, combined with his active nature, was put to good use in 1864, when, at several meetings, he promoted the Dingwall and Skye Railway to the public, for which he was commended by Alex Matheson at the line's inaugural banquet in 1870. As had been recorded by Robert Somers in 1847, MacLeod already had some experience in transport requirements from his operation of a coach service between Inverness and Dunvegan Castle - thus catering for the travelling public to and from the West with relative ease. When the railway was set to proceed in the direction of Skye, he was well aware that such an enterprising and essential scheme as this still required a sufficient degree of promotion to encourage the shares to be taken. He followed up his enthusiasm by becoming a Director and the Deputy Chairman of the Dingwall and Skye Railway, and though not having any official connection with the Highland Railway after the Skye company had been absorbed, he would certainly have been delighted to know that the Highland was intent on taking the line to the proximity of half a mile from his island. Unfortunately, as with Joseph Mitchell and Alex Matheson, Norman MacLeod was not to see the completion of the Skye railway to Kyle - the ambitious line to the West that they had helped to initiate three decades previously.

MacLeod's body was conveyed from Paris to Dunvegan Castle for burial. There were present a great many of the crofters from the extensive MacLeod estate, together with gentlemen representing other parts of the island, to offer their respect to a man who was considered eminently worthy of having held the position of chief of the clan MacLeod.

The first half of 1895 on the Kyle railway was dominated by tragic accidents to the navvies, as well as the inevitable incidents of brawling.

---

* i.e. the Central Board of Management of the Fund for the Relief of the Destitute Inhabitants of the Highlands.

In January, the *Ross-shire Journal*, with a heading of 'What they Say in Plockton', recorded:

> That the navvies are drinking, cursing and demoralising at a terrible rate.
> That it is a scandal to Christendom that such scenes should be allowed.
> That it is equally scandalous there is no police office or shed to put poor fellows in to preserve their lives, and to put foul-tongued scoundrels in to preserve the purity of others.

And the paper added in February that, at Dingwall, 'scarcely a week runs on but a visit is paid to the Sheriff Court by some of the navvy tribe, presently working at the Kyle Akin railway'.

There was an accident in mid-February at Erbusaig. While some of the navvies were carrying rails from the shore to the embankment, one of them - a young man called Lachlan MacLeod from Raasay - had one of his legs badly crushed by one of the rails falling on it. He was conveyed to his lodgings at Drumbuie, with Dr MacDonald of Plockton treating his injury such that a favourable recovery was able to be made.

At the end of February, the *North Star* contained the following report on some trouble that had occurred earlier in the month:

> Notwithstanding the long-continued storm, the navvies employed at the Kyle Akin railway were kept in constant employment at rock-cutting, and they have been consequently able to raise sufficient funds to enjoy themselves in a way dear to the heart of their species. At Dingwall on Monday, Sheriff Hill had no fewer than four of them before him for offences arising out of drunken brawls. They were named James Anglim, James Gorman, William Mackintosh and Michael Walsh - the names, in a curious way, suggest the nationality - and the charge against them was that of fighting with each other and conducting themselves in a riotous and disorderly manner on the public road near the Station Hotel, Strome Ferry, on Saturday, 9th February. On the night in question, there was, it appears, a general *mêlée* in the village, about 30 or 40 combatants being engaged, Highlanders versus Irishmen; and, as result of his efforts to quell the disturbance, the local policeman, David MacKenzie, had his leg injured by a stone.

On 2nd April, a serious accident occurred in a cutting at Badicaul, when an Irishman, Michael Green, aged 38, who was acting as powderman in the blasting operations, was badly injured in an explosion. Six blasts were ready to be fired by Green in the cutting, but the first fuse did not ignite properly, and after lighting the other five, he was in the act of reigniting the first when the others exploded. His companions found him prostrate among the debris, with his head and one arm mutilated, and he was carried on a stretcher to the navvy hut at Kyle, where he lay in a helpless condition for some time, as he was not in a condition to be moved. Dr MacDonald attended to the injuries as best as he could, but they were so serious, with permanent blindness feared, that they could not be treated at Kyle, and the doctor ordered him to be sent to the Ross Memorial Hospital at Dingwall.

Strangely, there was a similar accident two days later, as recorded by the *North Star*, when

> ... one of the navvies employed in the blasting operations at Erbusaig met with an accident which nearly proved fatal. The unfortunate man, O'Brien by name, had fired four of the five charges laid, and while searching his person for a match to fire the remaining fuse, the other four exploded with terrific force, mangling the poor fellow frightfully. It is a wonder, indeed, he was not killed outright. He was immediately afterwards attended by Doctors MacDonald and Duncan. It was feared that he would have lost his eyesight, but we understand that he has partially regained his vision.

Then came a fatal explosion on 9th April at Strome Ferry. The *Ross-shire Journal*, in reporting on this, also supplied a brief description of the progress of the line at Strome:

Another lamentable accident by explosives took place at the new railway works in the immediate vicinity of Strome Ferry Hotel on Tuesday forenoon last. A deep rock-cutting has been carried on near the beginning of the new line along the seashore below the hotel for nearly a twelve-month past. The works are gradually drawing near the road to Balamacara, passing in front of the hotel, until these are now close up to the road and only a very short distance from the hotel door. On Tuesday morning, the squad resumed work as usual at seven o'clock, and some three hours later, while the men were busy in the cutting, all of a sudden a mysterious explosion took place in their midst, killing one man, of the name James Brady, instantaneously and seriously injuring another, of the name James MacKay.

The cause of this terrible accident is, in the meantime, a profound mystery, as no explosives had been used in the cutting that day, and the only conjecture that can be arrived at is either that part of a former charge in the bottom of a hole did not explode and was unknowingly struck by poor Brady with his pick, which he was using at the time, or that a cartridge had been dropped in the cutting on the previous night and, it having got covered over, was struck and exploded before its presence became known. The miracle is that others of the men were not hurt, as there was a number of them in the near neighbourhood at the time. The Free Church Presbytery of Glenelg met on that day at Strome Ferry, and the Rev Mr Galbraith, Lochalsh, had a narrow escape, as he was at the time passing up the road. He says he was stunned for the moment. Gelignite is the explosive used at the works, and it is a most powerful and destructive substance. Extreme carefulness has to be used in the handling of it, and it is to be feared many of the navvies deal with it much too freely. A very just cause for complaint is the absence of prompt medical attendance when an accident does occur. In the case of the accident on Tuesday, there was no doctor on the spot for upwards of four hours after the accident, although two were telegraphed for, and the poor lad, MacKay, was in a pitiable condition, suffering fearful agonies. Brady was an Irishman and about 40 years of age.

Three days earlier, on the morning of Saturday, 6th April, at six o'clock, an Irish navvy, James Murphy, aged about 45, had been found dead by the roadside at Erbusaig. He had been working on the Friday afternoon until three o'clock, but when heavy rain put a stop to the work for that day, he went to the Kyle Inn, where he indulged too freely in drink. It was supposed that, having left Kyle in drunkenness at a late hour for his hut at Erbusaig, he somehow fell to the ground and slept, but, with the night being one of the stormiest in the district for some time, he succumbed to the cold.

An idea of the general progress of the railway works was provided at the half-yearly meeting of the Highland shareholders on 19th April, when Murdoch Paterson's report to the Directors was read. Having referred to the direct line from Aviemore to Inverness, which was in construction northwards from Carr Bridge, Paterson had noted that, with the milder weather on the west coast,

Mr Best was enabled to carry on his rock excavations with little interruption during January and February, when he had, on average, 700 men at work. The proportion of rock excavation executed and put to bank up to 28th ult. was 37 per cent. There are seven bridges in course of construction; and, considering the stoppages by gales and sea storms, good progress has been made with the pier at Kyle; 75 lineal yards of the east, and 32 yards of the west, side walls being well on to completion.

At the meeting, there was reference by the Highland's Chairman, Eneas Mackintosh, to a sum of £2,567 being spent on opposition to the Mallaig railway. It was very expensive, he said, but the Directors had thought it necessary because they believed that the harbour at Kyle Akin would meet the entire wants of the west coast, and they thought it right to defend their interest in that manner. The meeting also heard that the company, having now run for 40 years, had never experienced such a series of snow-blocks as had occurred in the past winter.

At the beginning of May, the *Ross-shire Journal* recorded from Strome Ferry that the locality had a spell of quietness in the fish traffic until the start of the Stornoway fishing a week later:

> Then the energetic and willing officials and porters at the railway station will have more than enough to do. The quiescence is, however, occasionally broken by that sociable neighbour, the navvy, who frequently sounds the trumpet of disorder and discord - a privilege for which he, at times, pays a decent fee.

Also in May, a sum of 43 shillings was collected by local subscriptions for the purpose of sending home to Arklow, County Wicklow, the Irish navvy, Michael Green, who had lost his eyesight in the explosion at Badicaul. However, yet another accident due to an explosion, and resulting in the death of a navvy, happened on 12th July at a cutting west of Drumbuie. The unfortunate man was George Hamilton, aged from 50 to 60, and resident at Duirinish, and the cause was a now-familiar one. Some bores in the cutting had been charged with gelignite, but one of them had not ignited. Hamilton was working with a hammer and a chisel at the charged bore, while the squad's ganger, by the name of Bricket, looked on. Referring to a wedge in the bore, Bricket called to Hamilton to 'strike it down', and then the explosion occurred, with Hamilton being killed instantaneously. At the public inquiry at Dingwall Sheriff Court on 30th July, under the Fatal Accidents (Scotland) Act, John Best junior stated before Sheriff Hill and a jury that he had engaged Bricket six weeks before the accident on the assurance that, having produced favourable certificates from former employers, he had good experience of blasting operations. After the accident, Bricket had admitted to Best that he did not have much acquaintance with explosives, and he had since ceased work, saying then that he would stay in the area until the investigation, but he was not seen again. The jury were unanimously of the opinion that Bricket, having been in charge of the squad, was to blame for the accident, either through ignorance or otherwise.

Meanwhile, in-mid July, the *Northern Chronicle* had briefly noted the progress of the railway and its terminal village:

> The Kyle railway works are being rapidly pushed forward, and in another year, at the present rate of working, very little will remain unfinished. In a few months, the line from Kyle to Erbusaig will be open for locomotive traffic. The quay at Kyle will, however, take about two years yet to finish. A number of people have taken up their residence at Kyle, and it has, at present, every appearance of being a summer resort.

The arrival of the railway would also improve an aspect of backwardness in Lochalsh which had been brought to attention in July through the *Ross-shire Journal*:

> A general complaint of the good folk here is that postal facilities are behind the age of modern times. No money-orders, no telegraphic communication, and no stamps are procurable, unless, in the latter case, our obliging postman will come to our aid with his very limited supply of stamps, which is entirely inadequate to meet one-third of the wants of the place. In fact, Kyle is as isolated in this respect as the last coral islands discovered.

For the half-yearly meeting of the Highland shareholders on 23rd October, Murdoch Paterson's report on the state of construction of the line and the pier, concentrated mainly on the latter:

Mr Best continues to make good progress with the works of the Strome Ferry and Kyle extension. The proportion of rock excavated and put to bank is 56 per cent of the total quantity contracted for; and 40 per cent of the bridges and culverts for roads and streams has been built. As regards the deep-water pier for steamers at Kyle, the east side-wall has been built to within 18 inches of its full height for 265 feet from the shore; and the remaining 98 feet, thence to the outer head, founded - 81 feet of which have been built upon the level of low water. The wall on the west side has been built to within 18 inches from the top for 106 feet from the shore, and the foundation laid for a further length of 106 feet seaward, of which 50 feet is built upon to above low water. On the whole, about one-third of the pier-works has been executed.

The October 1895 meeting was a significant but regrettable one for the Highland Railway, and for Andrew Dougall in particular, for then it was alleged by one of the Highland Directors that the General Manager had involved himself in a financial irregularity whereby he had made, or had intended to make, a profit of £21,000 for himself from a certain transaction involving Highland Railway stock. The allegation came from James Fletcher of Rosehaugh, on the Black Isle, who had been elected a Director only 18 months previously. Dougall denied the charge, saying that the £21,000 had been credited to the Highland Railway's account for the company, and not to himself.

This sum had been realised from the sale of £150,000 preference stock with which Dougall had speculated back in August 1893. As was usual, if not strictly correct, he had acted solely on his initiative, without first informing the Board, and in September 1893, the value of the stock had risen on the market by 14 per cent, so that, in then arranging for the stock to be sold, he had secured the £21,000 profit. It was only in April 1895 that the Board became acquainted with the transaction, and they appointed a committee to investigate the matter. The committee criticised Dougall, with the view that he was deserving of censure; but the Board thought that this expression was too strong, with their opinion that his action was most irregular and much to be regretted, and that steps would be taken to prevent the recurrence of such irregularity in future.

After the October 1895 meeting, Dougall explained his actions and his innocence in answer to what had been alleged by Fletcher. This was in a letter, dated 31st October, which was also sent to the newspapers. In justice to himself, Dougall pointed out,

... that the Board meet only once a month, and that it has consequently been usual and necessary for me at times to act on my own responsibility to the best of my judgement, and dispose of particular business between meetings on their behalf and in their name. What I have done in this way has, up till now, met with their full approval.

Referring to the stock having risen on the market, he wrote:

When I saw this, I decided that the profit should be paid to the company and, accordingly, I instructed the banks to remit the money direct to the company's bankers, which was done, and I mentioned the whole matter to the Chairman at the time.
Mr Fletcher, in regard to this matter, stated that I refused to withdraw all claim to the money, but he appears to have overlooked the fact that, several months ago, I intimated to the Board that I waived my claim to it, and placed myself unreservedly in their hands. I have not profited a penny by the transaction.

At the end of his letter, Dougall declared the concern that he had always shown for his company and how he felt at having had such an allegation thrust upon him:

In conclusion, I may be allowed to say that, during the long period of 40 years I have had the honour of conducting the business of the Highland Railway Company, I have done everything in my power to advance its prosperity, and have ever considered it to be my first duty to see that its interests were not allowed to suffer in my hands. Until now, I have worked in complete harmony with the Directors, and I deeply regret, when nearing the intended close of a long career in their service, that any one of these gentlemen should have felt called upon to make an attack and bring reproach upon me at a public meeting, without first giving me the slightest opportunity to explain the matters complained of. I feel conscious, however, that all my official acts have never, in a single instance, aimed at sacrificing the company for my own advantage.

Sympathy for Andrew Dougall was shown by the *Inverness Courier*. From it, firstly on 25th October, which was only two days after the half-yearly meeting, had come the comment in his defence that,

... it has, in fairness, to be borne in mind that Mr Dougall has not received the £21,000 which represents the profit on the purchase. No doubt, he held that he was entitled to that sum, but he seems to have waived his claim, and the shareholders have not actually suffered ... In any event, it will not be forgotten that Mr Dougall has been a valuable official to the company, and has fought for its interests with rare ability, determination and success.

Then, on 29th November, the paper, in repeated support, disclosed an ironical state of affairs:

There are, perhaps, some people who still imagine that Mr Dougall pocketed the £21,000 which was originally the cause of dispute. This, of course, is quite a mistake: the money was paid into the account of the company; it still remains there; and the Directors never manifested the slightest intention of parting with it. As regards the interests of the shareholders, the transaction was, in its results, the most satisfactory that has ever taken place in the company's stock.

Also in regard to Andrew Dougall, the *Inverness Courier*, on 3rd December, reproduced an extract from the *Elgin Courant*, which said in part:

The shareholders will have to give due weight to the defence Mr Dougall has placed in their hands. His 40 years' service to the company; the prominent part he has taken in developing it from small beginnings to its present magnitude; and the many successful Parliamentary fights he has made on its behalf ought not to be forgotten at the present time. He was the embodiment of the company - the great official into whose hands power naturally fell, and to whom the Directors - if not nominally, at any rate in reality - delegated much of their responsibility. It is from this point of view that Mr Dougall's action should be judged.

Nevertheless, due to the unfortunate situation that had arisen, Andrew Dougall felt compelled to make the decision to retire from the company, after having devoted 40 years of service to the railways of the Highlands. At the Board meeting on 4th December, he tendered his resignation, which was accepted with regret, but he was requested to continue in office, to perform all the duties of General Manager and Secretary, until further notice, and he agreed to this.

For the Highland Railway, Andrew Dougall had indeed been a splendid employee - remarkable in his dedication and loyalty to the company, earning himself high esteem. A native of Perth, he held a position there in the service of the Caledonian Railway before heading north to take up his appointment in the Highlands as General Manager of the Inverness and Nairn Railway in 1855. As the railway system expanded around Inverness, he took on the additional equivalent appointments for the successive railway companies that formed. He was General Manager and Secretary of the Inverness and Aberdeen Junction Railway from 1856 to 1865; General Manager and Secretary of the Inverness and Ross-shire Railway, 1860 to 1862; General Manager and Secretary of the Inverness and

Perth Junction Railway, 1861 to 1865; Secretary of the Dingwall and Skye Railway, 1865 to 1880; Secretary of the Sutherland Railway, 1865 to 1884; and Secretary of the Sutherland and Caithness Railway, 1871 to 1884. When the Inverness and Aberdeen Junction Railway and the Inverness and Perth Junction Railway were amalgamated into the Highland Railway in 1865, he naturally became General Manager and Secretary of the large, new company; and he would remain so for the next three decades, to attain a certain distinction in being the longest-serving British railway manager.

Like Joseph Mitchell, Alex Matheson and the third Duke of Sutherland, Andrew Dougall was, in a sense, a railway pioneer, with his ability and initiative for administration and business. Like Mitchell, Matheson and MacLeod of MacLeod, he was one of the several enthusiastic gentlemen in attendance at the two meetings in April 1864 for the inception of the Dingwall and Skye Railway, and it was inevitable that his first capacity of interim Secretary for the new concern would lead to him becoming the permanent Secretary, which occurred at the company's incorporation in the following year. His commanding presence, strong character and stentorian voice were features that ensured that his ideas and opinions were respected. At Board meetings and before Parliamentary committees, he was able to be relied upon to fight for the interests and rights of the Highland Railway or the constituent railway companies that he also represented. In spite of his stern exterior, he was a kind-hearted man who, while wishing to uphold the standards and regulations of the Highland company, was always willing to show leniency to those who had committed misdemeanours, and as such, he was regarded highly by his colleagues, from the Directors and officials to the railway workers.

At a meeting of the Highland Directors on 8th January, 1896, William Gowenlock was unanimously appointed Secretary of the company. He was an old and esteemed servant, having been employed for 38 years, of which the last 22 years were in the duty of Assistant Manager and Assistant Secretary to Andrew Dougall. However, it was now the aim of the Board to separate the position of General Manager and Secretary, and although at this time a new manager had not yet been decided, it was believed that the list of applicants had been reduced to three - these being George Thomson, the company's Goods Manager; David Deuchars, Line Superintendent of the North British Railway; and Charles Steel, Assistant Superintendent of the North Eastern Railway.

It was at a meeting of the Directors on 6th February in London that the appointment of General Manager was made, when Charles Steel would be the successor to Andrew Dougall. Steel was a native of the north of England and approaching 50 years of age, having been in the service of the York-based company for the last 20 years. At the same meeting, another important change was constituted as a result of Eneas Mackintosh of Raigmore having stated that he would retire as Chairman of the company, in which capacity he had acted in the five years since the death of the Hon. Thomas Bruce in late 1890. Raigmore, as he was usually referred to, was one of the spirited promoters of the first railway in the Highlands, from Inverness to Nairn, of which he was Chairman from 1857 to 1861; and when the Dingwall and Skye and the Highland companies came into existence, he became a Director of both. During the time of financial stress for the Highland - when Alex Matheson and his fellow Directors had to place their personal securities for advances to the extent of £1,000,000 - Eneas Mackintosh was one of the influential gentlemen who took part in this guarantee that tided over the young company. Now, at his time of life, aged 77, he found the duties of Chairman 'rather irksome'. His resignation was accepted with regret at the meeting, but in recognition of his long service on the Board, he was asked to remain a Director, which he agreed to do. Thereupon, Sir George MacPherson-Grant of Ballindalloch was unanimously elected Chairman of the company. Sir George had also been a Director for many years and

Deputy Chairman from 1890. He was not robust in health, but he had much business experience and he was deeply interested in the welfare of the company.

On 18th February, Charles Steel arrived in Inverness and visited the various departments of the Highland Railway in the presence of Andrew Dougall, who introduced him to the officials. Dougall had already addressed a circular to the heads of the departments, and this announced the ending of his services as General Manager and the appointment of his successor. In respect of his long connection with the company, the Directors recommended that a year's salary should be granted to him. Inevitably, it was with sadness that Andrew Dougall departed from the scene of the Highland Railway, and it was a pity that his association with the Skye railway was not able to continue until its completion to Kyle of Lochalsh.

On 27th April, some of the Highland Directors travelled by a special saloon carriage and engine from Inverness to Strome Ferry for the purpose of examining the progress of the works on the extension of the system to Kyle, and also present were Charles Steel and Murdoch Paterson. 'The peculiar feature of the work', commented the *North Star* in regard to the inspection, 'is the excessive and laborious amount of rock-cutting that has had to be executed'. The party observed that the work had been satisfactorily pushed forward, and they returned to Inverness in the evening.

The Highland Railway shareholders' half-yearly meeting was held two days later, and Murdoch Paterson's report was able to record a significant advancement from six months previously:

Mr Best has made most satisfactory progress with the works of this line, and he continues to push them forward with commendable energy. He has all along had a large force of men employed - consequent, no doubt, on the proximity of the works to the Isle of Skye and the Hebrides; also on the mildness of the climate, which differs greatly from that on the Aviemore line. Mr Best has excavated and put to bank 73 per cent of the total quantity of rock-cutting specified; has built 84 per cent of the bridges and culverts required for roads and streams; will shortly commence laying two considerable stretches of permanent way; and has erected about 30 per cent of the fencing. He has also made good progress with the works of the deep-water pier at Kyle. The walls on both sides of the pier have been founded to the outer head, which is 380 feet from the shore. The east wall has been built thereon to within 18 inches of its full height for 282 feet from the shore, and to the level of low water for a further distance of 64 feet. The west wall has been built to within 18 inches of its full height for 310 feet from the shore, and to the level of low water for a further distance of 35 feet. The works of the outer head, or cross wall, will shortly be begun, and for which additional plant is now on the way from the South. Approximately one-half of the works of the pier has been executed.

Back in the spring of 1895, a grievance had appeared in regard to an aspect of the building of the railway. This had come from the people of the village of Erbusaig, who were concerned about the embankment that was being built between their houses and the sea. The problem, which involved the question of the number of access bridges to be included in the embankment, was supported on behalf of the villagers by the MP for Ross and Cromarty, who was James Galloway Weir, a Liberal. He asked the Board of Trade whether a petition had been received from the village to the effect that, in the interests of this fishing and crofting population, there should be three openings in the embankment, instead of the one as planned, and whether steps had been taken to prevent the construction of the embankment without the necessary openings to the shore. To this, an answer from a representative of the Board of Trade in London read: 'I have received from the Secretary of Scotland the petition referred to by the Hon. Member, and will carefully consider the representations of the petitioners whenever the working drawings of the railway embankment are submitted to me by the Highland Railway Company, which has not yet been done'.

In the autumn of 1895, by which time the subject had been investigated to the dissatisfaction of the people of Erbusaig, the following letter of complaint, from a gentleman calling himself 'Bremmier', who was acting for the village, was dispatched to Edinburgh and addressed to Malcolm MacNeill of the Board of Supervision for the Relief of the Poor:

Dear Sir:
    I am instructed by the inhabitants of Erbusaig, parish of Lochalsh, in the county of Ross and Cromarty, to direct the attention of the Board of Supervision to the high-handed proceedings of the Highland company in the matter of the construction of the embankment over the foreshore of this village in connection with the new Kyle Akin railway.
    When the natives gave their consent to the company to construct the embankment referred to, they were led to understand that there would be three bridges, both for the convenience of their boats and on the higher ground of necessary sanitation - the village lying so low and near the water. Our complaint has special reference to the injury inflicted upon them in the latter respect, for, with one bridge, they are now so hemmed-in and confined that their health will doubtless be seriously interfered with, seeing that there is but one means of egress for the matter which will accompany each recurring tide. It is the opinion of parties most competent to judge that, in a short time, the stench caused by the superfluity of mud will become a most intolerable nuisance, which will assuredly be prejudicial to the health of the locality. I venture to submit that there is not a similar instance of such encroachment upon the rights of the people in either England or Scotland. Unless the railway comply with their wishes - while the embankment is still in course of formation - in regard to the granting of other two bridges, so as to admit a due supply of air, the exigency of the case will be such as to compel them taking action when it is too late. It is of the utmost necessity, ere matters proceed further, that the Board of Supervision institute an inquiry into their grievance with the least-possible delay, or instruct the County Council of Ross and Cromarty to adopt such proceedings as may be deemed advisable in the circumstances; and I have every confidence in your readiness to comply with their humble request.

This letter was also sent to the *Scottish Highlander* - another Inverness newspaper - and there was a response from the editor to the following effect:

Unless we are wrongly informed, the question, to which our correspondent properly draws attention, has already been very fully considered, both by the representatives of the residents of Erbusaig and the railway company, and we understand that the bridge accommodation which is to be provided will be such as will meet all the requirements of the village. We have no special brief from the Highland Railway Company to plead their cause, but would suggest that our correspondent should put himself into communication with the manager, who will, no doubt, be able to enlighten and satisfy him as to what is really to be done to meet the wishes and requirements of the people of Erbusaig.

James Galloway Weir again communicated with the Board of Trade in late March 1896, stating that the means of access to the foreshore were liable to be encroached upon by the construction of the railway. In return, he was informed that the Highland Railway had been requested to forward the necessary plans, and that the Board of Trade had undertaken to ensure that the interests of the population would be properly protected. It was on 10th June that another representative of the Board of Trade produced a final reply to the MP on the problem of Erbusaig:

Sir:
With reference to your letter of 28th March last, addressed to the president upon the subject of the method of constructing the Lochalsh railway at Erbusaig, which has been authorised by the Highland Railway Act, 1893, I am directed by the Board of Trade to acquaint you that they have given very careful consideration to your representations, as well as those of the inhabitants of Erbusaig, who have made a complaint to the Board in the matter. The Board have received from

the Highland Railway Company plans of the works in question, and have been in communication with the company with respect to the desired modification therein, and are informed that the crofters and others interested in this line of railway appointed, as their arbiter, Mr Donald MacRae, Balallan, to value the damage done to their subjects, and to decide what accommodation bridges and other works, including bridges in the sea embankments, should be given for their convenience. It appears that this gentleman, in company with Mr Donald Grant, the arbiter on behalf of the railway company, visited Erbusaig and heard the crofters on the spot, and that both arbiters were satisfied that the 50 feet bridge and other facilities referred to in their award and findings are sufficient for the needs of the locality. The Board of Trade, after careful examination of the circumstances of the case, have come to a similar conclusion, and are of opinion that the reasonable demands of the crofters have been fully met, and that no sufficient grounds have been shown for calling upon the railway company to make modifications in the works.

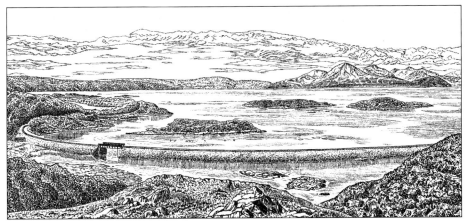

The view from above Erbusaig, looking west to the Cuillins of Skye, with the embankment or causeway carrying the Kyle railway across the bay. Out of sight is Erbusaig village to the left and the Erbusaig cutting to the right. *Drawing by Aurore McConnell*

Back in August 1895, the Highland Directors had 'considered the propriety of erecting a hotel at the Kyle terminus', after which they had instructed Messrs Ross and MacBeth, architects, Inverness, to prepare the plans for a suitable building. Their report, with the designs for the proposed hotel, were examined by the Directors in early January 1896, but it was resolved to postpone further consideration for the time being. On 1st July, it was decided that land - reported by Charles Steel to be available and suitable for the hotel, at the west side of the road leading to the pier at Kyle - should be acquired by the company. In early August, Steel reported 'that he was in communication with Sir Kenneth Matheson's representatives, in reference to the purchase of the land'; and on 2nd September, he was able to report 'that the site for the hotel at Kyle, together with Kyle House, which is situated upon the site, had been purchased for £1,500'.

At the Highland shareholders' half-yearly meeting on 28th October, it was remarked that 'the work at Kyle was in a fair state of progress', with no doubt that the line would be opened in 1897. Further details were supplied by Murdoch Paterson's report, as follows:

Mr Best continues to push forward the works in a very energetic manner. The quantity of rock-cutting remaining undone is 36,000 cubic yards - viz., 5,800 at Duncraig; 3,100 at Duirinish; 2,300 at Erbusaig; and 24,800 in the terminal station at Kyle, nearly all of which is of a very hard description. The bridges and culverts for roads and streams are rapidly approaching completion.

A construction train at Plockton station shortly before the opening of the Kyle Extension. The engine is HR No. 63, a 4-4-0 that was one of ten of this class designed by David Jones and built by Dübs & Co. of Glasgow in 1874.   *J.L. Stevenson*

The same construction train at Duirinish station.   *J.L. Stevenson*

Four miles of the permanent way have been laid in place and adjusted, and 12¾ miles of the fencing erected. The works of the deep-water pier at Kyle are far advanced. The two side-walls and the cross- or outer-head wall have been built to within 18 inches of the finished top, and preparations are in progress for the construction of the low-water landings.

A more descriptive account of the further advancement of the works followed from the *Northern Chronicle* in mid-November:

The extension of the Highland Railway from Strome Ferry to Kyle is so fast approaching completion that it is expected to be opened for fish traffic in the course of next summer. Considering that about one-third of the railway track had to be cut out of solid rock - some of which is 80 feet deep - the progress made by the enterprising contractor, Mr Best, is very remarkable. When Mr Best entered upon this contract, he seemed to have determined that the work should be pushed on, and he had as many as 800 men employed at one time. The pier at Kyle, which is now nearly finished, is a massive piece of workmanship. It is built of concrete, protected all round with huge piles, and will afford ample accommodation to a large number of fishing-boats and several steamers during the fishing season. There is a large 'island platform', with girder brides on either side, and Kyle station, when completed, will be large and comfortable, and finished with all modern improvements. The line proposes to be a favourable route for tourists. The scenery from Strome Ferry along by Duncraig Castle, the west-country seat of Sir Kenneth Matheson, is magnificent. Skye will now be brought much nearer to the mainland and the trip to Portree will be much shortened, while many of the Western Isles will also benefit by the opening of the line. Between six and seven miles of the permanent way are already laid, and the remainder of the work will, it is expected, be ready in a short time. The station for Plockton, now ready for the buildings, is situated about one mile west of that village. There will be another station at Duirinish. This work has been principally carried on by Mr Sloane, a courteous gentleman, who, as manager, seems to get on well with the men. Kyle bids well to become an important place; several buildings have lately been erected, the principal of which is an office for the Commercial Bank. This building is large and imposing, and will be ready for occupancy in May. The mason contractor was our townsman, Mr Thomas MacDonald, the others being Edinburgh contractors. During the progress of the railway works, a number of shops and stores have sprung up, and all seem to be doing a good trade.

The *Inverness Courier* had already mentioned, in mid-October, the development of Kyle. This was in a note relating to the Free Presbytery of Lochcarron, with 'the attention of the Presbytery having been called to the fact that the population of the proposed terminus of the Dingwall and Skye Railway is sure to increase greatly, and that many houses, banks and shops are in progress of building, or in prospect of being built, on the mainland side of the ferry of Kyle Akin'.

During the 1890s, the Skye railway was being worked by several of its own special locomotives. These were 'Skye Bogies', which resulted from the success of the 1873 and 1875 conversions of the Skye line's original 2-4-0s into 4-4-0s. David Jones, the Locomotive Superintendent, had received permission from the Highland Board to design a new 4-4-0 class, instead of modifying any further engines; and, thus, the first 'Skye Bogie' was completed in May 1882 at Lochgorm Works and given the number 70. It was found to be ideal for the Skye line, such that Jones was then authorised to construct three more 'Skye bogies' over several years. However, it was fully a decade after the construction of the first that the second appeared. This was No. 85, completed in August 1892; and it was followed by Nos. 86 and 87 in February and December 1893, and then by another, No. 88, in April 1895. These were the five 'Skye Bogies' to have been designed at Lochgorm by David Jones, who retired in October 1896, after 41 years of excellent service to the railways of the Highlands, from his commencement with the Inverness and Nairn line in 1855. His successor, in November 1896, was Peter Drummond.

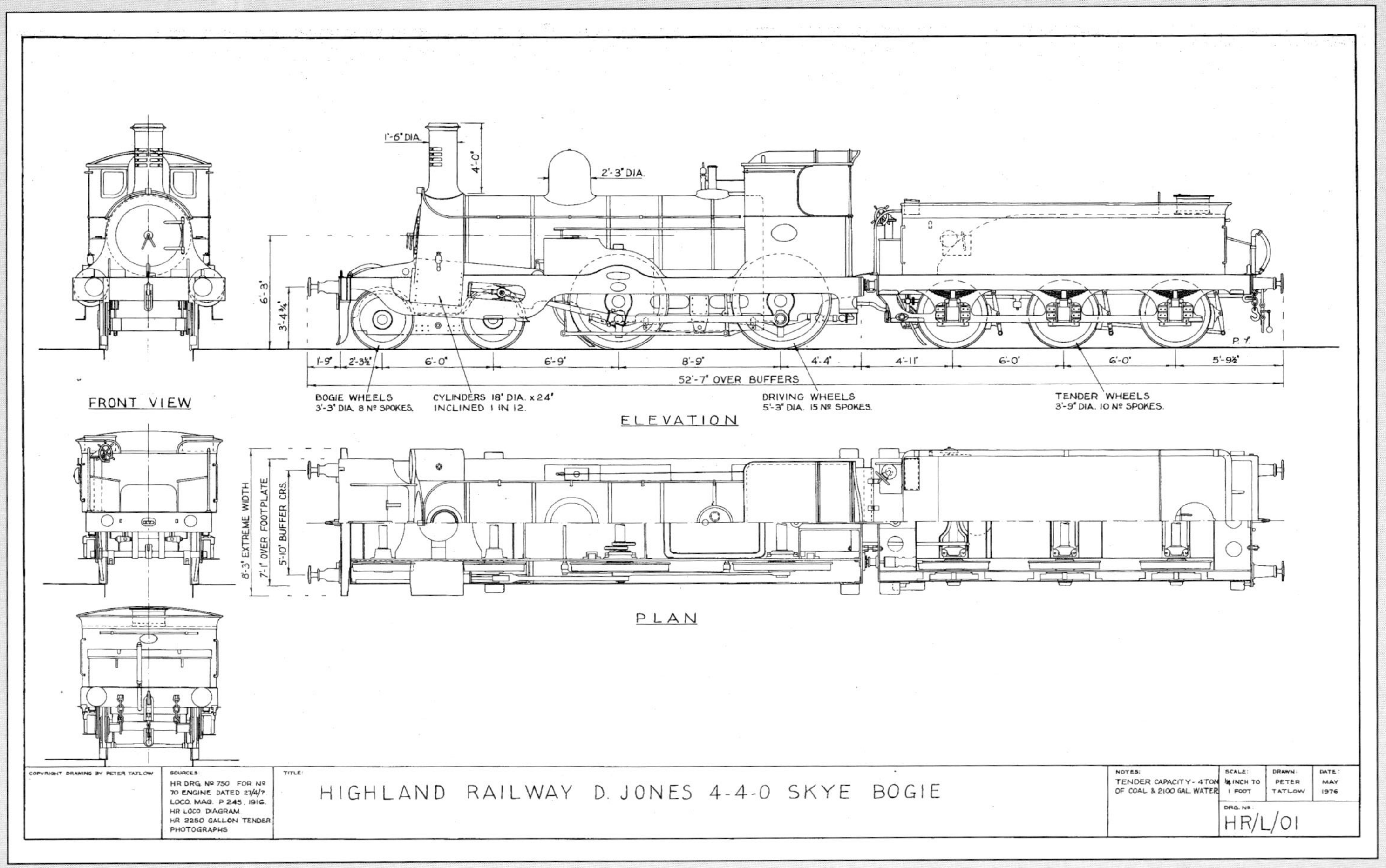

1'-6" DIA.
4'-0"
2'-3" DIA.
6'-3"
3'-4¾"
P. T.
1'-9"
2'-3½"
6'-0"
6'-9"
8'-9"
4'-4"
4'-11"
6'-0"
6'-0"
5'-9½"
52'-7" OVER BUFFERS
FRONT VIEW
BOGIE WHEELS
3'-3" DIA. 8 Nº SPOKES.
CYLINDERS 18" DIA. x 24"
INCLINED 1 IN 12.
DRIVING WHEELS
5'-3" DIA. 15 Nº SPOKES.
TENDER WHEELS
3'-9" DIA. 10 Nº SPOKES.
ELEVATION
8'-3" EXTREME WIDTH
7'-1" OVER FOOTPLATE
5'-10" BUFFER CRS.
PLAN
COPYRIGHT DRAWING BY PETER TATLOW
SOURCES:
HR DRG. Nº 750 FOR Nº
70 ENGINE DATED 27/4/?
LOCO. MAG. P 245, 1916.
HR LOCO DIAGRAM
HR 2250 GALLON TENDER
PHOTOGRAPHS
TITLE:
HIGHLAND RAILWAY D. JONES 4-4-0 SKYE BOGIE
NOTES:
TENDER CAPACITY - 4 TON
OF COAL & 2100 GAL. WATER
SCALE:
¼ INCH TO
1 FOOT
DRAWN:
PETER
TATLOW
DATE:
MAY
1976
DRG. Nº
HR/L/01

'Skye Bogie' sectional drawings

Drawings by P. Tatlow

Chapter Twelve

Completing the Line
1897

In February and March 1897, the Highland Directors considered the remaining tenders that had to be finalised. At a Board meeting on 3rd February, held in London, the offers received for the agents' houses and other dwellings at the stations were submitted, when it was resolved to accept that of Messrs Andrew Mackintosh and Sons, contractors, Muir of Ord, for all the buildings, as follows:

	£	s.	d.
Agent's house at Plockton	476	9	1
Block of 3 dwellings for men at Plockton	828	4	2
Block of 3 dwellings for agent and surfacemen at Duirinish	832	19	9
Block of 2 dwellings for surfacemen at Erbusaig	557	16	0
Agent's house at Kyle	529	8	5
Block of 4 dwellings for enginemen, guards and others at Kyle	1,111	15	5

At the same meeting, it was decided that the name of the station at Kyle was to be 'Kyle of Lochalsh'. At the next Board meeting on 3rd March, at Inverness, the offers received for the station-offices at Plockton and Duirinish, and for the goods shed at Plockton, were discussed, with the contract for these also being awarded to Mackintosh:

	£	s.	d.
Station offices at Plockton	577	8	2
Station offices at Duirinish	349	15	8
Goods shed at Plockton	240	0	0

There had been the death of another navvy on 5th February. Roderick MacAskill, aged 18, met his fate as a result of the jib of a crane falling upon him when he was engaged in loading sleepers onto a vessel in the bay at Duncraig. At the inquiry at Dingwall on 21st February, witnesses stated that they did not know what had caused the jib to fall, and from the evidence, the jury delivered a verdict to Sheriff Hill that MacAskill had been accidentally killed.

A significant amount of work had been carried out on the Kyle Extension during the winter and spring, as was in evidence from Murdoch Paterson's generally positive report, dated 2nd April, 1897, which was read at the Highland half-yearly shareholders' meeting on 28th April:

The length of this line, from Strome Ferry station to the outer head of the deep-water pier at Kyle, is 10¾ miles.

The excavations have been completed, with the exception of 2,000 cubic yards of rock at Kyle station; and the sides of the deep rock-cuttings along the line are being dressed down and made safe.

There are 42 bridges and culverts for roads and streams on the line, varying in span from 4 to 70 feet, all of which have been built, except two overline bridges at Duncraig.

The permanent way of the main line has been laid, except ⅞ mile. The extension of the loop-line at Strome Ferry and the sidings at Plockton have been laid and ballasted, but a considerable length of sidings and connections have to be laid at the stations and pier at Kyle.

The fencing has been nearly completed; and the seaward slopes of the railway embankments, at two of the most exposed points, are being made safe.

The works of the pier at Kyle were greatly delayed during the past half year by wet and stormy weather, and by frost, preventing the making of concrete.

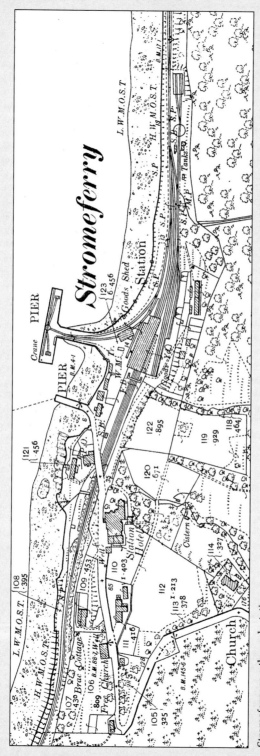

Reproduced from the 25", 1902 Ordnance Survey Map

Stromeferry as a through station.

The five low-water landings have been completed, and the fender-piles along the sides and outer head erected.

The works remaining undone are the concreting of 18 inches of depth on the top of the pier, and the laying of the main line, sidings, and turntables thereon.

Mr Best is making good progress with the works of the water-supply from Loch Scalpaidh, for Kyle station and pier.

The station offices and dwelling-houses for agents, porters and surfacemen at Plockton, Duirinish, Erbusaig and Kyle are being pushed forward with all speed.

From the late spring of 1897, more interest was gradually being taken in the Kyle extension as it was beginning to head towards its final stages.

On 14th May, the *Inverness Courier* reported that the laying of the permanent way had been completed a few days previously, and that the contractor's locomotives were now running regularly between Strome and Kyle. In stating that the line was expected to be opened in early July, the paper outlined some of the advantages that would then occur:

The opening of this track will be a great boon to the inhabitants of the west coast. It will bring the south of Skye within a short distance of Inverness. There will be no difficulty in spending a few hours in the Highland capital and getting back to Skye on the same day. As compared with the present circumstances, the fishing village of Plockton and the surrounding district will be placed in quite a different position. People will be carried at one penny per mile, instead of paying almost twopence per mile by steamer, and goods will be carried at half the rates now charged, without the risk of being damaged while being landed by boat. The facilities which will be afforded by the Highland Railway are sure to stimulate the fishing industry all along Lochalsh, and the people look forward with interest and pleasure to the opening of the line. This addition to the Highland Railway is sure to be very popular with tourists. It skirts the policies of Sir Kenneth Matheson of Lochalsh and Ardross, one of the finest residences in the north of Scotland. On several parts of the track, there are charming views of the hills of Skye, including the Cuillins.

Reference was made to the making of the line, with praise for the man in overall charge of the work:

Considering the difficulties the contractor had to contend with, it is a matter of congratulation to himself and his efficient staff that they got through the work so quickly. The quantity of rock-cutting on this extension is really one-fourth of the whole line, and some of it upwards of 80 feet deep. The station and sidings at Kyle had almost all to be blasted out of solid rock - some of it to a depth of 40 feet - and the quantity of explosives required for this huge piece of work was upwards of 45 tons. No person travelling on the line can have the slightest conception of the gigantic work accomplished, and almost within the time specified. Mr Best, the contractor, has pushed on this work with great energy. When in full swing, he had about 800 men working for a considerable time. The Highland Railway have been so fortunate in having the services of so pushing a man. Mr Best has several other large contracts in the South which occupied much of his attention, and the Kyle Extension was very much in the hands of Mr Best junior and his courteous manager, Mr Sloane, who is now giving the real Skye line its finishing touches.

And there was mention of the new, growing settlement at the terminus:

Kyle, where there were but two or three houses, has already become quite a village community. The Commercial Bank has built a large and commodious bank office. A post-office is being built, and several traders have built shops and stores. Building is still going on, and Kyle promises to become an important seaport in a few years. During the last three years, traders have had a good time of it and did a large stroke of business. Kyle Inn has often been taxed to its utmost capacity, but Mrs Finlayson and her courteous staff were always equal to the occasion.

On 21st May, the *Ross-shire Journal* published a description, in some detail, of the route

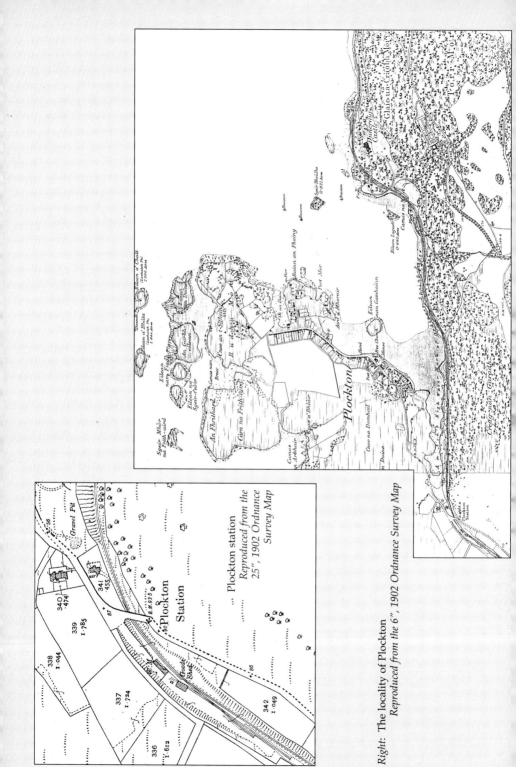

Right: The locality of Plockton
Reproduced from the 6", 1902 Ordnance Survey Map

... Plockton station
Reproduced from the
25", 1902 Ordnance
Survey Map

and works of the new railway and its terminus, from a correspondent who had travelled
on the line from Strome to Kyle:

The other day, through the kindness of the resident railway officials connected with Messrs John
Best and Sons, I, along with a friend, had the privilege of having a run over this most interesting
short line. The distance is only about 10 miles, but for grand and magnificent scenery, it has not
perhaps its equal anywhere else in Scotland.

After we had got comfortably seated in an open wagon, the engine moved slowly away, passing
under a large, iron, skew bridge carrying the district road over the railway - said road leading to
Balmacara, Dornie, etc. The line, for some distance, hugs closely to the seashore, while on the
other side is a thriving, young wood of fir, larch, etc. This is, as is all the ground through which
the line passes, the property of Sir Kenneth Matheson of Ardross and Lochalsh.

Immediately after leaving Strome Ferry, one gets some idea of the tremendous work entailed
upon the contractors, as rock-cuttings of from 20 to 40 feet in height are passed through, and this
even is as nothing almost compared with what is to be seen. A little further on, soon the hamlet
of Portchullin is passed, nestling between the railway and the sea. This place is best seen from the
Portree or Stornoway steamers while passing out of the Lochcarron firth. The houses are very
small and chiefly thatched with brackens. They look more like what is often to be seen in many
parts of Lewis or Skye. We never passed the place by sea, but it reminded us of a cluster of
beehives. There is just one slated house, and it gives one the idea that this must be the king's.

Shortly after passing, there is a quick curve in the line and Fernaig bridge is reached. There is a
heavy embankment on the other side, and this part gave the contractors much trouble. It was in
a rock-cutting just on the other side that the first serious accident by explosives took place - one
man being hurled from the cutting a great distance out into the sea, his mangled remains being
afterwards picked up out of the water, while several others were more or less injured. This, for
the first time, drew the attention of the Government to the works; and first, one official, and then
another, came down, including Colonel Majendie, Colonel Arthur Ford and others. The explosive
chiefly used in connection with the works was gelignite, one of the most powerful as yet known.
Afterwards, several deaths took place, and, on the suggestion of Colonel Majendie and under the
personal inspection of the local Inspector of Explosives (Mr Gordon, chief constable of the
county), a number of powder-magazines were erected at suitable points all along the line - there
being 11 in all, besides two large ones. The contractors and their 'gaffers' were seriously warned
and cautioned as to what they ought to do, and the result was, by the steps latterly taken, no
accident of a serious nature by explosives has taken place anywhere on the line for upwards of a
year past.

After leaving Fernaig, for some distance the line takes a somewhat sharp curve in order to get
well below Duncraig Castle, another of Sir Kenneth's seats; and right underneath the castle, the
second highest rock-cutting on the whole line is reached, it being 58 feet in height. All along here,
primroses everywhere abound in rich profusion, while the towers of the castle are seen through
the branches of the trees a short distance above. After getting clear of this cutting, a very good
view of the village of Plockton is got at some distance to the right, with a short arm of the sea
standing between. From this point, the village has a most interesting appearance, but we dare say,
like some other places, 'distance lends enchantment to the view'. A short distance above the
village, Plockton, the first station is reached; the substantial, concrete platform is well forward, as
is also the station master's house at a prominent point.

Passing on, there is not much of any great interest until Drumbuie, the second station, is reached.
At some distance, the village of the same name is seen away to the left. It appears to be of some
considerable size, and the villagers are in possession of good rigs of what appears to be well-tilled
land. Passing on for some distance, we come to the highest cutting on the whole line - that of
Erbusaig, 75 feet in height; and, looking up on either side, there is nothing seen above but the
clear, blue heavens. After passing through the cutting, the village of Erbusaig comes in sight on
the left. Mr Weir, MP for the county, the indefatigable questioner in the House of Commons, had
the interests of the villagers here at heart, as he took their case up and wanted more
accommodation for their boats, etc. There is one good, substantial bridge on the line opposite the
village, and to an outsider, it looks as if the people are better off than before, as the railway will
act as a shelter for their boats. Here, one feels the strong sea air coming in very fresh from the

Atlantic, and were the necessary accommodation to be had, this, of all others, is the spot for the worn-out and jaded city man of business as a complete place of rest.

A little further on, and after a good deal of more rock-cutting, another spot is passed where another death took place by rock-blasting. Almost immediately afterwards, we all at once come in sight of the village of Kyle, the terminus of our present journey. Let it be explained here that Kyle and Kyleakin are two different places - the former being in Ross-shire, the latter in Inverness-shire, on the opposite side of the entrance to Loch Duich - between the two places being a regular ferry. Kyleakin looks remarkably well and nicely-situated in the distance, having abundance of trees and shrubs, of which Kyle is destitute.

The new pier itself, we think, will always stand forth as one of the marvels of this short line. It has been recovered from the bed of the sea, and thousands of loads of rock, etc, have been buried there; and here, mountains have been removed and literally 'cast into the sea'. In the forming of the pier, hundreds of tons of cement have been used, and divers were specially employed for putting the tremendous blocks in position at the bottom. The biggest vessel afloat can now be moored at the quay. All the public offices, turning-tables, etc., are to be on the quay; and while we were there, workmen were engaged digging up the foundation in order to construct liquor-vaults in connection with the refreshment rooms. The quay, as we have already said, is most commodious. It has in it several cattle-creeps, where cattle, horses and sheep can be landed from the steamers at all states of the tide.

A considerable village is already springing up at Kyle - feus at reasonable figures being granted by Sir Henry MacAndrew, the commissioner upon the estates. A very commodious branch of the Commercial Bank of Scotland has just been finished and already opened for business. A site for a branch of the Caledonian Bank has already been secured. A shop and house intended for the post-office is also just about finished, and, though last not least, a police station is well forward. Let us hope that the occupants for this particular place will be few and far between.

We have thus given a hurried sketch of this wonderful, short railway, and we believe it will be a source of attraction to tourists and travellers from every part of the globe. It is hoped that it will be opened by the beginning of August, but there is much work in the way of finishing yet to be done - this more especially at the southern terminus and the pier.

At the Highland half-yearly shareholders' meeting back in April, the Directors had been confident that 'they would certainly be able to open the line to Kyle this summer'; but by the summer, there was still too much work to be completed. Nevertheless, on the evening of 22nd June, in connection with the first-ever concert and ball at Kyle, there was the novelty of the first-ever passenger train over the new line. The reason for the occasion was the celebration of the diamond jubilee, or 60th anniversary, of the accession to the throne, of Queen Victoria. The venue was the goods shed which was beautifully decorated for the occasion, and due to the kindness of William Sloane, the contract manager, a special carriage was run from Strome to Kyle for the convenience of those attending. Although the shed was large, it was inadequate for the accommodation of all of the 400 guests, but the enthusiastic dancing lasted until four o'clock in the morning.

Another journey - presumably by train, but this time of a formal nature - took place on 31st July, as reported by the *Inverness Courier*:

Through the courtesy on Saturday of the contractor, Mr Best, the officials of the Highland Railway Company at Strome Ferry paid a trip in the evening to the Kyle terminus. Including friends, about 150 took advantage of the trip. The company's and Mr Best's engineers, with their usual courtesy, accompanied the officials round the works, explaining the various arrangements of such.

On 7th August, a serious accident occurred, with the *North Star* recording that

. . . while a pilot engine was proceeding along the line near a place called Portnacloich, it came in contact with the contractor's engine, and three of the workmen were pitched out of a wagon and received severe injuries on the head and about the body and legs. Their names are: Duncan Finlayson, son of John Finlayson, Dornie; John Finlayson, Drumbuie; and Duncan MacMillan, Drumbuie. While their condition is very precarious, they are expected to recover.

In mid-August, work commenced on the new pier at Kyleakin, with the aim of the Highland Railway being to run a regular steam-ferry across the ½-mile narrows in time for the opening of the Kyle extension. However, the principal ferry communication for Skye would take place between Kyle and Portree, due to the faster steamer transport directly between the two places, compared to the horse-drawn vehicles over the poor road between Kyleakin and Portree. The pier at Kyleakin, which was to cost about £3,000, was being constructed of timber in such a manner that it could be extended if the traffic necessitated this. By early September, with the work being pushed forward rapidly, the piles had been driven in over the total length of the pier, of 240 feet, and it was expected that it would be completed in about a further six weeks.

Also in early September, a correspondent from Lochalsh noted for the *Inverness Courier* that the railway was in process of being ballasted and that the station master's house at Plockton was being plastered. 'A nicer station could not well be desired', he added, 'and the work done throughout is most satisfactory'. Then, in another note, dated 21st September, from Lochalsh, the writer and his friends were shown over the works of the harbour and the line, when they 'were astonished at the marvellous result exhibited':

> It is difficult to say which most to admire - the engineering skill on the one hand, or on the other, the courage of the contractor who undertook such a formidable work as making that harbour. The line itself was a sufficiently arduous business, but the harbour 'dings' it to mere nothingness, it may be said. The solidity of all that is visible, and not so visible, down deep in the water is something to set one thinking that very little is impossible to a capable engineer and contractor with plenty of money at their backs.

A second detailed, and a particularly descriptive, account of the line, the works and the terminus appeared in the *North Star* of 7th October from the paper's 'own representative':

> It was a bright October morning, and but for the purple of the hills and the gold of the bracken, one might have thought that the season was summer. The placid waters of Loch Carron, with its numberless, rocky islets, lay mirroring its rough, brown shores, and overhead, the barren hills rose in rugged grandeur, now gleaming bright in the play of light and shadow, and anon draped in gloomy mists and heavy belts of cloud. To the left, the hills rose in green slopes, with patches of cultivated land, and stretches of woodland and bracken, gleaming in all the variegated tints of autumn. Such is the entrance of the new Kyle Akin railway, the entire length of which is only 10½ miles.
>
> From beginning to end, it is one series of cuttings, and the total excavation has been estimated at 400,000 cubic yards. To accomplish this feat, nearly 70 tons of dynamite were used in blasting the impregnable rock. The line twists round from Strome station, passing along the side of the loch. At a distance of two miles, we reach the great Fernaig embankment, one of the engineering wonders of the line. Here, there waged for many months a strenuous battle with the sea, which has now been forced back 500 yards from the high-water mark. The accomplishment of this feat, however, was only a small portion of the difficulty with which they must contend, for now the great, frowning cliffs of Duncraig rose defiantly before them. The hardness of the red salt rock is indescribable, and no more despair-compelling work was ever engaged in. The boring was a laborious and painful task, and the dynamite charges were much heavier than was calculated upon. On the rugged sides of the cuttings, the evidences of the blasting are clearly perceptible.
>
> We pass through a series of cuttings. The hill-side on our left is clad with a profusion of wood and multitudinous clusters of fern, terraces of black rock overhung with rowans and beech, and

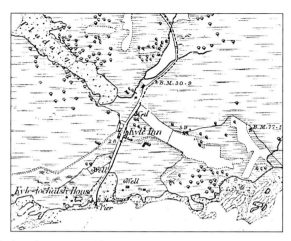

Kyle of Lochalsh before the coming of the railway.
Reproduced from the 6", 1874 Ordnance Survey Map

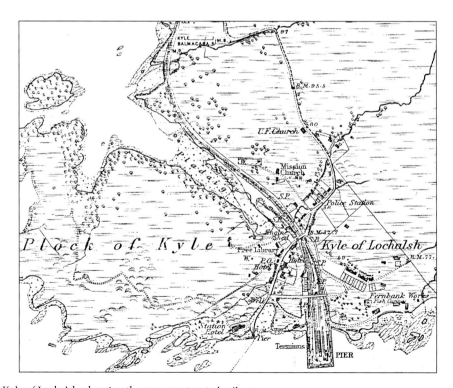

Kyle of Lochalsh, showing the now constructed railway.
Reproduced from the 6", 1902 Ordnance Survey Map

here and there, a waterfall hisses in our ears. We have now reached the great Craig cuttings, one of which is 65 feet high and 400 yards long. It is hewn out of red, salt rock, and 30 men were employed constantly for three years in accomplishing the work. Passing through woody patches, overtopped by ridges of brown rock, we catch a glimpse through the trees of the stately castle of Duncraig. The engine rumbles through another cutting, and to the right, at the bottom of a green brae, lies Plockton, a crescent-shaped village skirting the shores of a diminutive bay. The beach is rocky and dangerous, and is strewn with nets, boats and spars, and other evidences of the fishing industry, which will undoubtedly develop when the line is opened. The station is about a quarter of a mile distant from the village, and already, there are evidences of the village growing out in that direction, so that, in a few years, a greater Plockton may arise out of the ruins of the old.

Ascending the Strathie bank, there are visible evidences of cultivated land, and beyond, there is a little black peat-moss among the heath. The loch scenery now grows more wild, and beyond, in the distance, we catch a glimpse of the stone hills of Skye. We are rattled through a sharp cutting, and pass on our left a lonely glen, with a burn and a little bridge, peering through a rich profusion of dark fir. We are whirled through another cutting over a bare moor and reach the clachans of Drumbuie and Duirinish, little old-world villages scattered through a hollow among the hills. The little houses are built with the grey stones of the mountain and thatched with its brown heather, but they are mostly of that kind that are more picturesque than desirable. In front of the villages, there are poor little patches of cultivated land; solitary reapers cut and bind the grain and stook the little sheaves in a quaint, beehive-sort-of-shape. The womenfolks are digging out the potatoes, and one or two were raking rank-brown hay at the side of the burn. We saw a few fisherwomen on the road with creels on their backs, knitting loudly as they trudged along. We now pass the farm of Portnacloich, situated among mountain wildernesses; the sea prospect extends, and a glimpse is caught of a distant steamer among the misty islands of the West.

At length, the great Erbusaig cutting is reached, which is 600 yards long and 85 feet high. The hardness of its grey whin rock is indescribable, and, like the Craig cutting, the excavating and blasting was slow and laborious in the extreme. The line now curves round a crescent-shaped embankment similar to that of Fernaig, and on our left, the village of Erbusaig lies scattered in a deep valley on either side of a straggling burn. The biggins are similar to those in Duirinish and Drumbuie. One or two roofs, which have been newly thatched with decaying bracken, seem to assume the tints of autumn like the surrounding hills, and the effect is somewhat picturesque. There are a few trees on the banks of the little burn, and in the background appear one or two cultivated fields. The engine thunders through numberless cuttings, and here and there, the public road is built up and new bridges erected.

We now approach scenery of indescribable grandeur, and at length reach the Kyle of Lochalsh station, an island platform with five sidings on either side. We pass through a wide rock-cutting and step onto the platform. The station is large and commodious, and is fitted up with all modern conveniences; there are two refreshment rooms, ladies' and gentlemen's waiting-rooms, and steamer and railway booking-offices. The station master's room looks out on the pier and commands a fine view of the loch. The pier is 350 feet long and 225 feet in breadth. The depth of water at low tide is 25 feet, and there is a rise and fall of 18 feet. There are five low-water landings, constructed of granite and cement, for the convenience of passengers and other traffic. The arrangements on the pier are most complete. There are three turning-tables, and wagons can be run on at the right side and off at the left when they are loaded. The foundations were excavated by divers of all the loose material until a solid bottom of blue clay and rock was obtained. Huge blocks of cement, weighing seven or eight tons each, were built up to low water. Above this, they laid the liquid cement. The gravel for mixing purposes was taken up by excavators from a depth of 15 feet in Balmacara Bay, so that it was clean and hard, and entirely free from mud. The work has been carefully done and no crack or flaw is perceptible in the walls. The entire cost of the pier is roughly estimated at £40,000 to £50,000. The water-supply for the station and pier comes from an elevation of nearly 600 feet, at a distance of about three miles, and the Highland Railway Company have under consideration the working of the cranes on the pier by hydraulic power.

The village of Kyle of Lochalsh has already shown signs of life. There is a Commercial Bank, Victoria Buildings, and one or two villas of modern construction, while a new road has been cut on the side of the hill. Kyle House is to be fitted up as a temporary hotel, and a new building will at once be proceeded with. The prospect from the village is extensive and picturesque. On either side, the deep, narrow loch stretches out to the Atlantic; in front, overshadowing the ferry, rise the great stone hills of Skye. The little village of Kyleakin lies on the opposite shore; the ruins of Castle Moil, an old Highland fortress, rise on the left, and to the right, there is a patch of harvest field and a woody promontory. A wooden pier is being erected below the village, and a steamer is to ply on the ferry when the line is opened.

The contract of the new Kyle Akin railway is in the hands of Mr Best, the largest contractor north of Edinburgh. The work at first was principally under the control of Mr John Best junior, who showed exceptional ability and pushed the work on in all departments. His successor, Mr Sloane, is an admirable substitute, and he is an example of energy and skill. The whole engineering work has been done by Mr Murdoch Paterson, the veteran Engineer of the Highland Railway Company, and it is certainly a feat to be proud of. There are many great engineering feats on the Highland system, but the Kyle Akin line culminates all their efforts. Nowhere in the United Kingdom had greater difficulties to be contended with in the construction of such a short stretch of railway, while the undertaking as a whole has been accomplished with unprecedented success. It is expected that the railway will be opened for traffic within two months.

Back to the reality of the railway still having to be completed, there was a fatal accident at Plockton on 9th October when a navvy was run over by a train. He was Edward MacDonald, a 19 year-old native of Harris, and the circumstances of his death were as follows. Along with two other navvies, he had been in the last of the 11 wagons of a train that was engaged in ballasting operations over the line; and in a cutting about 400 yards south of Plockton station, while they were emptying the remaining small quantity of material onto the track, the slow-moving train gave a sharp jerk. At this instant, MacDonald lost his balance and fell onto the rails and under the wheels of the wagons, with the agonising result that, among other injuries, an arm was severed. Still alive, he was pulled to the side, but he survived for only 10 minutes longer. At the public inquiry at Dingwall Sheriff Court on 26th October, the jury recorded a verdict that he was accidentally killed.

At a special general meeting of the Highland shareholders back on 1st September, it had been explained that, while the Kyle line was approaching completion, the Directors had hoped that, by that time or very shortly afterwards, it would have been earning revenue for the company. Unfortunately, the contractor had been very much hampered by the great difficulty in obtaining labour because of the migration of men to the Mallaig and the Invergarry railways.* The belief held by the Highland company, having little knowledge of the social concerns of the navvies, was that they had left because these lines would be more pleasant for them to work on during the winter, but the real reason was the longer future of employment that they would secure on any materialising line than on one very near to completion.

Murdoch Paterson mentioned the departure of the navvies before the finish of the line, and he stated a further reason for this in his report of 1st October, to be read at the half-yearly shareholders' meeting on 27th October. He wrote:

> It was quite expected that this line would have been opened for traffic by now; and it would have been but for the scarcity of workmen. From early August till 20th September, a constant falling-off in the number of men took place. Many of them left for the Mallaig and Invergarry lines, and quite one-half of the remainder left about three weeks ago for harvesting the crops on their crofts. The permanent way has all been adjusted to line and level, but 4½ miles of it have to

* The West Highland Railway (Guarantee) Act, securing financial assistance from the Government towards the extension from Banavie to Mallaig, had been passed on 14th August, 1896, which was the same day as the passing of an Act for the independent, 24 miles-long Invergarry and Fort Augustus Railway, from Spean Bridge on the West Highland line, along the eastern side of the Great Glen, to Fort Augustus at the southern end of Loch Ness.

be top-ballasted and finished off, and it is at this work the scarcity of men is so much felt. Every effort is being made to have the line ready for the government inspector by the middle of the month, but much will depend on the number of men ballasting and the state of the weather. The station rooms and offices at Plockton, Duirinish and Kyle, with their water-supplies and other conveniences, are now ready for use.

The works of the new pier at Kyleakin, in Skye, for the new ferry steamer, are far advanced. The driving of the piles was completed on 23rd ultimo, and the bracing, joisting, flooring and low-water landing are so well advanced that the steam-ferry can be opened for public traffic at the same time as the line to Kyle.

The Highland Railway's half-yearly report, dated 6th October, recorded that the Kyle Extension was rapidly approaching completion and that it was expected to be opened about the beginning of November. By the time of the shareholders' meeting on 27th October, the building of the railway and pier had finished, and the government inspector was already in Inverness with the intention of proceeding over the line for its official inspection on the following day. The company was confident that he would pass the line as being fit for traffic, and if so, it would be opened on Tuesday, 2nd November. Meanwhile, by way of its issue of 27th October, it was now the turn of the *Northern Chronicle* to contain a further but shorter description of the line from the viewpoint of a correspondent recently having had the opportunity to make a trip from Strome to Kyle.

Through the kindness of Mr Sloane, manager for the contractor, the writer, with one or two others, had lately the privilege of travelling over the line, comfortably seated in a spring wagon which was driven by one of the contractor's tidy locomotives, *Lochalsh*. The day being fine and the atmosphere clear, the scenery was seen to great advantage.

Starting from Strome Ferry, the railway passes along the shores of Loch Carron for about a few miles, when it suddenly enters and skirts the policies of Duncraig Castle, the charming west-country seat of Sir Kenneth Matheson, and one of the finest residences in the north of Scotland. Unlike some other proprietors in the North, Sir Kenneth, much to his credit, encouraged, rather than objected to, this extension going through part of his policies, and his action in the matter is highly popular. A deep cutting through solid rock immediately below the castle prevents, however, anything more than a glimpse being obtained of the building. At the west end of the grounds, a substantial platform has been built for the special use of Sir Kenneth. From this point, there is a steep ascent to Plockton station, which is situated about three-fourths of a mile west of the village. The station buildings here are ample in accommodation, and are substantially built, with all the latest improvements. After passing this station, there is almost nothing to be seen - there being solid rock at every turning - until the train arrives at Duirinish station, a tidy little place, quite suitable for the wants of this district. Shortly after passing Duirinish station, and right on to Kyle, there is a charming view to be had of the headlands of Skye, including the Cuillins, which, on a clear day, can be seen with striking effect.

The train is now nearing the terminus, and in few minutes, we enter Kyle station. The buildings here are large and commodious. There is what is called an 'island platform', approached from the north and south sides, respectively, by two massive girder bridges, with easy approaches to the other different platforms, which extend several hundred feet, and are carried down close to the steamer landings. With the exception of a few yards, passengers can proceed on board steamer under cover - an advantage which will be much appreciated, especially on a stormy day. The pier is a large and massive piece of workmanship, the largest work of the kind on the west coast, and is built of concrete. It can accommodate several steamers at a time, to meet the requirements of the large fish traffic, which this pier is sure to command.

The correspondent also referred to the new settlement of Kyle and the increased tourist potential of the area:

Until lately, there were but three or four houses at Kyle, but it is now quite a flourishing village, with a bank, post-office, a number of shops, and a large kippering establishment, employing a

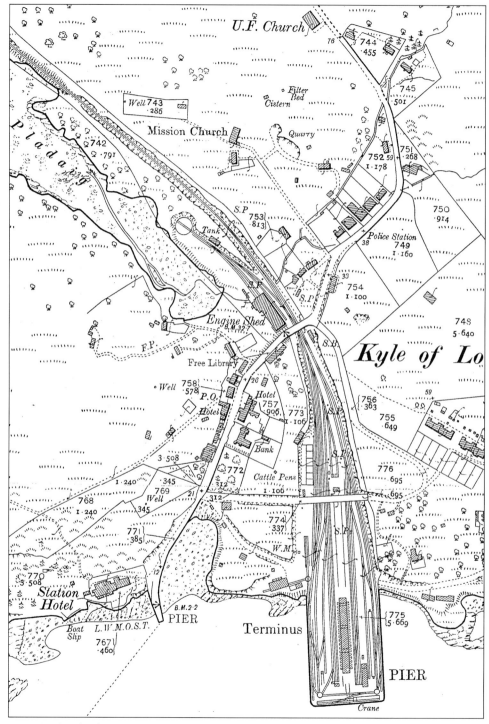

Kyle of Lochalsh terminus and village.   *Reproduced from the 25″, 1902 Ordnance Survey Map*

good number of men and women. Kyle, as a matter of fact, promises to become an important seaport in the near future. It need scarcely be said that Kyle pier will be a great acquisition in connection with the West Highland steamers. Tourists and others travelling by swift vessels during the summer and autumn can land here and complete the journey by rail. The Skye line has always been the admiration of tourists, and this addition will certainly add to its popularity.

The official inspection of the Kyle Extension took place on Thursday, 28th October, as arranged, when Major Sir Francis Marindin of the Railway Department of the Board of Trade went over the line. He was accompanied on a saloon carriage and engine by Sir George MacPherson-Grant, Chairman; Charles Steel, Manager; Murdoch Paterson, William Roberts and Alexander Newlands, Engineers;* William Garrow, Line Superintendent; Peter Drummond, Locomotive Superintendent; and John Best senior, contractor. Best had arrived in the district in early October in order to push forward the works in readiness for the inspection. The outcome of four years' work in making the railway was now in evidence before the inspector. He tested the bridges and the other features of the line thoroughly, and everything was found to be in excellent order, with Best having been congratulated upon the admirable manner in which he had carried out the contract. 'The Kyle line', as the *Inverness Courier* expressed the verdict, 'has received the official blessing of the Board of Trade, without which no British railway can be of any use to the public'.

The facts and figures of the Kyle Extension showed that it was something special in the British Isles. 'The new line is remarkable in many respects', declared the *Scottish Highlander*:

> It is 10¾ miles long, which distance, in itself, has nothing remarkable about it; but when it is stated that the line is a series of blast-cuttings through solid rock, skirting the sea, which, in several places, has been driven back many yards, the subject for remark is at once observed. It is believed that, in proportion to its length, no other line in the United Kingdom has such a great amount of rock-cutting in so short a distance.

As much as one-quarter of the length had to be forced through rock which was of the hardest description, being of the igneous or volcanic type, full of quartz, and very difficult to bore and blast. Some of the cuttings were extremely deep. The most impressive was that at Erbusaig, which was 85 feet deep, and from which 35,000 cubic yards had been excavated; while the other noteworthy ones were at Strome Ferry, at Craig, and at Duncraig; and there were numerous smaller but still significant cuttings that required much blasting. The site for the station, sidings and pier at Kyle had also to be cut out of solid rock to the extent of 100,000 cubic yards, with several parts being from 30 to 40 feet deep. The quantity of explosives used in the excavations for the railway and the pier exceeded 50 tons, and the sum expended for this was £6,000. The cost of the whole works amounted to £200,000, made up of £135,000 for the line and £65,000 for the pier. Thus, at an average cost of £12,800 per mile for the railway - or £19,400 per mile inclusive of the pier, which was an integral part of the scheme - the Kyle Extension became, in proportion to its length, the most expensive section of railway in the British Isles, being considerably more so than the £4,500 per mile of the original Skye line from Dingwall to Strome Ferry.

The steepest gradient on the extension was 1 in 60, which occurred on several short stretches between Duncraig and Portnacloich, but this was much less extreme than the longer 1 in 50 gradients on the original line. What was marginally the heaviest of the 1

---

* In 1891, Roberts had succeeded Paterson as Engineer of the Highland Railway's opened lines, with Paterson remaining Engineer for the lines under construction, while Newlands was the Resident Engineer on the Kyle Extension.

in 60 gradients on the extension formed most of the ascent from Duncraig that ran for just over half a mile, and carried the track dramatically along a ledge above the bay opposite Plockton to the station above the village. There were two minor summits - one being at Plockton station, immediately west of which was a half-mile descent at 1 in 60 as far as Strathie; and then there was a rise for ¾ mile, ending at 1 in 60, to a slightly-higher summit at the crossing of the Allt Dhuirinish, east of Duirinish station.

Praise was given for the excellent standard of construction and for those who had been responsible. 'The line is solidly and substantially built', commented the *Scottish Highlander*, which also stated that 'the workmanship reflects the highest credit on Mr Best, the contractor; on the able Engineer of the Highland company, Mr Murdoch Paterson, CE; and on the Resident Engineer, Mr Newlands.

The *Inverness Courier* acknowledged that 'the work of construction was admirably designed and admirably carried out by Mr Paterson', and that Mr Best had 'executed his contract to the entire satisfaction of the company and of Major Marindin of the Board of Trade', while adding:

> There is nothing shabby or shoddy about the Kyle railway. Not an ounce of lime mortar was used in its construction - nothing but Portland cement of sterling quality.

For the *Northern Chronicle*, the writer who had managed to make a trip on the line a short time previously had already provided words of commendation within his description:

> The Highland Railway Company is to be congratulated on having secured the services of so efficient a contractor. Mr Best, who had several other large contracts in the South, was unable to be much on the spot, and the work was carried on by his popular manager, Mr William Sloane.

The new pier and port at Kyle, in conjunction with the extension of the railway, would be a vast improvement over the facilities and conditions that had been in existence at Strome Ferry for the previous 27 years. The same writer for the *Northern Chronicle* had remarked: 'It is often impossible to get on board, without holding on by both hands, at Strome Ferry, and it is to be hoped this won't be repeated at Kyle'. The massive pier was 120 yards long by 75 yards wide, with a depth of water at low tide of 25 feet, and it contained five low-water landings for the various states of the tide. The Highland Railway had also built, as intended, a substantial timber pier at Kyleakin, at a cost of £3,000, for the use of the new steam ferry that would cross the 1,000 yards width between the mainland and Skye. As the *Inverness Courier* had declared in summarising the scheme:

> The extension of the Highland Railway system from Strome Ferry westwards to Kyle is a *fait accompli*. The Kyle line will considerably accelerate the journey from Portree and Stornoway, and the Western Isles generally, to Inverness and the South. Instead of coming up-channel to Strome - there to join the railway - the steamers from the West will put in at Kyle and practically drop their passengers into the Highland trains - thus evading a somewhat difficult waterway of over 10 miles. The splendid pier at Kyle is completed, and everything is in readiness for the transfer of the passengers from steamer to train. A steamboat has also been chartered by the Highland company to ply on the narrow ferry between Kyle and Kyleakin on the coast of Skye. There, then, you have the real 'Skye line'.

Chapter Thirteen

The Opening

The 'real Skye line' was to be opened on Tuesday, 2nd November, 1897, as planned; but like the opening of the original line from Dingwall to Strome Ferry in 1870, there would be no formal ceremony, although there was to be a banquet at Strome, as in 1870. Nevertheless, on a beautiful morning, great interest was shown in the new line and in the activities of the day by the inhabitants of the district and also by a large number of excursionists from Portree and Stornoway, who had been given the opportunity by David MacBrayne of cheap tickets for a sail to Kyle to witness the opening. The *Gael* steamer conveyed 300 passengers from Portree, where the day was observed as a holiday in honour of the occasion and of the delight at having a new Skye railway, while the *Lovedale* brought 200 from Stornoway. With the people of Lochalsh, the excursionists were then offered a run on the new line to Strome and back for a reduced fare. The first service train for passengers and mail had departed from Kyle at 6 am, and the first to head for the new western terminus had set out from Inverness at 8.35 am, leaving Dingwall at 9.35. The *Ross-shire Journal* recorded that this train left Strome 'about noon, a few minutes after the advertised time, and it was literally packed with young and old, anxious to participate in the first trip on the new railway', and that 'it was the first time for many of these people to have the privilege of a run in a train, so that their innocent and youthful behaviour was to many full of humour and interest'.

On the previous evening, some of the Highland Directors and officials had left Inverness by a special train, so that they would be present at Strome early on the Tuesday for the opening. On that morning, they went over the line to Kyle and then returned to Strome in time for the banquet. This commenced at half past twelve in the Station Hotel, with a large number of guests at the invitation of the Highland Railway. Presiding over the proceedings was Sir George MacPherson-Grant, the Highland's Chairman; and the other Directors in attendance were Sir Kenneth Matheson of Lochalsh, James Grant-Peterkin of Grange, and Francis Darwin of Muirtown. The officials of the company who were present included Charles Steel, Manager; William Gowenlock, Secretary; George Thomson, Goods Manager; William Garrow, Line Superintendent; William Roberts, Engineer; Alexander Newlands, Resident Engineer; and Peter Drummond, Locomotive Superintendent. Among the numerous guests were Sir Kenneth MacKenzie of Gairloch, John Best senior, John Best junior, William Sloane, and David Hope MacBrayne and Laurence MacBrayne, sons of the famous steamboat owner. Apologies for absence were received from David MacBrayne senior, Sir John Fowler, Murdoch Paterson, Sir Henry MacAndrew, and Sheriff Hill of Dingwall.

Sir George MacPherson-Grant, amid applause, referred to the expansion of the Highland Railway system from the Inverness and Nairn line in 1855 to what had now occurred with the opening of the Kyle Extension:

I will not go into the branches by which the present system is built up, but I will content myself by saying that, last year, the little 15 miles between Inverness and Nairn developed into 480 miles; and today, 10 miles are to be added to that distance. I am here to congratulate you and myself that we have been able to open this line to Kyle, which, I hope, will confer a benefit on the people of this part of the country. I am not a Socialist and I am not a Tory, but I should like to see a fair return for my money, and I should like to see the condition of the people on the west coast improved as much as possible. Some people are apt sometimes to be a little hasty. If the Highland Railway had launched into great and extensive schemes early in life, I do not know that the progress would be beyond that which we hail with such satisfaction today. Although blamed in

175

Kyle of Lochalsh from the west on the opening day of the Kyle Extension, with the *Lovedale* steamer at the pier. The station master's house stands prominently amid the rocky terrain. The road through the cutting on the left of the picture connects the station and pier with the main street of Kyle, which is out of view to the left. Further construction work for the new and expanding village is clearly visible near the centre. The view is along Loch Alsh towards the hills of the mainland, but part of Skye is seen at the extreme right. *British Railways*

Kyle of Lochalsh station and pier from the north, at the time of opening. This picture vividly indicates the degree of cutting that was required at the terminus. Skye and the 2,400 ft peak of Beinn na Caillich lie directly across Kyle Akin, with Castle Maol faintly visible near the right. From the station master's house on the left, a sea and mountain panorama, from west through south to east, is obtained. *British Railways*

some quarters for being slow, possibly there might have been occasions when that blame was not altogether undeserved; but our progress has been fairly sure, and I hope that this will be the sentiment in the future, as in the past, by which the Directors will be impressed.

As the present celebration is not only interesting in the life of the Highland line, and pregnant with great advantage and usefulness to the islands and the West, I cannot help referring for a moment to the progress and position of the Skye line. The Skye line was opened in 1870, and no one can mention the Skye line without mentioning the name of a man who did more than anyone else to bring the advantages of communication to this part of the country. I refer to the late Sir Alexander Matheson. And I am glad to see two sons of my old friend with us on this occasion. One of them is a dear and able colleague of mine on the Directorate of the Highland line, and a man who is certainly worthy to bear the mantle of his distinguished father, who did so much in opening up the Highlands. I might also say in passing that among those connected with the Highland Railway whom we miss on this occasion is our friend, Mr Murdo Paterson, who is absent through indisposition. He was the first Engineer of the Skye line, and he has been the Engineer until the finish.

The project of the line to Kyle of Lochalsh was not a new one. It was the original scheme of the Dingwall and Skye Railway, but owing to circumstances to which I need not allude, the line was not intended to go beyond Attadale, although it came to Strome Ferry. The idea of going on to Kyle was not abandoned, and today, you are here to see the idea fulfilled. I trust now that the people of the West will take full advantage of the new line. That is the crucial point. We have brought the line here. Will you, gentlemen of the West, take advantage of it? This line has been opened with no niggard hand, but, at the same time, you must remember the pockets of the shareholders. The more you patronise the line, the more good you will do to this company, to which you owe something; and the more you strengthen the hands of the company, the more you will put in our hands to advance the progress of the Highlands and islands.

You are living in a different dispensation from what you lived in yesterday. You are going home by train today. That train is run with the greatest punctuality, and if you are five minutes late, Mr MacBrayne will not guarantee you catching the boat! I have to congratulate you upon one fact. The remark, I may say, is not original, but it is that you have got the 'best' railway in the world. Whether Mr Best is responsible for it or not, I do not know!

Sir Kenneth MacKenzie of Gairloch, having outlined the improvements in the social conditions and the communications of the Highlands over the last century, remarked further that they in Ross-shire were proud of the fact that the islands had received their earliest communication with the railway system of the kingdom through Ross-shire, and that the head of the new extension was at Kyle, also in Ross-shire, which was the most central part of the west coast at which any railway could be placed. Sir Kenneth, however, had one 'complaint' to make, when he added:

I hope you will not think me ungracious if I pick a little quarrel with the Directors of the Highland Railway Company for the name that they have given to that historic place, Kyle Akin, in naming the station 'Kyle of Lochalsh', as it now appears on the timetables. Everyone who is a philologist knows that *kyle* is the Celtic equivalent for the Saxon 'strait' or 'narrows' - a passage of water. It does not mean 'land'. This particular kyle - this passage of water - had, from time immemorial, been identified with the name of King Haco of Norway. I have to confess I know nothing of Haco, except that he lived very long ago and has been immortalised in Kyle Akin. For this reason, I am sorry to see the name of Haco lost, and I regret our place-names should be deprived of their poetic interest. Lochalsh has a story of its own, as well as Kyle Akin. There was a Celestine of Lochalsh, a brother of one of the Lords of the Isles, who had figured in the history of the Highlands. Celestine of Lochalsh has long since passed into the realm of history, but Haco was a subject of history in the time of Celestine, and must have seemed to belong to antiquity, and perhaps to command veneration. At all events, Celestine never thought of changing the name, and he left to that monarch his full right in the name of the kyle; and the first attempt to deprive him of it seems to be made by the railway pioneers today. I hope the name of Kyle Akin is not to be lost by calling the station 'Kyle of Lochalsh'. I trust the Directors might find it possible to stick to the old name of Kyle Akin, or have 'North Kyle Akin' and 'South Kyle Akin'.

Highland Railway Directors, officials and guests at the opening of the Kyle Extension.

G.E. Langmuir

Kyle of Lochalsh on the opening day of the Kyle Extension. The engine is a 'Skye Bogie' 4-4-0.

D. St John Thomas

John MacPherson-Grant, son of Sir George, proposed the health of the Engineer, Murdoch Paterson, paying a high compliment to his outstanding ability in the construction of the line, and hoping that he would be able to witness the crowning achievement at the completion of the Aviemore line the following year. William Roberts responded on behalf of Paterson, stating that his work would bear the scrutiny of an expert; and he also referred to the excellent services of Alexander Newlands, the Resident Engineer, who had shown a great amount of ability and devotion in his work.

Charles Steel proposed the health of the contractor, John Best, adding that all who had been over the line would be unanimous in the opinion that he had done his work thoroughly and well. The railway would stand as an abiding memorial to the great ability and successful efforts of Murdoch Paterson and John Best. He had had the pleasure on Thursday of going over the line with the government inspector, such that no higher testimony could be given than this: that, at Kyle, when he asked Sir Francis Marindin for his conclusion, he was told, 'It is all right'. Then, when Steel asked, 'Can we open the line?', Sir Francis answered, 'Certainly'. Sir Francis Marindin was one of the most experienced government inspectors, added Steel, and to have his unhesitating assent to the line was a very high tribute to the contractor.

Sir George MacPherson-Grant announced that a telegram had been dispatched to Murdoch Paterson, congratulating him on the successful opening of the line, and that William Roberts had received the following telegram in reply:

My best thanks for your warm congratulations, and very sorry I am unable to be with you. Delighted to know your trip from Strome Ferry to Kyle, and by Gael to Kyle Akin and back, has come off so pleasantly and successfully. Hope you are all having a fine, clear day and are thoroughly enjoying your luncheon in the midst of the pure air of Lochalsh.

In conclusion, Sir George expressed the hope to his large audience that this was not be the last occasion upon which they would meet to celebrate the further advance of the Highland Railway Company.

After the banquet, the guests were conveyed over the highly-scenic line by the special train. 'The magnificent views of mountain peaks, bathed in sunshine, and placid waters perfectly reflecting the hills and rocky promontories were commented upon in enthusiastic language', said the *Inverness Courier*. At a number of vantage points along the route, including the stations of Plockton and Duirinish, flags and banners were displayed in honour of this great event in the history of Lochalsh, Skye and the West Highlands. Streamers were suspended from the bridge at Duncraig private platform, and flags were also displayed from Duncraig Castle, while some of the residents in the vicinity of the line had imposing flags floating over their houses. 'On arrival at Kyle', reported the *Northern Chronicle*, 'the scene was one of striking activity'; and here, 'where a splendid view was obtained of the magnificent scenery for which this new line is certain to become famed', the two steamers *Gael* and *Lovedale* were ready to return with their excursionists to Portree and Stornoway. A large crowd had gathered on the pier to witness the departure of the first passenger steamers from the new port of Kyle, with the *Ross-shire Journal* noting that 'the utmost bustle and animation were in evidence'. Hearty cheers were raised by the onlookers as both vessels, decorated with bunting, steamed away, and there was a response of rockets and gunfire from the seamen on board. In the evening, the Directors, officials and their guests returned from Kyle to Inverness by special train, and, said the *Inverness Courier*, they 'found themselves in a city of fog after spending the day in a beautifully-clear atmosphere'.

What was to be seen from the railway was most impressive, as had been described in the issue of the *Inverness Courier* on the opening date - this stating that the line

Kyle pier on the opening day of the Kyle Extension, with the MacBrayne Stornoway and Portree steamers, *Lovedale* and *Gael* respectively.   *G.E. Langmuir*

The *Gael* leaving Kyle pier for Portree with the 300 day excursionists who formed part of the celebrations of the opening of the Kyle Extension.   *G.E. Langmuir*

. . . stretches along the beautiful southern coast of Loch Carron, offering attractive lakeside views and glimpses of isles and islets. The loch is not very wide, and one may view the Applecross coast all the way to the sea. Striking views of Scalpay and Raasay are obtainable, and as one goes further Kylewards, Skye, their big brother, becomes the foreground of a noble picture of sea and mountain. The magnificent peaks of the Cuillins and other mountains of Skye are so near that nothing of their majesty is missed by the railway traveller, who can easily fancy that he is looking out upon the Sierra Nevada.

Not specific but nevertheless also highly praiseworthy were these words from the *Ross-shire Journal*: 'The scenery, in a sentence, along the new line ranks undoubtedly among the grandest and most picturesque in Scotland; in fact, along the route there is scarcely a yard but is romantic and inspiring'. The *Glasgow Herald*, in providing a good coverage of the day's events and the railway's features - considering the city's distance from Lochalsh - declared that the line 'will probably rank as the most remarkable piece of railway-engineering work in the country; while, for scenic attractions along its route, it is perhaps unapproachable in the British Isles alike for its rugged grandeur and variety of loch and mountain scenery'. In respect of the scenery, it was indeed appropriate that the meteorological conditions for the opening day were better than expected. The *Northern Chronicle* commented that 'the weather during the day was warm and pleasant, and the rugged scenery of the western seaboard was seen at its best'; while the *Inverness Courier* was more expressive in its weather report:

In regard to weather, which is often a matter of concern on the west coast, the day was perfectly delightful. The air was balmy and the sky was cloudless, the sun having a quite splendid effect in the afternoon. Seldom is the day so fine in the West in November, and if it be an augury of the fortunes of the new line, these must prove brilliant indeed.

Perhaps, the fine weather on this day was not too surprising in view of the fact that bright and dry conditions had also generally been the case for the previous two weeks - something that was considered unusual in the area at the beginning of winter. The day formed an admirable beginning for the new line, as was well summarised by the *Scottish Highlander*: 'On all sides, the greatest enthusiasm prevailed, and the day being one of the finest that could be desired, the opening of the Kyle Akin extension of the Highland Railway passed off with great *éclat*.'

The *Scottish Highlander* also reminded its readers of the convenience afforded by the extension, in that 'the Highland company are now able to run their trains right onto the pier at Kyle, which is almost within hail of the Misty isle, thus avoiding the slow and sinuous steamer journey from Strome', and that 'it is only a matter of a few yards to transfer from rail to steamer'. And, said the *North Star*:

Skye is practically an island no longer. From the terminus of the railway extension to Kyle of Lochalsh, it is but a leap across the water. Strome Ferry is now quiet and deserted-looking, and MacBrayne's steamers no longer sail up Loch Carron. But what the railway has taken away from Strome, it has conferred upon Kyle of Lochalsh, and the little village has been practically built in a day. Besides the new pier at Kyle, another has been erected below the village of Kyleakin on the opposite shore, and the Highland Railway are to run a steamer on the ferry. It will, therefore, be no longer a far cry to Skye.

The increased facilities are sure to improve the traffic on the Dingwall and Strome line, and when the herring-fishing season again comes round, the Highland will undoubtedly get the lion's share of the traffic. Compared with Kyle, the facilities for the loading and dispatch of traffic at Oban are much inferior. The former pier is larger and built specially for such traffic. The wagons can be run in at one end, loaded, turned at each corner, and run off at the other side. The cranes are to be worked by hydraulic power and will be very powerful. Then the low-water landings

Kyle pier and station from the east, overlooked by the station master's house, on the opening day. Skye is in the background.   *G.E. Langmuir*

An early postcard of Kyle of Lochalsh village, with a message written in 1901. This view from the north, taken above the Plockton road, shows the development of Kyle since the arrival of the railway in 1897. The main street lies beyond the large building in the centre of the picture, which is the engine shed. The steamer heading for the pier is the *Lovedale* from Stornoway; and in the background is Kyleakin village on Skye.   *J.L.Stevenson*

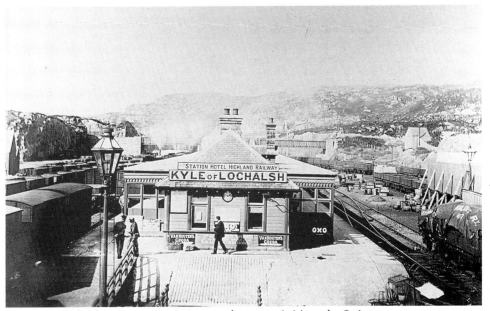

Kyle of Lochalsh station *c*. 1900, looking north, as recorded from the *Gael* steamer.

R. Charnley

Main Street, Kyle of Lochalsh *c*. 1900, looking north. The Kyle Hotel - initially the Kyle Inn, and one of the few buildings at Kyle before the arrival of the railway - is clearly seen on the right, and a small part of the Commercial Bank of Scotland - with its building dating from 1896 - is discernible on the extreme right.

R. Charnley

Strome Ferry *c.* 1900, showing the replacement station building, the cutting of the Kyle Extension below the hamlet, and the empty and largely disused pier.					*J.L. Stevenson*

An excursion train heading west along the shore of Loch Carron in the early 1900s.
					G.E. Langmuir

will enable passengers to come off and on the boats without experiencing the usual inconveniences at such piers. As the captain of the SS *Irene* said, 'It is the best pier north of Southampton'.

The railway was said to be equipped with everything necessary and modern that would ensure the smooth running of the trains. New signalling and interlocking arrangements were a special feature, especially at Kyle where several lines converged upon the pier and where the signal cabin contained more than 60 levers. The signalling machinery was made by Dutton and Co. of Worcester, whose proprietor, Mr Dutton, had been present at the banquet. The line was worked on the tablet system, by which only one train could be on a stretch of line at the one time, and which the Highland Railway was introducing beneficially on its other lines. The large pier, too, in being able to accommodate several steamers, contained excellent facilities in connection with these and the trains. Three large and powerful travelling-cranes had been erected, such that fish and goods could be transferred in a very short time. They worked on the hydraulic principle, with the water-supply coming from Loch Scalpaidh, 2½ miles distant and 600 feet high.

The Highland Railway, in constructing the Kyle Extension, had given much consideration to passengers and staff. At Kyle station, as well as there being the usual waiting rooms and offices, there was both a first class and a third class refreshment room. The intermediate stations of Plockton and Duirinish were considered to be smart-looking, substantial, commodious and up-to-date in respect of their requirements and comforts. At Duncraig, there was also the private platform for the use of Sir Kenneth Matheson and others going to and from the castle. For their staff, the company had built terraces of dwelling-houses at Kyle, Erbusaig, Duirinish and Plockton. At Kyle and Plockton, there was a separate house for the station master, and the elevated position of each house commanded a magnificent view - from Kyle, looking across Kyle Akin to Skye; and from Plockton, overlooking the bay towards Duncraig. The station masters for the extension were: Mr Douglas, at Kyle, having been transferred from Strome Ferry; Mr MacLeod, at Duirinish, from Achnashellach; Mr Fraser, at Plockton, from Grantown; and Mr Cameron, at Strome Ferry, from Pitlochry.

The Kyle Extension shortened the sea-journey to and from Portree by about an hour, compared to Strome Ferry, as the Isle of Skye in general, with its population of 15,000, was brought into more convenient and direct contact with the mainland. The south-eastern portion, especially, was now within a few hours of Dingwall and Inverness, and, similarly, it was possible for visitors from the two towns to spend some time on the island and return the same day. Unfortunately, for passengers crossing to and from Skye by Kyle Akin, only a large rowing-boat, called a 'gabbart' or 'garboard', that was fitted with a sail, constituted the ferry between the villages of Kyle and Kyleakin, instead of the steam vessel that had been anticipated and advertised. The ferry rights had been purchased from Lord MacDonald of Sleat by the Highland Railway, under the powers of the Highland Railway Act, 1893, and the ferry was leased to Captain Finlayson of Kyle, who operated the service with rowing-boats that were provided by the company. However, there was a once-a-day steamboat connection between Kyle and Kyleakin in each direction by way of David MacBrayne's Kyle-Portree passenger and mail service, with Portree forming the principal place of communication for the island's residents and visitors. Originally called *Kiltaraglen*, it became *Port an Righ* - from the Gaelic, meaning 'Port of the King' - after the visit of King James V of Scotland in 1540. 'Portree', said MacBrayne's 1895 guide-book *Summer Tours in Scotland*, 'contains 2,500 inhabitants, principally engaged in fishing and cloth-weaving. It has now four hotels, a post- and telegraph-office, and branches of three banks'. The town and the island were now

Kyle of Lochalsh station c. 1900, with a 'Skye Bogie' on a goods train.

Locomotive Publishing Co.

Kyle of Lochalsh station *c.* 1900, with a mixed train headed by 'Skye Bogie' No. 85.

Locomotive Publishing Co.

Kyle of Lochalsh station *c.* 1900. The engine of the goods train is 'Skye Bogie' 4-4-0 No. 70, the first of its class, and the steamer is the *Lovedale*. *R. Charnley*

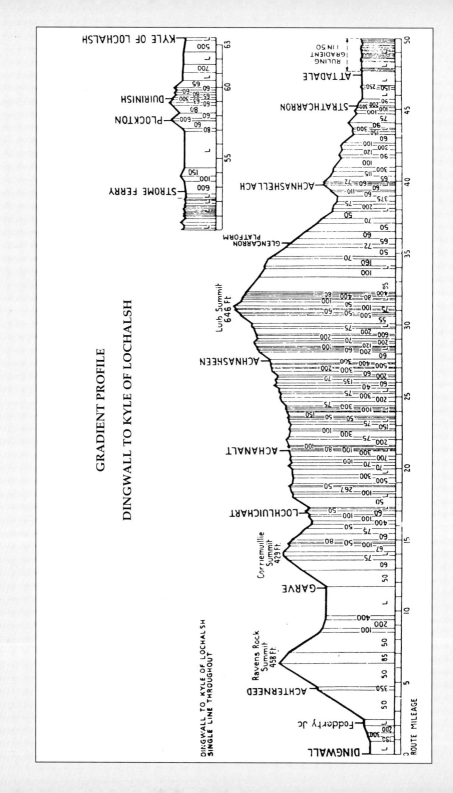

GRADIENT PROFILE

DINGWALL TO KYLE OF LOCHALSH

DINGWALL TO KYLE OF LOCHALSH
SINGLE LINE THROUGHOUT

served by what was truly the Skye railway; as was the largest town and port of the Hebrides and North-West Highlands - Stornoway, with its population of 3,000.

The new railway immediately began to provide an improvement in the conveyance of Stornoway fish. The *Inverness Courier* contained a note regarding the first cargo, taken on 3rd November:

Fish Traffic at Kyle. On Wednesday, the day after the opening of the Kyle railway, the first consignment of fish was carried over the line. The consignment, which came from Stornoway, arrived in Inverness in time to be sent on by the forenoon mail to London, where it arrived before the fish market yesterday. Previously, fish going by the same route did not reach London until some hours later.

The first timetable, in stating that the extension 'gives access to some of the grandest and most picturesque scenery in Scotland', communicated the information that a steam ferry-boat would ply between Kyle and Kyleakin. With three trains to and from Kyle per day, except Sundays, a composite version of the services, showing selected stations on the Skye line and the Strathpeffer branch, read as follows:

		am	am	am	am	am	pm	pm	pm
Inverness	d.			8.35		10.50		5.10	
Dingwall	d.	7.40	9.30	9.35	11.15	11.55	4.05	6.15	6.08
Strathpeffer	a.	7.50	9.40	-	11.25	-	4.15	-	6.18
Achterneed				9.47		12.10 pm		6.30	
Garve				10.06		12.30		6.58	
Achnasheen				10.45		1.05		7.40	
Strome Ferry				11.51		2.10		9.00	
Plockton				12.03 pm		2.22		9.17	
Duirinish				12.08		2.28		9.24	
Kyle of Lochalsh	a.			12.20		2.40		9.40	

		am	am	am	am	pm	pm	pm	pm
Kyle of Lochalsh	d.	6.00			10.30				4.55
Duirinish		6.11			10.41				5.10
Plockton		6.17			10.47				5.20
Strome Ferry		6.30			11.00				5.40
Achnasheen		7.30			12.00 pm				7.00
Garve		8.02			12.30				7.49
Achterneed		8.20			12.48				8.12
Strathpeffer	d.	-	8.35	10.15	-	1.25	4.25	8.05	-
Dingwall	a.	8.35	8.45	10.25	1.10	1.35	4.35	8.15	8.28
Inverness	a.	9.32			2.05				9.25

The Highland Railway also advertised the following MacBrayne's steamer services that connected with the trains at Kyle:

Portree and Kyle of Lochalsh:
 Leave Portree daily (Sundays excepted) at 6.45 am, calling at Raasay, Broadford and Kyleakin, and arriving at Kyle of Lochalsh in connection with the express train for the South at 10.30 am.
 Leave Kyle of Lochalsh daily (Sundays excepted) not earlier than 2.45 pm, calling at Kyleakin, Broadford and Raasay, reaching Portree about 5.45 pm.
Stornoway and Kyle of Lochalsh Direct:
 Leave Stornoway for Kyle of Lochalsh daily (Sundays excepted) at 1.00 am, to connect with the 10.30 am train.
 Leave Kyle of Lochalsh for Stornoway daily (Sundays excepted) not before 2.45 pm.

Stornoway and Kyle of Lochalsh via Portree:
Leave Stornoway for Portree every Monday and Thursday morning; thence Kyle of Lochalsh every Tuesday and Friday morning.
Leave Kyle of Lochalsh about 2.45 pm every Tuesday and Friday; Portree same evenings; reaching Stornoway every Wednesday and Saturday evening.
Portree, Gairloch, Aultbea and Poolewe:
Leave Portree for Gairloch, Aultbea and Poolewe after arrival from Kyle of Lochalsh every Friday evening. All goods for these ports should be at Portree on the Wednesday previous to sailing days to prevent delays.
Kyle of Lochalsh, Portree, Tarbert, Rodel, Lochmaddy and Dunvegan:
Leave Kyle of Lochalsh every Monday, Wednesday and Friday not before 2.45 pm; and Portree every Tuesday, Thursday and Saturday morning for Tarbert, Rodel, Lochmaddy and Dunvegan; returning every Monday, Wednesday and Friday morning.
Passengers and goods for the Highland and connecting lines are also conveyed via Kyle of Lochalsh and Portree by *Claymore*, *Clansman* or other steamer, leaving Portree, for Kyleakin, Balmacara, Glenelg, Isleornsay, Armadale, etc., every Tuesday and Friday not before 3.00 am. For Ullapool and Lochinver: from Portree every Tuesday evening, calling on the voyage to Stornoway.
On the west-coast steamers, breakfasts, luncheons, dinners and refreshments of all kinds can be had.
When, from any cause, the steamer from either Stornoway or Portree does not reach Kyle of Lochalsh in time for passengers or other traffic being forwarded from Kyle of Lochalsh by the connecting train, they will be forwarded by the first advertised train after arrival.
Note No. 1: The company do not guarantee time being kept by the steamers; and they reserve the power to call at intermediate places to suit the requirements of the traffic.
Note No. 2: Livestock is conveyed by the west-coast steamers solely at owners risk, and when not in bags, boxes, crates or hampers, will only be accepted for conveyance with some person in charge.
Note No. 3 Tickets for the steamers must be taken out before going on board at Stornoway, Portree and Kyle of Lochalsh.
Note No. 4: The company reserve the right of making alterations in the above arrangements at any time they find it necessary.

At the time of the opening of the extension, the hotel at Kyle was not ready for business, but it was brought into use on 18th December. The *Northern Chronicle*, in referring to an advertisement for the opening of the hotel, commented: 'The house, though not large, has been comfortably furnished, and the site is one of the loveliest on the west coast, and within five minutes' sailing of the island of Skye'. The advertisement read:

Highland Railway Company's Hotel, Kyle of Lochalsh, Ross-shire:
This hotel will be opened for the reception of visitors on Saturday, 18th inst. It contains coffee-, smoking-, and drawing-rooms, and a number of comfortably-furnished bedrooms.
Accommodation will be reserved on receipt of telegrams, which will be sent free of charge on application to the station master at any station on the Highland Railway.
Magnificent views of sea and land, and of the Isle of Skye, are obtainable from the hotel.
The hotel is only five minutes from the Isle of Skye, which can be reached by steam ferry.
Charges moderate.

Chapter Fourteen

The Highland Railway Era

An idea of the early success that had resulted from the railway and the port of Kyle was supplied by the *Inverness Courier* of 13th May, 1898, just over six months after the opening:

Heavy Traffic at Kyle. During the past 10 days, the traffic at the new pier of Kyle of Lochalsh, in transmitting all kinds of plant for the fishing industry at Stornoway, has been considerable, and the commotion has been great. From 10 to 12 new fish-curing firms will be represented in Stornoway this year, and every available piece of ground suitable for curing has been taken up. It is said that there is now, at the capital of the Lews, one of the largest fishing fleets ever seen there, and it is to be hoped their expectations will be realised. The Highland Railway Company, in extending their line to Kyle, have done much to develop the fishing industry on the west coast. The pier, being large and commodious, with the latest improvements for quick dispatch, cannot fail to be a great boon, especially to fish curers. The large kippering establishment, lately erected at Kyle, will be in full swing immediately, and will give work to a good many hands. Building, to a large extent, is still going on, and Kyle promises, in the near future, to become an important seaport. Passengers going per steamer have but a few yards to walk, which is much appreciated, especially in the rainy weather. The company's hotel is fitted up with every comfort. Its situation, overlooking the kyle, is charming; and to ascend the hill immediately behind the house is to view a scene of picturesque grandeur, including the famed Cuillins and the headlands of the misty isle.

In the summer of 1898, the train and steamer timetables were essentially similar to those at the opening of the extension, apart from a few alterations and additions. On the railway, there was an extra train in one direction only, departing from Kyle at 1.45 pm and arriving at Dingwall at 4.33, with a connection giving a 5.45 arrival at Inverness. On the Strathpeffer branch, there were two extra daily trains in each direction: from Dingwall at 1.45 pm and 9.5 pm, and from Strathpeffer at 3.45 pm and 9.25 pm; while there was also a Saturdays-only excursion departing from Inverness at 2.50 pm and Dingwall at 3.30, with the returning service leaving Strathpeffer at 7.40 pm. One minor change on the branch was a 4.35 pm departure from Strathpeffer instead of 4.25. The steamer timetable, now with an early-afternoon crossing from Kyle to Kyleakin and with services between Kyle and Oban, was as follows:

Portree, Kyleakin and Kyle of Lochalsh:
Leave Portree daily (Sundays excepted) at 7.15 am, calling at Raasay, Broadford and Kyleakin, and arriving at Kyle of Lochalsh in connection with the express train for the South at 10.30 am.
Leave Kyle of Lochalsh daily (Sundays excepted) not earlier than 2.45 pm, calling at Kyleakin, Broadford and Raasay, reaching Portree about 5.30 pm.
Leave Kyle of Lochalsh for Kyleakin daily (Sundays excepted) on arrival of the 8.35 am train from Inverness.
Stornoway and Kyle of Lochalsh Direct:
Leave Stornoway for Kyle of Lochalsh daily (Saturdays excepted) at 11.00 pm, to connect with the 6.00 am train.
Leave Kyle of Lochalsh for Stornoway daily (Sundays excepted) not before 2.45 pm.
Stornoway and Kyle of Lochalsh via Portree:
Leave Stornoway for Portree every Monday and Thursday morning; thence Kyle of Lochalsh on same nights not before 8.00 pm.
Leave Kyle of Lochalsh every Tuesday and Friday evening; Portree same nights; reaching Stornoway every Wednesday and Saturday evening.
Kyle of Lochalsh, Gairloch, Aultbea and Poolewe:
Leave Kyle of Lochalsh for Gairloch, Aultbea and Poolewe every Friday evening. All goods for

Dingwall shed in 1913, with, appropriately, a 'Skye Bogie' 4-4-0 discernible. The shed was established in 1870 in connection with the opening of the Dingwall and Skye Railway and the simultaneous emergence of Dingwall as a railway junction.   *Real Photographs*

Dingwall station from the north *c*. 1920. On the right is the third *Strathpeffer* engine, 0-4-4 saddle-tank HR No. 25, with the branch train. On the left is 'Small Ben' 4-4-0 HR No. 7 *Ben Attow* with either a Kyle or North line train.   *Real Photographs*

these ports should be at Kyle of Lochalsh on the morning of sailing day to prevent delay.
Kyle of Lochulsh, Portree, Tarbert, Rodel, Lochmaddy and Dunvegan:
  Leave Kyle of Lochalsh every Monday, Wednesday and Friday not before 2.45 pm; and Portree every Tuesday, Thursday and Saturday morning for Tarbert, Rodel, Lochmaddy and Dunvegan; returning every Monday, Wednesday and Friday morning.
Kyle of Lochalsh and Oban:
  Leave Kyle of Lochalsh for Oban by *Claymore* and *Clansman* every Tuesday and Friday at 4.00 am; and Oban for Kyle of Lochalsh every Tuesday and Friday at 8.00 am. Also by swift steamer, leaving Kyle of Lochalsh for Oban every Monday, Wednesday and Friday at 10.15 am; and Oban for Kyle of Lochalsh every Tuesday, Thursday and Saturday at 7.00 am.
  Passengers and goods from the Highland and connecting lines are also conveyed via Kyle of Lochalsh by *Claymore*, *Clansman* or other steamer, leaving Kyle of Lochalsh for Balmacara, Glenelg, Isleornsay, Armadale, etc., every Tuesday and Friday at 4.00 am. For Ullapool and Lochinver: every Tuesday evening, calling on the voyage to Stornoway.

There was sadness for the Highland Railway, in the second half of 1898, due to the death, firstly, of Murdoch Paterson as Principal Engineer, on 9th August, at the age of nearly 72, and then, of Sir John Fowler as Consulting Engineer, on 20th November, aged 81.

Murdoch Paterson was born at Dell of Inches, near Inverness, in 1826. At school, he showed an aptitude for mathematics, but after leaving, he obtained employment for two years as a clerk in Inverness, which was not indicative of the professional eminence that he was destined to attain, but which, nevertheless, enabled him to acquire a commercial knowledge that would be of some use in his later life. From 1846, however, he discovered what was to be his true vocation, when he was employed as an apprentice engineer under Joseph Mitchell, who, in soon realising the ability of his pupil, provided him with a comprehensive training for five years in his chosen profession. At this time, Mitchell was Chief Inspector and Superintendent of Highland Roads and Bridges, and the execution of his work meant that he and his assistants were called to all parts of the Highlands. Murdoch Paterson, being one of the most intelligent and enthusiastic of these assistants, performed a large share of the work that was allotted to Mitchell. In 1851, having served his apprenticeship, he left Mitchell's employment to work for a firm of contractors who were involved in the dredging of the River Ness at Inverness harbour; but in the following year, with this firm having become insolvent, he was appointed by Mitchell and the harbour trustees to complete the works, which he did successfully.

It was in 1854 - the year of authorisation of the first railway in the Highlands, from Inverness to Nairn - that Paterson began a railway-engineering career that was to form his most pleasing work and to last for the rest of his life. Having surveyed that first line with his brother, William, he was appointed Resident Engineer by Mitchell for the construction. From Nairn, there followed the successive expansions of the railway system to Keith by 1858 and to Invergordon by 1863, with Paterson as Resident Engineer; and still under Mitchell's overall supervision, he was left in charge of the great line from Forres to Dunkeld, which also opened in 1863, followed by the Ross-shire extension from Invergordon to Bonar Bridge in 1864. He also engineered the Perthshire branch from Ballinluig to Aberfeldy - only nine miles long, but heavy and expensive to construct - which opened in 1865. It was in 1862 that Mitchell had taken the two brothers into partnership with him, in the firm's name of Messrs Joseph Mitchell and Company, and this lasted for a few busy years. In 1866, William Paterson began business on his own; and then, in 1867, during the firm's involvement with the Sutherland Railway, Mitchell retired, and consequently, Murdoch Paterson entered his independent career in railway engineering.

This commenced with the building of the Dingwall and Skye Railway upon the plans of Joseph Mitchell and Co., with which Paterson was familiar, as he had already done

Dingwall station from the south in 1913.   *Real Photographs*

Achterneed in the early 1900s, looking west. Although the picture was taken after the opening of the branch into Strathpeffer village, the scene is representative of what was the Spa's only station from 1870 to 1885. The Kyle train is headed by a 'Small Ben' 4-4-0 engine, possibly *Ben Dearg*, HR No. 14.   *G.E. Langmuir*

much of the surveying work. Since the line was promoted locally and the capital was of a moderate amount, great economy was essential in the construction, and this was achieved because of the care and attention of Paterson in securing an easy route. Four years later, in 1874, he completed the 38 miles of the Caithness portion of the Sutherland and Caithness Railway from the County March to Wick and Thurso, and soon afterwards, he accepted the appointment of Chief Engineer to the Highland Railway, which he retained until his death. In addition to his responsibility in seeing to the maintenance of the lines, he took the leading part in the continuing extension of the Highland's system, which included the Strathpeffer branch, the Fortrose branch,* and, finally, the two major projects comprising the Aviemore direct line and the Kyle Extension. 'In all these works', said the *Northern Chronicle*, 'the deceased gentleman took an active part; in fact, not a single mile of the Highland line south of Inverness, and few, if any, to the north, but bear the impress of Mr Paterson's skilful labours. He knew not only every curve and gradient, every bridge and every level crossing, but every culvert and almost, it might be added without exaggeration, every drain on the system'. In total, he had been connected with the engineering of 500 miles of railways in the Highlands.

As well as being a loyal and highly-respected employee of the Highland Railway Company, Murdoch Paterson - or Murdo, as he was often known - held and maintained the utmost trust and confidence of all parties who sought his advice and assistance. He was one of the most genial and kindly of men who was appreciated by those under his charge. It was said that he knew almost every worker on the Highland system from Perth to Wick and Thurso and from Keith to Strome Ferry, and he always treated them with respect. 'Well, how are you getting on, bodach?' was a standard remark of his, whenever he met one of his workers, and it was said that he was seen at his best when among them on duty. In not having to show assertiveness, but still presenting his great independence of character, he knew how to obtain the most out of his men, without resorting to the role of a slave-driver. His adaptability was such that he joined them in the work, with his instructions usually in words like 'We'll do this, boys'. A long-standing friend wrote of him: 'Many a time, when the railway was snow-blocked at Scotscalder or Dalnaspidal, he battled with the storms on those exposed heights, as elsewhere, when duty called, with unsparing energy. Sometimes on such occasions, he would not have his clothes off for a week'. He was an abstemious man, but he knew that a 'dram' went a long way with the typical workman when called upon to produce more than the usual exertion amid the hardship of blizzard conditions, and he ensured that the snow-block train contained, in addition to foodstuffs, a copious supply of the 'water of life'.

His constitution, until shortly before his death, had been equal to all the demands, but his great exertions amid exposure to the elements of the weather in the work that he performed for half a century ultimately told upon him heavily. Of late, he had not been robust in health, and his friends observed that, through his lack of vitality, death was approaching him. He knew this and expressed the wish that nature would hold out until his last project was realised in the practical sense - that is, that he should live to see the Aviemore direct line opened - but this was not to happen. The 17 miles from Carr Bridge to Daviot had opened on 8th July, 1897 and the remaining section of 11 miles to Inverness was virtually complete. Over the total distance of 35 miles, which was cut through the Monadhliath Mountains to a summit of 1,315 feet at Slochd, there were heavy engineering works, and the most impressive structures were the large viaducts over two rivers, the Findhorn and the Nairn. The Findhorn viaduct, at a height of 142 feet above the river, was 1,335 feet long, consisting of nine steel lattice girders, each of

---

* This line opened from Muir of Ord, a distance of 13½ miles, on 1st February, 1894.

'Skye Bogie' 4-4-0 HR No. 48 - built in 1901 as the last of the famous class - below the impressive 250 ft-high Raven Rock.   *G.E. Langmuir*

130 feet span, that rested on eight piers and two end-abutments of masonry, with two arches of 25 feet-span within each of the abutments. The Nairn viaduct was not as high, at 130 feet above the river, but it was longer, at 1,785 feet, and more striking because of its line of 29 sandstone arches, 28 of which were of 50 feet-span, with the principal one, over the river, being of 100 feet. 'Not to mention the many difficulties which had to be overcome in carrying the railway over the Slochd and the adjacent districts', said the *Inverness Courier*, 'the Nairn and Findhorn viaducts form splendid monuments of the great skill of the engineer . . . In the Nairn viaduct, Mr Paterson had the greatest professional pride, and it is in the fitness of things that his death occurred in the station-house in the vicinity of the structure'.

The station-house referred to was that erected for the station master at Culloden Moor station, where Paterson had taken up residence for the summer in order to supervise the finishing touches of the Nairn viaduct and see the opening of the Aviemore direct line. 'This hope was not realised in the fullest sense', the *Inverness Courier* had to record, though adding with consolation, 'but to all intents and purposes, the new route from Inverness to Aviemore is completed, and he no doubt derived personal satisfaction from the knowledge of the fact that it would be brought into use by the company in the course of a few weeks'. And much feeling was evinced by the *Northern Chronicle* with these words: 'A few weeks more and, from his death-bed, the first through train might have been visible to him; but at last, the call came swiftly and peacefully; and there, close beside one of the grandest monuments that could be witness to his engineering skill and genius, he passed away, without a murmur that his work in this world was done'. One of those who was present at his bedside when he died was his fellow-engineer and former assistant, William Roberts, who had succeeded him as Engineer of the opened lines of the Highland Railway in 1891, from which time Paterson had confined his attention to the lines under construction. A last appropriate tribute, in short, also came from the *Northern Chronicle*, with the words that 'it is gratifying to think that so useful a life has so long been spared, and that Inverness has had so excellent a citizen'. Murdoch Paterson's last engineering monument, the Aviemore direct line, was opened on 1st November, 1898, with the result that Inverness, the West and the North now had a significantly-quicker connection with the South.

Throughout the Highlands, the name of John Fowler was well known and highly respected, as an engineer, as a landowner, and as a gentleman. Born near Sheffield in 1817, he began his career as an apprentice in hydraulic engineering and then ventured into railway engineering as an assistant in the construction of several lines, including the London and Brighton Railway. In 1839, he became Resident Engineer on the Stockton and Hartlepool Railway, and on its completion, he was appointed Engineer, General Manager and Locomotive Superintendent. In 1843, when he was 26, he started an independent career as a consulting engineer, and at this time, several railways were being promoted in Sheffield and in Lincolnshire, to which he was assigned as Chief Engineer, conducting them through Parliament and carrying them out. Having become established in London, and with his ability and increasing fame, all kinds of work flowed to him. Among the numerous railway enterprises that he had executed were these: London's original underground line, the Metropolitan; other lines in the city, such as the District; the St John's Wood; the Hammersmith; the Edgware, Highgate and London; and lines elsewhere, like the London, Tilbury and Southend; the Manchester, Sheffield and Lincolnshire system; the Oxford, Worcester and Wolverhampton; the Severn Valley; the Mid Kent; the Great Northern and Western of Ireland system; the Great Eastern extensions in Cambridgeshire and Essex; the Glasgow Union and City; Glasgow St Enoch station; and Liverpool Central station.

Garve station building in the early 1900s looking south-east.   *J.L. Stevenson*

Lochluichart station, with its original signal box, in the early 1900s, looking north-east. This was the original public station that replaced the private platform of Lady Ashburton in 1871. The only railway employee in the picture is the station master. The other gentlemen are probably forestry workers.   *G.E. Langmuir*

In 1866, Fowler was elected president of the Institution of Civil Engineers. In 1868, he went to Egypt because of health problems, and while there, he was appointed consulting engineer to the Egyptian Government, retaining this position for eight years and constructing many engineering works. In 1885, upon the recommendation of the Marquis of Salisbury, he became Sir John Fowler, being created a Knight Commander of the Order of St Michael and St George, in recognition of his 'important services and guidance of Her Majesty's Government in connection with Egypt'. Having entered into partnership with his engineering colleague Benjamin Baker in 1875, he proceeded to co-design what was universally acknowledged as the greatest railway bridge in the world, over the River Forth. After seven years of construction, the bridge was opened on 4th March, 1890, and as a result of its success and magnificence, Sir John Fowler was created a baronet.

Fowler's principal Highland connection was with his estate at Braemore, where the mansion house, situated on a lofty eminence, overlooked Loch Broom amid a picturesque setting. He was very attached to Braemore, and considering his busy professional life, he had still managed to spend part of every summer there since 1847. One of his other early Highland associations had been with the Dingwall and Skye Railway, when he became a Director in 1868; and, in 1869, with his engineering experience, he persuaded the Board that it would be better if the line was projected from Attadale to Strome Ferry, because the latter would be a better terminus. At the banquet at Strome for the line's opening, Alex Matheson praised John Fowler for his judicious suggestions in regard to the building of the line at its relatively-low cost. One other railway scheme of the Highlands, in which he was interested, the Garve and Ullapool Railway, did not materialise.

Fowler's name was honoured in railway engineering until death, as he was the Consulting Engineer to the Highland Railway, having worked harmoniously with Murdoch Paterson since their days of the Dingwall and Skye company. The inscriptions on the Nairn and Findhorn viaducts appropriately contained their names, thus: 'Sir John Fowler, Bart, KCMG, London - Murdoch Paterson, M Inst CE, Inverness - Engineers'. In addition, Sir John Fowler was the Consulting Engineer to several English railway companies, including the Great Western Railway and the Great Northern Railway. His life, in covering most of the century, was associated with some of the finest triumphs of engineering. He was also a Justice of the Peace and a Deputy-Lieutenant of Ross-shire and Inverness-shire. He died at his residence in Bournemouth, where he was spending the autumn because of his recent poor health, but in spite of this, his death was unexpected.

It was in the spring of 1901 that the 39½ miles of the Mallaig Extension of the West Highland Railway had opened from Banavie - after four years of construction through the scenic country associated with Bonnie Prince Charlie - thereby establishing the third line to reach the western sea and providing the North British Railway with access to the fishing grounds of the West. By the West Highland Railway (Guarantee) Act, 1896, the Conservative Government, under Robert Gascoyne-Cecil, had agreed to contribute to the expensive line. In recognising the importance of the scheme for the west coast, especially in the development of the fishing industry, and because of the small amount of traffic that would necessarily be conveyed, the Government guaranteed a dividend of 3 per cent annually upon £260,000 of the capital for 30 years, together with a further subsidy of £30,000 towards the construction of the pier and breakwater at Mallaig, costing £45,000.

The total cost in building the Mallaig Extension and the harbour was £540,000, or £13,500 per mile; but with an additional £40,000 for the land, the average cost amounted to £14,500 per mile. The principal general features of the construction were the many heavy rock-cuttings, embankments, bridges and tunnels, and the extent to which mass concrete was used in place of stone. At Glenfinnan, where Bonnie Prince Charlie began his gathering of the Highland clans in 1745 for the Stuart cause, was the largest structure

A 'Strath' or 'Glen' class 4-4-0 *Glenbruar*, HR No. 100, approaching Achanalt with a train from Kyle in the early 1900s.   *J.L. Stevenson*

Achnasheen station building and hotel in the early 1900s, looking north.   *Lens of Sutton*

- a spectacular, 1,248 feet-long, curved viaduct, comprising 21 arches of 50 feet-span, carrying the railway 100 feet above the valley. The three firms responsible for building the extension were from Glasgow. The engineers were Simpson and Wilson; the contractors for the line and harbour were Robert MacAlpine and Sons, with the head of the firm known as 'Concrete Bob'; and the contractors for the stations were Lawson and Co.

The opening was on Monday, 1st April, with the first train leaving Mallaig for Glasgow at 7.25 am, conveying passengers who had reached the new port and railhead from Stornoway. This was by the routine service that departed at 11 o'clock every night, except Saturdays, for Kyle - being the *Clydesdale* steamer in connection with the 6.10 am train to Dingwall - and the steamer was now extended to Mallaig, in connection with the West Highland Railway. There was a separate steamer for Skye - the *Lovedale* - which left Portree at 7.15 am, calling at Raasay, Broadford and Kyleakin, and arriving at Kyle in time for the 11 am train for Dingwall. The steamer then headed for Mallaig, calling at Isleornsay, and allowed the Skye passengers their opportunity to travel south on the second and final train of the day from Mallaig, departing at 1.21 pm. The first train of the new railway in the opposite direction left Glasgow at 5.55 am, reaching Mallaig in connection with the midday steamers to Stornoway via Kyle and to Portree via Isleornsay, Kyle, Kyleakin, Broadford and Raasay. The *Oban Times* outlined the scene at Mallaig for the arrival of the first train:

As the train steamed into the commodious terminus at Mallaig, the travellers were welcomed by a miscellaneous group of fishermen, natives and workmen employed on the line, amid a burst of warm sunshine. At the splendid pier, which connects with the station, lay the familiar red-funnelled steamers *Lovedale* and *Clydesdale* of the MacBrayne fleet with steam up - the former to take up passengers proceeding to Skye, and the latter to distant Stornoway. At Mallaig, a township is creeping up, although at present somewhat limited in extent, with a large and commodious hotel on a rising ground above, commanding a magnificent view of the Sound of Sleat and the mountains of Skye and adjacent isles.

There was a second train to Mallaig, which arrived at 5.30 pm, but this had no steamer connections. A Portree correspondent of the *Oban Express* summarised the steamer operations on the opening day, thus:

The Portree and Stornoway mail-steamers left their respective stations at the usual hours on Monday morning, and, after calling at Kyle of Lochalsh, proceeded to Mallaig. The Portree steamer left at 7.15 am with mails and passengers, and, having landed these, sailed to Mallaig, accomplishing the voyage in 1 hr 35 min.* The steamers *Lovedale* and *Clydesdale* lost no time after the arrival of the train from the South in starting on the return journey, and arrived at Kyle of Lochalsh in time to enable them to ship their respective cargoes and sail at the advertised time for Portree and Stornoway. The steamer *Lovedale* reached Portree at the advertised hour of 4.30 pm, so that, if this time is kept throughout, Skye, while it will have no acceleration of mail service, will be in no worse position than it has been for several years.

The establishment of the Mallaig Extension meant that, in effect, there were now two Skye railways, and the new line provided a quicker route between the South and Portree and Stornoway than did the original rail route via Inverness, so that a decline in the Highland's traffic in connection with the Kyle line inevitably occurred. Nevertheless, passengers still had a choice of travelling by sea to or from Kyle or Mallaig, because the Portree and Stornoway steamers called at both ports, with the advantage to David MacBrayne that his company now served two competing railways. The *Oban Times* explained the importance of the Mallaig line in relation to the Highlands in general:

* from Kyle.

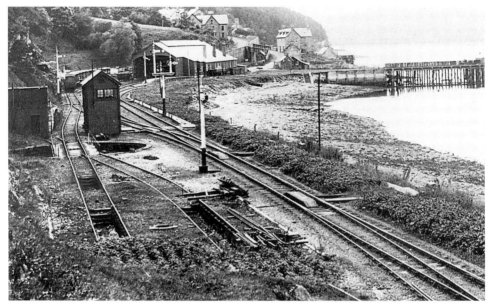

Strome Ferry in the early 1900s, after the goods shed had been demolished. The site of the engine shed is in the foreground, with the turntable, tracks and pits still in existence.

J.L. Stevenson

Strome Ferry station in the early 1900s, looking west from below the 'overall' canopy of the station building. However, no part of the platform on the left, resulting from the Kyle Extension, is contained within the canopy.   *J.L. Stevenson*

The railway comes as the friend of the present inhabitants of the West Highlands. It places within their reach the advantages that have ministered in a boundless degree to the happiness and prosperity of the country at large. In their isolation and their distance from the busy centres of life and industry, the Highlands need all the railway facilities they can get. The local industries of the Highlands are stunted and held down only because they have no outlet. There is no room for their growth. A fresh and speedy avenue to the great markets of the South puts a new weapon into the hands of the inhabitants, which they may use for their own advancement. The line to Mallaig will not work wonders in a day, especially as it serves a thinly-peopled territory of enormous area; but before long, it must come to play a large part in the life and work of the Highlands.

Neither the Highland Railway nor the North British Railway advertised each other's services and connections, but a basic, composite timetable, showing both together, for the spring and early summer of 1901, was as follows:

		am	am	am	pm
Glasgow	d.	4.20	5.55	7.15	
Fort William			10.00		3.45
Mallaig	a.		11.45		5.30
Inverness	d.	9.50		2.35 pm	
Dingwall	d.	11.10		3.40	
Kyle of Lochalsh	a.	1.50 pm		7.10	

Portree	a.	4.30 pm
Stornoway	a.	8.00

		pm	am
Stornoway	d.	11.00 (a)	
Portree	d.		7.15

		am	am	pm	am	pm
Kyle of Lochalsh	d.	6.10			11.00	5.00
Dingwall	a.	9.27			1.40 pm	8.19
Inverness	a.	10.45			2.35	9.30
Mallaig	d.		7.25	1.20		
Fort William			9.55	4.20		
Glasgow	a.		1.58 pm	9.00	9.25	8.42 am

Note: (a) Sun-Fri.

In the summer of 1901, alterations were made to the Kyle line timetable because the Highland Railway realised that, as a result of the opening of the Mallaig Extension, they had to provide a quicker service to and from the South, via Inverness, in connection with the Portree and Stornoway steamers. During the spring and early summer of 1901, the Highland Railway had not offered, at Inverness, a convenient train connection with the South for travellers on the 11 pm service from Stornoway. While the 6.10 am train from Kyle did allow a connection to the South, the arrival time in Glasgow of 6 pm was much too unfavourable in comparison with the 1.58 pm arrival time there via Mallaig and Fort William by the West Highland line. The changes took effect from July. With the steamer now departing from Stornoway at 10.20 pm instead of 11 pm, the first train from Kyle left 40 minutes earlier at 5.30 am, so that Inverness was reached in time to connect with the 8.50 am train for the South, allowing an arrival time of 1.45 pm at Glasgow, 1.51 pm at Edinburgh, and 10.45 pm at London. In the opposite direction on the Kyle line, in connection with the 4.20 am service from Glasgow and the 9.50 am service from Inverness, a new express train departed from Dingwall at 10.36, calling only at Garve, Achnasheen and Strathcarron, to reach Kyle at 1 pm.

The *Gael* steamer at Kyle pier in the early 1900s. *R. Charnley*

A scene at Kyle of Lochalsh station *c.* 1920, photographed by Duncan Macpherson. A 'Skye Bogie' is on a goods train, and a horse is on duty at the right of the view.

Dualchas Museums Service, Portree

The steamers, having come from Mallaig and calling at Kyle, were timed to reach Portree at 4 pm, which was half an hour earlier than before, and Stornoway at 6.55 pm instead of 8 pm. Three extra trains were also provided along the Kyle line in the summer of 1901. These were the 9 am and 6.10 pm from Dingwall to Kyle and the 1.25 pm from Kyle to Dingwall. With the establishment of the Mallaig Extension having resulted in much-improved Highland Railway services, the Kyle line timetable and its principal connections then read:

		am	am	am	am	am
Glasgow	d.		4.20		7.15	10.00
Inverness	d.	8.00	9.50	10.00	2.20 pm	5.10 pm
Dingwall	d.	9.00	10.36	11.10	3.30	6.10
Kyle of Lochalsh	a.	12.20 pm	1.00 pm	2.15 pm	6.05	9.25
Portree	a.		4.00			
Stornoway	a.		6.55			

		pm	am	pm	pm
Stornoway	d.	10.20 (a)			
Portree	d.		7.15		
Kyle of Lochalsh	d.	5.30 am	11.25	1.25	5.00
Dingwall	a.	8.00	1.54 pm	3.58	8.15
Inverness	a.	8.50	2.50	5.30	10.30
Glasgow	a.	1.45 pm	9.25	11.58	8.42 am

Note: (a) Sun-Fri.

In addition to the five 'Skye Bogie' locomotives that had been designed by David Jones, the Skye line had obtained a further four under the supervision of Peter Drummond. These were built at Lochgorm in August and November 1897, being numbered 5 and 6; in July 1898, being No. 7; and in December 1901, No. 48. And like the Skye line with its 'Skye Bogies', the Strathpeffer branch had continued to be operated mainly by its own locomotive, with David Jones having produced, in 1890, a second *Strathpeffer* to replace the 2-2-2 tank that had worked the branch since its opening in 1885. Built at Lochgorm Works, the new engine was a heavier 0-4-4 saddle-tank, which, in being numbered 13, incorporated the boiler of the previous No. 13, *Lovat* - renamed *Thurso* in 1874 - which had been withdrawn. Renumbered 53 in 1900, the second *Strathpeffer* was rebuilt by Peter Drummond at Lochgorm in 1901, with side tanks and a new boiler. In 1903, the engine was removed from the Strathpeffer branch and renamed *Lybster* for use on the 13¾ miles-long Wick and Lybster Light Railway, which opened on 1st July of that year.

Back in 1892, the Highland had obtained, from Dübs and Co. of Glasgow, two 4-4-0 tank-engines which had been built the previous year for a Uruguayan railway that ultimately did not accept them because of a financial problem, and they were sold to the Highland. In 1893, three more were purchased, and in 1899, one of these, No. 11, was renumbered 51. This locomotive worked the Strathpeffer branch in the summer of 1903 on the departure of No. 53 for the Lybster line. In an article for the *Railway Magazine* in 1904, entitled 'The "Farthest North" British Railway', which referred to the Highland, enthusiast T.R. Perkins provided an account of his travels over most of the Highland system in the summer of 1903, and this included a run to Strathpeffer and back behind No. 51. He and his wife travelled by steamer from Liverpool to Kyle of Lochalsh, and then by train to Dingwall behind an engine that was not a 'Skye Bogie'. It was a 4-4-0 of the 'Strath' or 'Glen' class that was one of 12 built in 1892 for the Highland by Neilson and Co. of Glasgow. In his description of the journeys on the Kyle line and the

The Station Hotel at Kyle - formerly Kyle House before it was acquired by the Highland Railway - photographed in 1914 by Duncan Macpherson.

R. Charnley

Strathpeffer branch, beginning with an arrival at Kyle by sea, Perkins also commented favourably on the Highland trains and stations:

Bidding farewell for a time to the steamer by which we had travelled from Liverpool, we stayed the night at a hotel in the village, returning to the station in time to resume our journey at the exhilarating hour of 5.30 the next morning. On arriving there, we found No. 100, *Glenbruar*, attached to our train, and during the few minutes before starting-time, had an opportunity of inspecting the station and rolling-stock. As to the latter, it was of such a character as would be calculated to satisfy the most fastidious traveller; every coach, except one, being on bogies; upholstery in both classes being equal in every respect to that of the best English railways, with a liberal allowance of lavatory accommodation. Indeed, on all the trains by which we had occasion to travel during our tour (excepting, of course, those on the short branches), the majority of the carriages ran on bogies and were provided with lavatories. Gas is the standard illuminant in the Highland Railway carriages, nearly all we saw being thus fitted.

During the last 18 months, changes have been made in the style of painting the Highland Railway rolling-stock, and both engines and carriages are now a very dark green, without any lining or picking-out whatever. The whole of our train was thus painted, most of the carriages being new. The locomotives, however, are not, in my opinion, improved in appearance by the change; the former colour - olive green, with black and white lines - seeming to me to give them a smarter look.

The terminus at Kyle, as also the approach to it for some distance, had to be blasted out of solid rock, entailing immense labour. The station has a single platform, with running-lines on each side, and is partly constructed of wood. The accommodation is, however, ample - a verandah roof extending almost the entire length of the platform on each side. The view from the platform is simply glorious, embracing the coastline both of Skye and the mainland for some distance, while the village of Kyleakin can be seen across the ferry.

For the first few miles, as far as Strome Ferry, which was until 1897 the terminus of the railway, the train closely hugs the seashore, winding about in a manner which affords the traveller most entrancing glimpses of the glorious scenery hereabouts. I say 'glimpses' advisedly, as the rocky coastline necessitated the construction of numerous cuttings, into which the train rushes for a few moments, only to emerge amid fresh scenes of beauty. Near Plockton, a private station may be seen on the right of the line. Strome Ferry, the former terminus, possesses a wooden station, with an 'all-over' roof; from this spot, the glory has now departed, and the engine-shed, which formerly stood near the station, has been demolished - the pit over which the locomotives stood being still visible.

Having referred to the severe gradients from Attadale to Achnashellach - 'as we soon noticed from the quick panting of our locomotive', and to the latter station's 'charming position on the side of the hill, the platforms being backed by belts of pine trees' - he summarised the Highland stations generally:

Unlike so many of the inconvenient, wooden erections met with on even important railways in England, Highland stations are almost invariably substantial, stone buildings, with platforms level with the carriage foot-boards, and having altogether an exceedingly-smart appearance. Even the name-boards, with their red letters on a cream-coloured ground, are pleasingly distinctive of this line.

The summit of 646 feet at Luib was approached:

Up this, in spite of a fairly-heavy load, *Glenbruar* mounted steadily - the sound of the heavy blast breaking the silence of the glen. Arrived at the summit, a 15-mile fall lay before us, down which we rattled at a good pace, stopping *en route* at Achnasheen and Achanalt. Leaving the broad valley soon after passing Achanalt station, we ran through a narrow gorge, with charming views to right and left; a few moments later, we obtained a passing glimpse of the Falls of Grudie - a roaring cascade of brown, foaming water - and, before reaching Lochluichart station, crossed the River Conon by a lattice girder bridge . . .

The second *Strathpeffer* engine, 0-4-4 saddle-tank HR No. 13, which took over the branch in 1890. It became HR No. 53 in 1900 and was rebuilt in 1901 with side tanks, as shown in this view.
G.E. Langmuir

The third Strathpeffer engine, 0-4-4 saddle-tank HR No. 25, which commenced operating on the branch in 1905.
G.E. Langmuir

Eventually, after having climbed for more than a mile at 1 in 50 from Garve 'through a bleak moorland' and past Raven Rock, there came into sight 'the fashionable spa of Strathpeffer in the valley below us':

Leaving Achterneed, formerly the station for Strathpeffer, we joined the branch from that place at Fodderty Junction, exchanging tablets at full speed by means of the apparatus fitted to most of the Highland locomotives. A mile farther on, we ran onto the main line from the North, and entered Dingwall station, 63½ miles from Kyle and 18½ miles from Inverness, where we alighted, resuming our journey by a later train.

The Strathpeffer branch train was drawn up in a bay at the northern end of the down platform, and, before proceeding southward, we took the opportunity of travelling over the branch, which is 4¾ miles in length. It may be of interest to mention, as showing the liberal treatment of passengers by the railway in this entirely-unopposed district, that the return third-class fare is only sixpence. A peculiarity of this train, which consisted of the oldest-type carriages - four-wheelers with straight sides - was the fact that the 'thirds' were in every respect similar to the 'firsts', even to the centre armrests.

Leaving the railway to Kyle on our right at Fodderty, where we obtained from the window a good view of the tablet-catching process, we crossed to the southern side of the valley, and in a few minutes, drew up in the single-platform station of Strathpeffer. The curative properties of the sulphur and chalybeate springs have made Strathpeffer Spa an increasingly-popular resort, and the little town is rapidly increasing in size. An excellent service of trains is run between Dingwall and the Spa - no less than 10 being provided daily in each direction, while Achterneed station, on the Kyle of Lochalsh section, is only a mile from Strathpeffer.

Two years after Perkins' tour, the third *Strathpeffer* engine appeared. Peter Drummond introduced a class of 0-4-4 tank engines that he had designed at Lochgorm for branch line working. Three of them were built in 1905, and there was a fourth in 1906, to be the last engines to come from the company's works; and it was the first of the four, No. 25, that obtained the honour of serving on the Strathpeffer branch and being named after the famous Spa.

Famous, too, was the Skye line, with its magnificent vistas that invited many travellers. A correspondent of the *North Star* journeyed over the route in late October 1910, and he was yet another to be impressed - his words acting as an encouragement for others to do the same:

A trip on almost any part of the Highland Railway in autumn is a treat of no ordinary kind, but a run over the section between Dingwall and Kyle is an experience not soon to be erased from the memory. The scenery, in its wild, rugged grandeur, cannot be well described effectively. It must be seen to be believed . . .

Then, there followed a description of what was observed in scenery as the train headed westwards. He was particularly excited by the stretch of the line beside Loch Carron, and, with a reference to the scenery at the terminus, he recommended a further excursion by sea:

From Attadale to Strome Ferry, the line runs along the edge of the loch, winding in and out, under the shadow of a huge, rocky hill which threatens to fall at many places and crush the train to matchwood or throw it into the deep, blue waters of the loch. This run is one of thrills to the newcomer and to all travellers who realise that little would send all into eternity. That no accident has befallen a train in the past (to our knowledge) is no guarantee that the same happy results will be enjoyed in the future. That nothing has happened must be put down to the extreme care of the railway officials. Flags waved by men on the lineside here and there along the most dangerous parts assure the driver that all is well. The truly-majestic, awe-inspiring scenery between Attadale and Strome Ferry has to be seen to be realised, and the wonder is that many more do not go, in

A Strathpeffer station scene in 1913, during the Spa's period of greatest prosperity. The engine is the third *Strathpeffer*, 0-4-4 saddle-tank HR No. 25. The station master's house is in view, and to the right of the engine, the signal box is visible. *L&GRP*

The third *Strathpeffer*, 0-4-4 saddle-tank HR No. 25, at the Spa, working the branch train in 1913. *L&GRP*

the summer time at least, to see Scotland at her best. There is nothing to be seen like it anywhere else in Scotland. This is indeed 'Scotia stern and wild'.

Kyle is a curious place. Perched on a rocky promontory, it has spread out wherever it has been able to obtain a footing. A deep cutting has let the station be placed right on the nose of the point and under the shadow of the Skye mountains. Wherever the eye wanders, it catches glimpses of scenes wild and grand. Here, the steamers call from Skye, Lewis, Oban and Glasgow, and from the signs of bustle when they call, do a good coasting trade. A sail to any of these places, following a run to Kyle on the railway, should form a fitting sequel to a delightful experience, in which town life, with all its multifarious and intricate ways, pale into insignificance and leave us face to face for a time with the grand, greater and higher realities of life, and the use we are making of it.

In the period from the opening of the Strathpeffer branch over the remaining 15 years of the 19th century, the Spa had continued to flourish. The coming of the railway directly into the village had created much of the impetus. It was in the two decades after the opening of the branch that the largest rise in the local population had occurred, with the majority of the villas having then been built to meet the growing demand for accommodation, as more people arrived to drink the waters and bathe in them to seek a cure for their ailments. The period of greatest popularity, activity and prosperity for Strathpeffer, and for the railway, occurred in the opening decade of the 20th century and the subsequent four years prior to World War I. During this era in particular, the Highland Railway did much to publicise the Spa. In 1908, a through carriage with sleeping compartments was introduced between London and Strathpeffer, running every night; and in 1909, the Highland, in recognising the need for still more accommodation facilities in the village, announced its intention to build a luxurious hotel there.

Construction having commenced in March 1910, the Highland Hotel was formally opened on 13th June, 1911. It occupied a commanding position on the rising ground behind the Spa, immediately west of and overlooking the pump-room, and also offering a fine view of the valley of the Peffery. The palatial building, costing £50,000, consisted of five floors, including a basement, and there were about 90 bedrooms, together with various sitting-rooms. One of the many modern features was a revolving entrance-door, which was only the second of its kind in the North. The first was the Highland's hotel at Dornoch in conjunction with the 7¾ miles-long Dornoch Light Railway, which had opened from The Mound on 2nd June, 1902. Both hotels had been designed by Messrs Cameron and Burnett, architects, Inverness.

The occasion of the opening of the hotel was celebrated by a luncheon held in the spacious dining-room and attended by a large section of guests from near and far, at the invitation of the Directors of the Highland Railway. Included were influential representatives from the medical profession and from the leading newspapers. Also in connection with the opening, the Highland had arranged exhibition golf at the Strathpeffer course, which involved two well-known amateurs - one each from Scotland and England - and they were followed by a large gallery of spectators.

The renowned and grandiose Strathpeffer Spa, bearing more resemblance to a continental watering-place than a Highland community, was different from any other village or town in Scotland. To promote it even further, the Highland Railway initiated a new service in the summer of 1911, by offering an improved travelling facility from the South. A brief explanation of this had been given by the Highland's Chairman, William Whitelaw, at the luncheon for the opening of the hotel:

Beginning the first Tuesday in July, and every Tuesday thereafter, a non-stop run will be made from Aviemore to Dingwall and thence to Strathpeffer. It will be the first train to run past Inverness, and I hope every effort will be made to make the new Strathpeffer train widely known. It will cut two hours off the run from Perth.

The 'Strathpeffer Spa Express', headed by 'Loch' class 4-4-0 HR No. 129 *Loch Maree*. The train's headboard can be clearly seen.

J.L. Stevenson

The new service commenced on 4th July. The 'Strathpeffer Spa Express', with its impressive carriages and locomotive carrying a headboard, started from Aviemore at 2.30 pm and, by-passing Inverness station by the spur of the South and North lines, called only at Dingwall, departing from there at 4.05 and reaching Strathpeffer at 4.15 pm. It ran over the direct line from Aviemore to Inverness via Carr Bridge, and at Aviemore, it connected with the 11.50 am service from Perth to Inverness which proceeded by Grantown and Forres. The service was worked by a much larger class of locomotive than the branch had known. This was usually a 'Loch' 4-4-0, of which 15 had been built for the Highland, from the design of David Jones, by Dübs and Co. in 1896. The 'Lochs' were well suited to hauling heavy passenger trains between Perth and Inverness, and they were the most powerful engines of the Highland Railway at this time and among the most powerful in Britain. There was no 'Strathpeffer Spa Express' in the reverse direction, but there was a Tuesdays-only through service to Inverness that departed from the Spa at 6.10 pm and called at all the intermediate stations between Dingwall and Inverness. The Strathpeffer branch timetable, together with the Kyle line services, for July 1911 can be seen on the following page.

The Highland Hotel was built and the 'Strathpeffer Spa Express' was operated with expectations of continuing prosperity, and for four summers, this was the case, as the village overflowed with visitors; but the arrival of World War I in August 1914 heralded the beginning of a decrease in the fortunes of the Spa that resulted in the 'Strathpeffer Spa Express' being withdrawn at the end of the 1915 season. Northern Scotland was of great strategic importance and became a restricted area, such that the public were prohibited from travelling northwards and westwards of Inverness without a permit, and this necessarily included the Kyle line and the Strathpeffer branch. Latterly, part of the defence of the British Isles from a possible German invasion across the North Sea comprised the establishment of a naval base at Scapa Flow in the Orkney Islands for the Grand Fleet and a repair base at Invergordon for the warships. Due to the immediate threat of a German advance by the autumn of 1917, and with the United States having entered the war in April of that year, the Allies decided to combat the danger by laying an extensive minefield, which was referred to as the Northern Barrage, across the North Sea from the Orkney Islands to Norway. In this operation, the Kyle line rendered a significant contribution.

For the assembling and laying of the mines, which was to be carried out by the Americans, one base was set up at Inverness and another at Dalmore, by Alness. Because the Kyle line conveniently connected Northern Scotland from the Atlantic Ocean to the North Sea, the mines from America were to be landed at Kyle of Lochalsh and then sent to Dalmore by rail. Work on the new base was commenced in January 1918, and the Railway Executive Committee, which had been established by the Government to take control of all the railways during the war, informed the public of the restrictions that would consequently be placed on the Kyle line, thus:

Notice is hereby given that, on and after Monday 18th February, 1918, the Highland Railway Company's pier at Kyle of Lochalsh, as well as the Dingwall and Kyle of Lochalsh section of the Highland Railway, will, as regards traffic for Lewis, Skye and the Outer Islands, only be available for passengers (with their personal luggage), mails, perishable traffic and Government stores.

The routes via Mallaig and Oban are not available, and all other traffic for Lewis, Skye and the Outer Islands will be conveyed via Glasgow.

By order, the Railway Executive Committee, February 1918.

Another announcement soon followed:

Strathpeffer Branch and Kyle Line Services
July 1911

		am	am	am	am	am	am	am	pm	pm	pm (a)	pm	pm	pm (b)	pm	pm	pm
Inverness	d.	5.40			7.45		9.50	9.55			2.00	2.35				4.55	8.00
Dingwall	d.	6.40	7.35	8.48	8.52	9.40	10.32	10.50	1.15	2.30	2.40	3.40	3.45	4.05	6.00	6.10	9.05
Strathpeffer	a.	6.50	7.45	8.58	-	9.50	10.42	-	1.25	2.40	2.50	-	3.55	4.15	6.10	-	9.15
Achterneed					9.05			11.05				3.56					6.32
Garve					9.22			11.23				4.13					7.00
Achnasheen					10.05			12.15 pm				4.55					7.45
Strathcarron					10.45			12.47				5.40					8.28
Strome Ferry					11.15			1.15				6.06					8.57
Plockton					11.25			1.24				6.16					9.12
Kyle of Lochalsh	a.				11.42			1.40				6.30					9.30

		am	am	am	am	am	am	pm	am	pm	pm	pm	pm (c)	pm (d)	pm	pm	pm
Kyle of Lochalsh	d.		5.00						10.50		12.50			4.50			
Plockton									11.05		1.04			5.04			
Strome Ferry			5.22						11.15		1.15			5.14			
Strathcarron			5.48						11.43		1.42			5.40			
Achnasheen			6.25						12.22 pm		2.17			6.20			
Garve			7.01						1.10		2.55			7.00			
Achterneed			7.17						1.31		3.16			7.20			
Strathpeffer	d.	7.12		8.30	9.15	10.15	10.55	12.40		3.10		5.40	6.10		8.00	8.15	9.25
Dingwall	a.	7.21	7.26	8.40	9.25	10.25	11.05	12.50	1.41	3.20	3.27	5.50	6.22	7.40	8.12	8.25	9.35
Inverness	a.	8.40	8.25		10.45		12.12 pm		2.58		4.40		7.05	8.55		9.30	

Notes:

(a) Sat only. Excursion from Inverness.
(c) Tues only.
(b) Tues only. From Aviemore 'Strathpeffer Spa Express'.
(d) Sat only. Return excursion to Inverness.

The Highland Railway

RUNS THROUGH

The Heart of the Highlands.

The Picturesque Line of the Empire.

A B C Illustrated Guide with Tourist Fares, &c., Posted on Application.

THROUGH CARRIAGES AND SLEEPING CARS FROM LONDON (EUSTON) TO STRATHPEFFER SPA, NIGHTLY.

CHEAP EXCURSION FARES TO STRATHPEFFER from London, Manchester, Liverpool, Birmingham, and Chief Cities and Towns in England every Friday night from June 11th to September 24th.

If you do not see announcement of Excursion Fares from your Town, and desire the Information, please send Post Card Enquiry.

Strathpeffer is a most charming centre for pleasure Excursions.

T. A. WILSON, General Manager.

Inverness, 1st June, 1909.

Notice is hereby given that the Highland Railway Company's route via Kyle of Lochalsh is closed for traffic by merchandise trains with Lewis, Skye and the Outer Islands, and places on the mainland, except for perishable traffic (in lots not exceeding 1 cwt) and Government stores for Broadford, Raasay, Portree, Stornoway, Tarbert (Harris) and Lochmaddy.

The passenger train service via Kyle of Lochalsh is still available for the conveyance of passengers (with their personal luggage), mails, perishable traffic (in lots not exceeding 1 cwt) and government stores for Broadford, Raasay, Portree, Stornoway, Tarbert (Harris) and Lochmaddy.

The routes via Mallaig and Oban are open for merchandise and passenger train traffic, but the steamer services are limited.

By order, the Railway Executive Committee, March 1918.

The whole of the Kyle railway from Dingwall, together with the Highland's pier and hotel at Kyle, the hotel at Strathpeffer, and the other hotels and boarding houses in the Spa, were requisitioned by the Admiralty. The first mines from America for Dalmore arrived at Kyle in May 1918, and ships continued at intervals of about a fortnight, with three or four trains running daily from Kyle to Dalmore thereafter for about a week. The public timetable for the Kyle line continued to be advertised, but sometimes, because of the necessity of the military traffic, only one passenger train per day in each direction was allowed to be run. Extra help was essential for the large military operation that had demanded too much of the Highland's limited resources. The military trains, which were usually hauled by one of four locomotives loaned by the London & South Western Railway consisted of a maximum of 11 wagons each, because of the heavy gradients, and these wagons were generally from 150 on loan from the South Eastern & Chatham Railway.

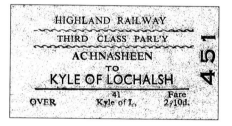

Highland Railway tickets.

I. Wilks

Chapter Fifteen

The London, Midland and Scottish Railway Period

After the war ended in November 1918, the Highland Railway's system inevitably had to contend with locomotives, rolling stock and track in poor condition, due to heavy use and reduced maintenance; but it was not only the Highland company that had been left with low morale from the war, for this was also the case with Britain's railways in general, as the individual companies attempted to return to their former state. However, it was agreed that the only way in which a recovery could take place was by re-organisation of the country's railways, and this was ultimately sanctioned by the Railways Act, 1921, in providing for the formation of four large, amalgamated companies. The system of the Highland Railway, and, thus, the Kyle line and the Strathpeffer branch, would be incorporated into the London, Midland & Scottish Railway, the largest of the four, which encompassed a route mileage of 7,500 miles, with the Highland supplying 500 miles. The Callander and Oban line, as part of the Caledonian Railway, would also be included in the LMSR, while the West Highland Railway and the Mallaig Extension, with the rest of the North British system, would form part of the London & North Eastern Railway. The 'Grouping', as the new mergers were collectively known, came into effect officially on 1st January, 1923, and from this date, the Highland Railway Company ceased to exist formally, though the eminent name would continue in memory. Under the LMSR, no significant differences in the operation of the Highland lines were anticipated, except that the overall control of them was now from London instead of Inverness.

An early account of the Kyle of Lochalsh railway after it had become settled in its new ownership was provided by enthusiast H.R. Stones in 1925, in a *Railway Magazine* article entitled 'The Dingwall and Skye Line, LMSR'. Having allotted much of the article to a basic description of the line, Stones portrayed the active terminus as it appeared over a quarter of a century after its establishment:

> Kyle of Lochalsh is a business centre and a fishing and shipping port on the extreme west coast of Ross-shire. It possesses ample banking facilities, shops, churches and hotels, including a small but extremely comfortable hotel owned and run by the LMSR. The hotel is only a few minutes' walk from the station, and is situated on the coast within a few feet of the high-water mark. It commands a magnificent view of the mountains of Skye. The village of Kyle, which was practically non-existent before the advent of the railway in 1897, is now an important interchange point for passenger and freight traffic for the island of Skye and the numerous other Hebridean islands. The mail steamers, belonging to the well-known shipping firm of David MacBrayne Ltd of Glasgow, ply regularly all the year round from Mallaig, on the West Highland section of the LNER, to Portree and Broadford on the island of Skye, and also to Stornoway and Lochmaddy in the Outer Hebrides. All the boats make Kyle a port of call in both directions. During the summer months, additional steamers are put into service, and excursions are made to neighbouring lochs around the coast, including the wild and beautiful Loch Coruisk. It may be also mentioned that, during the season, excursions by water are made from Glasgow and the Clyde to Mallaig, Kyle and the Hebridean islands.

Stones referred to the passenger service between Inverness and Kyle at the time of his visit. From Inverness, there were two trains per day, except Sundays: at 10.20 am and 3.45 pm, while a 9.35 am goods train also ran from Dingwall. From Kyle, there were three trains that conveyed passengers: at 7 am, 11 am and 4.30 pm. The journey time was 3¾ hours. Finally, he recorded that, at this time, the line was still usually worked by the

'Skye Bogie' 4-4-0 LMS No. 14284, ex-HR No. 7, with a Kyle of Lochalsh goods train near Fodderty Junction.   *J.L. Stevenson*

Achterneed in 1929, looking east, with the approaching Kyle of Lochalsh goods train hauled by 'Skye Bogie' 4-4-0 LMS No. 14279, ex-HR No. 86.   *J.L. Stevenson*

'Skye Bogie' 4-4-0 LMS No. 14279, ex-HR No. 86, at Kyle of Lochalsh in 1927.   *H.C. Casserley*

'Small Ben' class 4-4-0 LMS No. 14399 *Ben Wyvis*, ex-HR No. 3, at Kyle of Lochalsh in 1937.
H.C. Casserley

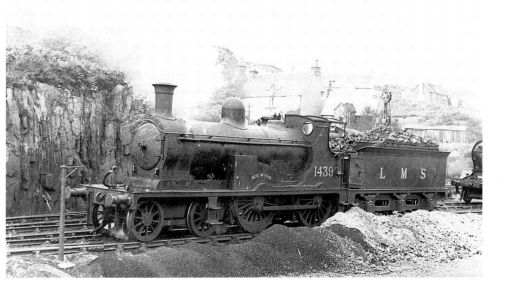

'Loch' class 4-4-0 *Loch Ashie*, LMS No. 14394, ex-HR No. 70, with a Kyle-Inverness train arriving at Achterneed *c*. 1930. This engine was one of three later 'Lochs' that were built, largely to the original design of David Jones, by the North British Locomotive Co. of Glasgow in 1917.

D. St John Thomas

'Loch' 4-4-0 *Loch Ehricht*, LMS No. 14381, ex-HR No. 121, at Kyle of Lochalsh *c*. 1930.

R. Simpson

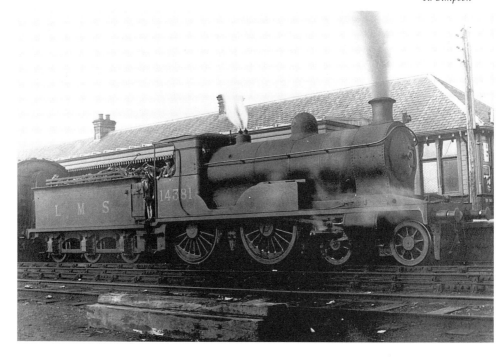

'Skye Bogies', though he did not use this name; but he added that engines of the 'Small Ben' 4-4-0 class, designed by Peter Drummond, were also used when required, and that one of these - No. 16, *Ben Avon* - had been regularly working on the line.

In the summer of 1932, the first-ever day excursion from Glasgow to Skye by railway took place, when the LMSR, in conjunction with the *Glasgow Weekly Herald*, operated a special train from the city to Kyle of Lochalsh. Because of the distance involved, the excursion consisted of two overnight rail journeys, and sleeping cars and a dining car were conveyed. Departing from Glasgow on Tuesday, 19th July at 11.50 pm, the train called at Stirling, Perth, Forres, Nairn, Inverness, Dingwall, Garve, Achnasheen, Strathcarron, Strome Ferry and Plockton, with an arrival time of 9.07 am at Kyle. The Skye steamer departed from Kyle at 9.35, and, calling at Broadford, reached Portree at 11.30. The return journey, comprising the same calls, commenced on the Wednesday evening with the departure from Portree at 8.15 pm and then 10.30 from Kyle, giving an arrival in Glasgow at 8.05 am.

Further information about Kyle and its railway in LMSR days was supplied by another enthusiast, C. Hamilton Ellis, in the January 1935 issue of the *Railway Magazine*, entitled 'Kyle of Lochalsh as a Traffic Centre'. By this time, motor cars and motor coaches had made a substantial impression in the West Highlands, though there was no serious threat of competition to the trains, especially for long distances, and the motor vehicles usually only complemented the railway for local convenience. Thus, in describing Kyle station and the awaiting transport there, Hamilton Ellis had no thoughts of potential rivalry to the railway:

After its spectacular passage from the other side of Scotland, the Skye line train slips quietly into Kyle through a bottle-necked rock cutting. A break in the cutting provides an entrance to the locomotive yard, turntable and steam shed, after which the tracks widen out, still in a cutting, into the yards of the terminus. Only after two overbridges have been passed, and the train is actually in the station, do the rocky walls fall away, and that is because the station is actually on the jetty, with deep water on three sides. On arrival, we shall probably find a short distance motor ship (the *Lochmor* or the *Lochnevis*) for Portree or Mallaig, and a larger boat (ss *Lochness* or *Lochbroom*) waiting to take on passengers for the Outer Isles. This applies to the summer time, when all the David MacBrayne* services are in full swing. In winter, the smaller ships, which have fully-equipped night accommodation for passengers of both classes, cover the long-distance work as well.

On the platform will be found the motor coach for Dornie - an indispensable, but by no means luxurious, equipage which awaits the arrival of passengers and mails from Inverness and the South. Quite a number of motor vehicles may be seen on the platform at once, for it is an island platform, approached by means of an inclined plane from the overbridge. The station buildings, which include public and staff rooms, a refreshment room and an office for the agent of Messrs MacBrayne Ltd, run down the middle of the island platform, while there are goods sheds at one end and a building housing the station's acetylene-lighting plant at the other. Goods sidings are laid out on both sides of the passenger station, next to the south-eastern and north-western sides of the jetty. The jetty itself is equipped with three 4-ton hydraulic cranes and two 3-ton steam cranes. Normally, the former do all the work of loading and unloading.

Hamilton Ellis briefly referred to the Kyle Akin ferry before describing another form of transport that was in operation for the conveyance of motor cars on the railway between Kyle and Strathcarron:

* From the original name of David MacBrayne Ltd, a new name of David MacBrayne (1928) Ltd had come into existence when, with the retiral of David MacBrayne senior in 1928 and with his son of the same name not continuing with the business because of financial difficulty, the company had been taken over jointly by the shipping firm of Coast Lines Ltd of Liverpool and the London, Midland & Scottish Railway Company.

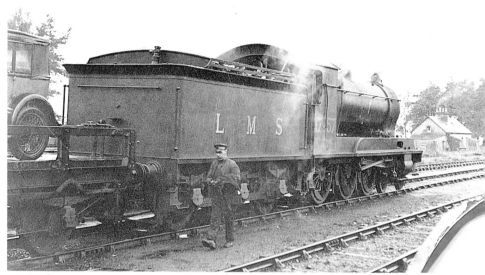

Strathcarron in 1931. Cumming 4-6-0 LMS No. 17957, ex-HR No. 82, has brought motor cars on the 'railway ferry' service between Kyle and Strathcarron, allowing the cars to avoid Strome Ferry.   *H.C. Casserley*

Cumming 4-6-0 LMS No. 17954, ex-HR No. 79, arriving at Achterneed with the 10.45 am Kyle-Inverness service in 1937.   *J.L. Stevenson*

Between the mainland and Kyleakin, there is a motor ferry service, and a considerable number of private cars make the passage during the summer season. The main road northwards involves crossing Loch Carron by another ferry - at Strome Ferry - and to enable motorists to avoid this, a 'railway ferry' service is operated, like that of the Great Western through the Severn Tunnel. For little more than the water ferry charge, in addition to the price of railway tickets for the passengers, cars are taken by rail, on carriage trucks, by the regular trains between Kyle and Strathcarron. In stormy weather, and when there is much motor traffic, involving a longer wait for the ferry proper than for the next train, there may be as many as a dozen or 20 loaded car trucks on the train. Opposite the small, stone jetty where the Kyle Akin ferry terminates, there is a big notice board advertising this facility and giving the times of trains to Strathcarron.

However, this was not a new service, for it had been introduced by the Highland railway early in the century, soon after the appearance of motor cars in the West Highlands, even though these new vehicles were few in number then. The service was in use by 1910, and the reason for its existence was to let car drivers avoid the difficulties and apprehension associated with their vehicles crossing by the ferry at Strome. In addition, there was the steep and winding road to contend with above Strome Ferry.

By the time of Ellis's visit, the renowned 'Skye Bogies' had disappeared from the line - the last of them having been withdrawn in 1930 - to be replaced mainly by two other classes. These were the Jones 4-6-0s and the Cumming 4-6-0s. During 1894, the Highland Railway had obtained, from Sharp, Stewart and Co. Ltd of Glasgow, a total of 15 bogie goods engines, built to the design of David Jones, and these became the first 4-6-0s to run in Britain - and for a time, they were the most powerful engines in the country. The Cumming 4-6-0s were named from Christopher Cumming, the Highland's locomotive superintendent since 1915, who had designed four other 4-6-0 goods engines in 1918 and a further four in 1919, with all of these having been built by R. and W. Hawthorn, Leslie and Co. Ltd of Newcastle.* Hamilton Ellis mentioned the locomotives of the Kyle line as follows:

The Jones 4-6-0s of 1894, which enjoyed nearly 40 years of life before ever they saw the west coast, are now regularly at work on the Skye line, and there are usually two to be seen at the Kyle. In September, the writer saw one of them take nine bogies and a six-wheeler, forming the morning train, from Kyle to Dingwall without losing time. The regular engine for this train was one of the larger Cumming 4-6-0 goods engines of 1918, which are the biggest allowed on the line. These two classes seem to be the regular Skye engines nowadays. Gone are the times when the brave little 'Skye Bogies' did nearly all the work, occasionally assisted by visiting giants in the form of a 'Strath' or a 'Small Ben'. The two former classes have gone forever, but the 'Bens' still turn up occasionally. So do the 'Lochs', though four-coupled locomotives are very rare on the line now. Sometimes, a 4-6-0 'Castle' puts in an appearance at Kyle.

The 'Castle' class, designed by David Jones but built under Peter Drummond's superintendency, comprised a series of 12 passenger engines for working heavy traffic between Perth and Inverness via Carr Bridge. The first six had come from Dübs in 1900, and the same firm produced four more in 1902, with the remaining two having been supplied by the North British Locomotive Co. Ltd of Glasgow in 1910 and 1911. Another type of engine to work on the Kyle line during the second half of the 1930s was the 4-6-0 'Clan' goods and passenger class, which had also been designed by Cumming, and built by Hawthorn, Leslie and Co. originally for the increasing traffic between Perth and Inverness. Four of them for goods traffic had been delivered in 1919, followed by a further four for passenger trains in 1921 and they became the last engines to be designed by Cumming and to be built for the Highland Railway.

---

* Hawthorn and Co. of Leith were originally the Scottish branch of Hawthorn, Leslie and Co. of Newcastle.

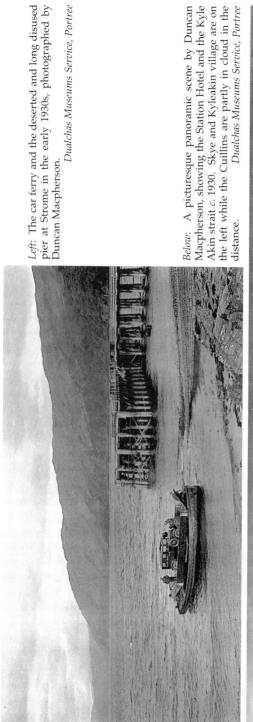

Left: The car ferry and the deserted and long disused pier at Strome in the early 1930s, photographed by Duncan Macpherson.

Dualchas Museums Service, Portree

Below: A picturesque panoramic scene by Duncan Macpherson, showing the Station Hotel and the Kyle Akin strait *c.* 1930. Skye and Kyleakin village are on the left while the Cuillins are partly in cloud in the distance.

Dualchas Museums Service, Portree

The arrival of the first Sunday excursion train at Kyle of Lochalsh in August 1929, as captured by Duncan Macpherson.   *Dualchas Museums Service, Portree*

A Duncan Macpherson photograph of Kyle of Lochalsh village *c.* 1930, from above the Plockton road that shows both the main street and the station and pier area, with the engine shed near the foreground, and Skye having a wintry appearance.   *Dualchas Museums Service, Portree*

Garve station in 1931 looking south. *H.C. Casserley*

Garve station in 1931, looking south-east to Loch Garve. The railway runs along the southern shore of the loch, from right to left into the distance. *St Andrews University Library*

Steam at Garve in 1937. In the foreground is Cumming 4-6-0 LMS No. 17956, ex-HR No. 81, with the 4.05 pm Inverness-Kyle service while 'Jones Goods' LMS No. 17930, ex-HR No. 117, approaches tender first with an eastbound goods, having passed below what was the only road bridge on the original Dingwall and Skye Railway. *H.C. Casserley*

Garve station in 1946, looking north. *J.L. Stevenson*

Achnasheen station *c.* 1930, looking north.   *J.L. Stevenson*

Achnasheen in 1935, looking south-west, showing the bleak and lonely aspect of the old staging post, initially for horse-drawn coaches and then for trains. The railway curves to the left to head south-west for Kyle, as does a road, while another road, to the right of the view, turns west for Kinlochewe and Gairloch. The brightness of the hotel at the station contrasts especially with the dark goods shed to its left.   *St Andrews University Library*

From 1933 names were given to two of the Kyle line trains by the LMSR. These were the 'Hebridean' and the 'Lewisman' and an example of their running times Mondays to Saturdays, was represented in the following basic timetable for 5th July to 26th September, 1937:

		'Hebridean' Restaurant Car	'Lewisman' Restaurant Car		
		am	*am*	*pm*	
Inverness	d.	7.25	10.15	4.10	
Dingwall		8.05	10.58	4.45	
Kyle of Lochalsh	a.	10.33	1.40 *pm*	7.13	
Portree	a.		4.30		
Stornoway	a.		7.30		

		'Lewisman' Restaurant Car	'Hebridean' Restaurant Car		
		pm	*am*	*am*	*pm*
Stornoway	d.	11.00 *(a)*			
Portree	d.		7.50		
Kyle of Lochalsh	d.	5.05 *am (b)*	6.10	10.45	5.35
Dingwall		7.23	9.23	1.40 *pm*	8.10
Inverness	a.	8.10	*10.11*	2.18	8.51

Note: (a) Sun to Fri nights. (b) 'Lewisman' through-carriages Kyle-Glasgow.

The Portree steamer called at Broadford and Raasay, and the Stornoway steamer called at Applecross.

The timetable for the same period on the Strathpeffer branch read thus:

								(a)
		am	*am*	*am*	*am*	*pm*	*pm*	*pm*
Inverness	d.	6.45		9.25	10.25			2.40
Dingwall	d.	7.50	8.45	10.20	11.18	1.55	2.47	3.45
Strathpeffer	a.	8.00	8.55	10.30	11.30	2.05	2.57	3.55

		(b)					SX	SO
		pm	*pm*	*pm*	*pm*	*pm*	*pm*	*pm*
Inverness	d.	2.40	4.10	5.00	6.00		8.15	8.25
Dingwall	d.	4.10	5.10	5.54	6.50	8.15	9.10	9.20
Strathpeffer	a.	4.20	5.20	6.04	7.00	8.25	9.20	9.30

		am	*am*	*am*	*pm*	*pm*	*pm*	*pm*
Strathpeffer	d.	8.30	9.25	10.45	1.10	2.25	3.15	4.27
Dingwall	a.	8.40	9.35	10.55	1.20	2.35	3.27	4.37
Inverness	a.		10.40		2.18	3.20		5.52

						SX	SO	SX	SO
		pm	*pm*	*pm*	*pm*	*pm*	*pm*	*pm*	*pm*
Strathpeffer	d.	5.35	6.25	7.45	8.35	8.35	9.30	9.40	
Dingwall	a.	5.45	6.35	7.55	8.45	8.45	9.40	9.50	
Inverness	a.			8.51	9.33	9.43			

Notes: (a) Until 14th August.   (b) From 16th August.
SX - Saturdays excepted.   SO - Saturdays only.

Achnashellach station in 1927, looking north-east, with the passing trains hauled by 'Skye Bogie' 4-4-0s. The approaching engine is LMS No. 14283, ex-HR No. 6.   *H.C. Casserley*

Achnashellach station in 1937, looking north-east. Cumming 4-6-0 LMS No. 17956, ex-HR No. 81, is shunting while working an Inverness-Kyle service.   *H.C. Casserley*

Another view of Cumming 4-6-0 No. 17956, ex-HR No. 81, as it shunts the siding at Achnashellach in 1937.   *H.C. Casserley*

Strathcarron station in 1934 with 'Jones Goods' 4-6-0 LMS No. 17919, ex-HR No. 106.
G.E. Langmuir

Strathcarron station *c.* 1930, looking north-east. The goods shed is visible to the upper right of the station house.
Lens of Sutton

Strathcarron station and hamlet in 1937 from the south. The goods shed is at the right, and the building at the left, partly hidden by trees, is the Strathcarron Hotel, established from the completion of the Dingwall and Skye Railway in 1870.   *St Andrews University Library*

The signal cabin at Stromeferry station in 1937, looking east.   *H.C. Casserley*

Plockton station *c.* 1930, looking south-west from the road bridge and showing the goods shed and sidings.   *Lens of Sutton*

'Small Ben' class 4-4-0 *Ben Avon* LMS No. 14412, ex-HR No. 16 and built in 1901, approaches Kyle with a mixed train from Dingwall in 1926. This was the first locomotive class to be designed by Peter Drummond, and of the 20 engines, the first eight were built by Dübs & Co. in 1898 and 1899, followed by nine at Lochgorm Works from 1899 to 1901, and the remaining three by the North British Locomotive Co. in 1906. *LCGB/Ken Nunn Collection*

The sidings near the engine shed at Kyle of Lochalsh in 1937, looking north-west. The Kyle line is on the right of the view, and the siding on the left - above which can be seen the top of the water tank - leads to the turntable. The engine is Cumming 4-6-0 LMS No. 17956, ex-HR No. 81. *H.C. Casserley*

In 1939, the Kyle line timetable from 1st May to 23rd September was similar to that for the summer-autumn period of 1937, and it was the last before the commencement of World War II in September 1939:

		(a)		(b)	(c)	(d)
		am	am	pm	pm	pm
Inverness	d.	7.25	10.15	4.05	4.10	5.00
Kyle of Lochalsh	a.	10.31	1.40 pm	8.05	7.13	8.53

		(c) ·			(e)	(a)
		am	am	am	pm	pm
Kyle of Lochalsh	d.	5.05	6.10	10.40	5.25	5.35
Inverness	a.	8.10	10.11	2.18 pm	9.35	8.51

Notes: (a) From 5th June. (b) SX. Until 30th June. (c) From 3rd July. (d) SO. Until 1st July. (e) Until 3rd June.

All of the trains called at Dingwall, Garve, Achnasheen, Strathcarron, Stromeferry* and Plockton, with the exception of the 5.05 am service from Kyle, which did not stop at Plockton.
By this time, over its four decades of existence, Kyle of Lochalsh had become, like Oban, a crossroads of the West Highlands, with trains and steamers running in conjunction. Thus, during the summer of 1939, there were the following services between Kyle, Portree, Stornoway and Mallaig:

	pm	am			pm	pm
Stornoway	11.00 (a)		Mallaig		12.00	
Applecross	3.15 am (b)		Armadale		12.25	
Portree		7.50	Glenelg		1.15	
Raasay	am am	8.20	Kyle of Lochalsh a.		1.45	
Kyle of Lochalsh a.	4.15 4.15	9.37	Kyle of Lochalsh d.	2.15 2.30	2.30	
Kyle of Lochalsh d.	6.15 5.45	9.50	Raasay		3.50	
Glenelg	6.45 6.15	10.20	Portree		4.30	
Armadale	7.45 7.15	11.10	Applecross	3.05 3.20		
Mallaig	8.15 7.45	11.30	Stornoway	7.30 8.00		
	(b) (b) (f)			(g) (h)		
	(c) (d)			(i) (i)		
	(e) (e)					

Notes: (a) Sun-Fri nights. (b) Mon-Sat. (c) June. (d) July-Sept. (e) Calls at Glenelg and Armadale Tu, Th, Sa. (f) June-Sept. Calls at Glenelg and Armadale Mon only 29th May-21st Aug. (g) June. (h) July-Sept. (i) Calls at Armadale and Glenelg M, Th, Sa.

The primitive Kyle Akin ferry - secondary to the Kyle-Portree passenger and mail steamer because of the poor state of the connecting roads in Skye - had continued to be worked in the same way for 17 years after the opening of the Kyle Extension, by the use of large rowing-craft that were fitted with sails. However, in the early years of the 20th century, cars were able to be conveyed on the Kyle Akin ferry, but there were few of them at the time. The car was secured on two planks that were attached laterally to, and extending over, the sides of the boat to carry the car, and the boat was towed by another rowing-boat that contained passengers. A car was subjected to a hazardous journey as it was rowed across the kyle, and the Highland Railway, acknowledging this, provided an insurance cover for every vehicle.

* Over the years, both spellings 'Strome Ferry' and 'Stromeferry' were used, with the latter gradually prevailing.

Kyle shed in 1937. The engine in the foreground is 'Jones Goods' 4-6-0 LMS No. 17925, ex-HR No. 112. The other engine is a Cumming 4-6-0.   *H.C. Casserley*

The northern part of Kyle of Lochalsh village *c.* 1930, photographed by Duncan Macpherson. A similar view exists today, even to the presence of the signal box.

Dualchas Museums Service, Portree

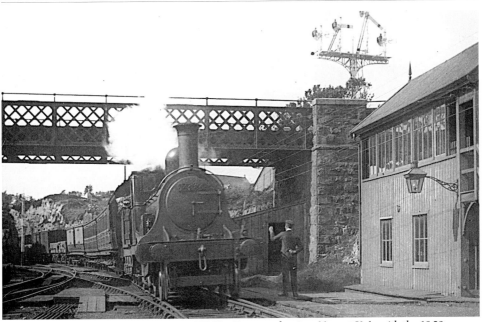

'Skye Bogie' 4-4-0 LMS No. 14284, ex-HR No. 7, passes the signal box at Kyle with the 10.20 am service from Inverness in 1926. *LCGB/Ken Nunn Collection*

'Skye Bogie' 4-4-0 LMS No. 14279, ex-HR No. 86, at Kyle of Lochalsh in 1927. *H.C. Casserley*

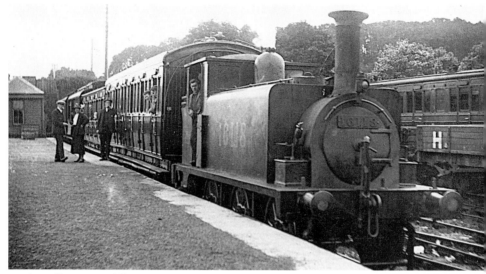

Stroudley 0-6-0 saddle-tank LMS No. 16118, ex-HR No. 56 and formerly named *Balnain*, at the Strathpeffer platform of Dingwall station, with the branch train in 1926. This engine, dating from 1869 was the first to be built at the Highland Railway's Lochgorm Works, and was one of only three designed by William Stroudley, the Highland's first Locomotive Superintendent. It was also the only one of the three to be completed while Stroudley was employed by the Highland - the other two having been built under the charge of his successor, David Jones - and, in being named *Dornoch* in 1902, it became the first engine to work on the Dornoch Light Railway.   *LCGB/Ken Nunn Collection*

The third *Strathpeffer* engine at Dingwall in 1928, as LMS No. 15051, ex-HR No. 25. The name was removed in 1920.   *H.C. Casserley*

In 1914, the first motor-boat, or motor-launch, made its appearance, under the ownership of Captain Finlayson of Kyle. A car mounted in the rowing boat was then able to be towed with ease behind the motor-launch. An improved, second motor-launch, which was given the name *Kyle*, arrived in 1916, and this was followed in 1922 by a third, called *Skye*, which was similar to *Kyle*. This method of conveyance remained in use throughout the 1920s, and then a further improvement occurred in 1930, with the introduction of the fourth motor launch, *Kyleakin*, which was equipped with a turntable and ramps, though it could still only carry one vehicle. By the beginning of the 1930s, larger vehicles, such as motor buses, merchants' vans and tourists' caravans, were risking the passage in slowly-increasing numbers, as confidence had grown in the ferry, while the roads in Skye had also been improved. From 1st January, 1935, the ferry was leased to David MacBrayne Ltd, and in 1936, came the fifth motor-launch, *Moil*, which was able to convey two cars.

From the commencement of World War II in September 1939, northern Scotland and its railways, including the Kyle line, again became strategically vital in the defence of Britain from Germany, with the area north and west of Inverness restricted to military personnel and local people. Once more, Kyle was transformed into a naval port of secrecy, in which the principal operations involved the movement of mines to there by way of the railway. The mines were stored along the line in specially constructed sidings, as at Duirinish, Stromeferry and Fodderty, before being conveyed to Kyle and loaded onto the ships of the British fleet. The naval base at Kyle was given the name *HMS Trelawney*, initially with the secret code name 'Port B' which was changed to 'Port ZA'. As in World War I, the Kyle line handled long, heavy naval trains, with the consequence that the service trains were restricted or cancelled, and special passes were required for travelling; but because of the greater resources of the LMSR, in comparison to those of the Highland Railway during the previous war, there was generally less disruption to the public. The line was also important for carrying the service personnel, arms and other equipment over the eastern portion of the line to and from Achnasheen, in connection with the port of Aultbea. It was in the safe, sheltered and deep waters from Aultbea to Ullapool that the convoys were assembled for their various war operations.

In the years between World War I and World War II, Strathpeffer had been a busy spa-resort, but by the onset of the war in 1939, the peak of the popularity of the village was long past and could not return. During World War II, Strathpeffer was again invaded by the military population, when the spa facilities were suspended and the train service dwindled to almost complete withdrawal. It was now also the era of the motor car and the motor bus, which, in offering greater convenience to both the visiting and local residents of Strathpeffer, had become such formidable rivals to the train. The railway had managed to endure the struggle of the new competition until World War II, prior to which a service of 12 trains per day in each direction had been maintained, similar to the timetable of 1937; but by the end of the war in May 1945, the situation was very different. In the 1945 timetable, the passenger service on the branch consisted of just one weekly train - the 11.25 pm Saturdays-only from Dingwall, arriving at 11.37 and returning empty. Connecting with the 10.30 pm Inverness to Tain service, it was used mainly by the Strathpeffer service personnel who had spent the evening carousing at Dingwall or Inverness.

For the next nine months, with Strathpeffer not having reopened as a spa-resort, this solitary passenger train, running at 11.25 pm on Saturdays, was all that continued to be available to the public on the branch until its quiet closure on the last Saturday in February 1946. In view of such a minimum service, which was the most infrequent in

Sentinel steam railcar, LMS No. 4749, at Strathpeffer station in 1928.   *H.C. Casserley*

The branch train at Strathpeffer in the early 1930s. The engine is 'Yankee' class 4-4-0 *Munlochy*, LMS No. 15014, ex-HR No. 102, which was one of two original tanks built by Dübs and Co. in 1891 for Uruguay. This engine was very similar to HR No. 11, renumbered 51, that worked the branch in 1903.   *L&GRP*

Britain - and there had been no increase during the summer of 1945 - the LMSR were determined that the line would soon cease to carry any passengers, though goods traffic, little as that was too, would remain. The *Railway Magazine* reported in its issue of September-October 1946:

> The LMSR closed the branch from Dingwall to Strathpeffer to passenger traffic on 23rd February. The services had been drastically reduced throughout the war years and had consisted latterly of one late-evening train from Dingwall on Saturdays only. The branch continues to deal with goods traffic, and Achterneed station, on the Dingwall-Kyle of Lochalsh section, affords an alternative for passengers.

The goods traffic, comprising the one daily train, lasted another five years, finishing in 1951 under the nationalised British Railways, which, had come into existence on 1st January, 1948. An announcement appeared in the *Ross-shire Journal* of 16th March, 1951, referring to the 'closing of Strathpeffer station for passenger train parcels and miscellaneous traffic and freight train traffic', and explaining that 'on and after Monday 26th March, 1951, the above-mentioned traffic, previously dealt with at Strathpeffer station, will be collected or delivered in Strathpeffer by Railway Executive road motor, based on Dingwall'. Thus, the Strathpeffer branch, after 66 years of operation, was the first railway in the Highlands to be closed under nationalisation. However, this new structure of the state taking control of the railways was ultimately necessary because of the ravages to them from German bombing raids during World War II, such that the constituents of the Grouping, having insufficient resources, could not remedy the situation properly in the form of investment and modernisation. Within the name of British Railways, there were six regions, determined geographically, of which the Scottish Region encompassed all of the lines north of the Border.

Various locomotives had operated on the Strathpeffer branch, the most famous being the three that were named *Strathpeffer*. The first of them, which was the 2-2-2 tank engine, HR No. 12, ex-*Breadalbane* and *Belladrum*, having worked the branch from its opening in 1885, was withdrawn in 1898. The replacement, the 0-4-4 saddle-tank, HR No. 13, which had taken over from 1890 until 1903, continued for most of its remaining life on the Lybster line, though it also worked latterly on the Dornoch branch. As LMSR No. 15050, it was withdrawn in 1929. The last engine to be named after the Spa, the 0-4-4 saddle-tank, HR No. 25, which had commenced working the branch in 1905, remained there until 1930, having become LMSR No. 15051, and then BR No. 55051 in 1949. Another type of locomotive to have been used on the branch largely in the LMSR period was the 4-4-0 'Yankee-Tank', built by Dübs and Co. of Glasgow. This was the class whose first two members had been originally bound for Uruguay in 1891, and which, instead, had been purchased by the Highland Railway in 1892, with the remaining three following in 1893. The unnamed No. 51, the third of the class, was the engine that had already worked the Strathpeffer branch train in 1903, in which T.R. Perkins had then travelled as part of his Highland Railway tour. One of the original two engines intended for Uruguay, LMSR No. 15014, ex-HR No. 102 and named *Munlochy*, worked regularly on the branch during the early 1930s until its withdrawal in 1934. Among various other classes to have been recorded on the line were the 4-4-0 'Small Bens' during the 1920s, the 4-4-0 'Lochs' during the 1930s, and the 0-6-0 'Barneys' during the 1930s. Of the 12 engines of the Highland's 'Barney' class, which was designed for goods traffic, the first 10 were built by Dübs in 1900 and 1902, while the remaining two were from the North British Locomotive Company in 1907.

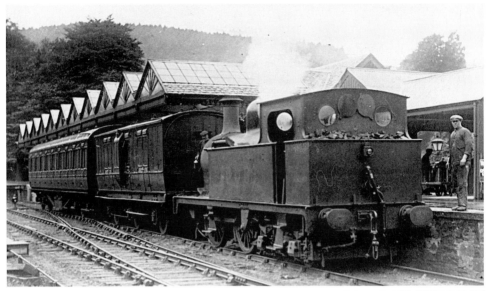

Above: Strathpeffer station in 1932. The engine is an ex-Glasgow & South Western Railway 0-4-4 tank, being one of three that worked in the Highlands from 1930 to 1932. *Lens of Sutton*

Right: An advertisement for the railway-owned Highland Hotel in Strathpeffer. *Ross-shire Journal*

Chapter Sixteen

The British Railways Years

Six years after nationalisation, a significant local change had been completed, in the spring of 1954, in regard to a short section of the Kyle line along the north-western shore of Loch Luichart. This resulted from the North of Scotland Hydro-Electric Board's Conon Valley project, which necessitated the raising of the loch by 25 feet, with the consequence that part of the railway, together with Lochluichart station, would be submerged. Thus, for a distance of about 1¾ miles, a new trackbed had to be made in such a way that it would form a diversion both horizontally and vertically in relation to the existing route. This meant that, because of the increased depth of the loch, the new line had to be built slightly to the north of, but also sufficiently higher than, the original. In addition to the laying of a new track and the construction of a new station, the work included other associated new features. There was the building of a ¾ mile-long stone embankment, north-eastwards from the station, to raise the railway along the side of the now-higher loch; a 100 ft-span bridge, replacing its predecessor of the same size, over the now-wider stretch of water that had been the River Conon; a 36 ft-span bridge beside the new Mossford Power Station, at the northern end of the embankment; a station master's house; and two cottages for surfacemen. The diversion, which extended from a mile north-eastwards to ¾ mile south-westwards of the stations, ran almost parallel with and close to the original route, such that the new station was built about 100 yards north of the previous one. The maximum separation of the two lines was in the vicinity of the stations for a short distance on either side of them, and over much of the 1¾ mile length, the diversion was as much in a vertical as a horizontal plane. The new line was 43 yards longer than the original.

Apart from the loss of the original 1¼ mile course of the River Conon from its beginning at the confluence of the River Bran and the River Grudie, another effect of the flooding from the scheme was the loss of the hamlet of Mossford, on the southern bank of the Conon. The Mossford inhabitants had been among those to petition the Dingwall and Skye Directors in 1871 for a public station, and due to the generosity of Lady Ashburton of Lochluichart Lodge, their request had been granted, with the public station near Mossford succeeding her private station near the Lodge. Over the years, many guests of Lady Ashburton had travelled by the Skye railway, using Lochluichart station, and among the more famous of them had been Thomas Carlyle, the Scottish philosopher and historian, and Robert Browning, the English poet.

On Monday 3rd May, 1954, which was 83 years after the opening of the second, but first public, Lochluichart station, the early morning train from Dingwall to Kyle switched over to the new track and drew up at the new, third station, built by the North of Scotland Hydro-Electric Board. The station building was of a modern design that contrasted with the older style of its predecessor and the other stations on the Skye line. The station master, Charles Garrow, was also the signalman, porter and sub-postmaster.

Prior to nationalisation, the LMSR had introduced another type of locomotive to the Kyle railway. This was the Stanier class '5' 4-6-0, which made its appearance on the line in 1946. Designed by William Stanier, who was the chief mechanical engineer of the LMSR, the engines originated from the mid-1930s and became known as 'Black Fives'. To accommodate them at Kyle, the 54 ft-long turntable there, which had replaced the original installation of 1897, needed to be superseded by one of 60 ft; and due to the lack of space that was available, the work for this had necessitated the blasting of more rock at the cramped yard of the terminus. The 'Black Fives' soon became popular with the

In this 1952 view at Kyle of Lochalsh, Cumming 4-6-0 No. 57956's tender is still lettered 'LMS', more than three years after nationalisation. *H.C. Casserley*

An eastbound train through bleak Strath Bran in 1952 approaches the skewed bridge one mile to the east of Achanalt station. The 200 ft-long bridge, of four 50 ft spans, is taking the train from the northern side of Loch Achanalt to the souhtern side of Loch a' Chuilinn. *H.C. Casserley*

Left: The eastern end of the Lochluichart diversion, in connection with the North of Scotland Hydro-Electric Board's Conon Valley project. The train is heading west on the original track in March 1954, prior to completion of the new line. *J.L. Stevenson*

Cemtre: Construction of the new station at Lochluichart, looking east, from the train leaving the original station in March 1954. The building nearest the train is the station master's house. *J.L. Stevenson*

Bottom: The new station at Lochluichart, looking west. Resulting from the Conon Valley project, this third Lochluichart station, being the second for public use, opened in May 1954. *Lens of Sutton*

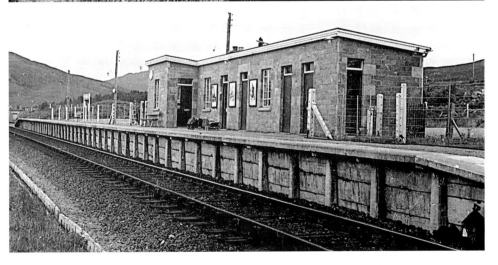

A Stanier class '5' 4-6-0 'Black Five' on the 60 ft turntable at Kyle in 1952. 'Black Fives' appeared on the Kyle line in 1946, and the turntable, installed that year to accommodate the class, superseded the previous one of 54 ft. *H.C. Casserley*

Class '5' 4-6-0 'Black Five' with the 10.45 am Kyle train at Inverness station's platform 7 in 1952. *J.L. Stevenson*

drivers and the other staff.

In 1955, as part of the plans for the modernisation of the British railway system, it was announced that steam locomotives would be replaced by diesel traction. The first diesel engines appeared in the Highlands in 1958, and by 1960, they had virtually taken over from the commonplace but well-liked 'Black Fives', which had given admirable service, although steam services continued on the Kyle line until 1961.

Two late, but special, occasions of a steam locomotive - or, more correctly, the same one twice - operating on the Kyle line, occurred in 1960 and 1961. The locomotive concerned was from the past - a Jones 4-6-0, or a 'Jones Goods', as it was known, that had been made available in 1934 for preservation. Towards the end of the 19th century, the Highland Railway had been in need of powerful locomotives that could work reliably over the long and tough distances of the Perth-Inverness and Inverness-Wick-Thurso lines, and David Jones provided the answer in designing what were Britain's first 4-6-0s. The 15 engines of this class, having been built in 1894 by Sharp, Stewart and Co. of Glasgow, were intended mainly for goods traffic but they were also capable of hauling passenger trains. They worked regularly on the Kyle line during the 1930s but departed before the onset of World War II.

It was the first of the 'Jones Goods' - originally HR No. 103, which became LMSR No. 17916, and then 103 again - that represented the temporary return of the class to the Kyle line. This was possible because, in an era when little thought had been given to preserving locomotives for posterity, the LMSR had decided to retain a 'Jones Goods' and a Caledonian 4-2-2 for that reason. The idea of their preservation was particularly forward-looking because both were still in service. They were kept at St Rollox Works in Glasgow for many years, but in 1959, the Scottish Region of British Railways restored them to full working condition for hauling excursion trains. In the summer of 1960, No. 103 was allowed the historic opportunity of working service trains on the Kyle line - these being the 5.45 pm from Inverness and the 6.15 am from Kyle - and advantage was taken by film cameramen from BBC Television for the 'Railway Roundabout' series of programmes. The film was completed in the summer of 1961, when No. 103, having brought its service train from Kyle to Dingwall, coupled with a 'Black Five' on the service from the North, and then led the latter train double-headed to Inverness. Scenes of the 'Jones Goods' on the Kyle line were shown on 'Railway Roundabout' in the spring of 1962.

During the late 1950s and the early 1960s, revolutionary changes had occurred in regard to methods of transport over Britain generally, and this included the Highlands and islands. Apart from diesel replacing steam on the railways, there was the increasing popularity of the motor car and the aeroplane, and these were seriously rivalling the train. By 1963, there was much pessimism about the future existence of the Kyle line, due to the threat from Dr Richard Beeching, who had been appointed Chairman of British Railways, with the aim of increasing efficiency by closing many of the lines, under the directive of 'Make British Railways Pay by 1970'. The dreaded Beeching report, entitled *The Reshaping of British Railways*, was published on 27th March, 1963. Having been prepared at the request of the Conservative Government, under the leadership of Harold Macmillan, the findings were contained in a booklet of 148 pages, accompanied by 12 maps, showing the intended closures and modifications of rail services throughout Britain. It brought shock to the whole country. Altogether, the plan proposed the withdrawal of 266 passenger services, in addition to 55 already under consideration before the report had been commissioned; and of these, 51 services were in Scotland. It recommended the closure of 1,928 stations, in addition to 435 previously considered, with 235 having already been closed; and of these, 439 were in

Achterneed station in 1956, looking east. *J.L. Stevenson*

Achterneed station in 1956, looking west. *J.L. Stevenson*

Achanalt East signal box in 1952, looking east.

H.C. Casserley

Achanalt station in 1961, looking west.

P. Tatlow

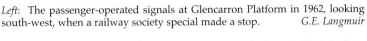

Left: The passenger-operated signals at Glencarron Platform in 1962, looking south-west, when a railway society special made a stop.   *G.E. Langmuir*

Below: A tranquil scene at the lonely Glencarron Platform in 1967, looking north-east, with the halt having closed in December 1964.   *M. Mensing*

Achnashellach station in 1954, looking north-east.   *J.L. Stevenson*

Strathcarron station in 1954, looking north-east. *J.L. Stevenson*

Attadale platform in 1954, looking north. *J.L. Stevenson*

Stromeferry station in 1954, looking east.   *J.L. Stevenson*

Duncraig platform in 1954, showing the octagonal waiting room and looking east through one of the largest cuttings on the Kyle Extension. The girls are students from Duncraig Castle College, situated on the high ground to the upper right of the view.   *J.L. Stevenson*

Scotland.* This would result in more than 40 per cent of the railway network and more than two-thirds of the stations in Scotland being closed.

The Highlands would suffer drastically, if the plans of the Beeching report were implemented. The principal features were the withdrawal of all passenger services north and west of Inverness, which meant to Wick and Thurso and to Kyle of Lochalsh; and there was to be closure of the Aviemore-Grantown-Forres line, but with the retention of the Inverness-Perth and Inverness-Aberdeen lines, involving the reduction of services and the closure of many of the intermediate stations that served the smaller communities. The northern half of the Highlands would suffer most, for, in the southern half, the Glasgow-West Highland lines to Oban, Fort William and Mallaig were to remain; but, while it was understood that what Beeching had produced was only a report and not a final decision, there was little doubt that the majority of the recommendations would be carried into effect. This cold and callous intended amputation of some of Britain's arteries was indeed devastating news for the future of the railways in general, as well as for the Highlands. There would now be many battles, like never before, by the British people, who were determined that their rail services would remain, and among the gallant fighters were to be those for the Kyle line.

The *Scotsman*, in Edinburgh, was one source of opinion that appreciated the value of the Kyle line above other railways, and the paper, on the day after the publication of Beeching's report, in commenting about the station closures, spoke for all of the line's supporters, near and far, with these words:

> Inconvenient these closures may be to some. But included in the list are names whose closures would be tragic to Scotland.
> Names like Kyle of Lochalsh. Without a railway, Kyle must die. It was built by the railway and has always lived by the railway. From Kyle, leaves the MacBrayne steamers - the life-blood of so many islanders. Let 99 in every 100 stations listed by Dr Beeching be closed - but *not* the hundredth, like Kyle. This is a clear case for a subsidy. A look at the map shows the lack of population, but a look at the map shows the potential tourist trade, and the vital role the railway plays. No bus substitution would be of use here.
> Similar cases must be made out for Wick and Thurso. It is only in recent years the drain of population has been arrested in Caithness and Sutherland. All the valuable progress made to date would be shattered without a railway link. There is no charity about a subsidy being given for this route. It is a right the people must demand.
> Kyle, Wick and Thurso - these three stations must be retained.

Not surprisingly, Beeching's plan of closure for the Kyle line was heavily criticised inside and outside the Highlands by authorities and individuals, amid the feeling of shock. There would be dire consequences for the village of Kyle, with its population of 600, and for the surrounding areas, because the railway was the largest source of employment there. This consisted of a labour force of 80, which represented one-third of the working population of Kyle, and there were more sources of employment - shops, banks, post office, other services, trades, etc. - which were dependent, to some degree, upon the stable economy that was provided by the railway, while the tourist industry over a large surrounding area would also suffer greatly. Thus, the potential loss of the Kyle line was seen as catastrophic to Wester Ross and Skye.

The crux of the matter concerned suitable alternative transport, or the lack of it, for there was none that compared with the railway. Indeed, the local people, having recovered slightly from the shock of hearing what the Beeching report had in store for

---

* Among the closures to passenger traffic, on 13th June, 1960, had been some of the intermediate stations between Inverness and Wick, with goods traffic remaining, while the Dornoch branch had closed to all traffic.

Plockton station in 1954, looking south-west from the road bridge. *J.L. Stevenson*

Plockton station in 1954, looking north-east, showing the road bridge that would have accommodated a loop, though this was never built. The station master's house is visible through the bridge. *J.L. Stevenson*

Duirinish station in 1954, looking south-west. Part of the village of Drumbuie is visible on the left.   *J.L. Stevenson*

Duirinish station in 1954, looking north-east.   *J.L. Stevenson*

'Clan' class 4-6-0 *Clan Mackinnon* is seen shunting at Kyle. It still carries its LMS number - 14767 - in this 1949 view. *J.L. Stevenson*

Kyle of Lochalsh station in 1952. The engine is Cumming 4-6-0 BR No. 57956 on the 5.35 pm service to Dingwall. *H.C. Casserley*

them, realised that they could be confident that no closure of the line would be enforced - at least in the immediate future - because there was no adequate system of road communication available at the time, and nor was there likely to be for a number of years to come. There were only single-track roads with passing-places, combined with steep gradients and sharp curves, and too often snow-bound in winter, so that no one believed that road haulage could provide as efficient a service as the railway. By road, there was no regular passenger or goods service between Inverness and Kyle. Nevertheless, while the immediate threat of the Beeching plan looked as if it might be able to be averted for reasons of social hardships, the shadow of the axe-man of the railways would, for the time being, cast gloom over the future of the Kyle line, and the people and authorities could not relax in their efforts to convince the Government of their resulting difficulties, if their rail connection was taken away.

There was concern that financial considerations were taking priority over social aspects in the proposed implementation of the Beeching plan. The Federation of Crofters' Unions issued the following memorandum, after receiving protests about the rail closures from the member unions:

Closure of Highland railways will mean the death-knell of crofting and other activities north* of Inverness. The Government must not give priority to soul-less economies over the welfare of the Highland people. If the Highlands are to be put on a profit-and-loss account, then the crofting counties might as well be written off. Destruction of Highland railways will mean a betrayal of the Government's promise in its White Paper, *Review of Highland Policy,* which stated the aim to 'provide social amenities and social services, so that viable communities may be established and retained there'.

Many roads in the Highlands are mere ribbons. Even if a massive crash programme of road alternatives was begun, blizzards will wipe out their usefulness for many weeks each year. Severe hardships will follow without railway lifelines. Priorities for the Highlands and the isles are industrial development, tourism, agriculture and fishing, together with the settlement of overspill populations. To achieve these, the Kyle of Lochalsh, Wick and Thurso railways from Inverness are vital and must be retained.

The Dingwall-Kyle of Lochalsh railway has the railheads Garve, Achnasheen and Strathcarron serving the small communities on the west coast of the country at Ullapool, Gairloch and the shore of Loch Torridon. In addition to serving the greater part of the mainland of Ross-shire, the route connects Aberdeen and the Moray Firth with the west coast and the Hebrides. From Kyle, there are daily steamer services to Stornoway, Portree, Raasay, Applecross and Mallaig, and thrice-weekly steamer services to Harris and the Uists. At peak-traffic periods, the 770 seats on trains are fully taken up. Despite heavy snowfalls in central Ross-shire, rail services are generally not interrupted.

Present overloaded narrow roads are totally unfit for the carryings of the railways. If alternatives for the railways are to be substituted, then the Beeching report should never have been published until a parallel report on alternatives was also issued. Ministerial assurances are inadequate to dispel the fear and dismay of the crofters of the Highlands and the isles.

The opinion of the National Farmers' Union of Scotland was also made known:

A first reading this report leaves the overwhelming impression that its conclusions have been based almost exclusively on commercial considerations. The summary sets out the main objectives as building up the well-loaded routes and closing down 'routes which are so lightly loaded as to have no chance of paying their way and to discontinue services which cannot be provided economically'. The commercial yardstick is used throughout, and this makes the report completely one-sided and certainly no answer in itself to the major problem of ensuring an adequate transport system in this country.

At the same time, it would be folly to think that the railway system can be run without reference

---

* Including west.

Achnasheen in 1958, with a class '5' 4-6-0 'Black Five' No. 45476 hauling the 10.45 am Kyle-
Inverness service.   *P. Tatlow*

A Stanier class '5' 4-6-0 is seen hauling a Kyle goods train at Achnasheen on 10th July, 1958.
                                                                                                    P. Tatlow

The view from Raven Rock, looking east and down towards the 9.10 am Inverness-Kyle service hauled by a class '5' 4-6-0 'Black Five' in 1960. *P. Tatlow*

A Kyle-Inverness goods train is effectively insignificant in size against the hills, though it stands out because of the contrast in tone and smoke. The bleak location is the north-eastern end, or upper part, of Glen Carron, and the year is 1960.   *P. Tatlow*

A class '5' 4-6-0 'Black Five' No. 45123 is seen at Luib Summit in 1960, with the 10.45 am Kyle-Inverness service.   *P. Tatlow*

to economics, and this is not the attitude of the Union. When proposals have been put up in the past for closing branch lines and reducing facilities in other ways, the farming community has proved itself understanding and co-operative.

What is needed is a balance between the right of the community to have a reasonably adequate transport service at reasonable cost and, on the other hand, the economics of operating particular services. To achieve this balance, a rational integration of all forms of public transport is needed. This was the theme of the Highland transport report, published in February, which made good sense for the country as a whole but which received all too little public attention.

And in conclusion:

We cannot accept the view that the provision of transport services should be judged only by the yardstick of profitability. This is a narrow and sectional approach to a major public problem.

Strangely, the Scottish Landowners' Federation was ready to accept the situation and felt that the 'proposed rail closures, although frightening, could be a blessing in disguise to the rural areas of Scotland' - a statement that was then explained in terms of improving the bus transport:

It is true that implementation of the proposals might have an adverse effect on employment and distribution of population in certain outlying districts. But this need not be so. In the remoter parts of the North and West, road-improvement work on a specific scale will be necessary, and this will mean substantial employment. Everywhere, greatly-improved bus services, including provisions for transport of heavy personal luggage, will be necessary. Also, modern equipment will have to be bought with a view to keeping the roads, instead of the railways, open in winter. Provided that this policy is carried out, no rural depopulation need necessarily follow the closure of railway lines. During the initial changeover period, there will inevitably be some hardship and personal inconvenience. Reasonable steps can, however, be taken to mitigate this.

The closure of the Inverness-Kyle line will deprive Skye and Wester Ross of a vital source of communication. Severance of this link must not be allowed until such times as a first-class new road has been completed. Further depopulation in such areas must be prevented. The Federation trust that the Government will not sanction withdrawal of any rail service before a satisfactory alternative is in operation. This is the crux of the Beeching bargain.

The *Stornoway Gazette*, in representing the viewpoint of the islands, expressed caution about closing the Kyle line on the assumption that alternative public transport would be provided, emphasising the importance of an integrated transport system; and within this, was the meaning that there was no point in retaining the railway without other improvements in transport communications taking place:

Ready for Beeching. The Highlands are better placed to meet the Beeching crisis than most parts of the country because we have an alternative proposal ready, which can be urged on the Government with a fair chance of success. The Government is at present considering the report of the Highland Transport Inquiry, which recommended the setting up of a supervisory body to advise on the general level of transport services (of all kinds) that are necessary to provide an adequate modern transport system for the Highlands, and to see that any subsidies given are distributed to the best advantage of the Highlands and the nation. To campaign for the adoption of the Highland Transport Inquiry's report makes sense. To raise a cry of 'Hands off the Kyle railway' certainly does not. To keep the Kyle railway would be a purely-negative achievement, but to get a government body charged with the task of seeing that the area has an adequate modern transport service would be something positive and permanent.

The damage which would result from the premature closure of the Kyle railway is obvious; so obvious that no government could take the risk - especially a government which may shortly be going to the country, and must hold every Parliamentary seat it can. For one thing, closure of the Kyle railway would make nonsense of the administrative counties of Ross and Inverness. On two

A view of the 'Devon Belle' observation car - the first such vehicle on the line - as the 9.10 am Inverness-Kyle service passes Rogie in 1961.   *P. Tatlow*

A railway society special, hauled by class '5' 4-6-0 'Black Five' No. 44978 in 1962, passes the north-western shore of Loch Luichart.   *P. Tatlow*

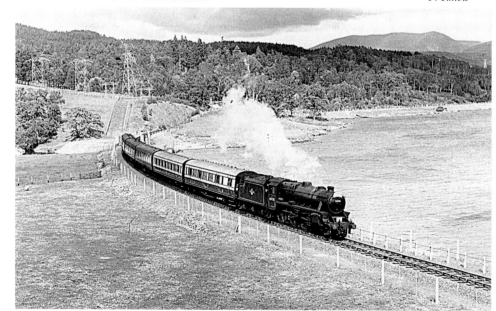

days a week, for most of the year, there is no air transport between Inverness and the Outer Isles, and on many days when the plane does fly, in summer, it cannot carry all the passengers who want to travel. Very often, people who have urgent business find themselves at the end of the queue because they cannot make bookings in advance. With no Kyle railway and no air service, the islands would be effectively cut off from contact with their respective county towns. The Government has deliberately tried over the years to build up Inverness as the capital of the Highlands; but without the Kyle line, or some really satisfactory alternative to it, Inverness will be more remote than Glasgow or even Edinburgh. Indeed, even now, it is often more convenient to travel to Glasgow than to Inverness.

There must be changes in the pattern of Highland transport, and the preservation of the *status quo* makes no more sense than it would have made to fight for the retention of the horse-and-trap after the motor car had appeared. What we need is some organisation which can ensure that the necessary changes are made in an orderly way, to provide an improving, rather than a diminishing, transport service. The one danger is that the Government is so thirled to the virtues of private enterprise, it may assume that bus services will spring up wherever railway services are withdrawn, to provide the necessary alternative. There is no justification whatever for such a view, especially in the Highlands, where so many bus services are themselves threatened with extinction by the increasing number of private càrs on the road. Everyone cannot have a private car, and some form of public transport is essential.

At the time of the publication of the Beeching report, the Kyle-line timetable, covering the period 10th September, 1962 to 16th June, 1963, Mondays to Saturdays, read as follows:

		(a)				(b)		(c)
		am	pm			am	am	pm
Inverness	d.	10.30	5.40	Kyle of Lochalsh	d.	6.00	10.45	5.30
Dingwall	a.	10.59	6.09	Duirinish		6.09	10.53	5.38
Dingwall	d.	11.09	6.14	Plockton		6.14	10.57	5.42
Achterneed		11.22	6.27	Duncraig		*6.18	*11.00	5.46
Garve		11.41	6.47	Stromeferry		6.29	11.11	5.56
Lochluichart		11.58	7.03	Attadale		6.45	11.28	6.13
Achanalt		12.10 pm	7.15	Strathcarron		6.53	11.36	6.19
Achnasheen		12.28	7.37	Achnashellach		7.09	11.52	6.34
Glencarron		*12.44	*7.53	Glencarron		*7.19	*12.01 pm	*6.44
Achnashellach		12.53	8.02	Achnasheen		7.40	12.23	7.05
Strathcarron		1.03	8.12	Achanalt		7.55	12.40	7.20
Attadale		1.09	8.19	Lochluichart		8.05	12.50	*7.30
Stromeferry		1.25	8.35	Garve		8.20	1.08	7.42
Duncraig		1.34	*8.44	Achterneed		8.39	1.27	8.01
Plockton		1.39	8.49	Dingwall	a.	8.50	1.37	8.11
Duirinish		1.43	8.53	Dingwall	d.	9.30	1.47	8.16
Kyle of Lochalsh	a.	1.53	9.03	Inverness	a.	10.00	2.17	8.30

Notes: (a) Observation car until 1st October. Restaurant car Inverness to Achnasheen.
(b) Restaurant car Achnasheen to Inverness.
(c) Observation car until 1st October. Buffet car.
* Request stop; with Duncraig Halt - originally private for the castle since 1897 - having entered the public timetable in 1949.

For the same period, there was the following MacBrayne's steamer timetable connecting Kyle with Stornoway, Portree and Mallaig:

	pm	am	am	am	am	am
Stornoway	11.45 (a)		12.15 (b)			
Portree					8.00	*9.00
Raasay					8.30	
Kyle of Lochalsh a.	4.00 am		4.30		9.47	
Kyle of Lochalsh d.		5.10		8.30 (c)		
Armadale						11.10
Mallaig		7.05		10.30		11.40

	am	pm	pm	pm	pm
Mallaig	10.15	12.15	12.30 (d)		1.30 (e)
Armadale	10.40	12.40			
Kyle of Lochalsh a.		2.00	2.45		3.30
Kyle of Lochalsh d.		3.00		2.45	
Raasay				4.05	
Portree		*3.15		4.45	
Stornoway		7.15			

Notes: (a) Mon.-Fri. nights. (b) Early Mon. mornings. (c) Mon. only. Also calls at Glenelg 9 am. (d) Thurs only. (e) Sat. only. * Motor coach from Armadale.

MacBrayne's Outer Isles service to and from Kyle read:

	am			pm	
Kyle of Lochalsh	6.00	Wed, Fri	Lochboisdale	*9.00	Mon.
Scalpay (Harris)	11.00		Lochmaddy	*12.30 am	Tu
Tarbert (Harris)	12.00 noon		Lochmaddy	5.30	Tu
Rodel (Harris)	2.00 pm		Rodel	7.00	
Lochmaddy (N. Uist)	4.00		Tarbert	9.30	
Lochboisdale (S. Uist)	7.00		Scalpay	10.00	
			Kyle of Lochalsh	2.45 pm	

* Sleeping berths were available.

Over the years since World War II, there had been gradual improvements to the Kyle Akin ferry service, and during this period, the names of the ferries had been traditionally consistent in accordance with local places. After *Moil* in 1936, *Cuillin* appeared in 1942, followed by *Coruisk* in 1947, which was for passengers only; and then came *Lochalsh* and *Portree* in 1951, and *Broadford* in 1953. *Portree* and *Broadford* contained a turntable device that could accommodate six cars. By the 1960s, the Kyle Akin connection was worked by the Caledonian Steam Packet Company Ltd, based in Gourock, Renfrewshire, and operating the Firth of Clyde steamer services. Their short Skye route was advertised as a 'frequent ferry service between Kyleakin jetty and Kyle of Lochalsh jetty for the conveyance of passengers, luggage, motor vehicles, livestock and merchandise'; and this included a 'special crossing from Kyleakin at 5.30 am, in connection with the early morning train from Kyle of Lochalsh'. There was no Sunday service.

In 1963, Kyle of Lochalsh and its railway were under possible threat not only from the Beeching report but also from the competition that could result in the port being superseded by two other new sea routes - one to the south and the other to the north. The first of these was the introduction of a car ferry from Mallaig to Armadale, due to come into service in 1964, with a road link to Uig in northern Skye and another ferry from there to Tarbert and Lochmaddy. Then there were plans for another new car ferry from Ullapool to Stornoway, though nothing was definite regarding this, of which the

Stornoway Gazette had commented in its article regarding the Kyle line and the Beeching report:

The threat to the Kyle railway gives new urgency to the proposal for a Stornoway-Ullapool ferry. Although we cannot visualise the Government closing the railway abruptly in the immediate future, it seems fairly obvious that it will go sooner or later, and we must consider what the alternative should be. A ferry to Ullapool would have obvious advantages for Stornoway, but it would also have advantages for Ullapool, and for the communities between Ullapool and Inverness, which are now served in part by the railway line and in part by local bus services. Without the Kyle railway, the Ullapool area could hardly hope to maintain adequate communications by bus, unless a good deal of the Stornoway traffic to Dingwall and Inverness and the South were routed along the same road. The Skye traffic should perform a similar function for the smaller communities along the route from Kyle to Inverness, provided we get a by-pass or a really adequate service at Stromeferry. It would be quite unreasonable to close the Kyle railway until the Stromeferry bottle-neck is cleared.

And in overall summary, the paper repeated:

In the meantime, the moral is obvious. There is no good in agitating for a Kyle railway, an Ullapool ferry, a better air service, the retention of the line from Inverness to Wick and Thurso, or any other individual project, however admirable it may seem. What we want is an authority charged with the responsibility of studying the picture as a whole and providing us with an efficient service and a flexible service which can change as the demand changes over the years.

One gentleman who was determined that Kyle should not be permitted to lose its importance - through the closure of the railway and the introduction of new ferry services - was the Lochalsh representative of Ross and Cromarty County Council. He was Torquil Nicolson of Plockton, who had shown his dissatisfaction to the proposals with these words:

We will not take this lying down. We will appeal to our Member of Parliament.

It is possibly unfortunate that the Mallaig-Armadale ferry service, as an integral part of the transport system, should have been approved before the Beeching report had received consideration and before a complete road survey had been made. What we need now is a Beeching report on the roads. I estimate that it would cost at least £4½-5 million to provide a double-track highway between Inverness and Kyle.

The railway should be given a minimum reprieve of 20 years. But if the Beeching plan goes through, it will mean disaster for Kyle. Redundancy would mean that one-third of Kyle's earning potential would go. The village would go back to the way it was before 1900, before it became a railhead - a hamlet of three houses.

The new ferry service will be another terrible blow to the community. I would think that more than half of MacBrayne's staff here would be slashed. Surely our village will be reprieved.

Amid the uncertainty of the future of the Kyle area, Mr Nicolson added that it was not generally realised that 'the maximum saving in mileage of the Mallaig route over the existing ferry at Kyle is only 17 miles, taking it from the Glasgow area; while for traffic coming in from the east of Scotland, the Kyle route is shorter, cheaper and more attractive'. Kyle also had a distinct advantage in that it provided a frequent shuttle service with Skye, which the more southerly route could never hope to provide; and he doubted that many people were aware of the full consequences of the provision of a Stornoway-Ullapool ferry: 'It is a matter of conjecture how many people in the island of Lewis would be prepared to sacrifice the direct sea route for one which would still land them 60 miles from Inverness and 60 miles farther from Glasgow'.

Ardent protests and logical reasoning from authorities and individuals inside and

Birmingham Railway Carriage & Wagon Co. (BRCW) Bo-Bo type '2' No. D5335 is seen shortly after leaving Kyle, in approaching Badicaul, with the 5.30 pm train for Inverness in 1965, and with the 'Devon Belle' observation car at the rear. *M. Mensing*

outside the Highlands ensured that the British Government fully understood how the closure of the Kyle and North railways would create great hardship throughout and beyond the communities that were directly served. Thus, for the near future at least, with short-term financial support from the Government, both lines would stay open, but no guaranteed long-term security was offered, and during 1964, some of the stations were closed to goods traffic. For the Kyle line, these began with Lochluichart and Achnashellach on 27th January, followed by Achterneed on 18th May, Stromeferry on 15th June, Plockton on 7th September, and Achanalt on 2nd November.* Moreover, the process of closure would be taken a step further at the end of the year, when passenger traffic was to cease at Achterneed and at the halts of Glencarron and Duncraig. With the complete closure of the Strathpeffer branch in 1951, Achterneed station had still remained to serve the village - albeit indirectly - in passenger and goods traffic, as it had done on its own from 1870 until 1885, though its use after World War II was much less significant than in those first 15 years. Now, before 1964 was over, Strathpeffer would lose all connection with the railway. In response to the closures, the following letter from a concerned observer was sent to the editor of the *Ross-shire Journal* and published in the issue of the paper for 4th December, 1964:

Sir:
On 7th December, Achterneed, Glencarron and Duncraig railway stations will be closed to passenger traffic. Why are the public not objecting? Do they not realise that there will be no substitute bus service? Do they realise that these closures will pave the way for the closure of certain stations and halts on the North line; then the closures of all stations north of Inverness; and finally of Inverness itself?
Why are British Railways closing Achterneed, Glencarron and Duncraig? Will these closures result in any saving by BR? The answer to the first question probably is - to pave the way for the eventual closure of the whole line. The answer to the second is - no, there will be no saving by BR. Neglecting, for the present, staff and signal costs, the only costs incurred by BR are painting (although this may not seem to be the case) and the erection of station signs (this was done shortly after nationalisation). Staff and signal costs can be dispensed with by making the stations unstaffed request halts. This means that if this is done, these stations will cease to be a liability (Glencarron is already a request halt).
No extra bus services are to be put on to replace the railway service. The alternative transport mentioned in the closure notice merely refers to the present Dingwall-Strathpeffer bus service.
These closures should not be allowed to proceed, although to stop them will be very difficult. All that can be done is to write to BR and the Minister of Transport.
Yours etc.,
Edward Acton,
Dingwall, 23rd November 1964.

Achterneed, Glencarron and Duncraig did close as planned; but two months later, Achterneed was brought back into use as an unadvertised and unstaffed request stop under a local arrangement. *Branch Line News* - the newsletter of the Branch Line Society - contained the following note in its issue of 24th February, 1965: 'Achterneed station, on the Dingwall and Skye line, which was closed to passengers on 7-12-64, re-opened as an unstaffed halt on 8-2-65'. Similarly, by the late summer of 1965, Glencarron and Duncraig were once again made available to the public - at least, to passengers who were aware that they could use them. All three stations were excluded from the timetable. Attadale, in remaining open for passengers, was closed to goods on 15th August, 1966.
During the remainder of the 1960s, the railways from Inverness to Kyle of Lochalsh and from Inverness to Wick and Thurso did not close. The power of the people of the western and northern Highlands had convinced the British Government that the lines

---

* Duirinish had already been closed to goods back on 1st February, 1954.

BR-built type '2' (later classified '24') Bo-Bo No. D5067 is seen at Achnashellach with the 'Hebridean' on its way to Kyle in 1967.   *M. Mensing*

The 'Devon Belle' observation car appears to have a full complement of passengers as it passes Achnashellach on the same train in 1967.   *M. Mensing*

A BR-built type '2' (later classified '25') Bo-Bo No. D5127 is at the head of a goods train at Strathcarron in July 1967. *M. Mensing*

BRCW type '2' Bo-Bo No. D5339 heads the down 'Hebridean' past Glencarron Platform in 1967, with the top of the passenger shelter just visible. *M. Mensing*

BRCW type '2' Bo-Bo (by now reclassified as class '26') is seen at Kyle of Lochalsh station on the 5.50 pm service to Inverness in 1971.   *J.L. Stevenson*

A Kyle-Inverness train, hauled by a class '24' Bo-Bo has almost crossed the embankment at Erbusaig Bay and is about to head through the largest cutting on the line. Erbusaig village is in the background of this 1974 view.   *P. Tatlow*

were a necessity and, in effect, they had shown Dr Richard Beeching that he was wrong in his decision to think about withdrawing such vital links between the Highlands and islands and the rest of Britain. The port of Kyle also survived the introduction of the Mallaig-Armadale roll-on roll-off car ferry, which had commenced in the spring of 1964, and the steamers continued to operate from Kyle to Stornoway, Portree and Mallaig; but, by the end of the 1960s, there was still the threat of an Ullapool-Stornoway ferry, and this formed part of the reason for another shadow of closure being cast over the Kyle railway. Ullapool was now seen as the future port for Stornoway, with the road from Garve to Ullapool intended to be improved to carry express buses that would allow a connection with Inverness.

In 1969, a new road was in process of construction from Strathcarron along the southern shore of Loch Carron towards and above Stromeferry, such that it would replace the road on the northern shore and, more significantly, the inconvenience of the ferry-crossing. The road was adjacent to the railway on the landward side, and for it to be accommodated at the foot of the cliffs, not only did some of the rock have to be blasted away but the railway itself had to be shifted seaward in places onto new embankments - a similarity to what had happened a century previously when Murdoch Paterson was engineering the line. While the road works were in progress, there were two resulting landslides at the most troublesome part, being a mile south of Attadale, which affected the railway. The first of these was in May, and for six weeks the services had to start and end at Strathcarron. Then, in early November, the second and more serious incident resulted in hundreds of tons of rock burying a length of over 200 feet of track. This time, the line was closed for 17 weeks, and the re-opening, in mid-March 1970, was on a partial basis, when the trains were allowed to pass Attadale only during daylight hours - meaning the 10.30 am service from Inverness and the 11.08 am and 5.50 pm services from Kyle. The 4.55 pm train from Kyle did not restart in the meantime, and continued to be replaced by a bus service through Glen Shiel, Glen Moriston and the Great Glen to Inverness; while the 5.40 pm from Inverness ran only as far as Achnasheen, with passengers having to travel the rest of the way by bus. To protect the road and the railway from future falling rock at this most vulnerable place, the works also involved the construction of a permanent avalanche shelter of concrete over a short length, together with steel-meshed netting draped over the cliffs and extending a further distance from each end of the shelter.

Back in 1965, a serious landslide had occurred on the eastern section of the Callander and Oban line, causing the early closure of the track between Callander and Crianlarich, which had already been listed by Beeching. Thus, from the landslide at Attadale, there were fears that the Kyle line would suffer the same fate, and while this turned out not to be the case, apprehension remained even after the service had been fully restored, because of the changed circumstances of transport communication in the West Highlands. Moreover, by 1970, virtually all of the intended Scottish closures of the Beeching report had been carried out, with only a few reprieved exceptions - notably the Inverness-Kyle, the Inverness-Wick-Thurso and the Ayr-Stranraer lines - so that there was still the anticipation of a forthcoming closure of the Kyle line.

The fears were eventually confirmed on 21st December, 1971. It was then from a Conservative Government, which had gained power again in 1970, with Edward Heath as its leader, that the Secretary of State for the Environment, after consultation with the Secretary of State for Scotland, consented to the proposal by British Railways that the Kyle line should close. British Railways was being forced to withdraw the service because the Government had announced that no further grant towards the line would be given after 31st December, 1973. However, this meant that the closure would not take

Duncraig platform from Creag nan Garadh in 1974. A small part of Duncraig Castle is discernible through the edge of the main clump of trees, above and to the right of the platform.
P. Tatlow

A Kyle-Inverness train, hauled by a class '24' diesel, runs along the edge of the bay between Plockton and Duncraig in 1974. Plockton village is in the background. *P. Tatlow*

place before that date, and, furthermore, the Government had stated that it would then happen only if a suitably improved bus service was provided to replace the rail service. The resulting reprieve of at least two years would allow the Kyle line supporters the opportunity to fight the closure again.

This time, the closure decision coincided with a revival of Scottish nationalism, which added impetus to the support, from the point of view that it was an insult that a part of Scotland - especially a scenic aspect - was to be destroyed. Throughout 1972 and 1973, many individuals, near and far, together with Members of Parliament, Highland authorities, railway societies, non-railway organisations, newspapers, and others, rallied to try to stop the closure. They were from the Highlands, from the Lowlands, from the rest of Britain and even from abroad. One set of official statements that the people would have to counteract in their protests was the alleged expense in keeping the line open. Thus, in 1972, British Railways produced figures stating that the estimated annual cost would be £318,000 for the line's operation, with the earnings from fares being £51,000, resulting in a deficit of £267,000 to be supplied by grants - but these figures were viewed with much suspicion.*

Torquil Nicolson, as leader and chairman of the 'Save the Kyle Railway Line Campaign' and as Chairman of Ross and Cromarty County Council Planning and Development Committee, continued in his determination to retain the line, as he had done for almost a decade, with the support of the local people. His efforts had indeed been appreciated, and the following letter to him, in early 1972 from Surrey, had also shown one woman's satisfaction regarding the two-years' reprieve:

Dear Mr Nicolson:
I felt I must congratulate you on the fact that the trains are being retained for another two years. I am sure this is due to your efforts to a very great extent.
I am very thankful for it myself - I am shortly retiring and will be spending quite a bit of time in Drumbuie, so was horrified at the idea of no trains, as I do not drive. Let's hope that, before the two years are up, the traffic will have increased to justify keeping the trains running. I just don't understand myself why they don't make more of that line. They used to have lots of trips - I can remember going on evening trips from Lochcarron by train, which connected with the boat for a trip up Loch Duich. I am sure that, with a bit more imagination, they could make that line pay.
Anyway, please accept my thanks for the present extension.
Yours sincerely,
Dolina Neilson.

Another letter - this time to the editor of the *Inverness Courier* - in the autumn of 1972 expressed how people from abroad were dismayed at what was to happen. Written from London, it was headed 'Frenchwoman's Tribute' by the paper:

Sir:
My family and I are on our way home to Lyon after our tour of Scotland. We have enjoyed most gratifying hospitality. The greatest excitement of our holiday was the journey by train from Inverness to Kyle of Lochalsh. The scenery is magnificent. It is unique. We have nothing to compare in France. We are going to tell all our friends to come to Scotland and experience this wonderful excursion. Then, at our hotel, we hear that, after 1973, there is no more railway - nothing. Impossible! We cannot believe this shall be true. We hope your country will never consent to part with such a great attraction for the visitors.
Yours etc.
Josephine Gallet.

---

* A significant example of such a deception occurred in regard to the closing of the Dumfries-Stranraer line in 1965, with the public having been informed that the closure would save £122,260 per year, whereas the true figure, which British Railways had kept secret from the public, was £29,940.

Achanalt station in the early 1970s, looking east to Loch Achanalt. The loop and the east and west signal boxes were removed in 1966.   *J.L. Stevenson*

Strathcarron station in 1974, looking south-west.   *P. Tatlow*

And in the spring of 1973, a letter from Ontario, Canada, to Torquil Nicolson further confirmed that people who lived so distant from the line, such that they would rarely, if ever, be able to use it, could still offer concern and support:

Dear Mr Nicolson:
    I am a Canadian of Scottish descent, deeply interested in the future of the Highlands. Reading in the *Oban Times* that the Kyle line is probably closing, I wish to urge you to renew your efforts to save the line. If the campaign committee is collecting subscriptions, I will be pleased to send my cheque. The Inverness-Kyle passenger trip is one of the great treasures of Scotland. It should be developed, not suppressed.
Yours sincerely,
Murdo MacKinnon.

The case for the retention of the Kyle line suffered a setback, formally, in the spring of 1973, with the ending of the Kyle-Stornoway ferry service on Saturday, 24th March, and Ullapool replacing Kyle as the mainland ferry terminal on Monday, 26th March. The former service was concluded and the new service was inaugurated by the *Iona* steamer of Caledonian MacBrayne Ltd - the name of the company having resulted from a merger between David MacBrayne and the Caledonian Steam Packet Co. on 1st January, 1973. The transfer from Kyle to Ullapool had been prepared well beforehand, based on the approval, in January 1971 by the Conservative Government's Secretary of State for Scotland. This had occurred partly from the premise that the Kyle line would close, but mainly because the Stornoway road hauliers wanted a roll-on roll-off ferry in connection with Ullapool, across the shorter sea distance, and an improved road link from Ullapool to Inverness, which was also shorter than from Kyle to Inverness. There were two ferry crossings in each direction per day, with coaches operating between Ullapool and Inverness via Dingwall.

It was a sad day for Kyle of Lochalsh when that last ferry connection was made between the Skye railway and Stornoway. The Stornoway route had been operated for virtually all of the previous quarter of a century by the familiar *Loch Seaforth* steamer, since its launch in 1947, but from May 1972 the *Iona* had worked the 103 years-old service that had begun at Strome Ferry with the opening of the Dingwall and Skye line in 1870. Now, with the transfer of the Stornoway ferry, there was, in a sense, a form of revenge for Ullapool over Kyle, in regard to the authorisation of 1893, when the Kyle Extension had been preferred to the Garve and Ullapool line, to the dissatisfaction of the people of Ullapool. In an article entitled 'By Rail to the Isles' in the June 1971 issue of the *Railway Magazine*, enthusiast K.S. Farr had criticised the planned, but controversial, move away from Kyle, and also the attitude of the Highlands and Islands Development Board, based in Inverness, in readily accepting the proposed closure of the Kyle line:

The Highlands and Islands Board appears apathetic towards retention of what could be a valuable tourist asset: instead of fighting all out against the proposed closure, the Board has merely stated that adequate 'alternative' facilities must be available. Even more amazing is the intended transfer of the Outer Isles steamer service from Kyle of Lochalsh, rail-served and with adequate anchorage facilities, to a new port at Ullapool! Naturally, such a proposal has created considerable opposition in Kyle, where it is felt that a sector of the town's employment would be lost, but also that a further excuse would be provided for closure of the rail link with the East. The Highlands and Islands Board considers that few of the passengers at present carried by the Kyle trains are bound for Lewis; yet one train, the 4.55 from Kyle, runs solely to connect with the Stornoway steamer!

By the summer of 1973, there were fresh hopes for the possible retention of the Kyle

Attadale platform in 1974, looking north-east.   *P. Tatlow*

Duirinish station in 1974, looking south-west. On the left is the village of Drumbuie.
                                                                  P. Tatlow

line because of a new and unexpected development. This was the beginning of the era of the North Sea oil production, and there was increasing competition to build large concrete drilling platforms that were required by the industry. Attention was directed towards construction sites on the deep-water coast of Wester Ross, and a joint application by the engineering firms of Taylor Woodrow Construction Ltd and John Mowlem Ltd resulted in the possibility of the chosen location being at Drumbuie, north of Kyle. From this proposal, there was a change of attitude by the Highlands and Islands Development Board over the future of the Kyle line. Optimistically, the Aberdeen-published *Press and Journal*, which was read all over the Highlands, reported in its issue of 14th June that 'another reprieve for the Kyle line loomed last night when the Highlands and Islands Development Board announced that the closure, scheduled for the end of this year, might be "premature and unsound" - because of offshore oil'. The matter had been discussed on the 13th at a meeting in Inverness with a deputation from the Kyle line campaign committee, led by Torquil Nicolson. Prospects for such an industrial development on the west coast were such that, although there was no certainty, the question of the decision to close the Kyle line had to be reconsidered, and the Board were preparing a memorandum on this to the Secretary of State for Scotland. Torquil Nicolson, in describing the meeting as 'very successful', was delighted at the reaction of the Board.

Two days after the Inverness meeting, Mr Nicolson was in Edinburgh, along with representatives of Inverness County Council, Ross and Cromarty County Council and the Scottish Council, to meet Lord Polwarth, Minister of State at the Scottish Office, who had taken responsibility for oil developments. Mr Nicolson impressed upon Lord Polwarth the view of the Kyle line campaign committee that the possibility of oil-related activity in Wester Ross justified the withdrawal of the consent that had been given to close the line. Lord Polwarth promised that the information supplied by the committee would be taken into account when the social, economic, industrial and environmental aspects of the subject were re-examined in the light of new developments.

To increase the publicity further, Ross and Cromarty County Council had commissioned the making of a documentary film about the railway, with the venture having the additional sponsorship of Inverness County Council and the Highlands and Islands Development Board. Produced by Films of Scotland Ltd, the 15 minutes-long film, called *The Line to Skye*, was to be shown to MPs in the House of Commons before being made available for the public.

A special feasibility study in connection with the Kyle line - or, more correctly, as an alternative to it - was carried out one day in August 1973, with the aim of assessing how a bus would perform on the route that ran parallel to the railway for most of the distance to Kyle. The bus set out from Inverness and, by way of Dingwall, Strathpeffer and Contin, wound its way south-westwards along the twisting single-track road, with passing places every 100 yards. British Railways had devised a timetable that allowed 3 hours 25 minutes for the journey, which the train covered in just over three hours; but the bus could not keep to the scheduled time, as Torquil Nicolson was pleased to state: 'The bus took 42 minutes longer, and that was through fairly-light traffic, and not allowing time for luggage to be sorted out, fares to be taken and passengers to get on and off'.

In the autumn of 1973, a provisional decision, having the backing of the Highlands and Islands Development Board, had been made in favour of Drumbuie for the proposed oil-rig construction site, at the bay known as Port Cam, where the railway very conveniently passed. The project, it was rightly said, would bring new employment to the area, but there were objections from the local people for environmental reasons, because of the visual intrusion seawards and because the scenic countryside in the vicinity of the bay, including the important crofting fields between Drumbuie and Duirinish, would be obliterated in accommodating the land construction site. A public inquiry, which drew much publicity to the area, began in November 1973, with opposition also coming from Ross and Cromarty County Council and from the National Trust for Scotland, who were the owners of the land. The outcome of the inquiry would be eagerly awaited by everyone for and against the project.

Meanwhile, some figures for the number of passengers and excursion trains lately to have used the Kyle line had been made available in the defence of retaining the route. There had been overwhelming support for the 'Save the Kyle Railway Line Campaign', and due to the increasing publicity, the trains were carrying more passengers in successive years. From a summer traffic of 25,000 passengers in 1965, the corresponding figure had become 102,000 in 1969, while recent spot checks by Ross and Cromarty County Council showed a continuing increase. Thus, by June 1973, there was a 40 per cent rise in the summer passenger traffic by the service trains, in comparison with the equivalent weeks of 1972, which had also been a considerable improvement over the same period in 1971. During the first week of June 1973, there were 670 passengers, compared with 480 for the same week in June 1972. In addition, the traffic from excursion trains was expanding significantly, with 21 specials having been run during the season of 1972, and 23 in 1973, carrying an average of 300 people each. The excursion trains came from various starting places, including Aberdeen, Glasgow, Edinburgh, Crewe, London, Bristol and elsewhere in Britain, to see the scenic railway that the Conservative Government was intending to close at the end of 1973. Amid the enthusiasm, there was sadness.

One railway society that had arranged enterprising trips over the Kyle line, when it needed such vital help during the early 1970s, was the *Wirral Railway Circle* of Cheshire. On hearing of the plight of the line, the Circle responded by organising a weekend tour in September 1971 from Crewe to Kyle on a train that it named the 'Hebridean Express'. After a journey of over 13 hours, the travellers were delighted to be welcomed into Kyle station by Torquil Nicolson and a large crowd, together with the Conchra Pipes and Drums. One and a half years later, in April 1973, the Circle proceeded a stage further, with one of the most ambitious excursions to have been planned by a railway society. This was the 'Grand Scottish Circular Tour', which, in again starting from Crewe, took the travellers either to Kyle on the 'Hebridean Express' or Mallaig on the 'Jacobite' and then, by the *Columba* steamer that had been chartered from Caledonian MacBrayne, along the Sound of Sleat, to Mallaig or Kyle respectively, so that both railways were able to be traversed by everyone. The monumental tour, involving the use of 17 diesel locomotives, 22 seated-carriages, eight sleeping cars and two restaurant cars, resulted in 800 people passing through Kyle - a number that was greater than the population of the village. The interest in the Kyle line from the Wirral Railway Circle was such that a third 'Hebridean Express' to Kyle ran in September 1973.

By the end of the autumn of 1973, there had still been no definite word from the Government about the future of the line, but before the end of the year, a decision - albeit one of a temporary nature - had emerged that brought relief and delight to the line's many supporters. In view of the North Sea oil developments and the intended oil platform construction in Wester Ross, the Government, in realising the possibility of the line being used to transport the associated heavy freight, concluded that closure of the line could not be implemented on 1st January, 1974. Instead, it was to be kept open throughout 1974, so that a proper decision in regard to the oil industry developments would be able to be made later, and the Conservative Government hoped that the present decision would be welcomed in the area. Indeed it was, but the outcome of what became, in effect, a second reprieve for the line was partly due to one of their own Members of Parliament. He was Hamish Gray, the MP for Ross and Cromarty, who had been leading the campaign in Parliament, and he had constantly expressed the view that it would be folly to close the line.

The security of the line now appeared to be solely dependent upon the oil industry. The inquiry for the proposal by Taylor Woodrow and Mowlem to obtain land at Drumbuie had continued from its commencement in November 1973, and the meetings lasted for a total period of over six weeks until the conclusion in May 1974. The Highlands and Islands Development Board had supported the application on the basis of new employment and an increased population to revitalise the area, together with the retention of the Kyle line, but the National Trust for Scotland, backed by Ross and Cromarty County Council and many of the local people, had protested. The case of the opponents was not only concerned with the visual result of the industry but was enforced by the fear of the social and economic impact that such a large-scale and relatively short-term industry would have on the small rural population. Furthermore, the land, as part of the Balmacara estate, had been declared inalienable, or non-transferable.

However, earlier in the year, there had been other developments. Another large business partnership had formed in 1973 that, by January 1974, had produced an independent application for an oil platform construction yard at Loch Kishorn, only five miles north of Drumbuie. The request had come from an Anglo-French consortium of the engineering firms of Sir John Howard and Co. and C.G. Doris,* to be known as Howard Doris Ltd. Then, in March, there was a new Government in power again, with the Labour Party, still led by Harold Wilson, having defeated the Conservatives at the general election. This was good news for the supporters of the Kyle line, since both of its closure proposals, in 1963 and 1971, had been introduced under a Conservative Government, with the first reprieve having come from Labour, although the Conservatives were now the creators of the second but temporary reprieve.

In June 1974, the preliminary findings of the Drumbuie inquiry were made known to the public, and these favoured the opponents of the scheme, such that a new oil industry there would be an intrusion to the landscape and to the local people. Initially, it seemed that this would be detrimental to the retention of the Kyle railway, but this was not the case, because of the growing support for the Kishorn project, instead of the one at Drumbuie. Ultimately, the late summer of 1974 was momentous for the Kyle line and its many supporters, and the wonderful news began on 31st July from the House of Commons when it was unexpectedly announced that the Labour Government had granted a permanent reprieve to the line. On the following day, the words of Aberdeen's *Press and Journal* recorded the success, with the heading 'On Right Line for Kyle':

The Highlands were jubilant last night, following the Government's reprieve of the Kyle of Lochalsh-to-Dingwall rail link. The news was greeted with relief and delight by the campaigners who had fought so long to save the line which has been threatened with closure for more than 10 years. Transport Minister Mr Fred Mulley told the Commons all action directed towards the closure of the line will stop 'in the public interest'.

'Saved: Kyle Line Stays', read the headline on the front page of the *Highland News*, of Inverness, with the paper stating:

---

* Compagnie Générale pour les Développements Opérationels des Richesses Sous-Marines.

The Kyle line has been saved - for the foreseeable future. Probably for good. The surprise and welcome announcement was made in the House of Commons yesterday, in answer to a Parliamentary question. The news was received with delight in the North last night and was regarded as a triumph for the Kyle line campaign committee, local authorities and others who have fought for years to retain the line, including British Rail.

In response, the leader of the fight, Torquil Nicolson, having referred to the Kyle line as 'the man who had escaped the hangman's noose three times and was freed', expressed his joy at the decision, but he also suggested what could be done to make the line better:

I am highly delighted. This justifies the fight we have had for all these years. It is a case of third time lucky. The line could have been closed in 1963; again in 1971; and in 1973, it was given a final year's grace, until this great news. British Rail might now improve the line by investing capital in it. They could improve the stations along the line and provide a new timetable. It would not be difficult to trim three-quarters of an hour off the journey from Inverness. They could re-arrange the crossing lines and improve the slower sections of the track.

Mr Nicolson emphasised the importance of the people in having fought to keep the line open:

This development really is a triumph for the campaign committee and all the bodies and individuals who have helped. I believe that this decision has been made as a direct result of pressure put to bear by the committee, which has been the main driving force in the struggle for the line's retention. The arguments for the line's retention have become stronger year by year, with passenger traffic constantly increasing. I think this is the main reason for the decision. Another strong argument for keeping it on has been the tremendous potential for oil-related industry at Kyle of Lochalsh.

For some time, Hamish Gray, the Conservative MP for Ross and Cromarty, had led the fight in Parliament, having pressed his own Government and Labour to drop the plans for closure, and he had promoted the Kyle line documentary film there. He, too, recorded his great satisfaction at the outcome:

This is first class. I wholeheartedly welcome the decision. Along with many others, I have campaigned for the retention of this line for a number of years, always maintaining that it is a vital link between the two sides of Scotland. I am delighted that our joint action and representations have persuaded the Government at last. British Rail can now proceed with improvements in the knowledge that they will be on a permanent basis. This is a great victory for all who fought for the retention of the line over many years. The efforts of the 'Save the Kyle Line Committee', so ably led by Mr Torquil Nicolson, have played a major part in this achievement. I am also convinced that the showing of the Kyle line film in the House of Commons recently also gained us much support among Members.

Even British Rail were delighted, with a spokesman in Glasgow saying:

It is great news that the doubt has been removed. We will be making an earnest endeavour to attract as many passengers as we can.

And from the area manager at Inverness, came these words:

This is a morale booster to the staff at Kyle and Inverness. It indicates conclusively the different eyes of Ministers of Transport when Mr Mulley is prepared to sweep aside the closure order. A week never passes without us receiving queries from the South about whether the line is still open.

The result of the efforts of the people, individually and collectively, were reflected in Fred Mulley's welcoming statement. The Kyle line was one of six railways - the other five being in England and Wales - that the Labour Government had decided to keep open, and the collective success of these was the first action under the Railways Act, 1974, which was authorised on 31st July. This was the date of Mr Mulley's statement that he had read as follows:

> The Secretary of State for the Environment has decided that it would be in the public interest if current action on the following closure cases should cease, and that the services should be covered by the obligation to operate a railway passenger network, which I shall be imposing on the Railways Board under Clause 3 of the Railways Bill, which is to receive Royal Assent today.

Then he listed the six lines that had been reprieved. The Railways Act, 1974, replaced the existing system of specific grants for loss-making lines with a general subsidy for the whole passenger network. For the Kyle line, the decision meant that the Government would continue to meet the operating loss of £200,000 per year, and the reprieve ensured that 70 British Rail workers would keep their employment. Soon, the line's friends derived further satisfaction when they read the British Railways public notice of retention of the Inverness-Kyle passenger service, with the last of the three sentences symbolising the great success that had been achieved from the long battle:

> The Scottish Region of British Railways refer to the public notice, dated 21st December, 1971, publicising the decision of the Secretary of State for the Environment to consent to the withdrawal of all railway passenger services between Inverness and Kyle of Lochalsh. The Secretary of State for the Environment has now decided that this railway passenger service will be covered by the first obligation to operate a railway passenger network, which he will be imposing from 1st January, 1975 on the Railways Board under Section 3 of the Railways Act, 1974. The Scottish Region of British Railways therefore give notice that they will not be implementing the closure decision, and railway passenger services will continue to operate between Inverness and Kyle of Lochalsh.

With the railway's permanent retention having been secured before the final decision had been reached regarding the Drumbuie inquiry, the latter's outcome, which seemed to be proceeding against the scheme, was now irrelevant to the future of the line. Indeed, on 12th August 1974, the Secretary of State for Scotland, Willie Ross, ended the inquiry by giving a verdict in favour of the opponents. The victory for the National Trust for Scotland was gained at a cost of more than £30,000, but £26,000 of this was donated by members and other supporters who were against the Drumbuie scheme. It was ironical that this scheme, which had initially prevented the closure of the Kyle line, and which had the support of some of the people in the area, had now been defeated; but the railway was safe.

While the case of the railway had become inconsequential to Taylor Woodrow and Mowlem, the situation was different for Howard Doris, whose scheme was receiving the general acceptance of the local people. This was because the proposed site, although only a short distance from Drumbuie, was the wild and lonely western shore of Loch Kishorn, where the impact of a large labour force would be less intrusive to the nearby villages of Ardarroch, Kishorn and Achintraid, on the eastern shore. A public inquiry was not necessary because sufficient information had already been obtained from the Drumbuie inquiry and because there was much less opposition. Approval for the Kishorn scheme was granted in September 1974, and in November a contract to build the massive Ninian Central Platform was awarded to Howard Doris. Also before the end of the year, work on an access road to the site was commenced, and plant was landed on the western shore to excavate a dry dock and to spread 1¼ million tons of rock and peat that would form the foundations for a new industrial village. In connection with the oil platform, the Kyle railway would play a vital part.

Meanwhile, as the early stages of the construction progressed at Loch Kishorn, there was another aspect of sadness for the Skye railway in the spring of 1975. Two years after the demise of the Kyle-Stornoway steamer service, and, more significantly, 105 years after the commencement of the Skye service in connection with the railway, there was the withdrawal of the Kyle-Portree mailboat. Circumstances were still changing. The continuing improvements to the Kyle Akin ferry and to the roads on Skye combined to make a ferry for passengers, light cargoes and mail between Kyle and Portree superfluous. Thus, on Monday, 17th March, the Kyle-Portree service was brought to a close by the small *Loch Arkaig* steamer, which was the recent regular vessel that connected both places with Mallaig. Raasay was the intermediate call for the Kyle-Portree service, but there were also plans for a car ferry for the island. Although not classed as a car ferry, the *Loch Arkaig* sometimes did convey cars between Kyle and Raasay and between Portree and Raasay, because there was no other suitable ferry; but from Tuesday, 18th March, a new temporary Caledonian MacBrayne ferry service for passengers began between Portree and Raasay, with two runs in each direction daily, except Sundays. This was prior to the proposed permanent car ferry between Sconser and Raasay, which had been delayed because of disagreements with the owner of Raasay. However, the Kyle-Mallaig service was retained, and for the period 18th March until 3rd May 1975, the timetable read:

	MWFO	FO		TThFSO
	am	*pm*		*pm*
Kyle of Lochalsh	9.15	3.30	Mallaig	12.15
Armadale	11.15		Armadale	1.00
Mallaig	12.00	5.30	Kyle of Lochalsh	3.15

Notes: MWFO - Mon, Wed, Fri only. FO - Fridays only. TThFSO - Tues, Thurs, Fri, Sat only.

Raasay obtained its car ferry with Sconser in April 1976.

In conjunction with the establishment of the oil platform construction yard at Kishorn, a 4½ acre site at Stromeferry, immediately east of the station, had been reclaimed from the sea in a period of six months in 1975, with more than 100,000 tons of infill having been transformed into a marine terminal and a rail depot, containing five sidings installed by British Railways. The sidings served four 70 ft-high silos for storing cement that was conveyed by rail. A condition of planning permission being granted to the Kishorn location was that it had to be treated as an island site, with the raw materials to be brought there by sea. Thus, the railway was able to play a vital role because, under such a condition, there was no advantage in road haulage when the final journey to the site was by sea. This brought new life in the form of much-welcomed freight traffic to the Kyle line. Every morning, except Sundays, a freight train left Inverness at 6.49 for Stromeferry. The train brought cement that had come by rail from Oxwellmains in East Lothian, pozzolan ash from Alloa in Clackmannanshire, pre-stressing material from Ayr, and other construction materials, such as steel. Howard Doris also had their own two 0-6-0 diesel-shunter locomotives within the site at Strome. The cement was transferred in barges that were called 'pontoon-mounted silo sets', each having a capacity of 1,000 tons. Many thousands of tons of heavy materials were shipped from Strome to Loch Kishorn; then to the 'Stage One' wet dock, opposite Airigh-drishaig on the south-eastern coast of the Applecross peninsula; and finally to the 'Stage Two' wet dock in the deeper water between the Crowlin Islands and the western coast of Lochalsh.

The Howard Doris industrial settlement of 3,000 people at Kishorn, which was representative of a Klondyke town, also brought extra revenue to the railway, with some of the workers using the trains between Strathcarron and Inverness when travelling to and from the South in connection with their periods off duty. In addition, the Kishorn yard provided employment for people in and around the Lochalsh peninsula, including Skye. The Ninian Central Platform was constructed between October 1975, when the first pour of concrete had taken place, and May 1978, when the successfully-completed colossal structure of 601,000 tons was towed by eight of the largest tugs in Europe from the Stage Two dock to its location, 575 miles distant, in the North Sea. Unfortunately, by this time, there was no longer a demand for large concrete platforms, and there was no further need for the use of Stromeferry as a rail terminal. The site had closed to the trains in September 1977, though, in the meantime, as if in anticipation of a return to fortuitous times, the railway sidings were left in connection with the Kyle line. Nevertheless, this formally brought another era in the history of the Skye railway to an end. Howard Doris remained at Stromeferry and at Kishorn, extending the latter yard in 1978 to build smaller drilling structures of steel and of steel and concrete combined. With the permission of Highland Regional Council, the materials were then reaching Strome by road, for transfer to Kishorn.

With the arrival of the 1980s, the Kyle line received some further visual publicity. For the British representation of the BBC television series and its accompanying book, both entitled *Great Railway Journeys of the World*, TV personality Michael Palin had travelled from London to Kyle of Lochalsh in the early summer of 1980, writing and presenting a documentary about his journey via Manchester, York, Newcastle, Edinburgh, Perth and Inverness. Prior to his run from Inverness to Kyle, he attended a Highland games, where he met a caber-tossing railwayman from the Kyle line - Alec MacKenzie, who was in charge of the station and signal box at Garve. Michael spoke to passengers on the Kyle train, including a young American woman who, in never having travelled by train there, was impressed by the observation coach in which she found herself, and he was informed by sprightly 99 years-old Jean MacKenzie of Plockton that, when aged 14, she had been taken by boat to Strome, and then by rail to Inverness and Glasgow. Michael noted that Jean had been travelling on the Kyle line since its year of opening in 1897, but, based on her own words, the specific journey that she recalled would have taken place even earlier, in 1895, before the completion of the Kyle Extension.

A book of British railway journeys, called *Stopping-Train Britain*, which included the Kyle line and the line from Glasgow to Mallaig, was published in 1983. Alexander Frater, as its author, had travelled from Inverness to Kyle, providing an account of his run in a chapter having the title of 'Skye Boat-Train'. He met some of the people who worked on the railway, including Alec MacKenzie, or 'Big Alec', at 19½ stones, who was still at Garve. There was also Mrs Barbara Pratt, an English carriage cleaner at Inverness who was the guide for the Kyle line observation car in summer, and who had been heard and seen, supplying the commentary, in the background of Michael Palin's programme. The author received further information about aspects of the line from two helpful employees on the train - Jack Rennie, ticket collector, and Francis Coghill, guard. He was intrigued to encounter the man in charge of Achnasheen station - Fred Field, known as 'Captain Birdseye' because of his long, white hair and beard, and his peaked cap. And at Balnacra level crossing, south-west of Achnashellach, he met Peter Roy, an English biochemist and Bachelor of Science - 'the best-educated crossing-keeper in Scotland', according to Jack Rennie.

The observation car - having been revived in 1979 by the use of this former Caledonian Railway saloon - is seen on the rear of the 10.30 am Inverness-Kyle train at Dingwall on 13th June, 1980. The train is being hauled by a class '26' locomotive.   *T. Heavyside*

Class '37' Co-Co No. 37 260 is seen leaving Achnasheen on an empty fertiliser train from Kyle on 18th July, 1983.   *T. Heavyside*

Class '26' No. 26 034 runs alongside Loch Carron on an engineer's train from Inverness on 19th July, 1983.   *T. Heavyside*

Class '26' No. 26 032 leaves Stromeferry with the 5.10 pm Kyle Inverness on 18th July, 1983. The remains of the disused Howard Doris sidings are in evidence.   *T. Heavyside*

Class '37' No. 37 260 and test car *Iris* are seen testing newly installed radio signalling near Attadale on 20th July, 1983. Across Loch Carron is the Slumbay part of the straggling village of Lochcarron, formerly called Jeantown   *T. Heavyside*

Achnasheen in 1986, looking south-west. In the cold light of a January dawn a class '37' diesel hauls the 7.10 am Kyle-Inverness service.   *J.L. Stevenson*

Observation car No. ADM 45028 is seen at the rear of the 10.55 am Inverness-Kyle train as it leaves Dingwall on 14th July, 1986. *T. Heavyside*

A class '37' on the 11.10 am Kyle-Inverness train in July 1986 approaches the junction at Dingwall, with the North line to Wick and Thurso on the right. *T. Heavyside*

Below dramatic cliffs, class '37' No. 37 417 with the 3.05 pm Kyle-Inverness service on 12th July, 1988, has just passed through the avalanche shelter, a mile south of Attadale, that protects both railway and road at this most troublesome part of the scenic run by Loch Carron. *T. Heavyside*

An important day in the history of the Skye railway occurred quietly on 10th July, 1983, when the first Sunday passenger train in service ran on the line - ironically, 100 years after the Strome Ferry riot.* Back in August 1929, the LMSR had run the first Sunday excursion train from Inverness to Kyle, amid signs of religious disapproval in the West, but without any trouble. Then, in June 1965, for the first Sunday ferry between Kyle and Kyleakin, a protest had been enacted by the local Free presbyteries and branches of the Lord's Day Observance Society, leading to one minister, who had made his demonstration by lying down on Kyleakin jetty, being carried away by four policemen. There were fears of a Sabbatarian protest at the new summer-only train service, which British Rail had arranged in response to the view of the Highlands and Islands Development Board that it would be of great benefit to Sunday tourists. In spite of outcries from the Free Church, the Free Presbyterian Church† and the Lord's Day Observance Society, British Rail decided to proceed with the service.

At around nine o'clock at Inverness station on the Sunday morning, there were no protesters for the departure of the busy train of 250 passengers, which also contained two plain-clothed railway policemen on board. The *Inverness and Highland News* provided a summary of the run to Kyle by what it called the 'Sunshine Special' on a beautiful day for an outing. There were interviews with, and photographs of, a few of the travellers and the train staff. One man who was eager to make the trip was a fruit farmer from Blairgowrie in Perthshire. He drove to Perth to catch the 1.40 am train for Inverness, reaching the Highland capital just after four o'clock, and having managed a few hours' sleep, he eventually boarded the Kyle train. 'The new Sunday service is ideal', he said, 'because it's the only day I have off from the farm. I always wanted to go to Kyle by train, and despite my early start and the fact I won't get home until eleven tonight, I feel it has been all worthwhile'. Also by the new service, a retired man from Dingwall, with his wife, obtained his first trip on the Kyle line. 'Every time I went to Kyle', he commented, 'I drove by road and missed much of the beautiful scenery'. Among the travellers were local people, tourists and Kishorn workers taking advantage of the service in having spent Saturday night in Inverness.

The train staff were also mentioned by the correspondent of the *Inverness and Highland News*. He noted that, as a measure of the meteorological conditions, ticket inspector Ian Leitch of Inverness 'soon had to doff his jacket in the sweltering heat, as he checked and issued tickets'; while from buffet attendant Paul Morris of Nairn, in a break from a constant stream of customers, he received the comment of 'It's good to see people enjoying themselves and supporting this venture'. Barbara Pratt provided the running commentary that was enjoyed by the passengers in the fully-booked observation car. The train was welcomed as it headed on its journey to Kyle. 'All along the route', wrote the correspondent, 'locals stood in the sun outside their cottage homes, as this Sunday "first" snaked its way through the hills, past rushing rivers and calm lochs, to pull in exactly on time just after midday, with driver David Fraser and his mate Ron Donaldson (both from Inverness) at the controls'.

On arrival at Kyle station, the travellers were further welcomed by almost 100 hand-clapping locals, with one Kyle lady saying 'It's the best thing that's happened to the place'. However, the shops of Kyle had not responded to the new service, and, apart from a kiosk, all of them remained closed, though the hotels and bars were open.

---

* *Branch Line News* referred to the service under the title of 'A Sunday Train Journey into Highland History Heading for the Wrath of Sabbatarians', and asked the rhetorical question: 'Was it just coincidence that the first regular Sunday trains on the Kyle of Lochalsh line should have run just 100 years and 37 days after the Strome Ferry riot of 3rd June, 1883?'

† In 1893, a disruption occurred within the Free Church and resulted in the formation of the Free Presbyterian Church.

The portable building on the station platform is the Dingwall Signalling Centre for the radio signalling of the Kyle and North lines, with the radio mast at the left of this July 1986 view.

T. Heavyside

The end of an era. These semaphore signals - the most northerly on the national railway network at the time - had a working life of only two more weeks when this picture was taken at Dingwall on 17th July, 1988. The radio signalling notice is already in place at this junction for the Kyle and North lines.

T. Heavyside

Class '101' diesel multiple unit driving trailer No. M54356 has been converted into an observation car and is seen at Dingwall at the rear of the 10.15 am Inverness-Kyle of Lochalsh service 'The Hebridean' on 13th July, 1987. The observation car returned on the 5.10 pm service from Kyle.   *P.A. Biggs*

Class '37' No. 37 415 departs Garve for Kyle on the 'Highlander', a special from London on 17th July, 1988.   *T. Heavyside*

Class '37' No. 37 156 stands at Kyle of Lochalsh station with the 5.05 pm train for Inverness on 29th August, 1991, with the view dominated by Beinn na Caillich on Skye.   *T. Heavyside*

Members of the press had been sent to Kyle for the train's arrival, because of the objections to the Sunday service and of the anticipated drama, based on history 100 years previously; but they had to wait for a further two hours, until just prior to the return journey, before there was anything to record, and this was very little, due to the commendable attitude adopted by a local Free Presbyterian minister. The *West Highland Free Press*, the local newspaper which was published in Skye and had no connection with either of the Free churches, reported on the mild demonstration under the heading of 'Calm Journey for First Sunday Train':

> The Sabbatarian protest which ensued was notable mainly for the youthfulness of most of those who took part, and for the absence of black-clad ministers. In fact, the only clergyman in evidence - Lochcarron FP minister, Rev John Walter Ross - was sensibly dressed in white shirt and tie in deference to the hot weather. He seemed to be on first-name terms with most of the media team, as he pressed leaflets on Sabbath observance on them and posed amicably for photographs.

The paper included a photograph of a smiling Mr Ross and his young helpers handing out the leaflets, suggesting that they, too, enjoyed the occasion. The friendly nature of the protest was much in contrast with what had happened at Strome Ferry 100 years before, and the services of the two railway policemen were not required. The feelings of the travellers were effectively summarised by an American tourist as he alighted at Inverness: 'It sure was a wonderful day out'.

The 1980s became a period of significant changes - mostly of a progressive nature - for the Kyle line. There had been the start of the Sunday trains in 1983, which, in national terms, was not significant, but in an area of the West Highlands where Sabbath observance had for so long prevented the operation of public transport on this one day, it was a revolutionary achievement. Sadly, there was a negative change from August 1983, when goods traffic officially ceased at the remaining stations to have handled this - these being Dingwall, Garve, Achnasheen, Strathcarron and Kyle. However, there had been good news for the line's future in the summer of 1983, with the announcement by British Rail that a new £415,000 scheme to provide radio signalling between Dingwall and Kyle had been approved, and that it would be in use by the following summer. In replacing the mechanical signalling that was expensive to manage, the radio signalling system would control all of the train movements over the 63½ miles of the Kyle line from a control centre at Dingwall.

With work on the installation of the equipment having begun in the autumn of 1983, the system was inaugurated by the British Rail Chairman, Sir Peter Parker, on 13th July, 1984, and brought into full operation on 28th October. Known as Radio Electronic Token Block, or RETB, it combined mobile radio facilities with recent developments in microprocessor technology, and it provided safe access, or 'token', for each train entering and leaving each section, or 'block', of the single-line track. With the use or spring points that were operated by the trains, there was no longer any need for signals and signalmen; while level crossings with automatic flashing lights superseded the signal box-operated and manual crossings. The train driver was able to be kept in communication with the control centre at Dingwall by VHF radio. The RETB system on the Kyle line was the first of its kind, having originated from the British Rail Research and Development Department at Derby, and it was funded by British Rail in conjunction with a grant from the European Regional Development Fund. While the new system unfortunately meant the loss of much of the human element in the operation of the line, the overall result of this more efficient and less costly scheme was a large gain in the railway's future security. Due to its success on the Kyle line, RETB was introduced on the North line from Dingwall in November 1985, and it was extended to Inverness in August 1988, with the control of the Kyle and North lines then being

The 10.45 am Inverness-Kyle service, of class '156' 'Sprinter', at Plockton station in November 1996.   *Aurore McConnell*

Another view of a typical two-car 'Sprinter' of the Kyle line at the often-deserted Stromeferry station. Only a basic passenger shelter remains, which stands behind the photographer.   *Aurore McConnell*

transferred from Dingwall to Inverness.

A further rail improvement in connection with Kyle of Lochalsh had been completed by the summer of 1987. In a £32,000 scheme that was funded by the Highland Regional Council and ScotRail - British Rail's Scottish network - the 90 years-old listed building at the terminus was extensively renovated. The waiting-room and ticket office, the parcels office, the staff amenities and the toilet facilities were modernised at what was now the only staffed station on the line. Left luggage lockers were provided, and the station lighting, signs and platform seating were renewed. To mark the completion of the scheme, a commemorative plaque, in English and Gaelic, was unveiled at the station by a representative of the Highland Regional Council with the English words reading: 'This modernised station was formally opened by Mr A.J. Russell, Convener, Highland Regional Council, on 17th June 1987'. Councillor Russell was accompanied by ScotRail's provincial manager, Chris Leah. 'Over the past few years', said Mr Leah, 'ScotRail have invested more than £22 million in improvement schemes at stations, large and small, throughout the country. Inverness has been extensively modernised; the stations on the route to Wick and Thurso have been refurbished, and now it is the turn of Kyle. These schemes demonstrate our faith in the future of the line, where, despite the relatively-poor summer last year, revenue was well up on the previous year'.

It was on the same day that Mr Leah announced yet another change for the Highland lines north and west of Inverness, which was that £20 million had been approved for new class '156' 'Sprinter' diesel multiple units to replace the large diesel locomotive trains.* At this time, it was foreseen that the 'Sprinters' would arrive sometime between August 1988 and May 1989, but it turned out that they were not able to reach their destination lines in the expected way. In February 1989, before their arrival, the Highlands suffered torrential rain on two consecutive days, and the resulting flood water of the River Ness, combined with a high tide, forced the collapse of the railway viaduct at Inverness on the third day, the 7th. This viaduct was the original stone structure of the Inverness and Ross-shire Railway of 1862 that connected the Highland capital with the North and West, and its demise meant that the Kyle and North lines were cut off from Inverness and the South. While there were, fortunately, sufficient sets of locomotives and coaches already on the separated lines to allow services on them to commence and terminate at Dingwall, the 'Sprinter' trains had to be transferred in the spring of 1989 from Inverness by road to a temporary maintenance depot at Muir of Ord, as did the observation car for the 1989 summer services on the Kyle line. ScotRail provided a bus connection between Inverness and Dingwall until the opening, on 9th May, 1990, of the replacement viaduct, which cost £3 million.

The achievements on the Highland lines during the second half of the 1980s, among others over the Scottish network generally, were the result of ScotRail's enterprise, and, in particular, of ScotRail's General Manager, Chris Green, who, with his progressive attitude, did much for the security of the Kyle and North lines.

The trend of summer services on the Kyle line during the first half of the 1990s consisted of four services in each direction on weekdays, where three of these were 'Sprinters' and the fourth was locomotive-hauled with observation car; while there were two services on Sundays each way, being of one Sprinter and one locomotive-hauled with observation car. From 1961 until 1965 and from 1979 until 1994, the observation car had been a successful additional attraction for tourists on the scenic line. Over the years,

---

* The diesel locomotives that had worked on the Kyle line from the 1960s to the 1980s were of Type 2, consisting, in today's identification system, which was introduced in 1968, of the following: initially, classes '24' and '25', succeeded by '26', with an occasional '27'; while class '37s', of Type 3, gradually took over from the '26s' during the remainder of the 1980s, with class '40s', of Type 4, hauling the excursion trains.

several vehicles operated the services, beginning with the former 'Devon Belle' saloon during the first half of the 1960s and ending with a converted diesel multiple unit coach from the 1987 season. Unfortunately, in February 1995, ScotRail announced that the service would be discontinued because of the high cost of using a locomotive capable of pulling the observation car and the regular carriages.

From the opening of the controversial Skye road bridge, with its excessive toll charges, in October 1995, the Caledonian MacBrayne ferry service ceased to operate, so that, at Kyle, the sole-existing boat connection with the past was the summer-only and passenger-only excursion run from Mallaig to Kyle and back to Mallaig on Caledonian MacBrayne's *Lochmor* vessel. In recent years, this service operated on Tuesdays, Thursdays and Fridays, but it is now on Fridays only. However, the 'romance of the Skye boat' returned in July 1996, when a new locally-owned passenger ferry, *Heather*, commenced running between Kyle and Kyleakin, as part of the strong protests against the bridge, and it is hoped that the ferry will continue to maintain the sea connection between Lochalsh and Skye.

Today, while there is no doubt that much still needs to be done to obtain the best from the Skye railway for the tourists who are its principal patrons, the line is in a relatively healthy state, especially in comparison to the circumstances in the precarious years of the 1960s and 1970s. Ultimately, the retention of the line was due to a combination of the people's determination in resisting the closure attempts and of the arrival of the North Sea oil industry - the latter's part being possible only because of the former's success - for each factor on its own would not have been sufficient over the whole decade of uncertainty. The line must continue to exist not just to *survive* but to *flourish* - as was the aim of the late Torquil Nicolson, friend of the line, who, with his enthusiasm and exertions, encouraged many other individuals and organisations to be the line's friends.

Kyle Line Timetable, 1st June to 27th September, 1997

		Mondays to Saturdays			*Sundays*	
			(a)		(b)	(c)
Inverness	08.10	10.45	12.35	18.00	10.45	18.00
Muir of Ord	08.26	11.01	12.51	18.16	11.01	18.16
Dingwall	08.36	11.11	13.01	18.26	11.11	18.26
Garve	09.00	11.32	13.28	18.49	11.35	18.47
Lochluichart*	09.09	11.41		18.58	11.44	18.56
Achanalt*	09.16	11.48		19.05	11.51	19.03
Achnasheen	09.27	12.00	13.55	19.16	12.03	19.14
Achnashellach*	09.45	12.18		19.34	12.21	19.32
Strathcarron	09.55	12.30	14.23	19.44	12.31	19.42
Attadale*	10.00	12.35		19.49	12.36	19.47
Stromeferry	10.13	12.48	14.41	20.02	12.49	20.00
Duncraig*	10.21	12.56		20.10	12.57	20.08
Plockton	10.25	13.00	14.53	20.14	13.01	20.12
Duirinish*	10.28	13.03		20.17	13.04	20.15
Kyle of Lochalsh	10.41	13.15	15.06	20.30	13.15	20.27

			Mondays to Saturdays		Sundays	
			(a)		(c)	(b)
Kyle of Lochalsh	07.20	11.45	15.20	17.05	09.52	15.20
Duirinish*	07.29	11.54		17.14	10.01	15.29
Plockton	07.33	11.58	15.33	17.18	10.05	15.33
Duncraig*	07.36	12.01		17.21	10.08	15.36
Stromeferry	07.45	12.10	15.45	17.30	10.17	15.45
Attadale*	07.57	12.22		17.42	10.29	15.57
Strathcarron	08.03	12.31	16.03	17.48	10.38	16.03
Achnashellach*	08.11	12.39		17.56	10.46	16.11
Achnasheen	08.31	12.59	16.31	18.16	11.06	16.31
Achanalt*	08.41	13.09		18.26	11.16	16.41
Lochluichart*	08.48	13.16		18.33	11.23	16.48
Garve	08.59	13.27	16.57	18.48	11.34	16.58
Dingwall	09.24	13.52	17.20	19.11	11.59	17.23
Muir of Ord	09.33	14.01	17.33	19.20	12.08	17.32
Inverness	09.49	14.23	17.49	19.38	12.24	17.48

Notes: (a) 30th June-6th September. (b) From 29th June. (c) 29th June-31st August.
         * Request stop.

With the line no longer serving Skye and the outer isles in the way that it did for most of its lifetime, it is unfortunate that its original reason for being - of trade between Skye and Inverness and the South - has disappeared. Nevertheless, the Kyle line must remain for what it does have left to offer in the form of tourism for Skye and Wester Ross. 'The railway proves a most enjoyable crossing of the Highlands scenically, and is very popular with visitors', recorded the late Alfred Wainwright,' the highly-respected English hill-walker, artist and TV personality. 'The last time I travelled on it', he added, 'there was standing room only. Closing it would be criminal folly'. Francis Coghill of Kyle, the long-serving and knowledgeable guard on the line, is as sure as it is possible to be that such a criminal act will not occur. 'They'll never close the Kyle line. They can't. It's the equivalent of a listed building, and they won't let you knock down listed buildings, will they?'

With dedication: to the enterprising gentlemen who planned the Skye railway in its two stages; to the brave and hardy navvies who built the line; to the tenacious people who fought to prevent it from closing; and to its appreciative and appreciated travellers of the future - let us hope that there will never be another attempt to close the Kyle line, and that its security will be assured to enable it to be present for its second centenary, and beyond.

Postscript

The opening of the centenary year, 1997, of the Kyle of Lochalsh railway has been momentus in a quiet way by the heralding of what, it is hoped, will be a permanent return of freight to the route. Within the debatable policy of the Conservative Government's privatisation of British Rail that has recently replaced nationalisation, English, Welsh and Scottish Railway, the country's large new freight operator, has taken the initiative in trying to encourage the transport of freight by rail in the Highlands, including along the Kyle and North lines. Thus, on Wednesday, 29th January, the first freight train for almost one and a half decades ran on the Kyle line and conveyed 400 tonnes of sawn timber from Kyle station to north-west England on a trial basis. The

Two views of Kyle of Lochalsh on 29th January, 1997, as 400 tonnes of timber are loaded onto the first freight train on the line for nearly 15 years. In the lower view, beyond the station, work is proceeding for the 'Kyle Prospect' environmental improvement scheme, while in the background is the controversial Skye bridge. *(Both) West Highland Free Press*

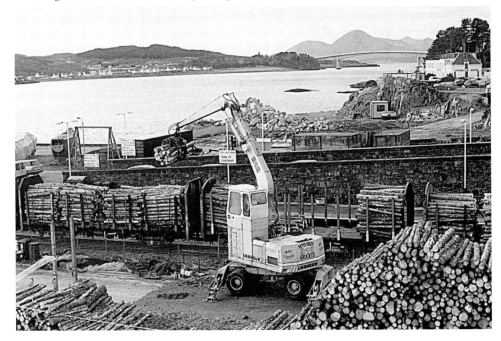

Kyle of Lochalsh station on 17th March, 1997, with 250 tonnes of Caithness flagstone having been brought in for the 'Kyle Prospect' environmental improvement scheme. A class '156' 'Sprinter' is at the far platform and the *Hebridean Princess* cruise ship, out of season, is at the pier.

West Highland Free Press

timber had reached Kyle by lorries from the plantations of Forest Enterprise at Kinloch on Skye and at North Strome on the mainland, and it was taken by rail from Kyle, in 18 wagons hauled by two class '37' Motherwell-based locomotives, to head for the Swedish-owned Iggesund Paper Board at Workington in Cumbria. A week prior to the commencement of the experimental service, the district manager of Forest Enterprise at Fort Augustus, Malcolm Wield, explained to the *West Highland Free Press*:

> This is an alternative form of transport for timber, to relieve congestion and to keep the thousands of timber lorries off the roads. This move is very encouraging. Before now, costs have prevented timber being put on the rails, but now, negotiations have secured a deal which shows that it can be done. Although next week's shipment is only a one-off at this stage, we are definitely looking to the future and are actively considering using rail transport as the main way to ship timber around the country. We are optimistic that there will be a repeat of this practice in the very near future, as the feasibility of the rail transport idea has been proved.

Highland Council's local representative, Bill Fulton, for Kyle and Sleat, was enthusiastic in welcoming the initiative:

> It is fantastic that timber is being put on the Kyle line at last, and I hope that it will continue. This also means that we could look at other goods that can be transported in, such as thousands and thousands of tonnes of fish feed, which are brought in by lorry.

A letter from an interested gentleman in Skye, Ron Shapland, appeared in the *West Highland Free Press* of 7th February, expressing satisfaction at the possibility of such a new freight service, but there was concern regarding another aspect:

> I hope the initiative to transport timber by rail from Kyle of Lochalsh, reported in your paper last week, is successful. A substantial increase in timber production from Skye and Lochalsh is likely over the next 15 years as plantations mature, and its transport by rail will not only improve the viability of the Kyle-to-Inverness rail link but remove many long-distance timber lorries from our congested roads. Unfortunately, this initiative could be undermined by the high tolls on the Skye bridge, as they are sufficient to turn harvesting operations from profit into loss. . .

And in the paper's issue of 21st February, there was the following letter from Mr V. MacLennan of Glasgow:

> I was delighted to read your paper on 31st January. The photograph of timber being loaded onto a freight train at Kyle station brought back memories to me. Having worked at Kyle station in the early 1950s, the photo brought back memories to me of how the station used to be. During my time at Kyle, we had two freight trains per day, as well as various fish and livestock specials. Kyle during that time was a very busy and friendly depot to work at. I hope now that we will hear more about freight on the Kyle line.

Indeed, more was soon to be heard about freight on the line. On Monday, 17th March, there was a freight train of 15 vehicles into Kyle, again hauled by two class '37' engines. This comprised 11 wagons carrying 250 tonnes of Caithness flagstone from Georgemas Junction in Caithness, with these having been joined at Inverness by four vans of fish feed. The flagstone was for the environmental improvement of the seafront at Kyle, between the pier and the former Skye-ferry jetty, in a scheme known as the 'Kyle Prospect'; while the fish feed was bound for onward transport by sea to salmon farms in the area. As a result of this incoming freight train to Kyle - in the sense that a train was already at Kyle - the opportunity was taken by English, Scottish and Welsh Railway in offering to Forest Enterprise a further shipment of timber by the train's outward journey, and it was readily accepted. On Monday, 24th March, this second load of timber left Kyle for the Iggesund factory in Workington, to become, after many years, the third freight train over the Kyle line within two months, in the line's centenary year. With the Highland Council and the Highlands and Islands Enterprise trying to encourage an increase in rail freight traffic as an effective and economical alternative to road transport and its congestion, hopes are high that freight will continue to be carried on the line.

Also in 1997 and within the programme of privatisation, the last of 25 British Rail franchises to pass from nationalisation into operation by private companies was finalised by the transfer of ScotRail to the National Express Group bus company. With the franchise period being seven years, the date of the formal exchange was 31st March, when the ScotRail network became part of National Express, as ScotRail Railways Ltd. It now remains to be seen what improvements will occur to Scotland's railways overall and, with particular interest to the subject of this book, to the Kyle line, in the next seven years of privatisation under National Express, and in the next five years under the Labour Government, as a result of the overwhelming victory at the general election on 1st May 1997.

The view from Badicaul, looking west across the Inner Sound, from the Cuillins of Skye on the left to the island of Raasay on the right, with the Black Islands close to the mainland, as a class '156' 'Sprinter' passes on the Kyle railway.   *Drawing by Aurore McConnell*

Appendix One

Two Runaway Trains

In 1892, an accident occurred at Achnashellach with a train that was hauled by a 4-4-0 locomotive of the 'Duke' class. This name originated from engine No. 67, *The Duke*, which was the eighth of the 17 members of the class. The first 10 were built in 1874 by Dübs and Co. of Glasgow and the remaining seven came from Lochgorm Works between 1876 and 1888. It was the 15th, No. 74, *Beaufort*, built in 1885, that was the engine of the Achnashellach runaway rolling stock of 1892.

The train was 'mixed' - meaning that it consisted of passenger and goods vehicles - and this was typical of the Highland Railway's operation, for economical reasons in regard to the large areas of limited population that the company served. The Board of Trade, in accepting the need for mixed trains, expressed disapproval towards the Highland for placing the passenger carriages at the rear of the trains. For the necessary shunting at the stations, this arrangement suited the Highland because of convenience and time-saving. However, the goods wagons, between the tender and the passengers, had no continuous brakes connected to the engine, and the continuous brakes which did exist on the passenger carriages, and which would have been able to be used from the engine, were rendered unusable because of the separation. Thus, the only available brakes were on the engine and on the guard's van as the last vehicle - these being satisfactory if the train remained together while in motion - but if there was a disconnection of a wagon coupling, only the guard's handbrake, which applied brakes to the passenger carriages, was left to try to stop any runaway rear portion.

The runaway train at Achnashellach was the 4.20 pm or evening service from Dingwall to Strome Ferry on 14th October. A stop had been made at Glencarron, with the guard having then found that the wheel of the brake-handle had broken off, so that there were no longer any brakes at the rear of the train. Nevertheless, the driver and guard considered that it was safe to proceed to Achnashellach, which was reached at seven o'clock. The approach to Achnashellach station from the east involved a steep ascent of 1 in 60 for nearly a mile, and engine No. 74 and its train surmounted this safely to reach the station. The procedure then involved the engine and tender being detached and moved forward from the rest of the train, so that two of the wagons could be hauled by rope into the siding. Unfortunately, the engine having eased backwards to slacken the coupling, and due to a misunderstanding among the four railwaymen of the scene, the train of wagons and carriages, on the falling gradient, began to slip away from the engine and tender. The four men watched helplessly as the train, with its passengers, soon disappeared into the darkness in the direction from which it had come.

A decision was made by the driver, that the engine, preceded by the tender, would have to set off cautiously in pursuit; and, in doing so and reaching the bottom of the 1 in 60 gradient, it began to make the first ascent, which was at 1 in 375. The driver then saw a light in the distance, and this was soon discovered to be the runaway train - but it was on its way back after having been halted, a mile and a half from Achnashellach station, by the next ascent of 1 in 75. A collision occurred. The runaway train's leading wagon, loaded with sleepers, crashed with the tender of No. 74 and was derailed, though the rest of the train remained on the rails. This was fortunate for the nine passengers on board, who, nevertheless, received minor injuries of cuts and bruises and were considerably shaken, and who managed to walk along the line to Achnashellach station. A doctor from Strathcarron was telegraphed for, and he attended to the injuries. A special train was dispatched from Strome Ferry to convey the passengers westwards, and an accident crane, with a staff of workmen, was sent from Inverness to clear the line quickly.

In spite of the accident at Achnashellach and the continuing pressure from the Board of Trade, the Highland Railway still placed the passenger carriages at the rear of its trains. This occurred even after the passing of a final deadline of 1st January, 1896, when the company was supposed to have complied with the Board of Trade's demand for the carriages to be placed in front of the wagons. It was only on 20th September, 1897 that Andrew Dougall informed the Board of Trade that the company would at last comply with the order; but on 25th September, a mixed train left Dingwall for Strome Ferry with the carriages behind the wagons, and this became another runaway train.

The service was again the evening one, which now had a departure time of 6.15 from Dingwall, and the engine was 'Skye Bogie' No. 88, with a heavily-loaded train having no continuous brakes for the carriages. It was a wet Saturday evening and the rails were very slippery. With difficulty, No. 88 successfully managed the ascent of the two miles at 1 in 50 from Fodderty Junction to Achterneed, but it was on the further climb of 1 in 50 over the next two miles towards the Raven Rock summit that serious trouble occurred. No. 88 came to a standstill when almost at the summit, and, resulting from the strain of the violent jerking that had occurred, a coupling broke between two of the wagons, splitting the train. Although the brake was applied by the guard at the rear, his runaway portion, containing between 40 and 50 passengers, began to run back down the steep gradient. Initially, there was no fear felt by the passengers or the guard, because it was believed that the train was intentionally returning to Achterneed, but they soon knew otherwise, as the speed increased and the situation became alarming before the station was reached. Several male passengers ventured onto the footboards of the carriages to jump off, but they quickly realised the danger of this against the rapid speed.

The runaway train swept past the station and rushed onwards at a terrific pace, heading for the sharp double curve of the Fodderty embankment, with the passengers resigning themselves to the train tumbling over. At the first curve, the carriages swayed violently but remained on the rails. The next danger in the minds of the passengers was that the points at Fodderty Junction might be set for the Saturdays-only Inverness special from Strathpeffer, but, fortunately, the signalman, having realised that something was wrong as he heard the sound of the train in its rapid descent from Achterneed, had set the points accordingly - though just in time, as the train had then reached the Fodderty bridges. The train took the second curve and rattled over the points at great speed, and still managed to keep to the rails. From here, the gradient eased considerably, but the train carried sufficient momentum to take it almost all of the way to Dingwall. The level crossing keeper at the west end of the town had also heard the noise of the train's approach, so that the gates were open here, but this was not the case with the second of the two crossings, at the road to the North. The train crashed through the gates, but soon afterwards, its speed began to slacken. This was due to the slight ascent in the line east of the second crossing, followed by the beginning of the sharp curve of the line towards the junction with the North line, causing a sufficient drag for the brake of the guard's van to take effect. The outcome was that the runaway train was eventually brought to a standstill a short distance before the junction.

After their arrival on firm land again, the passengers, though naturally shaken, were relieved to be able to joke over the terrifying experience. One example of this concerned a London gentleman, who, while unaware of what was happening, remarked that he should congratulate the Highland Railway Company upon the speed of their trains. He began to make a comparison between the speed of the Skye train and the London and North Western express, much favouring the former. 'We're having a good run', he said. This would beat the 'Flying Dutchman'. 'Oh yes' responded another passenger, 'we're having a good run - we've beaten the engine!' The Londoner would not believe what had occurred, and when the train stopped, he asked where they were. Having been informed that they were back at Dingwall, he remarked with satisfaction: 'Then, just what I said. The London trains would never beat that!'

When the driver discovered the disappearance of most of his train, he returned with the remainder to Achterneed to await news of the occurrence, and when he was told to continue to Dingwall, he was asked, on his arrival there, why he did not follow the train. His reply was that the signals were against him - after which a passenger answered him, to the merriment of the bystanders: 'I see, but weren't they against us too?' The passengers agreed to resume their journey, but only if the wagons were taken off, and, with the Highland Railway officials having to accede to this request, No. 88 and its train headed westwards again.

It had also been stated by one of the passengers on the runaway train that there had recently been an increase of wagons on this service, such that it was loaded much heavier than formerly. A further train was in trouble on the Achterneed slope and near Achanalt on 25th October, 1897, and a short report in the *North Star* showed that the Highland Railway had not learned the lesson of a heavily-laden train on the line. No information was given on where the carriages had been placed:

Another Railway Train Stuck. On Monday evening, the 6.15 pm mixed train from Dingwall to Strome Ferry stuck near Achterneed, on the part of the line known as the Fodderty bank. The train was so heavy that the engine was unable to take it further, and after tugging and backing for about a quarter of an hour, it had to proceed to Achterneed with only a portion of the train. The passengers, says a correspondent, were almost frightened out of their wits, as they feared there was to be a repetition of the runaway train experience. The train again came to a standstill about two miles beyond Achanalt station. About midnight, another engine arrived from Dingwall to take the train forward, and the Strome Ferry passengers were only brought to their destination about 2.30 am on Tuesday morning.

Until late 1897, the Highland Railway had run over 100 mixed trains daily, which amounted to almost half of the company's total services. However, from 1st November of that year, the number of mixed trains was reduced, with an additional 50 trains being brought into operation solely for passenger or goods traffic.

****

THE GREAT SNOWSTORM DEC: 1906.
CUTTING THROUGH A BLOCK ON THE SKYE LINE,
HIGHLAND RAILWAY AT ACHTERNEED, NEAR DINGWALL.
COPYRIGHT "URQUHART DINGWALL" SERIES. 124.

When the Skye railway suffers from the problem of snow, it is usually the eastern half that can become severely blocked. A notable example occurred at the end of December 1906, as in this view of a snow-plough train at Achterneed. Two Skye trains and one Strathpeffer train were stuck on the same day. The 10.00 am Inverness-Kyle service was halted on the notorious Achterneed incline for over 24 hours, and was only able to return to Dingwall - the passengers having forced their way through the heavy drifts to Achterneed station on the first day. The 5.00 pm train from Kyle, having been temporarily snowed in at Duirinish, came to a more permanent stop at Rogie, where 'the drift was a dozen feet deep', resulting in the passengers staying the night in the train, which could only return to Garve in the morning. Snow closed the Strathpeffer branch for the first time, after the 6.00 pm train from Dingwall ran into a drift soon after Fodderty Junction, and the passengers had to struggle across fields to reach the Spa several hours later in a tired condition.   *P. Strong*

Appendix Two

The Kyle Pharmacist
and his Village and Railway

In the summer of 1946, a book was published under the title of *Gateway to Skye*, in which the emphasis was on Lochalsh. Its author was a well known personality of Kyle of Lochalsh - Duncan Macpherson, born in Aberdeenshire in 1882, who had moved to Kyle in 1911. 'Setting foot on the rocky West in search of a livelihood and, even more vitally important, seeking after elusive health', as he stated in the book, he had chosen to settle in Kyle to help in his recovery from ill health, and, appropriately, his profession was synonymous with this. He had trained as a chemist in Aberdeen and had worked in England and at Strathpeffer, such that, in his new location, he was able to establish his own business in the form of the Kyle Pharmacy. His original, personal and sole copy of *Gateway to Skye* had been typed, illustrated and bound in 1939, but its publication had had to be postponed because of World War II. The book's popularity resulted in it being reprinted in 1946, 1947 and 1948. Another book of a similar nature, called *Lure of the West*, followed in 1950, and finally, there was a third, entitled *Where I Belong*, in 1964.

These books provided a valuable retrospective record of life in Lochalsh and its vicinity over the first half of the century. However, they were not Duncan Macpherson's only publications, for, since 1926, he had been producing an annual *Pocket Guide to Skye and Lochalsh*. He was known as 'the chemist', but he was much more than that. He was the most knowledgeable man in the area, and his pharmacy became the unofficial tourist inquiry office, where he readily answered the numerous questions from visitors. He was a progressive thinker and activist, and this characteristic, combined with his election as the councillor for Lochalsh, ensured that his ideas and efforts were directed at improving the village and parish. Moreover, in connection with his pharmacy, he was a professional photographer who not only recorded many views of the locality for his own interest and for posterity, but he also made some of them available as postcards for the tourists.

In his books, Macpherson outlined, amid tales of local people, aspects of the origin and early social history of his adopted village, as in *Gateway to Skye*, thus:

> Kyle of Lochalsh is built round its railway and harbour, and these are the main supports of its population. When I first came to live there, it consisted of about 80 dwellings. Several were comfortable, stone-walled buildings, but others were constructed of wood and corrugated iron. The village presented a new, out-west appearance. Houses had been erected on rocky hillside, in hollow or crevasse; in short, wherever the ingenuity of man or the avarice of landowner permitted. The inhabitants numbered about 350. Some had migrated from neighbouring townships. Many came from more distant parts of the country. There were English, Irish and Welsh, whom we classify as Sassenachs. There were Lowland Scots from Aberdeen, Fife and Glasgow, and these were also regarded as aliens - unless they spoke 'the Gaelic'.

> The railway cuts through the centre of the village and terminates at a square-built pier, at which steamboats call. This, in turn, is intersected by the highway from the East, which ends at the Skye ferry pier. From a window in my modest pharmacy, I looked in those early days across the ferry to the isle of Skye. I feasted my eyes upon the beauty of Beinn na Caillich, with its mantle of mist; I saw the ships as they passed daily to and from Portree and Stornoway. In summer, the bay was dotted with small boats. Captain Finlayson, owner of the first motor-boat in the district, was crossing and recrossing with passengers . . . From another window, I saw up the village street, one side lined with bank, post office and shops; the other with bank, hotel and gardens. In the distance, a heather-clad hill loomed up . . .

In the same book, he devoted a chapter to a train journey from Kyle to Inverness, and his account began as follows:

> A morning train leaves Kyle of Lochalsh station at five o'clock during the summer months. It connects with the Stornoway boat, due to arrive an hour earlier - the interval in the timetable being arranged to permit of a delayed crossing caused by bad weather or other circumstances. The train has a good connection at Inverness for those travelling south - London being reached

the same evening. For the eastbound traveller, however, the next train, leaving about six o'clock, provides an equally-good connection. It has the further advantage of getting into Inverness after the shops and other places of business are open . . . Hence, my reason for travelling by the six o'clock train. It would reach Inverness about 10, by which time the bulk of the inhabitants would be awake . . .

There was this reference to Stromeferry:

The wooden pier, at which steamboats called before the railway was extended, has now been removed. The old stone pier below the station is now used for the ferry which runs regularly - on weekdays only - to North Strome, half a mile distant.

After commenting on the halt at Attadale - 'a nicely-kept platform without much sign of activity', and having 'neither station master nor other railway employee' - he expressed his satisfaction with the quality of the rolling stock, but he also had one minor criticism:

We sometimes hear complaints about the old carriages put on branch railway lines. Now, I am perfectly certain that if any dilapidated, old carriage had been put into service on the Kyle line, that is the particular one in which I should have found myself. But no; my compartment was well-cushioned, warm and clean; and I could go out into the corridor to stretch my legs. Although the same carriages are probably used regularly on this route, the photographs which adorned the walls of my compartment consisted of Welsh beauty spots with unpronounceable names. To most travellers, and particularly to tourists, a strip-map of the district would have been more helpful.

At Strathcarron station, there was a tedious delay as a carriage containing motor cars was shunted into a siding and detached, due to several motorists having put their cars on the train at Kyle, to avoid crossing by the ferry at Strome. As well as further brief descriptions regarding the rest of the journey, some advice was provided: 'Achnasheen Hotel is conveniently placed alongside the station, but the traveller who leaves his carriage there for refreshment will be well advised to take the engine driver along with him'. Of Lochluichart station, he was decidedly unenthusiastic. 'The only interesting fact I can recall about this depressing station is that the station master's triplets - three girls, who probably comprised the entire juvenile population - journeyed daily by this train to school at Dingwall'.

It was in his account of the return journey that Duncan Macpherson communicated an interesting social aspect of the Kyle line service, because of the particular day that he had unwittingly chosen to make his trip to Inverness:

I had enjoyed the comfort of a compartment to myself on most of the outward journey - passengers usually, after one painful glance in my direction, hurrying off to find a seat elsewhere. But now, whether due to my newly-trimmed head or for some other reason, I could hardly find space for my long legs. The carriage-racks were filled with packages; boxes and cases were crammed below the seats; and even in the corridor, there were strangely-shaped articles wrapped in brown paper. And still more packages came. They were brought by message-boys from shops, who called out 'Mrs MacRae', 'Mrs MacKenzie', and many other names. These dames responded nobly. There were handshakes and last good-byes, and last minute messages, as the train moved slowly out. The return journey had commenced. The babel changed from English to Gaelic. I tried to read and dropped off to sleep.

We were an hour late on leaving Dingwall, but even then, I did not realise the cause of delay. At Garve, some of the passengers got out, and there was more room to breathe; but we had passed Achnasheen - the train still far behind scheduled time - before the painful truth dawned upon me. This was the last Saturday of the month! There may be someone to whom that conveys nothing. Then let him travel by the evening train to Kyle on that day. At every station, friends were meeting the housewives returning from their monthly shopping visit to Dingwall or Inverness. The train stopped not only at the stations but at many intermediate spots - it almost seemed wherever there was a dwelling. Then someone brought a chair and placed it by the side of the train, and, in leisurely fashion, the passenger descended. But this was not all. Packages had to be handed down; frequently, the wrong ones were given, and these had to be put back. There had been hours in which to have everything in readiness; but no; the stopping of the train always came as a complete surprise. Then the leave-takings took time. Guard and engine driver might fume, but they had to wait.

We halted at lonely shielings and wayside cottages; we halted, it almost seemed, to let the engine driver light his pipe. We halted to exchange greetings with a retired, octogenarian railwayman, living rent-free in one of the company's houses. Interesting at first, the continual stopping became monotonous. The novelty had worn off. I was tired and hungry when I arrived home, two hours late. I even felt that my hair, with the passage of time, had begun to grow long again.

In *Lure of the West*, Macpherson summarised the social backwardness of Erbusaig before the arrival of the railway there, but he was critical of how the resulting railway embankment had affected the Viking-named settlement, and his sympathy was evident:

Around Erp's Bay, there grew up the village of Erbusaig, known in those early days as Arbesak. A murmuring stream flowed past - its pure waters ministering to the comfort and well-being of the inhabitants. I like to picture this old-world village. I see its low-walled cottages, each built with native stone, with low doorway and windows. The people of Erbusaig were content to live happily, to rear large families and to die of old age. They were not interested in the spread of civilisation as we know it. They had no public hall or assembly room. They held no public meetings, appointed no committees, and held no conferences. They did not even slaughter their fellow creatures. In short, they were definitely old-fashioned.

In 1870, a dark cloud appeared on their sky. It may have been the smoke from the railway, opened at Stromeferry in that year. Many changes were taking place. The lands of Lochalsh had been bought by Sir Alexander Matheson, a descendent of the chief who had owned Lochalsh in the 15th century. The new laird erected Duncraig Castle on the high crags opposite Plockton. Well-engineered roads were built to connect the castle with Duirinish and Achmore. A post-gig travelled along the new thoroughfare, carrying mails from Stromeferry railway terminus to the Skye ferry at Kyle. The sight of this vehicle, 'dashing' along the highway above the village, produced a daily thrill for the people of Erbusaig; but, on the whole, life remained pleasant, serene and uneventful.

Then came the blow. The railway was extended westward from Stromeferry. The great headland separating Erbusaig from Portnacloich ('Port of the Stone') was sliced open as one might cut a chunk from a cheese, and the rock cuttings were dumped in front of this beautiful village. An aqueduct permitted the sea to penetrate at high tide; but never again, from many of the homes, would the isles of the seas be visible. Never again would an aged native of these shores view, from the window of his home, the waves dashing upon the rocky coast. All he might now see would be a sullen stream gurgling up from the base of that forbidding wall, as if from the bowels of a giant sewer. I have observed a rabbit burrowing into the hillside, and I have seen the black soil at the mouth of the warren. But, always, nature has taken a hand and atoned for the ravages of the rodent. Not so with man's bungling. It is 50 years since that obscuring embankment was built across Erp's Bay - yet today, there is still no sign of verdure. No tree or shrub has been planted on these barren slopes to relieve the stark ugliness of the scene.

In *Where I Belong*, Macpherson explained how he had obtained his plot of land from the Highland Railway at Kyle, in order to establish the pharmacy; and how, under nationalisation, he had refused to pay the sum then demanded for the land's yearly rental:

When I decided to settle at Kyle of Lochalsh, I found that the most suitable position for a pharmacy was on ground which the Highland Railway Company had acquired for railway purposes. I happened to be staying with my brother, Joseph, at the manse of Newmill in Banffshire at the time I wrote to Mr Sutherland, railway factor, Inverness, asking for an interview. This was readily granted, so I proceeded to Inverness where I was received most kindly.

I was told afterwards that Mr Sutherland was a church elder, and that, as I came from a manse, I was bound to be all right. Now, if I had written from my home, the name of a farm might not have been so effective.

Mr Sutherland informed me that, the Highland Railway Company having acquired the land specifically for railway purposes, it could not be feued or sold, but that, if I would sign an agreement to remove my premises when asked to do so, he could let me have a small piece of ground for an annual rent of £3. Actually, this 'ground' was a heap of loose stones which had been dumped upon the foreshore. So, upon these rocks, I built my modest pharmacy, and I remained very much 'on the rocks' for many years.

Meanwhile, various changes were to occur. The Highland Railway Company became merged in the London, Midland and Scottish Railway Company. Later, all were to be nationalised. Laws and agreements which had applied to companies and private individuals were apparently not binding upon a nationalised concern. In place of the kindly factor at Inverness, there arose, in Glasgow, 'a new king who knew not Joseph' or Joseph's brother. This modern Pharaoh had sent his emissary to Kyle to demand a ransom of £500 from me. I was asked to pay this sum for my heap of rocks, or quit. In a sentence of three words, I told the creature where to go. He returned to Glasgow.

A 'Kyle Pharmacy Series' view from Duncan Macpherson of the first version of the Kyle Akin car ferry prior to World War I, with the car placed upon planks that were attached to a rowing boat, which was then towed by another rowing boat. The jetty is at Kyle, beside the Station Hotel, and Kyleakin village is in the background. *R. Charnley*

Appendix Three

Trouble at Loch Carron

References have been made to the problem of the Skye railway having to run along the narrow shore of Loch Carron and below the cliffs that extend almost to the water's edge. Over the lifetime of the line, there have been many instances of landslides and falling rocks that have disrupted the services. One of these occurred near Stromeferry in 1953, and the story is related here directly as a tribute to Robert Simpson of Kyle, the driver of the train on that occasion; but indirectly, it also serves as a tribute to the line's other careful and observant drivers - past, present and future - in having to take their trains along this precarious part of the route. Francis Coghill, the experienced guard on the Skye line, kindly arranged for the author of the present book to meet Mr Simpson - known as Bob - at Kyle in November 1995, when the story was explained. Bob, who was born in 1903, also mentioned that he was probably the only surviving employee of the Highland Railway. He began his long railway career of 48½ years in 1919 at his home town of Forres as an engine cleaner. In 1923, he left Forres for Inverness, and in 1930, he moved to Kyle, and then in 1937 to Badicaul, becoming an engine driver in 1940. He retired in 1968, with the distinction of having 28 years of driving experience on the scenic Kyle of Lochalsh railway.

The incident involved the 5.5 am passenger service from Kyle to Inverness on 2nd September, after there had been torrential rain during the previous few days. Bob, who had the reputation of being one of the most reliable drivers in the North, had taken his train from Stromeferry station and was proceeding very slowly through the early morning darkness and rain, as he always did in such conditions on the dangerous stretch between Strome and Attadale. About a mile after Strome, the engine suddenly left the line and jolted to a stop. Daylight revealed the reason fully. Hundreds of tons of rock, loosened by the days of rain, had fallen from the cliffs during the night and had swept away the railway embankment, in two places, into the sea. Bob had managed to stop the train in time, for, otherwise - that is, if he had been travelling faster - the engine would have plunged down a 10 ft gap in the line and into the depths of Loch Carron, with the carriages overturning and also being dragged into the water. When another engine pulled the stranded carriages back to Kyle, the 40 passengers were full of praise for Bob. 'We owe our lives to the driver', said one lady with tears in her eyes. 'Had we been travelling the least-trifle faster, nothing could have averted a tragedy'.

The ironical aspect of the incident was that when Bob had told the train's guard that such a slow speed along Loch Carron would be necessary on that morning, the latter's response was one of displeasure: that they had a timetable to keep to; that they would be late for the London connection; and that he would have to report Bob for this. Fortunately, Bob had refused to take heed of the guard, and for his initiative, he was commended by grateful passengers, who informed his headquarters at Inverness. Thus, from the manager of the District Motive Power Office there, he received an official letter of praise - if somewhat terse - representing the Railway Executive of the Scottish Region of British Railways, and this read:

> 5.5 am passenger train, Kyle of Lochalsh to Inverness: derailed between Stromeferry and Strathcarron on 2-9-53.
>
> I have received correspondence from members of the public expressing commendation of the alertness while working the 5.5 am passenger train from Kyle of Lochalsh to Inverness on 2nd September, 1953 when the train became derailed between Stromeferry and Strathcarron.
>
> Your prompt action on this occasion has been appreciated very much by the public and by the Railway Executive.

However, that letter, in having been the only thanks that he was given from his employers, meant much less to Bob than the many other letters and phone calls of appreciation that had come from the passengers.

A further tribute to Bob Simpson was presented by the *West Highland Free Press*, in the form of a feature article, in February 1997. In response to this, a letter appeared in the paper in March from Victor MacLennan, the guard who had disagreed with Bob's slow speed on the morning of the incident; and again - at least, in retrospect - there was praise. Mr MacLennan wrote in part: 'I was delighted to read the *Free Press* interview with Bob Simpson . . . I was guard on the early morning train during 1953 when the line was washed away between Stromeferry and Strathcarron, and had it not been for Bob's careful driving, a disaster would have occurred'.

Landslides and falling rocks have continued to affect the railway between Stromeferry and Attadale. The problem, while always having been present since the original Skye line of 1870, was worsened by the inclusion of the road - steep in places - along the southern shore of Loch Carron, with the road's construction effectively weakening the sides of the cliffs. Indeed, prior to the road's opening, part of a letter of prophecy in the *Ross-shire Journal* in November 1969 provided a viewpoint - still expressed now - that a bypass should not have been built along this shore:

The natives and others in these parts are completely satisfied that the bypass ought never to have been built where it did. If the road is ever finished, there might always be the danger of trees and rocks falling and blocking both road and rail. The money the project has already cost is in the region of £750,000 . . . A bridge at the narrows of Stromeferry would have been the right decision and probably cheaper in the end.

In the late autumn of 1990, the *Highland Railway Journal* summarised another instance of trouble which caused blockage to the road and involved the road vehicles having to be specially accommodated over the adjacent section of the railway:

The Kyle line has had problems recently on the Stromeferry side of the avalanche shelter alongside Loch Carron. Apparently, the rock face is unstable, possibly as a result of heavy rain, and loose stone is having to be removed. This has blocked the roadway, which has been slewed for a short distance onto the railway track. To protect trains, two semaphore signals have been erected, controlled from a local 3-lever ground frame. From a passing observation, it would appear that road vehicles are only allowed along intermittently, in between knocking rock off the cliff-face. Presumably, everything stops for the trains. The work is believed to have started on 1st October and is expected to take six weeks.

In 1992, the *West Highland Free Press* reported on a further blockage of 18th April and on the importance of finding a diversion for the road:

Discussions by members of Highland Regional Council's transport committee on the future of the Stromeferry bypass will be given added urgency in view of the latest rockfall, which blocked the road at the weekend. Around 80 tons of rock crashed down onto the road, spilling onto the adjacent railway track, at around 7 am on Saturday. Drivers of cars, halted by the fall, set to with bare hands to clear a path until police and roads department workers arrived to start clearing up. In the meantime, the 06.50 train from Kyle to Inverness was halted at Duirinish but was allowed to proceed over an hour late, after ScotRail manager Alan Hope* had checked the line. Rockfalls have closed the bypass on a number of occasions in recent years, and local people, fearing that serious injury or loss of life is bound to result sooner or later, have called for Highland Region to act. The council have already backed a plan to re-route a section of the road to take it away from the unstable rock-face which towers above the road and the railway line alongside Loch Carron.

It was reported that the work would cost £82 million, but so far, there has been no diversion of the road, and, thus, there remains the high probability of further trouble at Loch Carron.

---

* Alan Hope was the station manager and traffic supervisor at Kyle, and upon his early retiral in 1995, he was not replaced, so that he became, in effect, the last 'station master' there; but his railway connection with Kyle remains, for he operates the station bookstall and another shop on the platform which sell railwayana, and he resides in the station master's house that was built for the opening of the line.

Appendix Four

Strathpeffer and the Proposed Ben Wyvis Railway

For several decades, many visitors reached the spa resort of Strathpeffer by railway, initially at the original Strathpeffer station at Achterneed and latterly, over a greater period, at the Spa's own station. Sadly, the attractive village, while still popular with tourists, is no longer a spa resort, and no longer does it have a rail connection. By the late 1970s - which was almost 30 years after the final closure of the Strathpeffer branch - the village station had fallen into a state of ruin; but because the basic structure of the building, canopy and platform had not been demolished, a £160,000 transformation was able to be brought about to restore some of the former glory. This successful scheme consisted of converting the station into several craft shops, and a plaque there reads: 'Strathpeffer Craft and Visitor Centre - siteworks and landscape work carried out by Scottish Development Agency - handed over to Highland Regional Council - March 1980'. It is satisfying that the beautiful little station can still be seen today, albeit without any trains, as can the Highland Hotel, perched above the village - both of them, as listed structures, representing a railway age now long gone. The trackbed of the branch is also clearly visible, especially from the Kyle line trains between the former Fodderty Junction and Achterneed; but of the hillside station, there are unfortunately no remains.

While Britain has generally shown no interest in the development of spas for the treatment of arthritis, rheumatism and other ailments - unlike the countries of the Continent, with some of them having hundreds of spa resorts in operation - the re-opening of Strathpeffer as a spa resort after World War II would not have ensured the retention of the railway amid the changing transport circumstances. However, during the 1970s and early 1980s, there were plans for a new railway scheme in the vicinity of Strathpeffer, which was intended to bring the stations of Strathpeffer and Achterneed back into service. This was the Dingwall and Ben Wyvis Railway that was to run almost to the mountain's summit. It meant making use of the existing rails of the Kyle line from Dingwall as far as an interchange station east of Raven Rock, from where an electrified rack railway, six miles long, would have proceeded by way of the slopes of Gleann Sgathaich, Cnoc nan Each Mor, Tom na Caillich, Coire na Faeriach, An Cabar and Glas Leathad Mor to the south-western summit ridge. Included in the proposal was a 1¼ mile-long railway from Strathpeffer station directly to the Kyle line at Achterneed. This would have made use of almost half a mile of the old trackbed from Strathpeffer before turning north to run immediately east of the Achterneed road; and, prior to reaching the small village of Achterneed, it would have curved sharply east and then north on a very steep incline, with the last few hundred yards having to be worked by rack, round to a new station at Achterneed on the site of the original one.

The idea of a railway running up Ben Wyvis originated in 1970 when the Kyle line was under serious threat of closure, and it was hoped that the new venture would play a part in preventing this taking place. The Ben Wyvis railway was not intended solely for the benefit of sightseers but was also to serve proposed ski-runs on the upper slopes of the mountain, while a ski-complex of hotels and chalets, costing £25 million, was visualised for the Raven Rock area. Unfortunately, in spite of initial encouragement from authorities such as Ross and Cromarty County Council, Highland Regional Council, and the Highlands and Islands Development Board, nothing has progressed of the railway beyond the surveying stage. As well as the main problem of where the financial support would come from, there was the difficulty faced from objectors who were firmly in favour of conservation. The whole project of the railway and the ski-complex was also questioned in terms of being further than Aviemore and the ski-runs of the Cairngorms from the centres of population in the South which would be expected to provide most of the skiers and, thus, the revenue. However, the Dingwall and Ben Wyvis line has not been officially abandoned, even if it seems unlikely to materialise, and if it was ever to become reality, it would bring a new railway era to the valley of the Peffery.

It is indeed a pity for Strathpeffer that MacKenzie of Coul had objected so strongly to the route of the Dingwall and Skye Railway; and while the Highland Railway did provide what can be called a consolation branch into the Spa, it is also a pity that the company did not, instead, dispense with the deviation line by Raven Rock and continue along the original route. In either case, Strathpeffer

- now the largest village in the vicinity of the Kyle line - would have had a station today, and one used by many travellers, especially tourists. Indeed, a new station should be established at Achterneed for the benefit of anyone who would want to make use of it - again, particularly tourists - as it would allow a rail connection between Strathpeffer and the West. All that is required is a basic request-only platform with a shelter, such that the cost would be minimal; and any stops at Achterneed would add little to the journey times, since a speed restriction is already in operation there because of the level crossing. A new station at Achterneed would be used by more passengers than some of the stations on the Kyle line and on the North line which have remained open but with trains rarely calling. The present lack of a station on the Kyle line for Strathpeffer further confirms that, overall, the Spa has had a raw deal in railway terms, but the facts have certainly provided it with an interesting railway history.

Strathpeffer station restored as a series of craft shops and seen here in 1993. The scene is particularly impressive with the roses beside the platform in their full growth and colourful bloom.
Author

Authorisation and Opening Dates
of Highland Railways

Line or Section of Line	Authorisation	Public Opening
Stanley Junction to Dunkeld,	10.7.1854	7.4.1856
and, thus, connection between Dunkeld and Perth		
Inverness to Nairn	24.7.1854	6.11.1855
Nairn to Dalvey, near Forres	21.7.1856	22.12.1857
Dalvey to Elgin	21.7.1856	25.3.1858
Elgin to Keith,	21.7.1856	18.8.1858
and, thus, connection between Inverness and Glasgow and Edinburgh via Aberdeen		
Inverness to Dingwall	3.7.1860	11.6.1862
Dingwall to Invergordon	3.7.1860	23.3.1863
Dunkeld to Pitlochry	22.7.1861	1.6.1863
Forres to Aviemore	22.7.1861	3.8.1863
(Public closure 18.10.1965)		
Aviemore to Pitlochry,	22.7.1861	9.9.1863
and, thus, connection between Inverness and Perth		
Invergordon to Meikle Ferry,	11.5.1863	1.6.1864
Meikle Ferry to Bonar Bridge	11.5.1863	1.10.1864
Bonar Bridge to Golspie	29.6.1865	13.4.1868
Dingwall to Strome Ferry	5.7.1865	19.8.1870
Callander to Oban, throughout	8.7.1865	1.7.1880
(Public closure Callander to Crianlarich 27.9.1965)		
Golspie to Helmsdale	20.6.1870	19.6.1871
Helmsdale to Wick and Thurso	13.7.1871	28.7.1874
Fodderty Junction to Strathpeffer	28.7.1884	3.6.1885
(Public closure 23.2.1946)		
Aviemore to Carr Bridge	28.7.1884	6.7.1892
Carr Bridge to Daviot	28.7.1884	8.7.1897
Daviot to Inverness,	28.7.1884	1.11.1898
and, thus, more direct connection between Inverness and Perth		
Craigendoran to Fort William	12.8.1889	7.8.1894
Muir of Ord to Fortrose	4.7.1890	1.2.1894
(Public closure 1.10.1951)		
Garve to Ullapool	14.8.1890	
Fort William to Banavie	20.7.1890	1.6.1895
Strome Ferry to Kyle Of Lochalsh	29.6.1893	22.11.1897
Banavie to Mallaig	31.7.1894	1.4.1901
Connel Ferry to Ballachulish	7.8.1896	24.8.1903
(Public closure 26.3.1966)		
Spean Bridge to Fort Augustus	14.8.1896	22.7.1903
(Public closure 1.12.1933)		
The Mound to Dornoch	13.8.1898	2.6.1902
(Public closure 13.6.1960)		
Wick to Lybster	27.11.1899	1.7.1903
(Public closure 1.4.1944)		

Appendix Six

Opening and Closing Dates
of Skye Railway Stations

In the case of some stations, the recorded dates of opening and closing do not necessarily represent the occurrence of the first or last services, and such dates may be official or inferred. See the following notes for stations marked.*

	Opening for:		Closing for:	
	Passengers	Goods	Passengers	Goods
Strathpeffer / Achterneed*	19.8.1870	4.8.1870	8.12.1964	18.5.1964
Garve	19.8.1870	4.8.1870	(open)	8.1983
Lochluichart,* 1st station	1870	-	30.6.1871	-
Lochluichart,* 2nd station	1.7.1871	1.7.1871	1.5.1954	1.5.1954
Lochluichart,* 3rd station	3.5.1954	3.5.1954	(open)	27.1.1964
Achanalt	19.8.1870	4.8.1870	(open)	2.11.1964
Achnasheen	19.8.1870	4.8.1870	(open)	8.1983
Glencarron*	1872	-	7.12.1964	-
Achnashellach*	1870	1870	(open)	27.1.1964
Strathcarron	19.8.1870	4.8.1870	(open)	8.1983
Attadale*	by 12.1877	1.3.1878	(open)	15.8.1966
Strome Ferry	19.8.1870	4.8.1870	(open)	15.6.1964
Duncraig*	2.11.1897	-	(open)	-
Plockton	2.11.1897	2.11.1897	(open)	7.9.1964
Duirinish	2.11.1897	2.11.1897	(open)	1.2.1954
Kyle of Lochalsh	2.11.1897	2.11.1897	(open)	8.1983

Notes:

Originally called Strathpeffer, **Achterneed** station, having closed to passengers on 7th December, 1964, was re-opened as an unstaffed halt on 8th February, 1965. Similarly, Glencarron and Duncraig were closed on the same day, to re-open at an unspecified time soon afterwards, but all three halts were not advertised in the timetable. They remained unpublicised but usable until the closures for Achterneed and Glencarron, also at an unspecified time, several years later, while Duncraig continued to be used and was re-instated to the timetable in 1976. A note in *Branch Line News* of 7th July, 1976 read:

Duncraig, Glencarron and Achterneed were officially closed to passengers from 7th December, 1964. By the summer of 1965, all three were in use under local arrangements, but, with realignment of the track through Achterneed station away from both platforms, the use of this 'station' ceased about 1968.

However, the statement of the cessation 'about 1968' is in disagreement with information that had previously appeared in the *Railway Magazine* for August 1969 from a correspondent who recorded that Achterneed was 'now used as a request stop', and that 'a 10 mph restriction over the adjacent level crossing means that a brief halt there is of little consequence'. With reference also to Glencarron and Duncraig, he added: All three halts are omitted from the public timetables, possibly in the mistaken belief that this would avoid the need to go through the closure machinery a second time, were services to be permanently withdrawn. Further to the note in *Branch Line News*, another in regard to Achterneed appeared in the issue of 11th May, 1977:

Despite its lack of a platform, Achterneed station has apparently seen use. The train in question is believed to have been the 17.50 from Kyle on 28th August, 1974, when one man alighted; he was not obviously a railwayman.

At a Board meeting of the Dingwall and Skye Railway on 15th July, 1871, a letter was read from John Shaw of the newly-constructed Glencarron Lodge, 'enquiring if the company will give him a platform near his new house, in the event of his trustees taking £1,000 of the stock of the company'. It was then 'resolved to give him a platform at his expense, provided he takes £2,000 of stock'. Shaw agreed to this, and the arrangement was approved by the Board on 6th September; but at a Board meeting on 3rd November, another letter from Shaw, together with one from his law agents, explained a delay in the payment of the £2,000. There was no further reference in the Dingwall and Skye minute book to the private platform, but Shaw appears to have obtained this by the spring of 1872, as a notice was issued then to the railway staff:

Please note that we have agreed to stop all ordinary trains run over the Dingwall and Skye Railway at Glencarron platform, either by signal or by notice given at Achnasheen or Strathcarron stations, as the case may be, for the purpose of setting down or picking up the proprietor or any member of his family, visitors or servants; also for all parcels or van goods belonging thereto which can be taken off or put into a vehicle by the guard.

The date of **Glencarron** becoming a request stop for the public is not known. It was listed as Glencarron Platform in the timetable that commenced on 1st July, 1885, but its public use possibly started well before this. Occasionally, trains stopped on request at Glencarron after its final but unspecified closure. The correspondent for the *Railway Magazine* of August 1969 stated that 'Glencarron closed on the same day as Duncraig, and trains now call by request only, mainly for the benefit of Glencarron Lodge'. *Branch Line News*, in its issue of 26th May, 1976, referred to Glencarron within the heading of 'Unadvertised Halts':

A booklet entitled *The Kyle Line* and published by a commercial firm, not BR, advises that trains can be stopped at Glencarron Platform, between Achnasheen and Achnashellach, by hand-signals, though, apparently, one is supposed to give advance notice to Achnashellach station. A correspondent says that he boarded a train at Glencarron in July 1974, after it had stopped to set someone down.

The booklet was a recent publication written by Tom Weir, a well-known Scottish hill-walker, author and TV personality, who, in mentioning the passenger-operated signals on the short platform, did imply, perhaps correctly, that the halt was still able to be used. He wrote: 'Glencarron lies under the peak of Moruisg, 3,026 ft, and one day, after climbing the rather featureless hill, I had the pleasure of running down to the halt to pull the hand-signal and stop the "up" train - one of the privileges of getting on at such a lonely spot'. In July 1982, the author of the present book travelled on a Kyle-Inverness train which made a stop at Glencarron to set down a passenger or passengers.

From the opening of the Kyle Extension, **Duncraig** was a private platform for the use of the owner of Duncraig Castle, Sir Kenneth Matheson, son of Sir Alexander. During the 1930s, the castle was the property of Sir Daniel Hamilton, who had purchased the Balmacara estate in 1918, and he and his wife made the provision that Ross and Cromarty County Council should ultimately take over Duncraig 'to establish a centre of practical and residential education for young people of the Highlands'. The castle was used as a military hospital during World War II, and with the war's ending, the county council were able to comply with the bequest, by the opening in September 1945, of a residential college for girls. Soon after this, the platform at Duncraig may have had trains stopping for the students and staff of the college, and it was eventually included as a public halt in the timetable from 23rd May, 1949. After having closed on 7th December, 1964, as with Achterneed and Glencarron, Duncraig was re-opened, but unadvertised, by the summer of 1965. It was the one intermediate station on the Kyle line with a regular supply of passengers, due to the college. The *Railway Magazine* correspondent of August 1969 explained that the closure of Duncraig halt

. . . caused considerable inconvenience to the 70 domestic science students at the castle, and in August 1965, Ross and Cromarty County Council agreed to pay BR £10 a year to cover the upkeep of the station. It is now a request stop, and is one of the busiest stations on the line.

From 3rd May, 1976, Duncraig was once again reinstated to the timetable, after what had become, in effect, a non-implemented closure, and it remains as an advertised request stop. This is in spite of the fact that, sadly, the castle had to be closed as a catering college by Highland Regional Council in the summer of 1989, because of the high cost of maintaining the large building for the falling numbers of students.

The platform at **Achnashellach** was in existence at or soon after the opening of the Dingwall and Skye line on 19th August, 1870, and, being initially private for Achnashellach Lodge, was used on 4th and 6th October of that year for the visit of the Prince of Wales. Achnashellach became a public station from the timetable that commenced on 1st May, 1871.

The first station at **Lochluichart**, which was a private platform for Lady Ashburton of Lochluichart Lodge, was opened at or soon after the opening of the Dingwall and Skye line. With Lady Ashburton's approval and expenditure, it was replaced by the public station that opened on 1st July, 1871. This was succeeded by the present station on 3rd May, 1954, in connection with the North of Scotland Hydro-Electric Board's Conon Valley project.

The opening date of the platform at **Attadale** is also not known, but it was some time between 1875 and 1877. No station is shown on the Ordnance Survey map that was surveyed in 1875, and the Minutes of a Board meeting of the Dingwall and Skye Railway on 4th December, 1877 referred to a 'proposed siding at Attadale, where there is already a passenger platform'. The platform would have been used mainly by Alex Matheson and his family for their Attadale estate, although it was also available for the public, but it is surprising that a station there to serve the Mathesons had taken so long to materialise.

The note in *Branch Line News* of 7th July, 1976, which referred to Duncraig, Glencarron and Achterneed, also outlined the state of the other intermediate stations at the time:

Use of Duncraig and Glencarron has, however, continued - both being included in the list of stations when the line was proposed for closure in 1975.* With installation of Calor gas lighting, similar to other unstaffed stations on the line, Duncraig has been advertised again from 3rd May, 1976. These Calor gas lighting installations are of interest because they have been installed in one of the original station lamps at most of the stations - thus preserving a connection with yesteryear. All trains now stop at Duncraig, and will do so at Glencarron on prior notice to the guard to be set down or to one of the staffed stations - usually Kyle of Lochalsh - if one wishes the train to stop to pick up. Indeed, Duncraig is the busiest intermediate station between Dingwall and Kyle, and Glencarron the quietest. One would have a hard job giving advance information to Achnashellach, as this station is now unstaffed, and, like Attadale,† the buildings have been completely removed - no shelter at all being available for intending passengers. Garve, Achnasheen and Strathcarron are all staffed by signalmen, who, while dealing with parcels traffic, do not issue tickets - the train guards being responsible for this function. The station buildings at Lochluichart, Plockton and Duirinish still stand and are used for other purposes, as are the buildings at Stromeferry; the latter are used by BR staff involved in working the oil-related traffic to the sidings for Howard Doris Ltd. The shelters at Attadale [*sic*] and Duncraig are still *in situ* in reasonable condition.

With Duncraig still in the timetable, Achterneed and Glencarron are the only stations on the Kyle line to have undergone effective closure.

Today, the station at **Kyle of Lochalsh**, with its listed building, appears generally similar to how it was at the opening of the line, except for the lack of sidings now; and there is still a magnificent view seawards, in spite of being lessened by the unpopular Skye bridge to the west. The sole-remaining signal box on the line is at Kyle, but with the use of RETB signalling controlled from Inverness, it is no longer used for its original purpose. At the single platforms of Duirinish, Attadale, Stromeferry, Achnashellach and Achanalt, only a basic shelter exists, with the last three stations having long lost their double-track and double-platform status, though the disused platforms are still in evidence but overgrown. Due to the Howard Doris construction yard at Kishorn having closed in 1986, Stromeferry station no longer has sidings, and it serves just a quiet hamlet again. At Plockton, the original station structure - also a listed building - is now used as a small restaurant and craft shop during the summer. When the tables are placed on the platform

---

*   This should have read either 1973, if referring to 31st December, or 1974, if referring to 1st January.
†   Achanalt seems to have been meant here.

under the canopy, an attractive scene is presented, and this forms a novelty for the diners, especially with the arrival of a train, when there is also a pleasant surprise for the onlooking passengers. Strathcarron, Achnasheen and Garve - each with its original but modified station house building that is no longer used for railway purposes - still have two platforms and two lines that form the only crossing loops on the whole of the Kyle railway. The station building at Lochluichart, from the 1954 diversion, still stands, and the remains of the old station platform, amid overgrowth, together with the old trackbed, can be seen.

Of the stations that underwent closure, nothing is left at Achterneed, but Glencarron is in a relatively good state, considering its duration of having been closed, with the short platform and the wooden shelter intact. Being the only closed station that is able to be seen, it can be reached by the original track that begins from the main road a short distance west of Glencarron Lodge and winds down the hillside. The re-opened Duncraig station - or, rather, the setting of the station - is the gem of the line. It is situated below the castle at the water's edge, and there is a wonderful view from the short platform that looks across the bay to Plockton, with a tree-lined island in the foreground, and with the line, heading westwards, curving sharply to the right to ascend the gradient to Plockton station, while the tops of the Cuillins may be seen in the distance. It is worthwhile making a trip - either by train or by other means - to stand on Duncraig's platform to see one of the best views from a railway station in Britain. On a fine, clear day or evening, it would, indeed, be a pleasure to wait here for a train that was late. Finally, in regard to Duncraig, a note in the Spring 1996 issue of the *Highland Railway Journal* read: 'Station lighting has now been provided, and, from Monday, 15th January, all services will stop when required. This removes the anomaly that trains only stopped during the hours of daylight, at least officially.'

Signal Boxes and Loops

Fodderty Junction - box opened 1885, closed 1936, re-opened 1940, closed 1944.
Achterneed - loop opened 1871; box opened 1893; box and loop closed 1966.
Garve - loop opened 1870; east and west boxes opened 1893, closed 1984; loop remains in use.
Lochluichart - box at original public station opened 1893; closure not known; no box at replacement station; no loop at either station.
Achanalt - loop opened 1870; east and west boxes opened 1893; boxes and loop closed 1966.
Achnasheen - loop opened 1870; east and west boxes opened 1893, closed 1984; loop remains in use.
Loan Crossing - see Appendix Fourteen.
Glencarron - no box and no loop.
Achnashellach - box opened 1893; loop opened 1900; box and loop closed 1966.
Strathcarron - loop opened 1870; east and west boxes opened 1893, closed 1984; loop remains in use.
Attadale - box opened 1893; closure date not known; no loop.
Strome Ferry - east box opened 1870; west box and loop opened 1897; boxes and loop closed 1966.
Plockton - no box and no loop.
Duncraig - no box and no loop.
Duirinish - box opened 1940, closed 1945; no loop.
Kyle of Lochalsh - box opened 1897, closed 1984; only remaining box on line, but not in use for signalling.

Data for boxes and loops courtesy of David Stirling of the Highland Railway Society.

Skye Railway Mileages

D - From Dingwall
I - From Inverness
S - From Strome Ferry
K - From Kyle of Lochalsh

	D	I	S	K
Inverness	-	-	71 ¾	82 ¼
Dingwall	-	18 ¾	53	63 ½
Fodderty Junction	2 ¼	21	50 ¾	61 ¼
Achterneed	4 ½	23 ¼	48 ½	59
Raven Rock Summit	6 ½	25 ¼	46 ½	57
Garve	11 ¾	30 ½	41 ¾	52 ¼
Corriemoillie Summit	14	32 ¾	39	49 ½
Lochluichart	17	35 ¾	36	46 ½
Achanalt	21 ½	40 ¼	31 ½	42
Achnasheen	27 ¾	46 ½	25 ¼	35 ¾
Luib Summit	31 ¾	50 ½	21 ¼	31 ¾
Loan Crossing	34	52 ¾	19	29 ½
Glencarron	36 ¼	55	16 ¾	27 ¼
Achnashellach	40 ¼	59	12 ¾	23 ¼
Balnacra Level Crossing	42	60 ¾	11	21 ½
Strathcarron	45 ¾	64 ½	7 ¼	17 ¼
Attadale	48	66 ¾	5	15 ½
Strome Ferry	53	71 ¾	-	10 ½
Duncraig	57	75 ¾	4	6 ½
Plockton	58	76 ¾	5	5 ½
Duirinish	59 ½	78 ¼	6 ½	4
Kyle of Lochalsh	63 ½	82 ¼	10 ½	-

Class '37' No. 37420 at Badicaul with the 5.10 pm Kyle-Inverness train on 14th July, 1986. The view is towards the Cuillins. *T. Heavyside*

Appendix Eight

Skye Railway
Selective Chronology

Events not previously mentioned are indicated by *.

1. *Dingwall and Skye Railway: Dingwall to Strome Ferry*

26.4.1864	Initiation of Skye Railway at first meeting of promoters, in London.
28.4.1864	Second meeting of promoters, in London: name changed to Dingwall and Skye Railway.
7.1864	Issue of Dingwall and Skye Railway Prospectus, by provisional committee, for line from Dingwall to Kyle.
15.7.1864	First promotional meeting of Dingwall and Skye Railway to public, at Inverness.
6.10.1864	First meeting of provisional committee of Dingwall and Skye Railway Company, at Inverness.
11.1864	Issue of Parliamentary notices for Dingwall and Skye Railway.
5.7.1865	Royal Assent of Dingwall & Skye Railway Act.
5.9.1867	Meeting of four shareholders at Jeantown: decision taken not to construct line beyond Attadale.
11.1867	Issue of Parliamentary notices for deviations regarding Strathpeffer and Achnashellach, and for new terminus and pier at Attadale.
29.5.1868	Royal Assent of Dingwall and Skye Railway (Deviations) Act.
2.9.1868	Commencement of building operations on Dingwall contract - Dingwall to Achanalt.
9.10.1868	Commencement of building operations on Loch Carron contract - Achanalt to Attadale.
23.3.1869	Board meeting: decision made to extend line from Attadale to Strome Ferry.
4.1869	Commencement of building operations on Strome Ferry extension - Attadale to Strome Ferry.
7.1870	Completion of constructional work of line.
27.7.1870	First run over whole line by locomotive, conveying wagons carrying contractors.
29/30.7.1870	Board of Trade inspection of Dingwall contract by Captain Tyler.
1/2.8.1870	Board of Trade inspection of Loch Carron contract by Captain Tyler.
4.8.1870	Opening of Dingwall and Skye Railway for goods: first run over whole line by special train and carriages carrying officials and guests; commencement of steamer services between Strome Ferry and Portree and between Strome Ferry and Stornoway.
8.8.1870	Communication received that Captain Tyler had refused to sanction opening of line to passengers, due to incomplete fencing.
19.8.1870	Opening of Dingwall and Skye Railway for passengers: commencement at Strome Ferry of full operations of train and steamer connections between Inverness and Portree and between Inverness and Stornoway.
7.9.1870	Grand banquet at Strome Ferry, in celebration of opening of line.
1.7.1871	Opening of Lochluichart station for public.
31.7.1872	Destruction of Strome Ferry engine shed by fire during early hours of morning, but with rescue of locomotive.*
24.4.1877	Royal Assent of Highland Railway (Steam Vessels) Act.
14.10.1877	Severance of line near Achnashellach, due to torrential flood water from exceptionally-severe storm.

2. Highland Railway: Strome Ferry to Kyle of Lochalsh. Other Proposed Railways

2.8.1880	Royal Assent of Highland and Dingwall and Skye Railways (Amalgamation) Act.
3.6.1883	Riot at Strome Ferry.
1883	Rejection of Glasgow and North-Western Railway Bill in Parliament.
3.6.1885	Renaming of Strathpeffer station to Achterneed, in connection with opening of Strathpeffer branch.
1.1889	Signing of petition by 1,020 men of Lochbroom and Assynt to appeal to Highland Railway for line from Garve to Ullapool.
12.1889	Appointment of royal commission by Government to examine transport needs of West Highlands and islands, with particular reference to which of six proposed railways would receive financial assistance.
4.6.1890	Board meeting of Highland Railway: interest expressed by Directors in extending line from Strome Ferry to Kyle, and in constructing pier at Kyle, for sum of £120,000.
14.8.1890	Royal Assent of Garve and Ullapool Railway Act.
8.1890	Publication of report of West Highland Royal Commission.
3.1891	Meeting between Andrew Dougall and Financial Secretary to the Treasury, regarding extension from Strome Ferry to Kyle; letters from latter to former stating that £45,000 would be contributed towards expense of extension.
6.1891	Cursory survey of proposed route of extension from Strome Ferry to Kyle.
6.1891	Appointment of railway committee by government to re-examine west coast railway schemes.
27.6.1891	Meeting of West Highland Railway Committee with several Highland Railway Directors: importance of extending line from Strome to Kyle stressed by latter to former, with promised support from Highland company.
7/8.1891	Inspection of six proposed railway routes by West Highland Railway Committee.
16.10.1891	Destruction of Strome Ferry station by fire during early hours of morning, also resulting in loss of carriages and vans, totalling 14.*
3.1892	Publication of report of West Highland Railway Committee.
14.10.1892	Runaway-train accident from Achnashellach.
11.1892	Issue of Parliamentary notices for Kyle Extension; issue of Parliamentary notices for Loch Maree and Aultbea Railway.
12.1892	Communication received by Highland Railway from Treasury that £45,000 would be contributed towards extension to Kyle.
29.6.1893	Royal Assent of Highland Railway Act, for Kyle Extension.
1893	Rejection of Loch Maree and Aultbea Railway Bill in Parliament.
24.8.1893	Royal Assent of Garve and Ullapool Railway (Abandonment) Act.
10.1893	Commencement of building operations on Kyle Extension.
3.2.1897	Board meeting: decision made that name of station at Kyle would be Kyle of Lochalsh.
22.6.1897	First run over extension by passenger train, consisting of special carriage for guests attending concert and ball at Kyle, in celebration of Diamond Jubilee of Queen Victoria.
31.7.1897	Run to Kyle by Highland Railway officials and friends, numbering 150, and inspection of works.
25.9.1897	Runaway-train accident from Raven Rock.
10.1897	Completion of constructional work of extension.
28.10.1897	Board of Trade inspection of extension by Major Marindin.
2.11.1897	Opening of Kyle Extension for passengers and goods: banquet at Strome Ferry in celebration; commencement at Kyle of Lochalsh of train and steamer services between Inverness and Portree and between Inverness and Stornoway.
1.4.1901	Commencement of Stornoway-Mallaig-Kyle steamer service, in conjunction with opening of West Highland Railway Mallaig Extension.
7.1901	Commencement of express train service from Dingwall to Kyle, calling only at Garve, Achnasheen and Strathcarron.

| 7.1914 | Opening of Loan Crossing loop. (See Appendix Fourteen.)* |
| 1.1.1923 | Cessation of Highland Railway Company and commencement of London, Midland & Scottish Railway Company under Grouping: establishment of Kyle line within LMSR. |

3. *British Railways*

1.1.1948	Cessation of London, Midland and Scottish Railway Company and commencement of British Railways under nationalisation: establishment of Kyle line within BR.
2.9.1953	Severance of line near Stromeferry, due to torrential rain.
1.2.1954	Closure of Duirinish station for goods.
3.5.1954	Opening of replacement Lochluichart station and replacement track, in connection with Conon Valley power scheme.
27.3.1963	Publication of Beeching report, recommending closure of Kyle line.
27.1.1964	Closure of Lochluichart and Achnashellach stations for goods.
18.5.1964	Closure of Achterneed station for goods.
15.6.1964	Closure of Stromeferry station for goods.
7.9.1964	Closure of Plockton station for goods.
2.11.1964	Closure of Achanalt station for goods.
7.12.1964	Closure of Achterneed, Glencarron and Duncraig stations for passengers.
8.2.1965	Re-opening of Achterneed station as unstaffed request halt for passengers.
15.8.1966	Closure of Attadale station for goods.
21.12.1971	Announcement of closure of Kyle line from 1st January, 1974.
24.3.1973	Cessation of Kyle-Stornoway steamer service.
26.3.1973	Commencement of Ullapool-Stornoway steamer service.
31.7.1974	Announcement of permanent reprieve for Kyle line.
17.3.1975	Cessation of Kyle Portree steamer service.
10.7.1983	Commencement of Sunday passenger services on Kyle line.
8.1983	Closure of Dingwall, Garve, Achnasheen, Strathcarron and Kyle of Lochalsh stations for goods.
13.7.1984	Inauguration of RETB signalling on Kyle line.
28.10.1984	Full operation of RETB signalling.
17.6.1987	Formal opening of renovated station building at Kyle of Lochalsh.

Class '37' No. 37 415 stands at Kyle of Lochalsh with the 5.00 pm to Dingwall on 21st July, 1989. The diesel multiple unit observation car is behind the engine. At the time this picture was taken, through trains had been suspended due to the closure of the Ness bridge because of severe flood damage.   *T. Heavyside*

Strathpeffer Railway
Selective Chronology

4.1864	Initiation of Dingwall and Railway, with line to pass through Strathpeffer village.
7.1864	Issue of Dingwall and Skye Railway Prospectus.
5.7.1865	Royal Assent of Dingwall and Skye Railway Act, with line to pass through Strathpeffer village.
29.5.1868	Royal Assent of Dingwall and Skye Railway (Deviations) Act, with line avoiding Strathpeffer village.
4.8.1870	Opening of Dingwall and Skye Railway for goods, and opening of Strathpeffer station at Achterneed for goods.
19.8.1870	Opening of Dingwall and Skye Railway for passengers, and opening of Strathpeffer station at Achterneed for passengers.
28.7.1884	Royal Assent of Highland Railway Act, for Strathpeffer branch.
2.6.1885	Board of Trade inspection of Strathpeffer branch by Major Marindin.
3.6.1885	Opening of Strathpeffer branch for passengers and goods, with original Strathpeffer station renamed Achterneed.
13.6.1911	Opening of Highland Railway's 'Highland Hotel' at Strathpeffer.
4.7.1911	Commencement of 'Strathpeffer Spa Express'.
23.2.1946	Closure of Strathpeffer branch for passengers.
26.3.1951	Closure of Strathpeffer branch for goods.
18.5.1964	Closure of Achterneed station for goods.
7.12.1964	Closure of Achterneed station for passengers.
8.2.1965	Re-opening of Achterneed station as unstaffed request halt. Date of final closure not known.

Strathpeffer station in LMS days. *G.E. Langmuir*

Appendix Ten

Deaths and Injuries to Navvies
on the Kyle Extension

A short chronology, based on the events that were publicised, herewith commemorates not only the unfortunate navvies on the Kyle Extension who lost their lives or who survived with some suffering, but these preceding words also express a tribute to the rest of the many brave and hardy men who physically transformed Ross-shire, from east to west, in building all of the Skye railway in its two sections, from Dingwall to Strome and from Strome to Kyle. Commendation is offered to them here because, in consideration of the fact that their spirited struggles and resulting successes were, strangely and unjustly, not honoured at the openings of the respective lines in 1870 and 1897, they deserve a formal acknowledgement for what they accomplished for the West Highlands and islands.

14.11.1894	Fernaig. Irishman Michael Poiner hurled into air from explosion during blasting operations, landing 40 yards from place of accident and being killed instantaneously. Three others, John MacDonald, John MacLeod and Malcolm MacAulay, all from West Highlands, injured, but not seriously.
2.12.1894	Plockton. Irishman found dead, having been in drunken state and having, presumably, stumbled and drowned in shallow pool by roadside.
2.1895	Erbusaig. Lachlan MacLeod from Raasay suffered badly crushed leg by a rail falling upon it, but recovery occurred.
2.4.1895	Badicaul. Irishman Michael Green mutilated in head and one arm, with loss of eyesight, from explosion during blasting operations.
4.4.1895	Erbusaig. Irishman named O'Brien mutilated during blasting operations, losing but regaining his eyesight.
6.4.1895	Erbusaig. Irishman James Murphy found dead, having been in drunken state and having, presumably, fallen to the ground and slept on a cold night.
9.4.1895	Strome Ferry. Irishman James Brady killed instantaneously in explosion. James MacKay seriously injured.
12.5.1895	Drumbuie. George Hamilton killed instantaneously from explosion during blasting operations.
5.2.1897	Duncraig. Roderick MacAskill killed by jib of crane falling upon him.
7.8.1897	Portnacloich. Three local workmen, Duncan Finlayson, John Finlayson and Duncan MacMillan, pitched out of wagon and seriously injured, when two engines collided.
9.10.1897	Plockton. Edward MacDonald from Harris killed after falling from ballast train and being run over by wagons.

Also, unpublicised, there were undoubtedly many other minor accidents, and there may have been other serious accidents and even deaths.

Appendix Eleven

Principal Skye Railway Steam Motive Power
A Summary by the late James Stevenson
of the Highland Railway Society

When the Dingwall and Skye Railway was due to open to Strome Ferry in 1870, the Highland Railway possessed 31 small 2-4-0s with coupled wheels of 5 ft 0 in or 5 ft 1½ in., and these were the only locomotives reasonably able to work the new line. However, all of them had a rigid wheelbase varying between 14 ft 6 in. and 15 ft 0 in., and this rigidity was expected to cause difficulties on some of the sharp curves of the line. David Jones had become the Highland's Locomotive Superintendent in 1870, and in quickly realising that 2-4-0 designs with a wheelbase of over 14 ft were ill-suited to the Skye line - which was inaugurated by two 'Seafield' class 2-4-0s dating from 1858 - he was determined to improve matters because of the Highland's precarious financial position.

Jones resolved to fit the two 'Seafields' with a leading bogie arrangement to provide enhanced flexibility, and he eventually prevailed upon the Board in October 1871 to authorise the conversion from 2-4-0s to 4-4-0s, but with the retention of the 5 ft 0 in. coupled wheels. The first of the two engines to be converted was HR No. 10 in June 1873, and it was followed by HR No. 7 in May 1875. The two converted 4-4-0s proved successful and were the mainstay of the Skye line during the 1870s and early 1880s, lasting until the end of the 1890s. This success prompted Jones to build a new class specifically for the line, and, incorporating his experience gained from Nos. 7 and 10, the first new 4-4-0 'Skye Bogie' appeared in 1882, being, in general, not dissimilar to Nos. 7 and 10. However, funds were short for some time, and it was not until 1892 that another 'Skye Bogie' was built. The famous class, eventually totalling nine by the end of 1901, had 5 ft 3½ in. coupled wheels. The 'Skye Bogies' were very successful and largely monopolised the Skye line, though some of the later and larger Highland 4-4-0s also appeared on occasions.

By the middle of the 1920s, in LMSR times, heavier rolling stock began to tax the 'Skye Bogies' severely, and thoughts turned to the use of six-coupled engines. In 1918 and 1919, the Highland had taken delivery of a class of eight 'Superheated Goods' 4-6-0s, designed by Christopher Cumming, with 5 ft 3 in coupled wheels, intended for freight traffic between Inverness and Perth;* and by 1928, standard LMSR engines had begun to arrive on the Perth line, such that the 'Superheated Goods' became available for trials on the Kyle line. They proved an immediate success, although much improvement to the track was necessary. After the 'Superheated Goods' came upon the scene, the 'Skye Bogies' - several of which had already been withdrawn between 1923 and 1927 - disappeared quickly from the scene.

Encouraged by the success of the larger engines, the LMSR began to make use of some of the famous Jones 'Big Goods' 4-6-0s of 1894. These were built with flangeless centre-coupled wheels, but flanges were provided for those used on the Kyle line, because of the sharp curves. However, all of the 'Big Goods' were withdrawn by 1940, and the 'Superheated Goods' were left to deal with the heavy traffic of the war years, with assistance mainly from 4-4-0s. From 1934, LMSR standard class '5' 4-6-0s - the William Stanier 'Black Fives' - had come to monopolise the rest of the Highland main lines, but they were precluded from working to Kyle by reason of the short turntable there. Originally 50 ft, which accommodated the 'Superheated Goods' and the 'Big Goods', the turntable was extended to 54 ft to enable the larger 'Clan' class passenger 4-6-0s to work the line on occasions, mainly during the war years. 'Black Fives' required a still-larger turntable, and one of 60 ft was eventually installed in 1946, involving heavy rock-cutting. Thereafter, they largely took over, but the 'Superheated Goods' were still seen at Kyle until 1952, while the 'Black Fives', as the last of the steam trains, continued until 1961.

Further Reading:
A History of Highland Locomotives, by P. Tatlow, OPC, 1979.
Highland Railway Locomotives, (2 Vols) by J.R.H. Cormack and J.L. Stevenson, RCTS, 1990.
Highland Railway Liveries, by H. Geddes and E. Bellass, Pendragon, 1995.

* These were the Cumming 4-6-0s of 1918 and 1919, which, in retrospect, were referred to erroneously, as 'Clans' - the 'Superheated' class being separate from the true 'Clans' of 1919 and 1921, which were also designed by Cumming. - DMcC.

'Skye Bogie' Numbers
and Dates of Operation

HR No.	Built	LMSR No.	Withdrawn
70	5.1882	14277	12.1929
85	8.1892	none	8.1923
86	2.1893	14279	10.1927
87	12.1893	14280*	12.1926
88	4.1895	14281*	12.1926
5	8.1897	14282	9.1929
6	11.1897	14283	8.1929
7	7.1898	14284	4.1930
48	12.1901	14285	10.1928

HR renumberings:

70: to	70A	in	12.1912	
then to	67	in	2.1923	by LMSR
85:	85A		4.1918	
	85		9.1919	
	85A		11.1919	
86	86A		4.1918	
	86		9.1919	
5	32		2.1899	
6	33		2.1899	
7	34		1899	

* Allocated number but not brought into use.

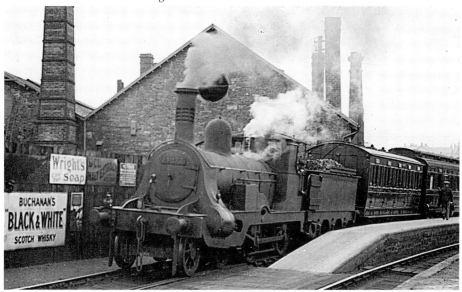

'Skye Bogie' 4-4-0 LMS No. 14277, ex-HR No. 70, with a Kyle train at Inverness station's platform 5 in the 1920s, against the background of Lochgorm Works.   *J.L. Stevenson*

Appendix Thirteen

Signalling on the Skye Line
by David Stirling of the Highland Railway Society

When the Dingwall and Skye Railway opened in 1870, railway signalling was at an intermediate stage of its development. Interlocking of the points and signals was known and used, but by no means universally. The Highland Railway installed proper interlocked signalling at the two largest stations, Dingwall and Strome Ferry, but that at the intermediate stations was more primitive.

At Dingwall, there were two cabins, at the north and south ends of the station, controlling the points and signals, while Strome Ferry had only one cabin. The equipment was supplied by McKenzie, Clunes and Holland of Worcester, the signal boxes being of their 'Type 1' design.* These installations were recognisably of the traditional British type, but with some early features. Instead of bracket signals, there were signal posts with several arms, including those on the home signal at the north end of Dingwall, where three arms, in line vertically, applied to trains from Bonar Bridge to the main platform, from Strome to the 'Skye arrival platform', and from Strome to the main platform.

At the intermediate crossing loops, there were station signals and distant signals. The distant signals were 'absolute stop signals', and drivers finding one at danger had to stop, after which, if the line was clear, they could proceed cautiously forward. The distant signals were regarded as protecting the station. They were not interlocked with the points in the conventional way, but the wires operating the signals detected that the points were in the correct position. The loop points were weighted to keep them in position for the left-hand line. At non-block stations with sidings, and probably those without sidings, distant signals only were provided, but no station signals. It is possible that the distants were controlled from a central 'cabin' of some sort, but evidence for this is very slight. There were sidings at Achnashellach and probably Strathpeffer (Achterneed), although the Board of Trade inspector did not mention the latter when the line opened - others appearing at Lochluichart (second station, being first for public) and Attadale in due course.

When the line was opened, it was worked on the block system, using dedicated needle block instruments, in the same way as the rest of the Highland Railway. No form of staff or token was used. The block sections were Dingwall-Garve-Achanalt-Achnasheen-Strathcarron-Strome, with each of these intermediate stations having a crossing loop and sidings. In October 1870, the Dingwall and Skye Railway Board agreed to convert the siding at Strathpeffer to a crossing loop, and this was done by the following summer, with the station dividing the Dingwall-Garve block section in two.

In 1885, the branch to Strathpeffer opened, with the earlier Strathpeffer station being renamed Achterneed. This introduced new interlocked signal cabins at Fodderty Junction and Strathpeffer, each with a brick base and wooden superstructure. McKenzie and Holland were the contractors. Fodderty had the simplest possible layout, with one point, and became a block post between Dingwall and Achterneed, although it was able to be switched out to give a longer section between Dingwall and Achterneed.

In 1893, under compulsion from the Board of Trade, the Highland Railway installed fully-interlocked signalling at the intermediate stations, including a new cabin at Strome. The signals were then of the current designs, with the boxes being of McKenzie and Holland 'Type 3' and the lever frames more modern than those already in use. At most of the crossing loops, two cabins were provided, in the Highland's usual practice, for most of its loops were too long to be worked by a single cabin. In these cases, the home signals were controlled by both cabins to prevent misunderstandings causing accidents, while the starting signals were controlled by the adjacent cabin and a lever in the station office, where the block instruments were located. Achterneed's crossing loop was short enough that it could be controlled by one cabin. At the non-crossing places with sidings - Lochluichart, Achnashellach and Attadale - a cabin was provided that controlled the signals and points. The layouts at the crossing stations were revised in 1894, and the example shown, of Achanalt, was typical (*see opposite*). Note the repeater signal beneath the home signal, to indicate the position of the starting signal ahead. The provision of shunting signals varied a little, with most stations having these at one end only, although Garve was so equipped at both ends. At about the same time, Achnashellach was made into a block post, splitting the very long Achnasheen-Strathcarron section.

* As described in *The Signal Box* by The Signalling Study Group, Oxford Publishing Co., 1986.

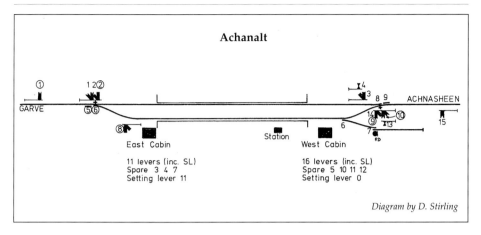

Achanalt

GARVE

ACHNASHEEN

East Cabin

11 levers (inc. SL)
Spare 3 4 7
Setting lever 11

Station

West Cabin

16 levers (inc. SL)
Spare 5 10 11 12
Setting lever 0

Diagram by D. Stirling

The Kyle Extension in 1897 introduced two novelties as far as the signalling was concerned: a new signalling contractor, and a new method of working the single line. The contract for the signalling of the Extension had been awarded to Dutton and Co. of Worcester, having done work elsewhere on the Highland Railway. Two signal cabins were involved, at Strome Ferry West and Kyle of Lochalsh, being of the Dutton 'Type 3' design, while the outdoor signals were on lattice posts, which were very rare on the Highland Railway. Otherwise, the signals conformed closely to the McKenzie and Holland designs.

The single line between Strome and Kyle was controlled by the tablet system - that is, there were metal discs, suitably engraved for the section, and the driver of each train was required to be in possession of one of these before running in the section. The tablets were kept in instruments at each end of the section, electrically interlocked so that only one tablet could be out of the instruments at any time, and thereby giving additional protection against a head-on collision. The tablet system was approved by the Board of Trade, whereas the Highland's method of control by block instruments only was not. The tablet itself was used to unlock the ground frame that controlled the siding points at Plockton, avoiding the need for signals there. The old block instruments east of Strome were retained until 1899, when the whole line was converted to tablet operation. Tyer's No. 6 tablet instruments were used. Unusually for a non-crossing station, Achnashellach retained its block post when the tablets were introduced, and it was upgraded to a crossing loop in 1900. The loop here was short enough that only one signal cabin was needed to control it. Once the tablet had been introduced, a few more sidings appeared between stations, with the first two being Achnasheen Ballast Pit and Portchullin Ballast in 1903.*

The tablet system dispensed with the need for signals at the intermediate sidings, and in due course, the signals at Lochluichart and Attadale were taken out of use, and the associated cabins made redundant, early in the 20th century. Around the same time, passenger-operated double-armed signals appeared at some request stops, such as Glencarron.

A further crossing loop was added, for Admiralty traffic, in 1918 at what was called Loan Crossing. This had a brick-built cabin, capable of being switched out to give a long Achnasheen-Achnashellach section when not required. Loan was at the same place as Luib Siding, being accessible by means of a ground frame unlocked by the long section tablet.

The Highland Railway had long been in the habit of banking trains to Raven Rock Summit from Dingwall, with the bank engine detaching from the train there and making its return from the summit. This procedure was placed on a safer and more regular basis in 1921 when a banking key

---

* As listed in the Highland Railway Society's booklet *Highland Railway Station Locations and Dates*, the other sidings, westwards from Dingwall, were as follows: Scottish Oil (Meiklefield), also known as Council Siding and Harper's Siding, opened in 1920 and closed in 1959; Fodderty Timber Siding, opened 1913, closed by 1915; Raven Rock Siding, opened 1924, possibly closed 1952; Tarvie, opened 1914, no closure date stated; and Loan, opened 1914, no closure date stated, but see Appendix Thirteen; with no closure dates stated for Achnasheen Ballast Pit and Portchullin Ballast. - DMcC

was installed for the Achterneed-Garve section. The train engine carried the Achterneed-Garve tablet and the banker carried the special key, with the instruments being locked so that it was not possible to signal another train until both the tablet and the banking key had been returned to their respective instruments.

The LMSR era saw little change at first, except that, in the late 1920s, the tablet instruments on alternate sections were replaced with key token instruments, as on the rest of the Highland system. However, in 1936, Fodderty Junction cabin was closed, with the junction points becoming motor-operated from Dingwall North cabin. The points were electrically interlocked with the tokens for the Dingwall-Achterneed and Dingwall-Strathpeffer sections, so that it was possible to change the points only when the tokens for both sections were in their instruments, and only the token for the section that corresponded to the lie of the points could be withdrawn from the instruments. A Tyer's occupation key was used for the Dingwall-Strathpeffer section. It was possible to restore the key to the instrument at Strathpeffer while a train was there, to allow traffic to work between Dingwall and Achterneed. As Strathpeffer cabin was closed at the same time as Fodderty, the points at the terminus were controlled by a ground frame, but there was a new sand drag and a starting signal there to prevent a train starting from Strathpeffer in error without the section key.

In 1940, the effects of another war appeared on the Kyle line, with armaments depots being set up at Duirinish and near Fodderty Junction, where a new cabin, on an extension of the base of the old one, was opened in 1940. The occupation key was transferred to control trains between Fodderty and the storage sidings, and a single staff controlled the meagre traffic to Strathpeffer itself. Trains from the storage sidings could be worked by two locomotives, one at each end, reversing at Fodderty, with the one that had been leading to Fodderty becoming the banker to Raven Rock. At Duirinish, there were extensive sidings, and a new block post was introduced here, without a crossing loop, between 1940 and 1945.

After the war, the block posts at Fodderty and Duirinish were removed, with the working control of the points at Fodderty reverting to Dingwall, although by this stage, it was no longer possible to allow Kyle traffic to pass while a train was at Strathpeffer. In the 1960s, the chill wind of retrenchment eliminated the crossing loops at Achterneed, Achanalt, Achnashellach and Stromeferry. In connection with an oil-rig construction project, Strome later acquired sidings, with an intermediate key token instrument to allow trains to be shut in while traffic passed on the main line.

Semaphore signalling, and even the Highland Railway's old pattern of having two cabins at each station, survived until the signalling was drastically simplified in 1984. All signals were removed and train-operated points - a modern version of weighted points - were installed, with the sidings being controlled by small ground frames unlocked by keys carried on the locomotives. This was part of the installation of Radio Electronic Token Block (RETB), which arrived in 1984. It was initially computer-controlled from a centre in Dingwall and later in Inverness. As its name suggests, it issues a virtual electronic token to drivers - or to the permanent way squads, for one of its great advantages is the ability to protect the PW men effectively. There were, inevitably, substantial teething troubles with RETB, which were not helped by the government enforcing a change to less favourable radio channels. Because of its nature, it is simple and cheap to introduce non-crossing block posts with RETB, and the simplified arrangements make this necessary near junctions - so that one of the consequences is that under RETB, Fodderty is once more a block post!

The level crossing that replaced the bridge at Garve, looking north-west in 1992, with RETB in operation.   *J.L. Stevenson*

Appendix Fourteen

Loan Crossing Loop

On the original Dingwall and Skye Railway, there were crossing loops at Garve, Achanalt, Achnasheen and Strathcarron from 1870, and at Achterneed from 1871, with none at Lochluichart, Glencarron and Attadale. A loop at Strome Ferry was established from the opening of the Kyle Extension, but no station crossings were found to be necessary at Duncraig, Plockton and Duirinish, although the road bridge over the line at Plockton station was built to a length that would have accommodated a loop there, if required later. With a loop having been opened at Achnashellach in 1900, there was one other loop which was not at a station. Initially having been a siding, it lay at the head of Glen Carron, at the western end of Loch Sgamhain, such that the location was 2¼ miles north-east of Glencarron Platform and 34 miles from Dingwall. The crossing was originally called Luib Crossing, although it was 2¼ miles from Luib Summit, but it latterly became known as Loan Crossing, from the Gaelic *lòn*, meaning 'marsh'. Useful information about the crossing has been provided through the Highland Railway Society. In the Society's booklet *Highland Railway Station Locations and Dates* - 1995 revised edition, but also in the original of 1990 - the following note briefly explained the reason for the crossing's existence:

Luib/Loan Siding was used to stable part of a train if it had to be divided on the bank. When Loan Crossing was built, the siding was retained for use when the loop was switched out.

In the Summer 1990 issue of the *Highland Railway Journal*, society member David Stirling supplied a good description of what he referred to as Loan's complicated story:

The first feature to appear here was a siding for the purpose of splitting fish trains which had stalled on the ascent to Luib Summit. This was called Luib Relief Siding in the minute authorising its construction in February 1914. The aim was to cut down the delay in dividing a stalled fish train and in taking the first portion to Achnasheen; so presumably, the first portion was taken to the new siding, and the engine then returned for the rest, joining the two at the siding. As the worst of the bank, the parts at 1 in 50, lay west of the siding, this would be a practical proposition, and it would save a 13 miles round trip to Achnasheen. The site is near the west end of Loch Sgamhain and involves a very wet crossing of a bog to reach from the road.

With the extra traffic in connection with the North Sea Barrage, the Admiralty wished an extra loop on the Kyle line to split the 12 miles Achnashellach-Achnasheen section. This was agreed to, at the Admiralty's expense, in the HR minute of 10th April, 1918, when it was referred to as Luib Crossing Loop. The plan of the loop was sent to the Board of Trade and provisionally approved on 10th May, while the tender for slating the signal box roof was accepted on 4th June. On 10th July, the HR Board decided it was to be called Loan. As the HR was not wont to waste money, this presumably indicates that the box was not then in use, for otherwise, all the tablets would have had to be re-engraved. The annual report of 31st December, 1918 records the loop as having been finished.

The signal box was of the brick-built HR pattern, and there was a loop and siding. The old siding was lifted (it was in the way of the loop) and replaced on the south side of the line, operable from a two-lever ground frame, released by the long-section Achnashellach-Achnasheen tablet. This siding could not be used while the box was switched into circuit, which is eccentric but would save some money. The catch point at the west end of the loop was provided so that, if a train had to be split while the box was open, the vehicles brought up could safely be left in the loop.

The closure date of this box is a problem. It switched out, so no action was needed other than not to switch it in; there would be no great changeover to remove it. The 1920 Appendix* marks this box as 'when open'; so it was, at most, open seasonally, perhaps not at all, by that time. On 4th May, 1919, the HR Board considered a letter from the Admiralty on the subject, so it was presumably out of use by then; the HR left Mr Newlands† to negotiate the purchase of the loop,

---

* *Highland Railway Appendix to the Working Timetable, 1st May, 1920*, reprinted by the Highland Railway Society.

† Alexander Newlands, Engineer.

which was settled (for £2,000) by 12th November. Presumably, the HR were interested in the materials, for it cannot have wanted the loop itself. No staff were ever specifically allocated to the loop, so it must have been manned by relief men when it was used.

David Stirling added that Loan Relief Siding survived into BR days and that the signal box 'had its upper portion removed and was made into a permanent way hut, and there was an intermediate key token instrument here for a time to allow PW trolleys to be shut in to the siding'.

BRCW Bo-Bo type '2' No. D5321 is seen at the head of the 11.20 am Kyle-Inverness service in 1967 as it runs through the bleak country alongside the River Bran, four miles east of Achnasheen.

M. Mensing

'We'll Keep the Train to Kyle

The effects of the proposed severance of the Kyle line under Dr Richard Beeching's surgery, and how the local people would respond to it, were vividly represented in a lyrical manner, which was the work of a music teacher for the schools of the area, Miss Milner, who took up residence at Duncraig Castle College in 1949. For ease of reading and consistency of style, the version here has minor differences, without changes of meaning, from the original that was circulated at the time of the Beeching plan. The reference to 'Sir Alec' meant Sir Alec Douglas-Home, who succeeded Harold Macmillan as the Conservative Prime Minister in 1963.

We'll Keep the Train to Kyle

Oh dear dear, and don't you hear
The news I heard today.
They say they're going to take the train
That runs to Kyle away.
Our goods and friends no more will come,
Our trade no more will boom.
The closing of this Highland line
Will spell our district's doom.

Oh, I met with Dr Beeching,
He received me with a smile.
He said, 'I'm very sorry,
There will be no train to Kyle'.
It's the most appalling blunder
That has happened for a while.
They're going to close the railway line
That takes the train to Kyle.

It takes the goods to Lewis,
To North Uist and to Skye,
And little districts in the West,
It does not pass them by.
Without it, we shall lose our trade,
Our population too,
For none can live without
This transport, very true.

The evictions turned our people off,
They died in '45.
And now they're going to take the train
That keeps the West alive.
Committees and the Tourist Board
Profess to love the West,
But they're taking off the train to Kyle
That serves the people best.

We have friends in Inverness,
The outer isles, Portree,
And relations all along the line
To Glasgow and Dundee.
In serried ranks, we'll muster
And forget our feuds awhile,
For the West will be forgotten
If they close the line to Kyle.

We'll oppose that Dr Beeching
And Sir Alec's rank and file.
We'll unite to fight the tyrants
Who would close the line to Kyle.
It's the most appalling blunder
That has happened for a while.
But we'll fight, and we'll conquer, and
We'll keep the train to Kyle.

And they did.

A dramatic view from the 5.30 pm Kyle-Inverness service in 1960 as it ascends Glen Carron.

P. Tatlow

Meanings of Selective Gaelic and Norse Place Names

It should be noted that this list of simplified meanings of place names, which are mentioned in the text or shown on the maps, is not definitive, and that some of the names, in having only possible intepretations here, have alternative meanings.

Achanalt	field of the streams
Achilitibuie	field of the yellow-haired lad
Achilty	high place
Achintee	field of the attack
Achintraid	field of the shore
Achmore	big field
Achnandarach	field of the oaks
Achnasheen	field of the storms
Achnashellach	field of the willows
Achterneed	high ground above the valley
Airigh-drishaig	shieling of the thorns
Applecross	mouth of the River Crossan
Ardaneaskan	promontory of the mussels
Ardarroch	promontory of the oaks
Ardelve	promontory of the fallow land
Ardnarff	promontory of the corn
Ardross	high promontory
Attadale	valley of the fighting
Auchtertyre	high part of the land
Aultbea	stream of the birches
Aultguish	stream of the firs
Avernish	bulky headland
Badicaul	clumps of hazel
Balmacara	township of the sons of Cara
Balnacra	settlement of the enclosures
Broadford	broad fjord
Bundalloch	foot of the two lochs
Conchra	place of the enclosures
Corriemoillie	corry of the mill
Corrieshalloch	corrie of the willows
Coulags	little nook
Craig	the rock
Dingwall	place of the Norse council
Dirrie More	great ascent
Dornie	pebbly place
Dubh-aird	black promontory
Duirinish	deer headland
Drumbuie	yellow ridge
Duncraig	fort of the rock
Dunvegan	small fort
Erbusaig	Erp's bay (personal name)
Fernaig	bay of the alders

Fodderty	lower ground
Gairloch	short loch
Garve	rough place
Glen Carron	narrow valley of the heaps of stones
Glen Docherty	narrow valley of cleansing
Glenelg	narrow valley of Ireland
Glen Sgathaich or Sgaich	narrow valley of the lopped branches
Gorstan	enclosure of arable land
Grudie	gritty place
Inverlael	estuary of the river of low hollows
Inverness	estuary of the roaring river
Kinlochewe	head of the lake of the yews
Kirkton	church settlement
Kishorn	bulky headland
Kyleakin	strait of Haakon (personal name)
Kyle of Lochalsh	strait of the rolling lake
Kylerhea	strait of Rheidh (personal name)
Lairg	the pass
Leckmelm	Mailm's gravestone (personal name)
Letterfearn	hillside of the alders
Loan	the marsh
Loch Alsh	rolling lake
Loch Broom	lake of the drizzle
Loch a' Chuilinn	lake of the holly
Loch a' Chroisg	lake of the crossing
Loch Carron	lake of the heaps of stones
Loch Droma	lake of the ridge
Loch Duich	black lake
Loch Dughaill	Dougald's lake (personal name)
Loch Gowan	lake of the blacksmith
Lochinver	lake of the estuary
Loch Laxford	lake of the salmon fjord
Loch Luichart	lake of the palace
Loch Maree	lake of Maelrubha (personal name)
Loch Scalpaidh	lake of the ships

Loch Sgamhain	lake of the lungs	Skye	winged island
Luib	the bend	Slattadale	flat valley
		Sleat	the plain
Mallaig	shingle bay	Slumbay	small bay
		Stornoway	steerage bay
Nostie	the inn	Strath Bran	wide valley of the drizzle
		Strathcarron	wide valley of the heaps of stones
Pladaig	flat bay		
Plockton	settlement of the lump	Strathpeffer	wide valley of the radiant water
Poolewe	settlement of the yews		
Port-an-eorna	port of the barley	Strome Ferry	ferry of the current
Port Cam	curved port		
Portchullin	port of the holly	Talladale	valley of the ledges
Portnacloich	port of the stone	Taodail	valley of the pastures
Portree	port of the king	Tollie	place of hollows
		Toscaig	tumulus bay
Raasay	roe-deer island	Tournaig	hillock bay
Rogie	splashing water		
		Ullapool	Ulli's settlement (personal name)
Shieldaig	herring bay		

Part of the view from Duncraig platform, looking west. Plockton village lies beyond the island, and on a clearer day, the Cuillins of Skye are seen above the lowest part of the terrain in the distance, where Plockton station and the upper part of the village are situated. To the left of the platform, the railway curves sharply, to run by the edge of the land, upper left to centre, on a gradient of 1 in 60 to Plockton station. *Author*

Acknowledgements

For kindness in permitting the use of photographs, other illustrations, and quotations - with all of these contributing greatly to the story of the Skye railway and being essential to the publication of this book grateful - appreciation from the author goes to:

Aurore McConnell, Plockton - for photographs, including colour cover photograph; for painstaking drawings which were produced specially for the book; and for inspiration for such a historical project, originating from her love of the Kyle railway and, in particular, its coastal scenery.

Richard Casserley, Berkhamsted, Hertfordshire - for photographs taken by H.C. Casserley, his late father, the renowned railway photographer.

Peter Tatlow, Hambledon, Surrey - for photographs, and for his 'Skye Bogie' sectional drawing.

Tom Heavyside, Bolton, Lancashire - for photographs.

Bob Charnley, Preston, Lancashire - for photographs from his large collection of postcards.

Michael Mensing, Fareham, Hampshire - for photographs.

David St John Thomas, Nairn - for photographs.

Bob Simpson, Kyle - for photograph, and for information on the 1953 Stromeferry derailment.

Anthony Lambert, London - for photograph.

Bill Ramsay, Kyle - for photograph.

Paul Biggs, Loughborough, Leicestershire - for photograph.

Paul Strong, Chedworth, Gloucestershire - for photograph.

Ian Wilks, Holywell, Clwyd - for ticket reproductions.

David Stirling, Reading, Berkshire - for writing an Appendix on signalling, and for allowing reproduction of his notes on Loan Crossing, which appeared in the *Highland Railway Journal*.*

Tony Jervis, Dunfermline, Fife - for information from *Branch Line News,* of which he is editor.†

Isobel Nicolson, Plockton - for providing information from the papers of Torquil Nicolson, her late husband.

Mary Hudson, Kyle - for allowing extracts to be used from the books of Duncan Macpherson, her late father.

Dualchas Museums Service, Portree - for colour cover photograph; for photographs from the collection of Duncan Macpherson, and for Parliamentary plans of the Kyle Extension.

Lens of Sutton, Surrey - for photographs.

Locomotive Club of Great Britain - for photographs from the Ken Nunn Collection.

Aberdeen University Library - for photographs from the collection of George Washington Wilson, the late 19th century photographer.

St Andrews University Library - for photographs from the collection of Valentine's of Dundee.

British Railways Board, London - for photographs.

West Highland Free Press, Broadford - for photographs.

Railway Magazine, London - for photograph.

Colour-Rail, Chesham, Buckinghamshire - for colour cover photograph.

Hunting Aerofilms Ltd, Borehamwood, Hertfordshire - for photograph.

British Library Newspaper Library, Colindale, London - for reproductions from newspapers.

Inverness Public Library - for reproductions from newspapers.

Ross-shire Journal, Dingwall - for advertisement illustrations.

D.C. Thomson and Co. Ltd, of Dundee - for drawing of the Strome Ferry riot, which illustrated an article by the author in the June 1993 issue of *The Scots Magazine*.

The author sadly records the death of Graham Langmuir of Glasgow in 1994 and James Stevenson of Kilmacolm, Renfrewshire, in 1997, and regrets that both gentlemen, as Highland Railway enthusiasts, were not able to read the story of the Skye railway in this book, which they helped to illustrate so significantly.

---

* The *Highland Railway Journal* is published quarterly by the Highland Railway Society, whose Membership Secretary is Sandy Harper, The Saplings, Weir Road, Hanwood, Shropshire, SY5 8LA.
† *Branch Line News* is the fortnightly newsletter of the Branch Line Society, whose Membership Secretary is Karen Noakes, 17 Blakes Terrace, New Malden, Surrey, KT3 6ET. This society has the aim of furthering knowledge of branch lines and minor railways, with special attention to news of services, unusual occurrences, and closures, openings and reopenings of stations and lines.

Chronological Index

Index to Illustrations

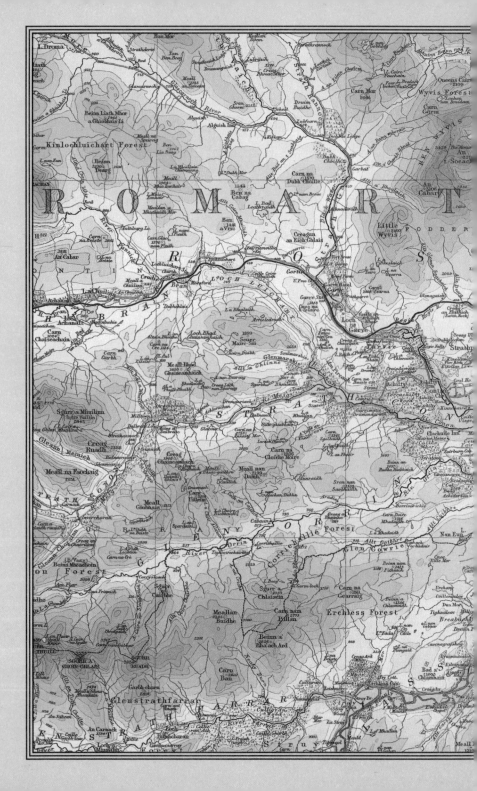